Melbourne

David McClymont

WITHDRAWN FROM STOCK

LONELY PLANET PUBLICATIONS
Melbourne • ris

MAP 1 – MAP INDEX

Brunswick
Jewell
Sydney Rd
Glenlyon Rd
Merri Park
Croxton
Fairfield
Ivanhoe
Eaglemont
Eaglemo
Ivanhoe
Lower Heidelberg
To Museum of Modern Art at Heidi (5km)
Darebin
BRUNSWICK
Fitzroy North
Holden St
Merri
Northcote
Victoria St
Separation St
Orange Rd
Alphington
Darebin Parklands
Alphington
Darebin
Royal Pde
Princes Park
Rathdowne St
Lygon St
Nicholson St
St Georges Rd
Rushall
Dennis
Fairfield
Heidelberg Rd
Westgarth
Chesworth Park
Ivanho Public Golf Club
Melbourne General Cemetery
Edinburgh Gardens
Queens Pde
Clifton Hill
Fairfield Boathouse
Yarra River
Green Acre Golf Club
Lamble Golf Club
Kew Golf Club
CARLTON
Fitzroy
Clifton Hill
Quarries Park
Yarra Bend Park
Eastern Fwy
Kilby Rd
University of Melbourne
Map 3
Map 5
Victoria Park
Yarra Bend Park
Yarra Bend Public Golf Course
Chandler Hwy
Earl St
Harp St
Kew
Carlton Gardens
Map 2
Melbourne Central
Collingwood
Collingwood
Hoddle St
Studley Park
Studley Park Rd
Princess St
High St
Boroondara Cemetery
Normanby Rd
Victoria St
Flagstaff Gardens
Parliament
Flagstaff
Fitzroy Gardens
Abbotsford
North Richmond
Victoria St
East Melbourne
Swanston St
Flinders Street
Yarra Park
Jolimont
West Richmond
Richmond
Bridge Rd
Church St
Glenferrie
Burwood Rd
Auburn
Rathmines Rd
Glenferrie Rd
Burke Rd
Cotham Rd
Barkers Rd
Richmond
East Richmond
Swan St
Map 6
Hawthorn
Power St
Map 7
Burnley
Burnley Golf Course
Riversdale Rd
Camberwell
Royal Botanic Gardens
CityLink
Como Park
Heyington
Hawthorn
Auburn Rd
Pleasant Rd
Anderson Park
South Melbourne
Kings Way
St Kilda Rd
Queens Rd
Fawkner Park
Punt Rd
South Yarra
South Yarra
Toorak Rd
Chapel St
Heyington
Toorak
Kooyong
Glenferrie Rd
Toorak Rd
Kooyong
Camberwell
Albert Park Lake
Albert Park Public Golf Course
Canterbury Rd
Commercial Rd
Hawksburn
Malvern Rd
Prahran
Prahran
Toorak
Malvern
Tooronga
Monash Fwy
Gardiner
Glen Iri
Middle Park
Windsor
High St
Windsor
Malvern Rd
Harold Holt Swimming Centre
High St
Glen Iris
Map 9
Armadale
Orrong Rd
Kooyong Rd
Glen Iris
St Kilda Pier
Fitzroy St
St Kilda Rd
Barkly St
St Kilda
Dandenong Rd
Williams Rd
Alma Rd
Glenferrie Rd
Wattletree Rd
Tooronga Rd
Burke Rd
Gardiner
St Kilda Beach
Balaclava
Marine Pde
St Kilda Botanical Gardens
Brighton Rd
Balaclava
Inkerman St
Malvern
Dandenong Rd
St Kilda Marina
Balaclava Rd
Caulfield Park
Elwood
Ripponlea
Balaclava Rd
Hawthorn Rd
Kambrook Rd
Caulfield
Waverley Rd
Elwood Canal
Glen Huntly Rd
Glen Eira Rd
Dandenong Rd
Caulfield Racecourse
Carnegie
Elwood Beach
Elsternwick
Elsternwick
Caulfield

Melbourne
3rd edition – October 2000
First published – March 1993

Published by
Lonely Planet Publications Pty Ltd ABN 36 005 607 983
192 Burwood Rd, Hawthorn, Victoria 3122, Australia

Lonely Planet Offices
Australia PO Box 617, Hawthorn, Victoria 3122
USA 150 Linden St, Oakland, CA 94607
UK 10a Spring Place, London NW5 3BH
France 1 rue du Dahomey, 75011 Paris

Photographs
Many of the images in this guide are available for licensing from
Lonely Planet Images.
email: lpi@lonelyplanet.com.au

Front cover
Reflected and refracted city, from the Adelphi Hotel (John Hay)

Title page of map section
Aerial vista south over Albert Park Lake (Tony Wheeler)

ISBN 1 86450 124 3

text & maps © Lonely Planet 2000
photos © photographers as indicated 2000

Printed by Colorcraft Ltd, Hong Kong

Contents – Text

The Author

David McClymont

David McClymont grew up in a small fishing village on the west coast of Scotland. After studying graphic design in Glasgow, playing pop star in London and working as a vegetarian chef in Paris, in 1989 he accidentally boarded an Air India flight to Sydney. He has lived in Australia ever since. David was a main contributor to Lonely Planet's *Out to Eat – Melbourne 2001*, and his fiction and journalism have appeared in various publications. David lives in Melbourne with his wife and two grey cats.

FROM THE AUTHOR

Everybody within earshot became a sounding board for this update. As my wife Janet was always there, even in the wee small hours, my biggest thanks goes to her. I'd also like to thank Katie Cody and Mary Neighbour for getting me started, Rebecca Turner and Ron Gallagher for keeping me going, Jay Kranz for getting me around, Leonie Mugavin for getting me away and my editor, Hilary Ericksen, for pulling everything together and coming up with some additional ideas when I thought I'd already crossed the finish line. A huge thanks also goes to everyone in the Fuji unit, to Maria Vallianos in design, and to all in the Mercury department – my Lonely Planet family. Lastly, I'd like to thank Supergrass and the Smiths for keeping me company on the way.

This Book

David McClymont researched and wrote this 3rd edition of Lonely Planet's Melbourne guide, and apparently gained not a pound of weight while researching the city's numerous cafes and restaurants. Reformed architect Brett Moore penned the aside on Melbourne's contemporary architecture, and Paul Clifton advised on information and venues for gay and lesbian travellers.

From the Publisher

This book was produced in Lonely Planet's Melbourne office. Editing was coordinated Hilary Ericksen, with editorial assistance provided by Arabella Bamber and Rebecca Turner; proofing was the domain of Bruce Evans and Evan Jones. With the help of Lonely Planet's Knowledge Bank team, Pablo Gastar mapped the city and then eased the book through design and layout. Jane Hart turned an expert eye to the colour wraps and advised on all matters visual. The ever-patient Maria Vallianos produced the stunning cover design, and Matt King liaised with artists Mick Weldon and Kate Nolan, who drew the book's illustrations. Knowing the quirks of Quark inside out and upside down, Tim Uden ironed them out for us. He and Jenny Jones also assisted with the maps during the book's layout.

Acknowledgments

Grateful acknowledgment is made for reproduction permission:
Yarra Trams and Swanston Trams: Metropolitan tram system map
Bayside Trains and Hillside Trains: Metropolitan train system map
Land Victoria: Melbourne city and inner-suburban map data

Lonely Planet would also like to thank the following readers for
sending their anecdotes, suggestions and recommendations to us:

Alan & Shirley Martin, Ana Lamo, Andras Gefferth, Aoife Colligan,
Beatrice Santha, Bill Warren, Carl Schedlich, Caroline Anderson,
Charles Russo, Cheyenne Morrison, Chris Renner, Christine & Philippe
Ledoux, Christine Gray, Clair Thomas, Darina Eades, Darren Edwardes,
Darren Southgate, Dean Smith, Deirdre Keating, Dr Debbie Puxley,
Fiona Fraser, Gina Pastega, Glen Bath, Haiko de Boer, Jas Fielding,
Jason Miles, Jeannnie Ong, Jesse Holliday, Jim Lennon, Johnathan
Littell, Katherine Duffy, Lars Axelsson, Lee Parker, Leo Hawkins, Lisa
Humphries, Loretta Feeney, Madeleine Fleischander, Maria Bloom,
Melanie Osborne, Paola Belfiore, Pete Golding, PJ Ellis, Pui-Sing
Wong, Robert Bender, Russell Robinson, Sacha Wong, Sally Collins,
Simon Cobley, Simon Perry, Tim Broome, Tony Brzozowski, Tracy
Kershaw

Foreword

ABOUT LONELY PLANET GUIDEBOOKS

The story begins with a classic travel adventure: Tony and Maureen Wheeler's 1972 journey across Europe and Asia to Australia. Useful information about the overland trail did not exist at that time, so Tony and Maureen published the first Lonely Planet guidebook to meet a growing need.

From a kitchen table, then from a tiny office in Melbourne (Australia), Lonely Planet has become the largest independent travel publisher in the world, an international company with offices in Melbourne, Oakland (USA), London (UK) and Paris (France).

Today Lonely Planet guidebooks cover the globe. There is an ever-growing list of books and there's information in a variety of forms and media. Some things haven't changed. The main aim is still to help make it possible for adventurous travellers to get out there – to explore and better understand the world.

At Lonely Planet we believe travellers can make a positive contribution to the countries they visit – if they respect their host communities and spend their money wisely. Since 1986 a percentage of the income from each book has been donated to aid projects and human rights campaigns.

Updates Lonely Planet thoroughly updates each guidebook as often as possible. This usually means there are around two years between editions, although for more unusual or more stable destinations the gap can be longer. Check the imprint page (following the colour map at the beginning of the book) for publication dates.

Between editions up-to-date information is available in two free newsletters – the paper *Planet Talk* and email *Comet* (to subscribe, contact any Lonely Planet office) – and on our Web site at www.lonelyplanet.com. The *Upgrades* section of the Web site covers a number of important and volatile destinations and is regularly updated by Lonely Planet authors. *Scoop* covers news and current affairs relevant to travellers. And, lastly, the *Thorn Tree* bulletin board and *Postcards* section of the site carry unverified, but fascinating, reports from travellers.

Correspondence The process of creating new editions begins with the letters, postcards and emails received from travellers. This correspondence often includes suggestions, criticisms and comments about the current editions. Interesting excerpts are immediately passed on via newsletters and the Web site, and everything goes to our authors to be verified when they're researching on the road. We're keen to get more feedback from organisations or individuals who represent communities visited by travellers.

> Lonely Planet gathers information for everyone who's curious about the planet – and especially for those who explore it first-hand. Through guidebooks, phrasebooks, activity guides, maps, literature, newsletters, image library, TV series and Web site we act as an information exchange for a worldwide community of travellers.

Research Authors aim to gather sufficient practical information to enable travellers to make informed choices and to make the mechanics of a journey run smoothly. They also research historical and cultural background to help enrich the travel experience and allow travellers to understand and respond appropriately to cultural and environmental issues.

Authors don't stay in every hotel because that would mean spending a couple of months in each medium-sized city and, no, they don't eat at every restaurant because that would mean stretching belts beyond capacity. They do visit hotels and restaurants to check standards and prices, but feedback based on readers' direct experiences can be very helpful.

Many of our authors work undercover, others aren't so secretive. None of them accepts freebies in exchange for positive write-ups. And none of our guidebooks contain any advertising.

Production Authors submit their raw manuscripts and maps to offices in Australia, the USA, the UK or France. Editors and cartographers – all experienced travellers themselves – then begin the process of assembling the pieces. When the book finally hits the shops, some things are already out of date, we start getting feedback from readers and the process begins again...

WARNING & REQUEST

Things change – prices go up, schedules change, good places go bad and bad places go bankrupt – nothing stays the same. So, if you find things better or worse, recently opened or long since closed, please tell us and help make the next edition even more accurate and useful. We genuinely value all the feedback we receive. Julie Young coordinates a well-travelled team that reads and acknowledges every letter, postcard and email and ensures that every morsel of information finds its way to the appropriate authors, editors and cartographers for verification.

Everyone who writes to us will find their name in the next edition of the appropriate guidebook. They will also receive the latest issue of *Planet Talk*, our quarterly printed newsletter, or *Comet*, our monthly email newsletter. Subscriptions to both newsletters are free. The very best contributions will be rewarded with a free guidebook.

Excerpts from your correspondence may appear in new editions of Lonely Planet guidebooks, the Lonely Planet Web site, *Planet Talk* or *Comet*, so please let us know if you *don't* want your letter published or your name acknowledged.

Send all correspondence to the Lonely Planet office closest to you:

Australia: PO Box 617, Hawthorn, Victoria 3122
USA: 150 Linden St, Oakland, CA 94607
UK: 10A Spring Place, London NW5 3BH
France: 1 rue du Dahomey, 75011 Paris

Or email us at: talk2us@lonelyplanet.com.au

For news, views and updates see our Web site: www.lonelyplanet.com

HOW TO USE A LONELY PLANET GUIDEBOOK

The best way to use a Lonely Planet guidebook is any way you choose. At Lonely Planet we believe the most memorable travel experiences are often those that are unexpected, and the finest discoveries are those you make yourself. Guidebooks are not intended to be used as if they provide a detailed set of infallible instructions!

Contents All Lonely Planet guidebooks follow roughly the same format. The Facts about the Destination chapters or sections give background information ranging from history to weather. Facts for the Visitor gives practical information on issues like visas and health. Getting There & Away gives a brief starting point for researching travel to and from the destination. Getting Around gives an overview of the transport options when you arrive.

The peculiar demands of each destination determine how subsequent chapters are broken up, but some things remain constant. We always start with background, then proceed to sights, places to stay, places to eat, entertainment, getting there and away, and getting around information – in that order.

Heading Hierarchy Lonely Planet headings are used in a strict hierarchical structure that can be visualised as a set of Russian dolls. Each heading (and its following text) is encompassed by any preceding heading that is higher on the hierarchical ladder.

Entry Points We do not assume guidebooks will be read from beginning to end, but that people will dip into them. The traditional entry points are the list of contents and the index. In addition, however, some books have a complete list of maps and an index map illustrating map coverage.

There may also be a colour map that shows highlights. These highlights are dealt with in greater detail in the Facts for the Visitor chapter, along with planning questions and suggested itineraries. Each chapter covering a geographical region usually begins with a locator map and another list of highlights. Once you find something of interest in a list of highlights, turn to the index.

Maps Maps play a crucial role in Lonely Planet guidebooks and include a huge amount of information. A legend is printed on the back page. We seek to have complete consistency between maps and text, and to have every important place in the text captured on a map. Map key numbers usually start in the top left corner.

Although inclusion in a guidebook usually implies a recommendation we cannot list every good place. Exclusion does not necessarily imply criticism. In fact there are a number of reasons why we might exclude a place – sometimes it is simply inappropriate to encourage an influx of travellers.

Introduction

The wayward child of Victorian England, Melbourne was little more than a colonial outpost until the discovery of gold in 1851. The settlement grew quickly to become one of the most impressive Victorian-era cities in the world. In the 20th century, subsequent waves of immigrants struggled and thrived according to the city's changing fortunes, creating a lively and exciting multicultural Melbourne that would have the Anglo-Saxon founding fathers turning in their graves.

Melbourne and Sydney appear to be the Jekyll and Hyde of Australian cities. The latter's fast pace and relaxed attitude are in striking contrast to Melbourne's high-brow culture, Victorian architecture, ordered grid plan and sophisticated, European ambience. But don't be fooled by this conservative exterior: Melbourne tends to be a secretive city, playing down its treasures rather than wearing them on its sleeve. The heart of the city is a perfect example, where a honeycomb of rediscovered arcades and laneways resemble a city within a city, and an eclectic array of shops, restaurants, cafes and bars pulsate with a style and life of their very own.

Melbourne's reputation as the arts, culinary, sporting and shopping capital of Australia is as strong as ever, and Melburnians' unbridled enthusiasm for these pastimes is impressive. One of the city's most striking features for visitors is the sheer abundance (and quality) of places to eat and drink, both in the city centre and in the inner suburbs.

Everything from Italian, Greek, French and Lebanese to Japanese, Vietnamese, Thai and Indonesian can be found here. And then there is the new wave of Australian cooking, which blends a variety of styles, flavours and the freshest of fresh produce to create a unique hybrid. If coffee's your poison, look no further. Melbourne has a vibrant cafe scene, and the best coffee you'll find just about anywhere outside of Italy – and believe me, this statement isn't made lightly.

Like many major cities, Melbourne has had to bear the brunt of questionable development decisions. Thankfully, much of the grandeur of the city's architecture remains intact, making it perfect for heritage walks and tours or to just wander around and marvel at the architectural splendour. The inner-city satellite suburbs of Fitzroy, St Kilda, South Yarra and Richmond, to name but a few, are all rich in architectural, cultural and culinary diversity, making a trip to the inner suburbs a prerequisite for any visitor to the city.

It's impossible to write an introduction to Melbourne without mentioning the trams. They are to the city what the yellow cab is to New York and the double-decker bus is to London. The friendly tram conductors may have gone (and are sadly missed), and the ticket machines will no doubt bamboozle you, but jumping on a tram remains the best way to get around the city and is a quintessential Melbourne experience. So buy your ticket to ride, and use it!

Facts about Melbourne

HISTORY
Early Aboriginal History

Aborigines journeyed from South-East Asia to the Australian mainland at least 50,000 years ago. Victoria's Aboriginal people, or Koories, lived in some 38 different dialect groups (also known as tribal groups, or *wurrungs*) who spoke 10 separate languages. These dialect groups further divided into clans and subclans, each with its own customs and laws. Each clan held ownership of a distinct area of land, the Aborigines' complex traditional culture being largely based on their close spiritual bond with the land. The Yarra Valley region was occupied by members of the Woiwurrung clan known as the Wurundjeri.

Koories led a semi-nomadic existence, migrating according to the seasons. In Victoria, they coped with the winter climate by sheltering in simple huts, wearing possum-skin cloaks and warming themselves with small fires. The coastal tribes' diet included a wide variety of plants and vegetables, supplemented with fish and turtles. Shellfish were collected and eaten on the beaches – evidence of these feasts, in the form of huge shell middens, has been found all along the Victorian coast.

The Europeans

While Captain James Cook is popularly credited with Australia's European discovery in 1770, it is thought that Portuguese navigators sighted the Australian coast in the 16th century.

The First Fleet sailed into Botany Bay in January 1788 to settle Australia. But it was not until October 1803 that a small party of convicts, soldiers and settlers under the command of Captain David Collins set sail for the south, arriving at Sorrento on the Mornington Peninsula to establish Victoria's first European settlement. The venture was short-lived, however, as Collins was unable to find a supply of fresh water with which to sustain a settler community. Less than a year after his arrival Collins sailed for Van Diemen's Land (Tasmania), little knowing that Surveyor-General Charles Grimes had just found the Yarra River.

Victoria remained unoccupied by white settlers for years after European arrival in Australia, but as the pastoral runs of New South Wales (NSW) and Van Diemen's Land became overcrowded, pastoralists began to look farther afield for fertile lands that they could farm. In what has been called 'the greatest land grab in British imperial history', pastoralists and settlers flooded into Victoria. The precedent was set by Edward Henty who, with family and sheep, left Van Diemen's Land for Portland in 1834, becoming Victoria's first permanent white settlers. Within 10 years Europeans outnumbered the region's original inhabitants.

Aboriginal Responses

Estimates suggest that in 1834 around 15,000 Aborigines were living in Victoria, but by 1860 there were only around 2000 survivors. Their traditional culture was disrupted by the arrival of white settlers, who regarded the Aborigines as a hindrance to settling and 'civilising' the land. Aborigines were dispossessed of their lands and killed in their thousands – first by introduced diseases, such as smallpox, dysentery and measles, and later they were massacred by gunfire and poison.

At a local level, individual Aborigines resisted the sure encroachment of settlers, and a number of warriors were for a time feared by the colonists who settled in their areas. However, without any legal right to the land, as this was conceived by the ruling colonists, many Aborigines were driven from the lands they once lived on, while others voluntarily left to travel to the fringes of settled areas to obtain new commodities such as steel and cloth, and to experience hitherto unknown drugs such as tea, tobacco and alcohol.

Founding of Melbourne

Two Tasmanian men, John Batman and John Pascoe Fawkner, are widely acknowledged as the founders of Melbourne.

In 1835 a group of Launceston businessmen formed the Port Phillip Association with the intention of establishing a new settlement on Port Phillip Bay. In May of that year, company representative John Batman rowed up the Yarra River to the site where central Melbourne now stands, and uttered the immortal phrase: 'This will be the place for a village'.

Batman purchased around 240,000 hectares of land from the local Aboriginal clans, and a settlement was established on the north side of the Yarra River. The concept of buying or selling land was completely foreign to the Aborigines, but in return for their traditional land Batman offered a bargain-basement assortment of blankets, knives, tomahawks, looking-glasses, scissors, hand-kerchiefs, various items of clothing and 50 pounds of flour.

John Pascoe Fawkner and a group of Tasmanian settlers joined Batman and other members of the Port Phillip Association in October 1835. Fawkner became a driving force behind the new settlement. The son of a convict, he was a man of vision and worked tirelessly as a publisher, publican and self-taught bush lawyer. He spent 15 years on the Legislative Council of Victoria, where he campaigned vigorously for the rights of small settlers and convicts, and for the ending of transportation. By the time of his death in 1869, Melbourne was flourishing and he was known as the 'Grand Old Man of Victoria'. More than 15,000 people lined the streets to bid him farewell at his funeral.

History doesn't remember John Batman as kindly. Within four years of his dodgy deal with the Aborigines, Batman was dead,

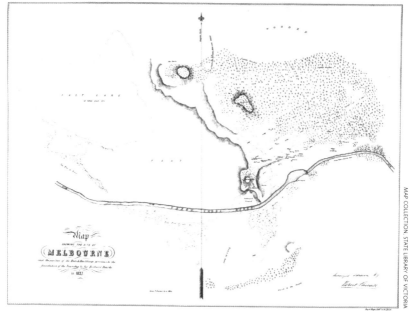

Robert Russell, *Map shewing* [sic] *the site Melbourne…1837*. As shown here, Russell drafted the outline of the city grid prior to surveyor Robert Hoddle detailing the city centre.

a victim of his own excesses. In his *History of Australia* historian Manning Clark described Batman as '...a man who abandoned himself wantonly to the Dionysian frenzy and allowed no restraint to come between himself and the satisfaction of his desires'.

Early Days

The settlement developed with astonishing speed, and became a packing-case village of tents and hovels almost overnight. While the initial treaty with the Aborigines had no legal basis, by 1836 so many settlers had moved to Port Phillip that the administrators of NSW had to declare the area open to settlement.

Some order to the pell-mell development was provided in 1837, when military surveyor Robert Hoddle drew up plans for the new city, laying out the distinctive geometric grid of broad streets that characterises the central city area today.

By 1840 there were over 10,000 people settled in the Melbourne area. As the new community grew in size and confidence, its members began to agitate for separation from NSW.

Separation & Gold Boom

In 1851 Victoria won separation from NSW, and Melbourne became the capital of the newly proclaimed colony. In the same year, gold was discovered at Bathurst in NSW. Fearing the young city's workers would desert for the northern goldfields, a committee of Melbourne businessmen offered a reward to anyone who could find gold within Victoria – but even in their wildest dreams they couldn't have foreseen what followed. The first gold strike was at Warrandyte in May 1851, and during the next few months massive finds followed at Buninyong and Clunes near Ballarat, Mt Alexander near Castlemaine and Ravenswood near Bendigo.

The subsequent gold rush brought a huge influx of immigrants from all around the world. The Irish and English, and later Europeans, Americans and Chinese, began arriving in droves. Within 12 months there were about 1800 hopeful diggers disembarking at Melbourne each week.

Melbourne became chaotic. As soon as ships arrived in the harbour, their crews would desert and follow the passengers to the goldfields. Business in Melbourne ground to a standstill as most of the labour force left to join the search. Once again, shanty towns of bark huts and canvas tents sprung up to house the population, which doubled within a decade. In 1852 the *Sydney Morning Herald* peevishly asserted:

...that a worse regulated, worse governed, worse drained, worse lighted, worse watered town of note is not on the face of the globe; and that a population more thoroughly disposed in every grade to cheating and robbery, open and covert, does not exist; that in no other place does immorality stalk abroad so unblushingly and so unchecked...that, in a word, nowhere in the southern hemisphere does chaos reign so triumphant as in Melbourne.

A generation later, and bolstered by the wealth of the goldfields, 'Motley Melbourne' had matured into 'Marvellous Melbourne', one of the world's great Victorianera cities. Melburnians took some pride in the fact that theirs was not a convict settlement, and they used their new-found wealth to build a city of extravagant proportions. Among the new migrants came tradespeople from Europe who were well trained in the great traditions of Renaissance building, and the city's architects readily put them to work. Large areas were set aside and planted as public parks and gardens. By the 1880s Melbourne was referred to as the 'Paris of the Antipodes'.

This period of great prosperity lasted for 40 years. The 1880s were boom times for Melbourne, but affluence soon led to recklessness. Money from the goldfields and from overseas was invested in real estate and building works, and speculation led to spiralling land prices that couldn't last. In 1880 Melbourne hosted the Great Exhibition in the opulent Royal Exhibition Building in the Carlton Gardens. No expense was spared in the buildings' construction or the exhibition itself, but this flamboyant showing-off to the world was to be the swan song of Marvellous Melbourne.

LA TROBE PICTURE COLLECTION, STATE LIBRARY OF VICTORIA

Francois Cogne, *Queens Wharf (Yarra Yarra)*, 1864. Customs House, on Flinders St in the mid-picture, is now home to the excellent Immigration & Hellenic Antiquities Museums.

In 1889 the property market collapsed under the increasing weight of speculation. In 1890 a financial crash in Argentina led to the collapse of several financial institutions in London; overnight, investment in Australia dried up. The 1890s was a period of severe economic depression, and it was years before Melbourne recovered. The city never entirely regained its glowing reputation of the 1880s.

Federation & Depression

On 1 January 1901, Victoria became a state of the new Australian nation. Melbourne was the country's capital and the seat of government until 1927, when the Australian capital was relocated to Canberra. The federal Parliament sat at the state's Parliament House, and the state Parliament moved to the Royal Exhibition Building.

The city again flourished in the early decades of the 20th century, but construction and development came to a shuddering halt with the Great Depression, which hit Australia hard. In 1931 almost a third of breadwinners were unemployed and poverty was widespread. During the Depression the government implemented a number of major public works programs, including the Yarra Boulevard, the Shrine of Remembrance, St Kilda Rd and the Great Ocean Rd.

WWII to the Present

White Australia's overwhelmingly Anglo-Celtic makeup was challenged in the 1930s and 1940s with the arrival of non-British migrants, fleeing the upheaval in Europe. The Australian government hoped that the increase in population would strengthen Australia's economy and contribute to its ability to defend itself. 'Populate or Perish' became the catch phrase. Between 1947 and 1968 more than 800,000 non-British European migrants came to Australia. The majority of migrants came by ships that docked first in Melbourne, where a large percentage of the new arrivals settled. With the demise of the government's insidious 'White Australia' policy in the 1970s, migrants began to arrive from South-East Asia, adding further to the multicultural mix. (See the Population & People section later in this chapter.)

Melbourne's Victorian heritage was irrevocably altered by the post-war construction boom, a period in which architectural aesthetics worldwide hit rock bottom. The city hosted the Olympic Games in 1956, and hectares of historic buildings were bulldozed as the city prepared to impress the hordes of visitors with its modernity. Construction continued in the 1960s under the Liberal premier Henry Bolte, culminating in the boom years of the 1980s. Reflecting the trends of 100 years earlier, land prices rose continuously throughout the decade, and in the competitive atmosphere of the newly deregulated banking industry, banks were queuing up to lend money to speculators and developers. The city centre and surrounds were transformed as one skyscraper after another sprang up, leading some overexcited architects to refer to Melbourne as the 'Chicago of the southern hemisphere'. Even the worldwide stock market crash in 1987 didn't slow things down, but in 1990 the property market collapsed, just as it had 100 years earlier. By 1991 Australia found itself in recession once again. Unemployment was the highest it had been since the early 1930s and Victoria was the state hardest hit.

In October 1992, a Liberal-National party coalition led by Jeff Kennett was elected in a landslide victory – ousting the mismanaged Labor party, which had been in power for 10 years. The Kennett government ruled the state with an iron fist. Its policies succeeded in turning around the state's economy, but at the same time Kennett's belligerence and his government's failure to properly address social-welfare and infrastructure issues alienated large segments of the community. A new phrase entered the Melbourne lexicon: to be 'Jeffed' meant that one had been well and truly shafted.

Kennett's casino-led recovery changed the face of Melbourne, both culturally and socially. Along with several high-profile construction companies, he changed the skyline, transformed pubs into identically costumed, jangling gambling dens, and temporarily left the city with neither art gallery nor museum, concentrating instead on new 'cultural events' such as the Grand Prix and other sports extravaganzas.

Kennett won a second term in 1996, and although discontment was growing, the 1999 state election looked like a one-horse race. To everyone's surprise, however, the election turned out to be a nail-biter and the result went right down to the wire. The huge swing in popularity to little-known Labor leader Steve Bracks was enough to seal a minority victory for Labor and finally see an end to a deflated Kennett's autocratic reign. With the coalition ousted, accusations of mismanagement have been rife. Bracks' pledge to clean up the house, listen to the electorate and run a more honest government, concentrating on welfare issues such as health and education, is now being put to the test.

GEOGRAPHY

The city perches at the top of Port Phillip Bay, with an urban sprawl spreading more than 70km to the north and more than 50km east to west, spreading down towards the Mornington and Bellarine Peninsulas. This sprawl covers a massive 1700 sq km. This is mainly attributable to the 'great Australian dream' – where every family wanted to own their own home on their own quarter-acre block. Melbourne's population density is thus a mere 16 people per hectare, in comparison with cities such as Paris (48) and London (56).

This trend results in increasingly greater pressures on the urban infrastructure, and planning authorities are encouraging higher-density housing in both inner and outer suburbs. With the ever-increasing number of cars on the road, traffic congestion has also become a major concern in and around the city. In an attempt to combat this growing problem, the ambitious and controversial CityLink project (see the Getting Around chapter) was devised. The largest private urban infrastructure in the country, when completed it will connect the city's main freeways to form a continuous expressway. The project has been hampered from the very beginning, with accusations ranging from the choice of materials used on the new Bolte Bridge to ongoing problems with the leaking Burnley tunnel to confusion surrounding the world's first boothless tollway, where tolls are paid on an electronic debit system.

The metropolitan area is predominantly flat. In 1837, the city was laid out in a geometric grid one mile (1.61km) long and half a mile (805m) wide. This street grid is now at an angle to the main metropolitan grid. Note that long streets often start renumbering addresses at the start of a new suburb.

Melbourne is fairly easy to get around; it has the benefit of many broad, tree-lined avenues and is surrounded by public gardens and parklands. The city centre isn't so much the focal point of Melbourne as the hub of the wheel, surrounded by clusters of interest within the inner suburbs. The Yarra River divides the city geographically and socio-economically. Traditionally, the northern and western suburbs are more industrial and working class, while areas south of the Yarra and to the east have been the domain of the more affluent, and the setting for the most prestigious housing.

CLIMATE

Victoria's seasons are the opposite of those of the northern hemisphere, so that January is the height of summer and July the depth of winter.

Melbourne has four seasons, with no great extremes. It rarely snows, the mercury only rises above 35°C a few times each year, and Melbourne has half the average rainfall of Sydney and Brisbane. In summer the average temperatures range from a high of 26°C to a low of 14°C; in winter the average maximum is 13°C and the minimum 6°C; in spring and autumn average highs and lows range from around 20°C to 10°C.

Of course, averages and statistics never paint the true picture. They smooth out the inconsistencies, of which there are plenty. Those four seasons don't always stick to their allocated timeslots either. You are just as likely to have a sunny, blue-sky day in winter and a sudden thunderstorm in summer as you are vice-versa. Or worse still, all four seasons will visit in one day! The saying goes that if you don't like the weather in Melbourne, just wait a couple of minutes. The guiding principle is to expect the unexpected – that way you're prepared for whatever comes over the horizon.

GOVERNMENT & POLITICS
Australian Government

Australia is a federation of six states and two territories, and has a parliamentary system of government based on the British Westminster model. There are three tiers of government: federal, state and local.

Australia's two main political groups are the Australian Labor Party (ALP) and the coalition between the Liberal Party and the National Party. In theory, the ALP is traditionally socialist, having grown out of the workers' disputes and shearers' strikes of the 1890s; the Liberal Party is traditionally conservative, representing the interests of free enterprise, law and order and family values; and the National Party (formerly the National Country Party) is traditionally the party of rural interests, having originally been formed to represent conservative farmers.

In practice, however, the distinctions that have long separated the major parties have become somewhat blurred as political expediency and holding onto office have increasingly taken priority over traditional party values. Particularly since the early 1980s, the ALP and the Liberals have converged on the political middle ground, relinquishing conventional left and right ideology respectively, and embracing economic rationalism and the free market.

The Australian Democrats are another important political group, formed, as its first

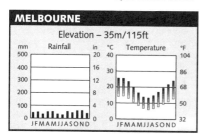

MELBOURNE
Elevation – 35m/115ft

federal leader, Don Chipp, said, to 'keep the bastards honest'. Independent and Green representatives are also playing an increasingly important role in national politics.

At the time of writing Australia had a Liberal-National coalition government, under the leadership of John Howard.

Victorian Government

Victoria's state government is based in Melbourne and is made up of the Legislative Council (the upper house) with 44 elected representatives and the Legislative Assembly (the lower house) with 88 elected representatives. Elections for the lower house are held every four years. Voting is by secret ballot and is compulsory for everyone aged 18 years and over.

The Labor Party, under the premiership of Steve Bracks, currently governs in Victoria, after a massive swing away from the Kennett coalition parties in the 1999 election. See WWII to the Present in the History section earlier.

ECONOMY

Melbourne's depressed economic state of a decade ago is thankfully a thing of the past. The city has entered the new millennium thriving once again and attracting large-scale investment and high-profile construction projects such as the Docklands development. Spending is up, but so also are interest rates.

Victoria may be Australia's smallest mainland state, but it's also the most densely populated and the most intensively farmed, producing more than 20% of the country's agricultural products. The state's manufacturing industries contribute around 25% of Australia's Gross National Product. The major industries are clothing and footwear, textiles, automotive and transport equipment, paper, metal, coal and petroleum products.

Around 70% of the state's workforce is employed in the tertiary sector, particularly in wholesale and retail trade and in community services such as education and health. As with the rest of Australia, tourism is of growing economic importance.

A Republic: Not If but When

International visitors to Melbourne and Australia may be as confused as the locals as to why an ageing 'marm' wearing a crown of jewels still holds a sceptre over the Australian people from her once great Britannia. A combination of apathy and an 'if it ain't broke why fix it' attitude saw the first referendum on the republic, held in 1999, fail. Most Australians believe that a republic is an inevitability. Not such a safe bet, however, is when it will happen. Will Australians still be swearing allegiance to the queen even after the Brits have thrown her to the dogs?

MICK WELDON

The city's ever-increasing cafe and restaurant scene seems to be Melbourne's biggest growth industry, with punters spending substantially more on dining out in 1999 than they did the year before. The number of newly opened venues is prodigious, but saturation point is surely only another caffè latte away.

POPULATION & PEOPLE

Melbourne has a population of over three million people, made up of many different nationalities and with almost a quarter of them born overseas. There are around 20,000 Koories and Torres Strait Islanders living in Victoria; more than half of whom live in Melbourne's inner suburbs.

The city is a meeting place for people and cultures from all over the world. The first wave of white settlers were predominantly Anglo-Celtic, but during the gold rush

Royal Exhibition Building and fountain, Carlton

Victorian Arts Centre

Trundling trams along Melbourne's central axis, Swanston Street

Fitzroy Gardens Conservatory

Dame Edna does it with flower power

A bird's-eye view of Melbourne

diggers came from all over the world. In the aftermath of WWII, thousands migrated from Europe. Many were Jewish, survivors of the holocaust who wanted to start again as far away from the horror as possible. Melbourne's large percentage of Greek, Italian and Jewish peoples dates from this time, with many others coming from far-flung places such as Turkey, Lebanon, Malta, Poland and the former Yugoslavia.

Since the mid-1970s, most immigrants have come from South-East Asia and the Pacific, many being refugees from Vietnam and Cambodia.

Today, one of Melbourne's greatest strengths is its cultural diversity.

ARTS

Melbourne is regarded by many people as the cultural capital of Australia. A town that unleashed on the world people as diverse as Barry Humphries, Kylie Minogue, Sir Sidney Nolan, Olivia Newton-John, Nick Cave, Rupert Murdoch, Dame Nellie Melba, Peter Carey and Germaine Greer can't be all beer and horse races.

For details on theatre in Melbourne, see that section in the Entertainment chapter.

Aboriginal Art & Culture

Relatively few traces remain of the Aboriginal tribes that lived and thrived in the Victorian region before white settlement. The Aboriginal Heritage Walk in the Royal Botanic Gardens is a fascinating introduction to the close bond between the Aboriginal people and the land (see Walking Tours in the Things to See & Do chapter).

The new Melbourne Museum in the Carlton Gardens incorporates an Aboriginal Centre called Bunjilaka, which hosts exhibitions, performances and activities celebrating indigenous culture.

The National Gallery of Victoria's (NGV) collection of contemporary Aboriginal art is to be re-housed in the new Museum of Australian Art in Federation Square (see the Things to See & Do chapter), which is expected to open in May 2001. There are also several private galleries in Melbourne that display the work of Aboriginal artists (see Other Art Galleries in the Things to See & Do chapter).

The Koorie Heritage Trust Inc (☎ 9639 6555), Level 1, 234–36 Flinders Lane offers an interesting program of activities and events relating to Victoria's living Koorie culture. Admission to the gallery is by donation.

Architecture

Victoria's earliest buildings were built in the Old Colonial style (1788–1840), a simplified version of Georgian architecture. The earliest settled towns such as Portland, Port Fairy and Port Albert are the best examples of this period. In Melbourne few examples remain – St James' Cathedral (1840) in King St is the oldest public building.

Somewhat appropriately, the most prominent architectural style in the state is Victorian (1840–90), which was an expression of the era's confidence, progress and prosperity. It drew upon various sources including classical, romantic and Gothic, and as the era progressed designs became more elaborate, flamboyant and ornamental. Melbourne is widely acknowledged as one of the world's great Victorian-era cities and features many outstanding examples of Victorian architecture in the city centre and inner suburbs such as Carlton, Parkville, East Melbourne, South Melbourne and St Kilda.

With the collapse of Melbourne's land boom in the early 1890s and the subsequent severe economic depression, a new style of architecture evolved, which came to be known as Federation. Federation style was in many ways a watered-down version of Victorian architecture, featuring simplicity of design and less ornamentation. Its evolution was mainly driven by economic necessity, but it was also influenced by the pending federation of Australia (in 1901) and the associated desire to create a more distinctive and suitably 'Australian' style of design.

From around 1910, the most prominent style of residential architecture was a hybrid of Federation and California Bungalow styles. The Art Deco style was also prominent from the 1920s, but following the Great Depression architecture became increasingly functionalist and devoid of decoration.

In recent years, appreciation of these older styles has increased to the extent that councils have actively encouraged residents to restore houses and buildings in sympathy with the period in which they were built. However, with the boom in medium-density housing, many of Melbourne's beautiful 19th- and early 20th-century houses and gardens have been replaced with a glut of graceless mock-Georgian 'townhouses'.

The city centre has fared little better, with much modern-day architecture remaining fixed in the grip of internationalism, leaving little room for vernacular expression.

Visual Arts

Melbourne's National Gallery of Victoria houses one of the most comprehensive art collections in the southern hemisphere. The Australian collection contains a significant number of works by Australian impressionists. Based at a bush camp in Heidelberg in the 1880s, Tom Roberts, Arthur Streeton, Frederick McCubbin and Charles Condor were the first local artists to paint in a distinctively Australian style rather than in imitation of European styles.

In the 1940s, another revolution in Australian art took place in Melbourne's east, at Heide, the home of John and Sunday Reed in suburban Bulleen. Under their patronage, a new generation of bohemian young artists (including Sir Sidney Nolan, Albert Tucker, Arthur Boyd, Joy Hester and John Perceval) redefined the direction of Australian art. Today, you can visit the Museum of Modern Art at Heide, which exhibits the work of many significant artists. See Other Art Galleries in the Things to See & Do chapter for details of Heide and other key galleries around the city.

In the late 1970s, 1980s and 1990s, artists such as Jenny Watson, John Nixon and the late Howard Arkley, along with the anti-establishment group Roar, were at the forefront of a new wave of local artists challenging the conventions of the art marketplace.

In more recent times, Melbourne hit the art-world headlines for all the wrong reasons, when a couple of delinquents attacked the controversial and quite beautiful work *Piss Christ*, by American artist Andres Serrano, on exhibition at the NGV. This large photograph of an effigy of Christ submerged in the artist's own urine was construed as blasphemous and was subsequently banned, sparking a furore over issues of freedom of expression. The gallery's decision to remove the work was seen by many observers worldwide as a cowardly one. Here at home, this display of staid conservatism was as embarrassing as it was worrying.

Music

Melbourne's rich musical heritage covers the spectrum from rock to classical. The lively rock-music scene has been the launching pad for bands such as Men at Work, Crowded House and Nick Cave & the Bad Seeds, while two Melburnians who achieved international fame on the classical stage were singer Dame Nellie Melba and composer Sir Percy Grainger.

The city hosts a wide range of music festivals throughout the year, featuring everything from jazz and blues to chamber music and alternative rock. Melbourne's music festivals include the Montsalvat Jazz Festival and the Melbourne Music Festival. The Port Fairy Folk Festival and the Wangaratta Jazz Festival are just two of many excellent music festivals held in country Victoria.

Indigenous music is one of the Australian music industry's great success stories of recent years. Yothu Yindi (from the Northern Territory) is one of the country's best-known Aboriginal bands, but Melbourne also has some great indigenous musicians, including Archie Roach, Ruby Hunter and local band Tiddas.

Melbourne's dynamic music scene has consistently produced many of Australia's outstanding bands and musicians. Local artists well worth checking out include Paul Kelly, Chris Wilson, Rebecca's Empire, Vika and Linda Bull, the Dave Graney Show, Stephen Cummings, the Black Eyed Susans, Magic Dirt, Living End, Snout, the Dirty Three, Crackpot, Pollyanna and Underground Lovers – to mention but a few!

If dance music is more your thing, Melbourne should keep you happy – there are a huge number of local DJs and electronic acts, and clubs and dance parties galore.

To find out what's happening music-wise, check out gig guides such as the *EG* (in Friday's *Age* newspaper), street papers *Beat* or *Inpress*, or smaller street magazines *TR* and *Groovine* – otherwise, pick up a few local CDs or tapes to provide the perfect soundtrack for your visit.

Cinema

Melbourne is the birthplace of the Australian film industry, and the base from which Australia began to create a distinctively home-grown style of cinema. Cinema historians regard Australia's *Soldiers of the Cross* as the world's first 'real' movie. It cost £600 to make and was originally screened at the Melbourne Town Hall in 1901. It was shown throughout the USA in 1902.

The next significant Australian film, *The Story of the Kelly Gang*, was screened in 1907, and by 1911 the industry was flourishing. Low-budget films were made in such quantity that they could be hired out or sold cheaply. Over 250 silent feature films were made before the 1930s when the talkies and Hollywood took over.

In the 1950s, *On the Beach* was shot in Melbourne. One of its stars, Ava Gardner, was less than enchanted by her surroundings and made the comment that Melbourne

---

Cultural Melbourne

As Australia's cultural capital, Melbourne presents a wide range of music, opera and theatre performances.

The arts precinct, at the city end of St Kilda Rd, should be your first stop for major artists in the classical fields, with opera, ballet and orchestral concerts held year round (except January). The Melbourne Symphony Orchestra (MSO) performs almost every week between February and December, with most performances held at the Melbourne Concert Hall. The season always includes internationally known guest artists.

The Victorian State Opera has merged with the Australian Opera, but a full opera season is still held here. If the Chamber Made Opera company is presenting a new work while you're here, it's one not to miss.

Dozens of theatrical productions are staged each week, ranging from amateur productions to the latest experimental work. The major mainstream drama companies are the Playbox and the Melbourne Theatre Company (see Theatre in the Entertainment chapter for more details). Handspan Theatre, an innovative puppet theatre, produces exciting shows for adults, as well as excellent kids' shows.

Musicals, from Gilbert and Sullivan to the latest international shows, are almost always playing. The Princess Theatre, Her Majesty's Theatre and the Regent Theatre are the venues for big touring shows.

The art of filmmaking will be celebrated by Cinemedia in Federation Square when the centre's huge new premises opens in 2001. Australia's first cultural institution solely dedicated to screen culture will house facilities for film, television and digital media, with public access to Cinemedia's extensive digital and analogue collection via individual and group viewing spaces, and three cinemas.

Melbourne also has a rich dance scene but no company has a permanent venue. You'll catch ballet in the Arts Precinct, but for modern works you'll need to keep your eye on the entertainment section of the daily newspapers or ask at the Victorian Visitors Information Centre, which usually has a listing of events.

The 'Readings' and 'Hear This' sections of the *EG* liftout in the Friday edition of the *Age* newspaper has listings of book launches, religious discussions, educational lectures and public debates.

Although there are very few 'high art' performances from non-Western cultures, there are plenty of opportunities to see folk performances.

was the perfect place to make a film about the end of the world – at the time she may have been right. The wheel turned full circle in 1999 when a re-make of *On the Beach* was shot in Melbourne.

With government interest and a large injection of funds, the Australian film industry enjoyed a renaissance in the 1970s and the films of this period came to be known, somewhat over-ambitiously, as the New Wave. Some landmark Victorian productions from this period were *The Adventures of Barry McKenzie*, *Monkey Grip*, *Picnic at Hanging Rock* and *The Getting of Wisdom.*

In recent years Australian directors and actors have become much sought after in Hollywood. There has been a great deal of concern that Hollywood is muscling in on our territory by opening a Fox Studio in Sydney – a little like the corner cafe making way for McDonald's. Whether or not the Australian film industry will become nothing more than a Hollywood outpost has yet to be seen.

If you're specifically interested in films made in or about Melbourne, the following are all home grown, available on video and well worth seeing: *Malcolm* (a simple genius builds a one-person tram) and *The Big Steal* (taking revenge on a dodgy used-car dealer) are both made by local filmmakers Nadia Tass and David Parker; *Death in Brunswick* is a black comedy about life in Melbourne's seedy underbelly; *Spotswood* is a nostalgic look at life and industrial relations in Melbourne in the 1950s, set in a moccasin factory; *Proof* is a poignant film about a blind photographer, set in St Kilda and Elwood; *Dogs in Space* is an entertaining and often ludicrous look at the punk-grunge side of Melbourne, starring a very young Michael Hutchence; *Hotel Sorrento* is an adaptation of Melbourne playwright Hani Rayson's original stage play of the story of three sisters and their reunion at a beach house in Sorrento; *Love and Other Catastrophes* is a quirky portrayal of student life set in and around the University of Melbourne; *Angel Baby* is a tragic love story about a schizophrenic couple; and *Head On* is a coming-of-age tale of gay sex,

drugs and futility, starring small-screen star Alex Dimitriades.

Uncompromising local director Geoffrey Wright's films include the savage *Romper Stomper*, about a neo-Nazi skinhead gang based in the Melbourne inner suburb of Footscray, and *Metal Skin*, about teenage boys in Melbourne and their love affairs with fast cars and women.

Literature

Victoria has produced plenty of outstanding writers. Some of the classic works of Victorian literature are *For the Term of His Natural Life* by Marcus Clarke, *The Getting of Wisdom* by Henry Handel (Florence Ethel) Richardson, *Picnic at Hanging Rock* by Joan Lindsay and *My Brother Jack* by George Johnston. Also, look for the work of Charmian Clift, Hal Porter, Alan Marshall and Frank Hardy.

Among Victoria's contemporary writers, the best-known is probably Peter Carey (now living in New York), who won the Booker Prize in 1988 for his novel *Oscar & Lucinda*. Helen Garner's works are mostly set in Melbourne and include *The Children's Bach*, *Postcards From Surfers*, *Cosmo Cosmolino* and *Monkey Grip*. Other contemporary Melbourne writers to look out for include Kerry Greenwood, Morris Lurie, Carmel Bird, Barry Dickins, Gerald Murnane, Robert Dessaix and Rod Jones. Recent novels with a Melbourne bent include Shane Maloney's *Stiff*, Andrew Masterton's *Last Days*, Elliot Perlman's *Three Dollars* and Neal Drinnan's *Pussy's Bow*.

In recent years, Melbourne has produced many promising new writers, including Andrea Goldsmith, Christos Tsiolkas, Claire Mendes, Fiona Capp and Michelle de Kretser. Melbourne is also the locus of Australia's literary 'little magazine' culture, with publications including *Meanjin*, *Landfall* and *Australian Book Review*, all of which publish well-known and lesser-known writers.

RELIGION

A shrinking majority of people in Victoria are at least nominally Christian. Most

Protestant churches have merged to become the Uniting Church, but the Church of England has remained separate. The Catholic Church is popular (about 30% of Christians in the state are Catholics), with the original Irish adherents boosted by the large numbers of Mediterranean immigrants.

Non-Christian minorities also abound in multicultural Melbourne; the main faiths being Buddhist, Jewish and Muslim.

LANGUAGE

Melbourne contains many surprises for those who think all Aussies speak some weird variant of English. For a start many Australians don't even speak English – they speak Italian, Lebanese, Vietnamese, Turkish or Greek.

Those who do speak the native tongue are liable to lose you in a strange collection of Australian words. Some words have completely different meanings in Australia to the meanings they have in English-speaking countries north of the equator; some commonly used words have been shortened almost beyond recognition. Other words are derived from Aboriginal languages, or from the slang used by early convict settlers.

There is a slight regional variation in the Australian accent, while the difference between city and country speech is mainly a matter of speed. Lonely Planet publishes an *Australian phrasebook*, an introduction to both Australian English and Aboriginal languages. For those wanting to make a more in-depth study of Australian English, the *Penguin Book of Australian Slang (A Dinkum Guide to Oz English)*, by Lenie Johansen, is a comprehensive and entertaining guide to the Australian vernacular.

Aboriginal Language

At the time the First Fleet arrived to establish the first European settlement in Australia, there were around 250 separate Australian languages spoken by 600 to 700 Aboriginal 'tribes', and these languages were as distinct from each other as English is from French. Often three or four adjacent tribes would speak what amounted to dialects of the same language, but another adjacent tribe might have spoken a completely different language.

It is believed that all the languages evolved from a single language family as the Aboriginal people gradually moved out over the entire continent and split into new groups. There are a number of words that occur right across the continent, such as *jina* (foot) and *mala* (hand). Similarities also exist in the sometimes complex grammatical structures.

Following European contact the number of Aboriginal languages was drastically reduced. At least eight separate languages were spoken in Tasmania alone, but none of these was recorded before the native speakers either died or were killed. Of the original 250 or so languages, many of which were mutually unintelligible, only around 30 are today spoken on a regular basis and taught to children.

There are a number of terms that Aborigines use to describe themselves, and these vary according to the region. The most common term is Koorie, used for the people of south-east Australia. Murri is used to refer to the people of Queensland, Nunga for those from coastal South Australia, and Nyoongah is the term used in the country's south-west.

Facts for the Visitor

WHEN TO GO

Melbourne's temperamental climate is often the brunt of jokes. There are four seasons, but some might say that you have them all in one day. The motto is be prepared.

The summer, from December to February, is the most popular time for visitors. You can expect good beach weather, particularly during late summer, and the occasional scorcher when the thermostat bubbles past 40°C.

The autumn months, particularly March and April, are the best time of year climatically. The days are warm and long and the changing seasons are highlighted to great effect in the city's parks and gardens.

Winter temperatures average a maximum of 13°C and a minimum of 6°C. It's a great time of year to take advantage of the city's proximity to ski resorts, with snowfields only two- to four-hours' drive from the city. Mischievous parakeets playing in gum trees laden with snow is one of the stranger sights overseas visitors might see.

Spring in Melbourne, from September until November, means a few different things – the weather can live up to its reputation of unpredictability, the parks and gardens come to life and the Melbourne International Festival, the city's major arts event, begins.

Along with the climate, it's worth bearing in mind the school-holiday periods. The school year is divided into four terms, and holidays are generally as follows: the longest break is the Christmas holiday from mid-December until the end of January; the three two-week holiday periods vary from year to year, but fall approximately from late March to mid-April, late June to mid-July and mid-September to early October.

ORIENTATION

Melbourne's suburbs sprawl around the shores of Port Phillip Bay, with the city centre sited on the north bank of the Yarra River, about 5km inland from the bay.

Many of the inner suburbs have their own distinctive characters. Most of the places and attractions covered in this book are within the city and inner-suburban areas – all easily accessible by public transport.

City Centre

The city centre is set out on a grid pattern, bordered by the Yarra River to the south, the Fitzroy Gardens to the east, Victoria St to the north and Spencer St to the west. The main streets, running east-west, are Collins and Bourke Sts, crossed by Swanston and Elizabeth Sts, all of which are interspersed with narrower roads and a maze of little alleys and lanes.

If you're arriving in Melbourne by long-distance bus or on the airport bus, you'll arrive in the city at either the Spencer St coach terminal on the west side of town (V/Line, Skybus, Firefly and McCafferty's buses) or at the Melbourne Transit Centre, at 58 Franklin St (Greyhound Pioneer Australia and Skybus buses) at the north end of the city.

On the Bourke St Mall, between Swanston and Elizabeth Sts, you'll find a tourist information booth, the Myer and David Jones department stores, and, on the corner of Bourke and Elizabeth Sts, the main post office (GPO).

Swanston St runs north-south through the city and crosses the Yarra River, where it becomes St Kilda Rd, a tree-lined boulevard running all the way south to St Kilda.

Beside the river on the corner of Swanston and Flinders Sts is Flinders St Railway Station, the main station for suburban trains. The other major station, for country and interstate services, is the Spencer St train station at the western end of Bourke St.

Inner Suburbs

To the north of the city centre are North Melbourne, home to the YHA hostels; Carlton, an area known for its gracious Victorian-era architecture and home to Melbourne's Italian community; Parkville, home to the University of Melbourne and the Royal Melbourne Zoo; and Fitzroy, a thriving lifestyle centre with an abundance of cafes and restaurants.

East of the city, Richmond is dominated by the local Greek and Vietnamese communities, while to the south-east is stylish South Yarra with its upmarket fashion boutiques.

South of the city, St Kilda is a cosmopolitan seaside suburb, while Williamstown, south-west of the city at the mouth of the Yarra River, has a historic maritime feel.

Greater Melbourne

The Yarra River wends its way through Melbourne from the Upper Yarra Reservoir (about 90km east of the city centre) to the head of the bay, dividing the city into two halves.

Most places of interest to travellers are either within the inner-suburban area or beyond the urban fringe. There are a few exceptions, such as the Museum of Modern Art at Heide in the north-eastern suburb of Bulleen, but generally there isn't too much that will lure you to the suburbs.

MAPS

Tourist information offices hand out free maps that cover the city and inner suburbs. If you're staying a while, more detailed maps, free to members, are available from the Royal Automobile Club of Victoria (RACV), and Lonely Planet publishes the *Melbourne City Map* ($7.95).

Comprehensive street directories are produced by Melway, UBD and Gregory's, and are available at bookshops and newsagents. The best option for travellers is probably *Compact Gregory's* ($16.95). The Melway street directory (around $37) is such a Melbourne institution that places are often located by simply stating the relevant Melway page and grid reference.

Map Land, at 369 Lonsdale St, has the city's most comprehensive range of maps.

TOURIST OFFICES
Local Tourist Offices

The excellent Victoria Visitor Information Centre (Map 2; ☎ 9658 9745), located in the Melbourne Town Hall on the corner of Swanston and Little Collins Sts, is the city's main tourist office. The centre also provides tours and accommodation bookings and information. It's open from 9 am to 6 pm weekdays, 9 am to 5 pm weekends. Multilingual computer touch-screen information is available at the City Experience Centre, also in the town hall. The centre is open from 9 am to 7 pm Monday to Friday, 9 am to 5 pm weekends. Tourism Victoria (☎ 13 2842 from anywhere in Australia) is also located in the town hall.

There are also information booths with lots of free information as well as maps and monthly calendars of events, staffed by friendly and helpful volunteers, some of whom are multilingual. The Bourke St Mall and Flinders St Railway Station booths are open seven days a week. The international terminal at Melbourne airport also has a tourist information booth.

For information about Melbourne's public transport, ring the Met (☎ 13 1638) between 7 am and 9 pm daily or visit the Met Shop (Map 2) at 103 Elizabeth St.

Another good spot to visit is Information Victoria (Map 2; ☎ 1300-366 356) at 356 Collins St, a government-run bookshop which stocks a wide variety of publications about Melbourne and Victoria.

Parks Victoria has an information service (☎ 13 1963) and will mail out brochures; it's Web site is at www.parks.vic.gov.au and has plenty of useful information.

Free Publications

There are a number of free information guides circulated in Melbourne, most of which are available from tourist offices and the RACV. They include *This Week in Melbourne* and *Melbourne Events*, which have handy 'what's on' listings.

The best giveaways are those published by Tourism Victoria (☎ 13 2842). Its *Melbourne & Surrounds Official Visitors' Guide* has all sorts of helpful information, including a calendar of events, transport maps, attraction and accommodation listings, and a useful information section at the back. Tourism Victoria also produces excellent glossy regional guides to Victoria. You can obtain these from its office in the town hall.

It's worth picking up a copy of the Victorian edition of *For Backpackers by Backpackers* or *TNT Magazine*, a small publication which lists cheap accommodation and eateries, attractions and events. Both publications are available free from hostels and information centres.

Interstate Tourist Offices

Tourism Victoria has an interstate office in New South Wales (☎ 02-9299 2288), at 403 George St, Sydney; otherwise call the nationwide service on ☎ 13 2842. Tourism Victoria can provide information about Melbourne and Victoria, book accommodation and advise you on how to get there. Its Web site is at www.tourism.vic.gov.au.

Tourist Offices Abroad

The Australian Tourist Commission (ATC) is the government body established to inform potential visitors about the country. It produces a useful free booklet called *Travellers' Guide to Australia*, which is a good introduction to the country, its geography, flora, fauna, states, transport, accommodation, food and so on. This literature is intended for distribution overseas only and can be ordered through its Web site at www.australia.com. From the Web site you can also access 10,000 pages of information on Australia and link to other useful sites.

DOCUMENTS

Visas

Visitors to Australia must have a valid passport and a visa to enter the country. New Zealanders need only have a valid passport, and a 'special category' visa will be issued on arrival.

There are several types of visas issued, depending on the reason for your visit, but most holiday visitors will require a standard tourist visa. Unless you have access to the Electronic Travel Authority (ETA) system, outlined later in this section, you'll need an application form, which is available from Australian diplomatic missions overseas and many travel agents. You can apply either by mail or in person.

Visa regulations change from time to time. Your travel agent or Australian diplomatic mission will tell you of any changes. Alternatively, you could check the Australian government's Web site at www.immi.gov.au for updated information.

Tourist Visas Australian consular offices abroad issue tourist visas; these are the most common type of visa and are valid for a stay of either three or six months from the date of arrival. Tourist visas obtained from outside Australia attract a $60 fee, though note that the fee is likely to be reviewed in mid-2000. After you arrive in Australia, you can apply to extend your visa for a total visit of up to 12 months (see the section on Visa Extensions). If you intend staying less than three months, the visa is free; otherwise you are subject to the processing fee. You'll need to provide your passport and a passport photo with your application.

Electronic Travel Authority Visitors from certain countries who require a tourist visa for three months or less can apply through an ETA-registered travel agency. There are no forms or fees and your travel to Australia can be authorised within a few minutes, as your ETA is computer generated.

ETA is available to citizens of the UK, the USA, Canada, most European and Scandinavian countries, Korea, Malaysia and Singapore. Other nationalities will probably be added to the list in the future. You'll find the list at www.immi.gov.au/eta/countries.htm.

Working Holiday Visas Young visitors from the UK, Ireland, Canada, the Netherlands, Malta, South Korea and Japan may be eligible for a 'working holiday' visa. 'Young' is fairly loosely interpreted as being between 18 and 25 years. You can work either full- or part-time for as much of the 12 months as you want (or are able to), but you can't work for the same employer for more than three months. Visitors aged between 26 and 30 years can also apply for a working visa, but the qualifying conditions are much stricter – you have to be able to prove that your work here will be 'mutually beneficial' to both Australia and your home country.

See the section on Work later in this chapter for further information.

Visa Extensions The maximum stay allowed for visitors to Australia is 12 months, including extensions.

Visa extensions are made through the Department of Immigration & Multicultural Affairs (DIMA) offices in Australia. As the process can take some time, it's best to apply about a month before your visa expires. There is a nonrefundable application fee of $150 (or $170, depending on the length of your stay) – even if they turn down your application they can still keep your money!

To qualify for an extension you must take out medical insurance and have a ticket out of the country. Some offices might want to see proof that you have enough money to stay in Australia, or statements from friends or relatives that you'll be staying with them.

The central Melbourne office of DIMA (Map 2) is at 2 Lonsdale St in the city. Phone ☎ 13 1881 for information or ☎ 9235 3030 for a 24-hour recorded information service.

If you intend staying longer than 12 months in Australia, the book *Temporary to Permanent Residence in Australia* (Penguin) might be useful.

Other Documents

Foreign driving licences are valid as long as they are in English or are accompanied by a translation. An International Driving Permit, obtainable from your local automobile association, must be supported by your own licence, so remember to bring both with you.

Bring proof of your automobile association membership, which will give you reciprocal rights to the services of the RACV, including breakdown services.

A student card will entitle you to a variety of discounts throughout Victoria. The most common of these cards is the International Student Identity Card (ISIC) issued by student unions, hostelling organisations and some travel agencies.

It's also worth bringing your youth hostel membership card (eg, HI, YHA) if you have one. As well as entitling you to various discounts, your card is valid for membership of the Australian YHA.

Copies

All important documents (passport data and visa pages, credit cards, travel insurance policy, air/bus/train tickets, driving licence etc) should be photocopied before you leave home. Leave one copy with someone at home and keep another with you, separate from the originals.

It's also a good idea to store details of your vital travel documents in Lonely Planet's free online Travel Vault in case you lose the photocopies or can't be bothered with them. Your password-protected Travel Vault is accessible online anywhere in the world – create it at www.ekno.lonelyplanet.com.

EMBASSIES & CONSULATES
Australian Embassies Abroad

Australian consular offices overseas include:

Canada (☎ 613-236 0841, fax 236 4376) Suite 710, 50 O'Connor St, Ottawa K1P 6L2; also Toronto and Vancouver

France (☎ 01 40 59 33 00, fax 40 59 33 10) 4 Rue Jean Rey, Paris, Cedex 15

Germany (☎ 030-880 08 80, fax 88 00 88 99) Friedrich-Strasse 200, 10117 Berlin

Greece (☎ 01-645 0404) 37 Dimitriou Soutsou, Ambelokpi, Athens 11521

Hong Kong (☎ 2827 8881) 23/F Harbour Centre, 25 Harbour Rd, Wanchai, Hong Kong Island

Indonesia (☎ 21-522 7111, fax 526 1690) Jalan HR Rasuna Said, Kav C15-16, Kuningan, Jakarta 12940; also in Denpasar

Italy (☎ 06-85 2721) Via Alessandria 215, Rome 00198; also in Milan

Japan (☎ 03-5232 4111) 2-1-14 Mita, Minato-ku, Tokyo 108; also in Osaka

Malaysia (☎ 03-246 5555, fax 241 5773) 6 Jalan Yap Kwan Seng, Kuala Lumpur 50450

Netherlands (☎ 070-310 8200) Camegielaan 4, The Hague 2517 KH

New Zealand (☎ 04-473 6411, fax 498 7135) 72–78 Hobson St, Thorndon, Wellington; also in Auckland

Singapore (☎ 863 4100, fax 737 5481) 25 Napier Rd, Singapore 258507
South Africa (☎ 012-342 3740) 292 Orient St, Arcadia, Pretoria 0083
Thailand (☎ 02-287 2680, fax 287 2029) 37 South Sathorn Rd, Bangkok 10120
UK (☎ 020-7379 4334, fax 7465 8217) Australia House, The Strand, London WC2B 4LA; also in Manchester
USA (☎ 202-797 3000, fax 797 3168) 1601 Massachusetts Ave NW, Washington DC, 20036; also in Los Angeles, Honolulu, Houston, New York and San Francisco

Foreign Consulates

Most foreign embassies are in Canberra, although many countries also have consulates in Melbourne. They include:

Canada (☎ 9811 9999) 123 Camberwell Rd, Hawthorn East
France (☎ 9820 0921) 492 St Kilda Rd, Melbourne
Germany (☎ 9828 6888) 480 Punt Rd, South Yarra
Greece (☎ 9866 4524) 34 Queens Rd, Melbourne
Indonesia (☎ 9525 2755) 72 Queens Rd, Melbourne
Italy (☎ 9867 5744) 509 St Kilda Rd, Melbourne
Japan (☎ 9639 3244) 360 Elizabeth St, Melbourne
Malaysia (☎ 9867 5339) 492 St Kilda Rd, Melbourne
Netherlands (☎ 9867 7933) 499 St Kilda Rd, Melbourne
Switzerland (☎ 9867 2266) 420 St Kilda Rd, Melbourne
Thailand (☎ 9650 1714) 277 Flinders Lane, Melbourne
UK (☎ 9650 4155) Level 17, 90 Collins St, Melbourne
USA (☎ 9526 5900) 553 St Kilda Rd, Melbourne

Addresses of other foreign consulates can be found in the Melbourne *Yellow Pages* phone book under 'Consulates & Legations', or in the *White Pages* under 'Consuls'.

CUSTOMS

When entering Australia you can bring most articles free of duty, provided that customs is satisfied they are for personal use and that you'll be taking them with you when you leave. There's the usual duty-free quota of 1 litre of alcohol, 250 cigarettes and dutiable goods up to the value of A$400.

With regards to prohibited goods, there are a few things you need to pay particular attention to. Of course Australian Customs has a positive mania about drugs, and they can be extremely efficient when it comes to finding the stuff.

Animal and plant quarantine is also an issue. You will be asked to declare all goods of animal or vegetable origin – wooden spoons, straw hats, flowers, seeds – and show them to an official. The authorities are naturally keen to prevent weeds, pests or diseases getting into the country. Fresh food is also unpopular, particularly meat, sausages, fruit and vegetables.

Weapons and firearms are either prohibited or require a permit and safety testing. Other restricted goods include products made from protected wildlife species (eg, ivory), nonapproved telecommunications devices and live animals.

When you leave, don't even consider smuggling out protected flora or fauna. Australia's unique birds and animals are prized possessions for overseas collectors, and customs come down hard on this kind of illegal activity with huge fines and jail sentences as a penalty.

MONEY
Currency

Australia uses the decimal system of dollars and cents (100 cents to the dollar). There are $100, $50, $20, $10 and $5 notes, and $2, $1, $0.50, $0.20, $0.10 and $0.05 coins. Although $0.05 is the smallest coin in circulation, prices are often still marked to the single cent. Shops should round prices to the nearest $0.05 on your *total* bill, not on individual items.

There are no notable restrictions on importing or exporting currency or travellers cheques, except that you may not take out of Australia more than A$5000 in cash without prior approval.

Note that unless otherwise stated all prices quoted in this book are in Australian dollars (A$).

Exchange Rates

Over the years the Australian dollar has fluctuated quite markedly against the US dollar, from above US$0.75 to below US$0.58.

Approximate exchange rates at the time of writing were:

country	unit		rate
Canada	C$1	=	A$1.13
European Union	€1	=	A$1.57
France	10FF	=	A$2.40
Germany	DM1	=	A$0.80
Hong Kong	HK$10	=	A$2.10
Japan	¥100	=	A$1.57
New Zealand	NZ$1	=	A$0.82
Singapore	S$1	=	A$0.95
UK	UK£1	=	A$2.62
USA	US$1	=	A$1.64

Exchanging Money

Changing foreign currency or travellers cheques is no problem at most banks. Generally, you'll find that banks are open from 9.30 am to 4 pm Monday to Thursday, 9.30 am to 5 pm Friday.

There are foreign-exchange booths at Melbourne airport's international terminal, which are open to meet all arriving flights. Most of the large hotels will also change currency or travellers cheques for their guests but the rate might not be as good.

You'll also find foreign-exchange booths in the city centre. These places are OK for emergencies – they have more convenient opening hours than the banks – but their rates generally aren't as good. The downside of changing money in banks is the transaction fee – around $5 to $7 per transaction.

Thomas Cook has four foreign-exchange offices in Melbourne's city centre, including one at 261 Bourke St, which opens daily. American Express (AmEx) has two city offices; the one at 233 Collins St opens from 8.30 am to 5.30 pm weekdays, 9 am to noon Saturday.

Travellers Cheques

American Express, Thomas Cook and other well-known international brands of travellers cheques are all widely used in Aus-

tralia. A passport is usually adequate for identification.

Commissions and fees for changing foreign currency travellers cheques seem to vary from bank to bank and month to month. It's worth making a few phone calls to see which bank currently has the lowest charges. Different banks charge different fees for different types of cheques. Most banks don't charge fees on Visa brand travellers cheques.

Credit Cards

The most commonly accepted credit cards in Australia are Visa, MasterCard, American Express and, to a lesser extent, Diners Club.

Credit cards are a convenient alternative to carrying cash or large numbers of travellers cheques. There are automatic teller machines (ATMs) throughout the country, and a credit card, preferably linked to your savings account back home, is the ideal way to organise your money for travelling. Visa and MasterCard are commonly accepted by ATMs – most machines display the symbols of the credit cards they accept. Cash advances are also available over the counter from all banks.

Foreign Banks

Quite a few foreign banks have branches in Melbourne. These include the Banque Nationale de Paris (☎ 9670 9500), at 90 William St; the Bank of New Zealand (BNZ; ☎ 9641 4300), at 395 Collins St; and the Hong Kong Bank (☎ 9618 3888), at 99 William St.

Costs

Compared to the USA, Canada and European countries, Australia is cheaper in some ways and more expensive in others. Manufactured goods tend to be more expensive but food is both high quality and relatively low cost. Accommodation is also very reasonably priced.

How much you spend daily will depend mainly on where you're staying and how you like to satiate your appetite. At the budget end of the spectrum (staying in hostels and doing most of your own cooking) you should reckon on at least $35 a day. If you're bedding down in a B&B or mid-range hotel and regularly eating out, reckon on about $80 a day. These costs really pertain to accommodation, meals and transport, so entertainment, tours etc will add to these estimates.

Tipping
In Australia tipping isn't 'compulsory' as it is in the USA or Europe. It's only customary to tip in restaurants, and only then if you want to. If you do decide to leave a tip, 10% of the bill is considered reasonable. Taxi drivers don't expect tips, although rounding off the charge isn't unusual.

POST & COMMUNICATIONS
Post
Australia's postal services are relatively efficient and a new electronic coding system should improve the service further.

It costs $0.45 to send a standard letter or postcard within Australia. Australia Post has divided international destinations into two zone: Asia Pacific and the Rest of the World. Air-mail letters cost $1/1.50 respectively. Postage for postcards and aerograms is the same to any country: $1 and $0.80 respectively.

Generally, post offices are open from 9 am to 5 pm weekdays. The GPO (Map 2), on the corner of Bourke and Elizabeth Sts, is open from 8.15 am to 5.30 pm weekdays, from 10 am to 1 pm on Saturday (for stamp sales and poste restante only). Stamps are also available from most newsagents.

Receiving Mail All post offices will hold mail for visitors. But be warned that the poste restante section at the GPO can get fairly hectic, especially in summer, and you may have to wait a while for your mail. Post offices will hold mail for one month before returning it to the sender, although for a small fee you can arrange to have mail forwarded to you. If you have an American Express card or buy AmEx travellers cheques, you can have mail sent to you c/o American Express Travel, 233 Collins St, Melbourne 3000.

Telephone
The area code (or STD number) for Melbourne and Victoria is ☎ 03. Dial this number first if calling from outside Victoria.

Australia's phone system was until recently solely owned and run by the government-owned Telstra (formerly Telecom), but these days the market for long-distance and international calls has been deregulated. Telstra's main competitor is Optus but a number of smaller companies are emerging.

Note that telephone numbers that are prefixed by ☎ 1800 attract no call fee, while numbers with the ☎ 13 prefix are charged at the local-call rate (even if they connect to an interstate number).

Public Phones & Phonecards Local calls from public phones cost $0.40 for an unlimited amount of time. You can make local calls from payphone booths and from the gold or blue phones often found in shops, hotels, bars etc.

There's a wide range of local and international phonecards available. Lonely Planet's eKno Communication Card is designed specifically for independent travellers and provides budget international calls, a range of messaging services, free email and travel information – for local calls, you're usually better off with a local card. You can join online at www.ekno.lonelyplanet.com, or by phone from Australia by dialling ☎ 1800-674 100. Once you have joined, to use eKno from Melbourne or anywhere else in Victoria dial ☎ 9909 0888. Check the eKno Web site for joining and access numbers from other countries and updates on local economy access numbers and new features.

Long-distance or Subscriber Trunk Dialling (STD) calls can be made from virtually any public phone. Many accept Telstra phonecards, which are very convenient. These cards come in $5, $10, $20 and $50 denominations and can not be recharged. They are available from retail outlets, such as newsagents and pharmacies, which display the Phonecard logo. Otherwise, have plenty of $0.10, $0.20, $0.50 and $1 coins ready, and be prepared to feed them through at a fair old rate.

Some public phones are set up to take only bank cash cards or credit cards; these too are convenient, although you need to keep an eye on how much the call is costing as it can quickly mount up. The minimum charge for a call on one of these phones is $1.20.

Rates for STD calls are charged according to distance, and vary depending on when you call. Currently Telstra's lowest rates are on weekends and after 7 pm during the week.

International Calls Almost all public phones allow you to direct dial international numbers. Dial ☎ 0011 for overseas, followed by the country code, the city/area code (codes can be found at the back of the *White Pages*) and then the local telephone number. Have a phonecard, credit card or plenty of coins on hand. It will cost you more to make an international call from a public than a private phone. If you want to know in advance how much your call will likely cost or the cheapest time to ring, phone ☎ 12 552.

The cost of making an international call from a private phone can vary dramatically. It depends on the company you use and if they have any special deals, which country you're calling, the time of day or week you're making the call and whether or not your phone is registered with a pricing plan. Call Telstra (☎ 1222) or Optus (☎ 1300-300 937) to find out its current deals. At the time of writing, a standard Telstra call from a private phone cost $0.28 a minute to the USA, and $0.34 a minute to the UK, anytime of the week using the ☎ 0011 prefix. If you use the ☎ 0018 Telstra prefix, a 30 minute call to either the USA or UK will cost $6 for 30 minutes.

Country Direct The Country Direct service gives travellers in Australia direct access to operators in more than 50 countries, in order to make collect or credit card calls. Country Direct includes:

Canada	☎ 1800-881 150
France	☎ 1800-881 330
Germany	☎ 1800-881 490
Japan (ITJ)	☎ 1800-881 143
Japan (KDD)	☎ 1800-881 810
New Zealand	☎ 1800-881 640
UK (BT)	☎ 1800-881 440
UK (Mercury)	☎ 1800-881 417
USA (AT&T)	☎ 1800-881 011
USA (MCI)	☎ 1800-881 100
USA (Sprint)	☎ 1800-881 877
USA (WorldCom)	☎ 1800-881 212

For a full list of the countries hooked into this system, check any local telephone book.

Operator Assistance Some useful telephone numbers include:

Emergency (nationwide)	☎ 000
International directory assistance	☎ 1225
National directory assistance	☎ 1223
Reverse charges	☎ 12550

Telephone Interpreter Service A free telephone interpreter service is available in 23 different languages. To access the service, call ☎ 13 1450 from anywhere in Australia, 24 hours a day.

Fax

You can send a fax from any post office, either to another fax machine or to a postal address. A fax to anywhere in Australia costs $4 for the first page and $1 for each subsequent page. A fax to a postal address within Australia will be delivered by the postal service, usually the next day. Overseas faxes cost $10 for the first page and $4 for each subsequent page.

You can also send faxes from many business services, photocopying shops and newsagents. Rates at these places are usually much cheaper than at post offices.

Email & Internet Access

Melbourne has many Internet cafes where you can collect your email or surf the Internet while enjoying a cuppa and a bite to eat. Access charges range from $6 to $10 an hour. Internet cafes include:

e:fifty five (Map 2; ☎ 9620 3899) Downstairs, 55 Elizabeth St, Melbourne
The Lab Internet Cafe (☎ 9639 7500) 490 Elizabeth St, Melbourne
Myer RMIT Internet Cafe (Map 2; ☎ 9661 1700) Myer Electric, Level 4, 295 Lonsdale St, Melbourne
Travellers Uni Net Shop (☎ 9326 6418) 211 Victoria St, West Melbourne
Net City (☎ 9525 3411) 7/63 Fitzroy St, St Kilda

Some places to stay, especially hostels, also offer email and Internet access. All public libraries are connected to the Internet.

INTERNET RESOURCES

The World Wide Web is a rich resource for travellers. You can research your trip, hunt down bargain air fares, book hotels, check on weather conditions or chat with locals and other travellers about the best places to visit (or to avoid!).

There's no better place to start your Web explorations than the Lonely Planet Web site (www.lonelyplanet.com). Here you'll find succinct summaries on travelling to most places on earth, postcards from other travellers and the Thorn Tree bulletin board, where you can ask questions before you go

or dispense advice when you get back. You can also find travel news and updates to many of our most popular guidebooks, and the subWWWay section links you to the most useful travel resources elsewhere on the Web.

Other useful sites include:

Australian Tourist Commission This site has plenty of information and some good links.
www.australia.com
Beat Magazine Everything you need to know about Melbourne's nightlife from *Beat Magazine*. It covers clubs, pubs and the arts, and includes a comprehensive gig guide.
www.beat.com.au
Cinemedia The site details Cinemedia's ambitious plans for its Federation Square centre. It also has information on Melbourne Cinémathèque's program of festivals.
www.cinemedia.net
Heritage Victoria A comprehensive guide to Victoria's many heritage-listed places.
www.heritage.vic.gov.au
Information Victoria This government site is intended to help Victorians, so it's more practical and informative than the tourism body's site.
www.infovic.vic.gov.au
National Trust An informative site with up-to-date listing of National Trust properties.
www.nattrust.com.au
Parks Victoria Here you'll find details of all the state's parks.
www.parks.vic.gov.au
The Age CitySearch A comprehensive guide to what's happening in Melbourne.
www.melbourne.citysearch.com.au
Tourism Victoria An informative, but not comprehensive site.
www.tourism.vic.gov.au
VicTrip Details of the public transport system and how to use it, including information on metropolitan, country and interstate services.
www.victrip.com.au

See Email & Internet Access earlier for a selection of handy locales at which you can access the Internet.

BOOKS
Lonely Planet

Apart from the comprehensive city guidebook in your hand, Lonely Planet also publishes guidebooks to Victoria and Australia, both of which have excellent information on all aspects of travel. The *Australian phrasebook* takes a tongue-in-cheek look at the Aussie lingo, and also covers Aboriginal languages. Lonely Planet's new Out to Eat series was launched in 1999 with *Out to Eat – Melbourne*, an invaluable guide to the city's restaurants, cafes and bars.

Other Guidebooks

Meyer Eidelson's *The Melbourne Dreaming – A Guide to the Aboriginal Places of Melbourne* is an illuminating guide to the city's hidden history.

Philip Goad's *Melbourne Architecture* is an invaluable guide to the built spaces of the city, chronologically covering styles and buildings from settlement to the late 1990s.

For the ambler, Helen Duffy & Ingrid Ohlsson's *Walking Melbourne* details numerous walks in and around Melbourne.

Those on a tight budget might want to pick up a copy of *Free and Low-Cost Melbourne*, by Joel Becker & Giacomina Pradolin.

Aborigines (Koories)

Henry Reynolds' *The Other Side of the Frontier* uses historical records to give a vivid account of Aborigines' experience of European arrival and takeover of Australia.

Historian Geoffrey Blainey's award-winning *Triumph of the Nomads* chronicles the life of the country's original inhabitants, and convincingly demolishes the myth that the Aborigines were 'primitive' people trapped on a hostile continent.

Koorie Plants, Koorie People, by Nelly Zola & Beth Gott, is an excellent publication by the Koorie Heritage Trust (☎ 9669 9058), detailing the traditional food, fibre and healing plants used in Victoria.

Diane Barwick's *Rebellion at Coranderrk* (Aboriginal History Inc, 1998) gives a history of the 19th-century Coranderrk Aboriginal Station at Healesville, on Melbourne's outskirts.

Australian History

For a good introduction to Australian history, read *A Short History of Australia*, a most accessible and informative general history by the late Manning Clark, the much respected historian. Robert Hughes' best-selling *The Fatal Shore* is a colourful and detailed account of the history of transportation of convicts.

Melbourne History

A number of books deal specifically with Melbourne's history. Michael Cannon's *Old Melbourne Town*, *Melbourne After the Gold Rush* and *The Land Boomers* provide a detailed history of the city, covering the early years, the effects of the gold rush and developments experienced during the prosperous 1880s.

Bearbrass – Imagining Early Melbourne, by Robyn Annear, is an unconventional and intriguing history. Annear 'reinvents' the Melbourne of 1835 to 1851 and integrates the history with her own experiences of contemporary Melbourne.

Graeme Davison's *The Rise and Fall of Marvellous Melbourne* takes a scholarly and fascinating look at the boom and bust of the 1880s and 1890s.

The city of the past comes alive in *Edwardian Melbourne in Picture Postcards*, by Alexandra Bertram & Angus Trumble. WH Newnham's *Melbourne – A Biography of a City* takes a classic 1950s look at the city's history, giving weight to Barry Humphries' wonderful autobiography *More Please*, which brilliantly captures the mid-century decades when Melbourne was the capital of 'wowserism'.

The many books devoted to Melbourne's vibrant inner suburbs take a closer look at the city's development and character. Try seeking out *St Kilda Heritage Sketchbook*, by Bill Brodie & Stan Marks, *Struggletown – Public and Private Life in Richmond*, by Janet McCalman, *Fitzroy – Melbourne's First Suburb*, published by Hyland House, and *Melbourne's Grand Boulevard – The Story of St Kilda Road*, by Judith Buckrich.

FILM

Sydney may have the new Fox Studio, but Melbourne is seen to be the birthplace of the country's film industry. See Arts in the Facts about Melbourne chapter for an overview of significant films about the city or from its filmmakers.

NEWSPAPERS & MAGAZINES

Melbourne has two major daily newspapers. The *Age* gives reasonable coverage of international news. The Saturday and Sunday editions have review sections with plenty of weekend reading; there are other interesting pull-out sections during the week. The *Herald-Sun* is a tabloid-style paper published in several editions throughout the day. The *Australian*, a national daily, is also widely available.

International publications are available at the larger city newsagents such as McGills (Map 2; ☎ 9602 5566), at 187 Elizabeth St. Papers from the UK, USA and South-East Asia are widely available and typically about three days behind. International papers such as the *International Herald Tribune* and the *Guardian Weekly* are available from larger newsagents.

A large number of foreign-language papers are also published in Melbourne. The *Melbourne Trading Post*, published Thursday, is a good place to look if you want to buy or sell anything. It's available at all corner stores, known in Australia as 'milk bars'.

Weekly magazines include an Australian edition of *Time* and the *Bulletin*, a conservative and long-running Australian news magazine which incorporates a condensed version of the US *Newsweek*.

You'll likely encounter, at least once during your stay, a street vendor selling *The Big Issue*. This weekly magazine supports the homeless and gives an alternative spin on various issues.

Gay & Lesbian Publications

For an introduction to the gay scene in Melbourne, pick up a copy of the fortnightly *Brother Sister*, or the weekly *Melbourne Star Observer (MSO)*. Both are free and available from gay cafes, bars and clubs. Also worth looking out for are *Lesbiana*, a monthly magazine for lesbians, and the handy *Gay & Lesbian Melbourne Map*.

RADIO & TV
Radio

Melbourne has more than 20 radio stations. Most of the commercial stations on the FM band flog the standard 'hits and memories' format.

Two excellent noncommercial FM stations that feature alternative and independent music, current affairs and talk-show programs are 3RRR (102.7) and 3PBS (106.7). Triple J (107.5) is the Australian Broadcasting Corporation's (ABC) national 'youth network'. It specialises in alternative music and young people's issues and has some interesting talk shows. ABC Classic-FM (105.9) plays classical music as does the noncommercial 3MBS (103.5), while 3ZZZ (92.3) and 3SBS (93.1) are both multicultural stations broadcasting in a variety of languages.

On the AM band, ABC's Radio National (621) covers a diversity of topics with often fascinating features. It has a 10-minute world-news service every hour on the hour. The Melbourne-based ABC station 3LO (774) has regular talkback programs, an excellent news service on the hour and a world-news feature at 12.10 pm every weekday. The ABC's News Radio (1026) broadcasts nonstop news when it isn't broadcasting the proceedings of federal Parliament.

3CR (855) is a noncommercial community radio station, and 3SBS (1224) is a multicultural foreign-language station. Radio for the Print Handicapped (1179) broadcasts readings of daily newspapers and other useful programs, and between 11.05 pm and 6 am broadcasts the BBC World Service.

TV

Melbourne has six TV stations. The three commercial networks – Channels Seven, Nine and Ten – are just like commercial channels anywhere, with a varied but not particularly adventurous diet of sport, soap operas, lightweight news and sensationalised current affairs, plus plenty of sitcoms (mainly American).

Channel Two is the government-funded, commercial-free ABC station. It produces some excellent current affairs shows, documentaries and a more informed news service as well as screening its fair share of sport and sitcoms (mainly British). The

Flinders Street Station (detail)

Cafe signage, Brunswick Street

Letting it all hang out, Brunswick Street parade

Tiled wall mosaic, Melbourne Concert Hall

Cappuccino with the lot

Marvellous Melbourne

Modern angles and Victorian curves

Melbourne by night

Melbourne by day

ABC also has a knack for making good comedy and drama that receive critical acclaim but low ratings.

The best international news service is at 6.30 pm daily on the publicly funded Special Broadcasting Service (SBS, channel 28, UHF). SBS is a multicultural channel that has some of the most diverse and best programs shown on TV, including serious current affairs, interesting documentaries, Spanish soap operas, and great films (with English subtitles when necessary).

For something completely different tune into community-based Channel 31, which pays its bills by broadcasting horse racing but also produces some quirky, amateur local programs.

VIDEO SYSTEMS

Australia uses the PAL system (unlike Japan and the USA), so prerecorded videos purchased here might not be compatible with your system at home. Check before you buy.

PHOTOGRAPHY

In the city centre, there's a cluster of photography and video equipment shops along Elizabeth St between Bourke and Lonsdale Sts. Little Bourke St (west of Elizabeth St) is another good area to look for camera gear.

If you need your camera repaired, the Camera Clinic (☎ 9419 5247) at 19 Peel St in Collingwood, has an excellent reputation and services all brands except Kodak and Hanimex. In the city, there's Vintech the Camera Service Centre (☎ 9602 1820) on the 5th floor at 358 Lonsdale St.

The Melbourne Camera Club (☎ 9696 5445), in South Melbourne on the corner of Ferrars and Dorcas Sts, meets every Thursday night at 8 pm and welcomes visitors.

Film & Processing

Including developing costs, 36-exposure Kodachrome 64 is around $25 and Fujichrome 100 slide film around $28. With a little shopping around you can find slide film for less, and it can be cheaper if you buy it in quantity.

There are plenty of camera shops in Melbourne and standards of camera service are high. Developing standards are also high, with many places offering one-hour developing of print film. While print film is available from just about anywhere, slide film can be harder to find. Camera shops in the larger towns are usually the best bet for finding Kodachrome or Fujichrome.

Technical Tips

Remember that film can be damaged by heat, so allow for temperature extremes and do your best to keep film as cool as possible, particularly after exposure. Other film and camera hazards are dust and humidity.

During the summer months, allowances should be made for the light intensity, which can wash out colour between mid-morning and late afternoon. In winter, the sky can be quite overcast and grey so you'll need to use a fairly fast film.

As in any country, politeness goes a long way when taking photos or videos; ask permission before photographing people.

TIME

Australia is divided into three time zones. Victoria is in the Eastern Standard Time (EST) zone which is 10 hours ahead of Greenwich Mean Time (GMT/UTC). Tasmania, NSW and Queensland are also in this zone.

From the last Sunday in October until the last Sunday in March daylight-saving time is in operation in Victoria, during which time clocks are turned forward one hour.

ELECTRICITY

Voltage is 240V and the plugs are three-pin, but not the same as British three-pin plugs (which are larger). Users of electric shavers or hair dryers should note that, apart from in fancy hotels, it's difficult to find converters to take either US flat two-pin plugs or the European round two-pin plugs. Adaptors for British plugs can be found in good hardware shops, chemists and travel agents.

WEIGHTS & MEASURES

Australia has used the metric system since the early 1970s, although imperial measurements are still used from time to time.

(A conversion chart is included on the inside back-cover of this guide.)

LAUNDRY

Most accommodation places provide laundry facilities for their guests. There are no self-service laundries in the city centre, but there are quite a few in the inner suburbs. They include the City Edge Laundry, at 39 Errol St in North Melbourne (opposite the town hall), and the St Kilda Beach Laundrette, at 7 Carlisle St in St Kilda. Others are listed in the *Yellow Pages* under 'Laundries – Self-Service'.

LUGGAGE

There are luggage lockers on the ground and 1st floors of the international terminal at Melbourne airport, which cost $4 a day.

In the basement at Spencer St train station, left-luggage lockers cost $2 per day but must be cleared by 10 pm, or $6 and $8 for 24 hours. There are also left-luggage facilities at the Elizabeth St entrance of Flinders St Railway Station costing $5, $8 or $10 for 24 hours.

HEALTH

As long as you haven't visited an infected country in the past 14 days (aircraft refuelling stops do not count) no vaccinations are required for entry to Australia.

Medical care is first class and only moderately expensive. A typical visit to the doctor costs around $35. If you have an immediate health problem, contact the casualty section at the nearest public hospital (see Medical Services later in this chapter for addresses of some hospitals) or a medical clinic. Don't forget to bring any medication you're already taking, and include prescriptions with the generic rather than the brand name (which may not be available locally).

Visitors from the UK, New Zealand, Malta, Italy, Finland, Sweden and the Netherlands have reciprocal health rights in Australia, and can register at any Medicare office.

Travel Insurance

Ambulance services in Australia are self-funding (ie, they're not free) and can be frightfully expensive, so you'd be wise to take out travel insurance. Make sure the policy specifically includes ambulance, helicopter rescue and a flight home for you and anyone you're travelling with, should your condition warrant it. Also check the fine print: some policies exclude 'dangerous activities' such as scuba diving, motorcycling and even trekking. If such activities are on your agenda, you don't want that policy.

Health Precautions

Travellers from the northern hemisphere need to be aware of the intensity of the sun in Australia. During summer, those ultraviolet rays can leave you burnt to a crisp even on an overcast day, so if in doubt wear protective cream, a wide-brimmed hat and loose-fitting cotton clothing that gives maximum skin coverage. Australia has the world's highest incidence of skin cancer, a fact directly connected to exposure to the sun. Be careful.

The contraceptive pill is available on prescription only, so a visit to a doctor is necessary. Doctors are listed in the *Yellow Pages* phone book or you can visit the outpatients section of a public hospital. Condoms are available from chemists, many convenience stores and often from vending machines in pub toilets.

Basic Rules

Heat Victoria has its fair share of hot weather during the summer months with an average daily maximum of over 30°C in some areas. The sensible thing to do on a hot day is to avoid the sun between mid-morning and mid-afternoon. Infants and elderly people are most at risk from heat exhaustion and heat stroke.

Water People who first arrive in a hot climate may not feel thirsty when they should; the body and 'thirst mechanism' often need a few days to adjust. The rule of thumb is that an active adult should drink at least four litres of water per day in warm weather, more when walking or cycling.

Melbourne has one of the highest standards of tap water in the world. Tap water is safe to drink in most other parts of Victoria, but in the more remote areas it may be bore water that's unfit for human consumption – check with the locals.

Sexually Transmitted Diseases

There are numerous sexually transmitted diseases (STDs), for most of which effective treatment is available. If you suspect anything is wrong, go to the nearest public hospital or visit the Melbourne Sexual Health Centre (☎ 9347 0244, 1800-032 017) at 580 Swanston St in Carlton – visits are free and confidential, and don't require a referral.

The AIDS Line (☎ 9347 6099, 1800-133 392) provides information on AIDS and AIDS-related illnesses.

Medical Services

The Traveller's Medical & Vaccination Centre (Map 2; ☎ 9602 5788), on Level 2, 393 Little Bourke St in the city, is open from 9 am to 5 pm Tuesday, Wednesday and Friday, 9 am to 9 pm Monday and Thursday, and from 9 am to 1 pm Saturday. It has excellent information on the latest vaccinations needed for most countries. Appointments are necessary.

The Melbourne Sexual Health Centre (see previous section) provides free check-ups and other medical services. The Victorian AIDS Council & Gay Men's Health Centre (☎ 9865 6700), at 6 Claremont St, South Yarra, provides education, information and support for AIDS sufferers, and operates a health centre for gay men. The Positive Living Centre (☎ 9525 4455), at 46 Acland St, St Kilda, provides support services for people with HIV or AIDS.

Melbourne's major public hospitals are:

Royal Children's (Map 4; ☎ 9345 5522)
Flemington Rd, Parkville
Royal Melbourne (Map 3; ☎ 9342 7000)
Grattan St, Parkville
Royal Women's (Map 3; ☎ 9344 2000) 132
Grattan St, Carlton
St Vincent's (Map 3; ☎ 9288 2211) 41 Victoria
Pde, Fitzroy
The Alfred (Map 7; ☎ 9276 2000) Commercial
Rd, Prahran

See Dangers & Annoyances later in this chapter for information on emergency services.

WOMEN TRAVELLERS

Melbourne is generally a safe place for women travellers, although you should avoid walking alone, especially late at night. Sexual harassment is rare, although the Aussie male culture does have its sexist elements. Don't tolerate any harassment or discrimination. Female hitchhikers should exercise care at all times.

The following organisations offer advice and services for women:

Royal Women's Hospital Sexual Assault
Centre (☎ 9344 2000) 132 Grattan St, Carlton
Women's Domestic Violence Crisis Service
(☎ 9329 8433, 1800-015 188)
Women's Health Victoria (☎ 9670 0669) Level
3, 373 Little Bourke St, Melbourne
Women's Information & Referral Exchange
(☎ 9654 6844) 247 Flinders Lane, Melbourne

GAY & LESBIAN TRAVELLERS

Homosexuality is legal and the age of consent, equal to that for heterosexuals, is 16.

The attitude in Melbourne towards gays and lesbians is, on the whole, open-minded and accepting. In regional Victoria there's still a strong streak of homophobia, and violence against homosexual people, in particular gay men, is not unknown.

Melbourne has an increasingly lively gay and lesbian scene, with numerous bars, cafes, nightclubs and accommodation places in the inner-city suburbs of Fitzroy, Collingwood, Prahran, South Yarra and St Kilda. Around the state, places such as Daylesford and Hepburn Springs, Phillip Island, Bright, the Mornington Peninsula, Echuca and Lorne have accommodation catering for gays and lesbians.

The highlight of the local calendar is the Midsumma Festival held each January/February. It showcases a wide range of theatrical, musical, artistic and sporting events, such as the Midsumma Carnival Street Party in Commercial Rd, Prahran, the Pride March down Fitzroy St, St Kilda, and Red Raw, a dance party held on the Saturday of Australia Day weekend. The Midsumma

Web site (www.midsumma.org.au) has more information.

If you're visiting towards the end of March, an event worth checking out is the Melbourne Queer Film & Video Festival. The festival Web site is at www.mqfvf.also.org.au.

The following organisations offer a range of advice and services for gays and lesbians.

Gay & Lesbian Switchboard (☎ 9510 5488) A telephone information service with trained counsellors who offer advice and counselling (or you can just ring for a chat). It operates between 6 and 10 pm nightly, from 2 to 10 pm Wednesday.

Gay & Lesbian Switchboard Information Service (☎ 0055 12504) A 24-hour recorded-information service, covering the entertainment scene as well as social and support groups.

DISABLED TRAVELLERS

Victoria provides an exciting range of attractions that are accessible to travellers with special needs. Highlights outside the city centre include the Penguin Parade (☎ 5956 8691) at Phillip Island, *Puffing Billy* (☎ 9754 6800) in the Dandenong Ranges and Healesville Sanctuary (☎ 5962 4022), east of the city.

Easy Access Australia – A Travel Guide to Australia, available from PO Box 218 Kew, Vic 3101 for $24.85, has a chapter devoted to Victoria, and you'll find the Access Melbourne Web site (www.accessmelbourne.vic.gov.au) a useful resource.

The following organisations offer a range of services for people with special needs:

Assist Travel (☎ 1800-809 192) This travel agent specialises in travel for people with disabilities. You can write to Assist Travel at c/o PO Box 83, Lara, Vic 3212.
Association for the Blind (☎ 9599 5000)
Disabled Persons Information Bureau (☎ 9616 7704) The bureau can refer you to a specific service provider.
Independent Living Centre (☎ 9362 6111) The centre may be able to help with equipment rental and relevant information for disabled people.
National Industries for Disability Services (☎ 9690 2266) This service, operating through the Australian Council for the Rehabilitation of the Disabled (☎ 9362 0800), 85 Cowper St,

Footscray, produces information sheets for disabled travellers, including lists of state-level organisations, specialist travel agents, wheelchair and equipment hire and access guides.
Paraplegic & Quadriplegic Association of Victoria (Para Quad; ☎ 9415 1200, 1800-805 384) Para Quad can provide advice on access, equipment hire and attendant care.
Traveller's Aid (☎ 9654 2600) Located at Level 2, 169 Swanston St, Traveller's Aid is helpful and friendly, and has a lounge, cafe, wheelchair-accessible toilets, showers and a telephone. It is also located on the lower ground floor of Spencer St train station (☎ 9670 2873).
Travellers Aid Disability Access Service (☎ 9654 7690) Part of Traveller's Aid (see above) and available to people with any disability, this service also offers meal, toilet and communication assistance, minor wheelchair repairs and computer and Internet facilities.
Victorian Deaf Society (☎ 9657 8111)

See also the Libraries section later in this chapter and the Places to Stay and Getting Around chapters for additional information.

SENIOR TRAVELLERS

Many organisations offer discounts to seniors, but usually only to those with a government pension or senior card, available only to residents.

Discounts of 10% are available to pensioners for most express bus fares and bus passes. Travellers over 60 years of age can get up to 70% off regular air fares. These discounts apply to both Australians and to visitors. To qualify, present current ID showing your age.

MELBOURNE FOR CHILDREN

The *EG* (Entertainment Guide), published in Friday's *Age* newspaper, has a 'Children's Activities' section that details what's on for children each weekend – eg, pantomimes, animal nurseries, sanctuaries and museum programs. *Melbourne Events* also has a children's section in its free monthly magazine.

Some of the favourite places to take kids include the Royal Melbourne Zoo in Parkville, Luna Park on the Lower Esplanade in St Kilda, the Fun Factory in South Yarra, the IMAX Theatre in Carlton, Scienceworks museum and the Planetarium in Spotswood, any of the city's public swimming pools, the Polly Woodside Maritime Museum at Southbank, the Melbourne Aquarium opposite the Crown Entertainment Complex on the Yarra, and *Puffing Billy*, a vintage steam-train that runs through the Dandenong Ranges (see the Excursions chapter).

Collingwood Children's Farm (☎ 9205 5469) is a great place for the kids to learn how to milk a cow and find out more about farm animals. It's open from 9 am to 5 pm every day.

If you want to get rid of the kids for the day, Kids Tours (☎ 9337 1192) is an excellent way to do it. They specialise in half- and full-day tours of sights in and around the city.

The Melbourne City Council runs a child-minding centre (☎ 9329 9561), at 104 A'Beckett St in the city, for children up to five years old. It charges $3.50 an hour or $35 a day.

LIBRARIES

The historic State Library of Victoria (Map 2) is at 328 Swanston St in the city. Other public libraries in the inner suburbs include the Port Phillip Library (Map 9), at 150 Carlisle St in St Kilda; the Braille & Talking Book Library, at 51 Commercial Rd in South Yarra; the East Melbourne Library, at 122 George St; the Fitzroy Library, at 201 Napier St; the Carlton Library (Map 4), on the corner of Newry and Rathdowne Sts; and the Port Melbourne Library, at 147 Lidiard St.

UNIVERSITIES

Major universities within Melbourne's inner suburbs include the University of Melbourne (Map 4; ☎ 9344 4000) on Grattan St in Carlton; the Royal Melbourne Institute of Technology (Map 2; ☎ 9662 0611), known as RMIT, at 124 Latrobe St in the city; and the Victoria University of Technology (☎ 9248 1000), which has a campus at 300 Flinders St in the city, though its main campus is at Footscray Park.

Melbourne's other two major universities are both over half an hour's drive from the city: Monash University (☎ 9905 4000) is on Wellington Rd in Clayton, and La Trobe University (☎ 9479 1111) is on Kingsbury Drive in Bundoora.

DANGERS & ANNOYANCES
Emergency

In the case of a life-threatening emergency, dial ☎ 000. This call is free from any phone, and the operator will connect you to either the police, ambulance or fire brigade. Otherwise, you can call these services direct:

Ambulance	☎ 11 440
Fire Brigade	☎ 11 411
Police	☎ 11 444

In the city centre, there are police stations at 228–32 Flinders Lane (☎ 9247 6666) and 637 Flinders St (☎ 9247 5347); both are staffed 24 hours a day.

Traveller's Aid, on the lower ground floor at Spencer St train station (☎ 9670 2873), offers assistance for stranded travellers, information, advice, showers, toilets and, if you're in need, a cup of coffee and a sandwich. The service is free and is open on from 7.30 am to 7.30 pm weekdays, 7.30 to 11.30 am weekends. There is also a branch at Level 2, 169 Swanston St (☎ 9654 2600), with a lounge, cafe, wheelchair-accessible toilets, showers and telephone. It is open from 8 am to 5 pm Monday to Friday.

Other useful emergency numbers include:

Accidents
  State Emergency Service (☎ 9696 6111)
  Poisons Information Centre (☎ 13 1126)
Chemist
  My Chemist (☎ 9386 1000) 28 Sydney Rd, Coburg, open 9 am to midnight
  Leonard Long Pharmacy (☎ 9510 3977) cnr of Williams Rd and High St, Prahran, open 9 am to midnight
Dentist
  Dental Emergency Service (☎ 9341 0222)
Interpreter Service
  Translating & Interpreting Service (☎ 13 1450) operates 24 hours
Life Crisis
  Crisis Line (☎ 9329 0300) 24-hour telephone counselling

Lifeline Counselling (☎ 13 1114, 9662 1000) 24-hour service available in six languages
Mechanical Breakdown
  Accident Towing Service (☎ 13 1176)
  RACV Emergency Roadside Service (☎ 13 1111)

Theft

Melbourne is a relatively safe city to visit, but you should still take reasonable precautions. Don't leave hotel rooms or cars unlocked, and don't leave money, wallets, purses or cameras unattended or in full view through car windows. Most accommodation places have a safe where guests can store their valuables.

If you're unlucky enough to have something stolen while on holiday, immediately report all details of the theft at the nearest police station. If your credit cards, cash card or travellers cheques have been taken, notify your bank or the relevant company immediately (most have 24-hour 'lost or stolen' numbers listed under 'Banks' or 'Credit Card Organisations' in the *Yellow Pages*).

Trams

In Melbourne, passengers should be *extremely* cautious when stepping on and off trams. A lot of people have been hit by passing cars, so don't step off without looking both ways. Pedestrians in Bourke St Mall and Swanston Walk should watch for passing trams too.

Car drivers should treat Melbourne trams with caution (see the Getting Around chapter). Cyclists should be careful not to get their wheels caught in a tram track and motorcyclists should take special care when tram tracks are wet.

Swimming & Boating

Port Phillip Bay is generally safe for swimming – the closest you're likely to come to a shark is in the local fish and chip shop (where shark is rather euphemistically called 'flake').

The blue-ringed octopus is sometimes found hiding under rocks in rockpools on the foreshore. Its sting can be fatal, so don't touch it under any circumstances! Many of the bay and coastal beaches are patrolled by life-savers in summer – patrolled beaches have a pair of red and yellow flags which you should always swim between.

If you happen to get caught in a rip when swimming and are being taken out to sea, try not to panic. Raise one arm until you have been spotted, and then swim parallel to the shore – *don't* try to swim back against the rip; you'll only tire yourself. Boating on Port Phillip Bay can be hazardous, as conditions tend to change dramatically and without warning.

Spiders

Victoria's most dangerous spider is the redback. It's a small black spider with a red stripe and a very painful bite – apply ice and seek medical attention. The white-tailed spider should also be avoided. Some people have an extreme reaction to this spider's bite and gangrene can occur.

Insects

In summer, you'll have to cope with flies and mosquitoes. An insect repellent such as Rid or Aerogard will help, but at times you may have to resort to the 'Great Australian Wave' to keep them at bay.

Stingose is a very good spray for relieving the sting of mosquitoes or sunburn.

BUSINESS HOURS

Standard shop trading hours are from 9 am to 5.30 pm Monday to Thursday, 9 am to 9 pm Friday, 9 am to 5 pm Saturday and 11 am to 5 pm Sunday. Bookshops often stay open as late as 9 or 10 pm. Places such as milk bars are open till around 8 pm, and many supermarkets stay open late. Coles supermarkets are open 24 hours.

Most offices and businesses open from 9 am to 5.30 pm Monday to Friday, although some government departments close at 4.30 or 5 pm. Normal banking hours are from 9.30 am to 4 pm Monday to Thursday, 9.30 am to 5 pm Friday. Pub bottleshops generally stay open until 11 pm from Monday to Saturday, but many close by 8 pm on Sunday.

PUBLIC HOLIDAYS

On public holidays, government departments, banks, offices, large stores and post offices are closed. On Good Friday and Christmas Day newspapers are not published and about the only stores you will find open are the 24-hour convenience stores. Also note that some consulates close for 10 days over the Christmas-New Year period.

Victoria observes the following nine public holidays:

New Year's Day 1 January
Australia Day 26 January
Labour Day March – the first or second Monday
Easter March/April – Good Friday, Holy Saturday and Easter Monday
Anzac Day 25 April
Queen's Birthday June – the second Monday
Melbourne Cup Day November – the first Tuesday
Christmas Day 25 December
Boxing Day 26 December

When a public holiday falls on a weekend, the following Monday is declared a holiday (with the exception of Anzac Day and Australia Day).

SPECIAL EVENTS

Melbourne has a great love of festivals. The city streets and venues play host to events year round, with themes ranging from film, comedy, arts, theatre, sports, food and wine.

'What's on' lists are available from tourist information offices as is *Melbourne Events* monthly calender. Tickets to most major events can be booked through Ticketmaster (☎ 13 6100) or Ticketec Victoria (☎ 13 2849).

January

Australian Open Grand Slam tennis, held at the Melbourne Park Tennis Centre.
Hanging Rock Horse Races Held annually at Hanging Rock since the 1870s.
Midsumma Festival Held in January/February, it is the premier gay and lesbian event, showcasing a wide range of theatrical, musical, artistic and sporting activities.
Montsalvat Jazz Festival This eclectic jazz festival is held over three days at a picturesque

KAREN TRIST

Beating out a Moomba tattoo at Southbank

artists' colony in Eltham and various other venues around town.
Summer Music Festival Based at the Victorian Arts Centre, the festival features everything from the classics to rock music.

February

Asian Food Festival Held in Chinatown, Little Bourke St.
Australian Matchplay and **Australian Masters** These golf tournaments are held on the great sandbelt courses.
Chinese New Year Celebrated most spectacularly in Chinatown.
Great Melbourne Bike Rides 20km and 45km bike rides.
Harvest Picnic Enjoy the pick of the crop of Victorian produce at Hanging Rock.
Melbourne Music Festival Local musicians showcased at various venues.
St Kilda Festival A week-long celebration of local arts and culture – food, art, music and writing.
Victoria St Festival Vietnamese culture is celebrated on Victoria St Richmond.

March

Antipodes Festival Held in Melbourne's small Greek quarter in Lonsdale St, between Swanston and Russell Sts, the festival celebrates Greek art, culture and music.

Formula One Grand Prix Motor racing at Albert Park.

Irish Festival Held at venues all over the city, reaching a climax on St Patrick's day (17 March) with an open air concert in the gardens.

Melbourne Food & Wine Festival This main gastronomical event of the year takes place from mid-March to early April.

Moomba Festival 10 days of carnival, with fireworks, an outdoor art show, water-skiing and a Dragon Boat Festival; all on the Yarra River.

April

Anzac Day Held 25 April, the day begins with a dawn service at the Shrine of Remembrance, followed by a march along St Kilda Rd into the city.

Bells Beach Surfing Classic The world's best surfers rip, tear and lacerate at Bells Beach, just south of Torquay.

Heritage Week Organised by the National Trust, the week is devoted to increasing appreciation of Melbourne's rich architectural heritage.

International Comedy Festival Locals are joined by a wealth of international acts performing at venues all over the city.

International Flower & Garden Show Held annually in the Carlton Gardens.

May

Next Wave Festival At various city venues, Next Wave presents over two weeks of visual and performing arts from a new generation of artists.

St Kilda Film Festival Showcasing contemporary Australian short films and videos.

July

Maverick Arts Festival An alternative event featuring the work of visual and performance artists, writers, singers and comedians in various small venues and pubs.

Melbourne International Film Festival Two weeks of the newest and the best in local and international film.

August

Exhibition of Victorian Winemakers Celebrating local food and wine.

Melbourne Writers' Festival Held at the CUB Malthouse in August/September, this 10-day festival ranges over literary genres and issues.

Sip 'n' Sup Wine & Food Festival Held in Sunbury, just out of Melbourne.

September

Grand Final The Australian Football League (AFL) final is played on the last Saturday in September.

Melbourne Fringe Arts Festival Starting late September with a parade and street party on Brunswick St, it continues to mid-October.

Royal Melbourne Show The country comes to town for this large-scale agricultural fair at the Royal Melbourne Showgrounds, Flemington.

October

Herald-Sun Tour A 10-day professional cycling race.

Lygon St Festa Italian culture is celebrated with food stalls, bands and dancers on Lygon St.

Melbourne International Festival The city's major arts event has a program that covers theatre, opera, dance and music.

Melbourne to Warrnambool Classic A professional cycling race that most riders refer to as the 'Holy Grail'.

Oktoberfest A three-day festival styled on the Bavarian festival of the same name, held at the Royal Melbourne Showgrounds, Flemington.

November

Hispanic Community Festival Melbourne's small Spanish and South American communities take over Johnston St for a lively celebration of Latin culture.

The Spring Racing Carnival This begins in October and runs into November. The two feature races: Caulfield Cup (Caulfield Racecourse) and the Melbourne Cup (Flemington Racecourse).

December

Carols by Candlelight Christmas carols under the stars in the Sidney Myer Music Bowl.

International Test Match Cricket Held at the Melbourne Cricket Ground (MCG), the first day of the international competition is Boxing Day.

Outdoor Theatre Evening performances of plays such as *A Midsummer Night's Dream* and *Romeo & Juliet* in the Royal Botanic Gardens.

DOING BUSINESS

Business and finance publications to look out for are the *Australian Financial Review* and *Business Review Weekly (BRW)*.

Most top-end hotels and serviced apartments provide business facilities such as conference rooms, secretarial, fax and photocopying services, use of computers, private office space and translation services.

Old meets new on Collins Street

Historic Como, South Yarra

The giant tuning fork, aka Bolte Bridge

Captain Cook's Cottage, Fitzroy Gardens

Melbourne Cup madness

Mecca for many Melburnians, the Melbourne Cricket Ground on Grand Final day

Qantas Club and Ansett Golden Wing at Melbourne airport offer business travellers a range of services, including meeting rooms and individual workstations equipped with telephone, fax, modem point and photocopier.

The Public Office (Map 2; ☎ 9321 6500), on the top floor at 100 Adderley St, West Melbourne, offers not just a great view but good office facilities for casual users. It's open from 8 am until late seven days a week. This unconventional workspace has a bar and cafe to help keep you fortified while at work (see the Entertainment chapter).

WORK

If you come to Australia on a 12-month 'working holiday' visa you can officially work for the entire 12 months, but can only stay with the one employer for a maximum of three months. On the other hand, working on a regular tourist visa is strictly prohibited. Some travellers do find casual work, but with the state's unemployment rate around 8% it's not easy to get a job – legal or otherwise.

To receive wages you must have a Tax File Number (TFN), issued by the Australian Taxation Office. Application forms are available at all post offices, and you must show your passport and visa. Finding work is usually tough, and those who succeed are very determined but not too choosy about what they do. The more common jobs found by travellers include factory work, bar work, waiting or washing dishes, nursing and nanny work, telephone sales, fruit picking and collecting for charities.

The staff at the Centrelink job centres can advise you on how to go about looking for work and what's available, but be prepared for long queues. Try the classified section of the daily papers under 'Situations Vacant', especially on Saturday and Wednesday. The staff and notice boards at some of the backpacker hostels can also be good sources of information.

Getting There & Away

AIR

Melbourne's airport services both domestic and international flights. It is Australia's second busiest airport, after Sydney. Flights can be heavily booked during the Christmas high season or on particularly popular routes such as Hong Kong or Singapore to Melbourne. The airport is at Tullamarine, 22km north-west of the city centre – about a 30-minute drive, although you should allow more time in peak-hour traffic.

Departure Tax

A departure tax of $30 applies to everyone leaving Australia; the tax is added automatically onto the price of your air ticket.

The UK

Airline ticket discounters are known as 'bucket shops' in the UK. Despite the somewhat disreputable name, there is nothing under-the-counter about them. Discount air travel is big business in London. Advertisements for many travel agents appear in the travel pages of the weekend broadsheets, such as the *Independent* on Saturday and the *Sunday Times*. Look out for free magazines, such as *TNT*, which are widely available in London – start by looking outside the main train and underground stations.

For students or travellers aged under 26 years, popular travel agencies in the UK include STA Travel (☎ 020-7361 6161), which has an office at 86 Old Brompton Rd, London SW7 3LQ, and other offices in London and Manchester. Visit its Web site at www.statravel.co.uk. Usit Campus (☎ 020-7730 3402), 52 Grosvenor Gardens, London SW1W0AG, has branches throughout the UK. The Usit Web address is www.usitcampus.com. Both of these agencies sell tickets to all travellers but cater especially to young people and students. Other recommended travel agencies include:

Trailfinders (☎ 020-7938 3939) 194 Kensington High St, London W8 7RG

Warning

The information in this chapter is particularly vulnerable to change: Prices for international travel are volatile, routes are introduced and cancelled, schedules change, special deals come and go, and rules and visa requirements are amended. Airlines and governments seem to take a perverse pleasure in making price structures and regulations as complicated as possible. You should check directly with the airline or a travel agent to make sure you understand how a fare (and ticket you may buy) works. In addition, the travel industry is highly competitive and there are many lurks and perks.

The upshot of this is that you should get opinions, quotes and advice from as many airlines and travel agents as possible before you part with your hard-earned cash. The details given in this chapter should be regarded as pointers and are not a substitute for your own careful, up-to-date research.

Bridge the World (☎ 020-7734 7447) 4 Regent Place, London W1R 5FB
Flightbookers (☎ 020-7757 2000) 177–78 Tottenham Court Rd, London W1P 9LF

Discounted, low-season return tickets between London and Melbourne start at about £459. High-season return fares start at around £700. Britannia Airlines runs a charter flight between London and Melbourne from November to March, with prices as low as £399 return. From Melbourne, return fares to London start at A$1800/2400 during the low/high season with Qantas, Singapore Airlines and British Airways.

North America

Discount travel agents in the USA are known as 'consolidators' (although you won't see a sign on the door saying Consolidator). San Francisco is the ticket consolidator capital of America, although some good deals can be found in Los Angeles, New York and other big cities. Consolidators can be found through the *Yellow Pages* or the major daily newspapers. The *New York Times*, the *Los Angeles Times*, the *Chicago Tribune* and the *San Francisco Examiner* all produce weekly travel sections in which you will find a number of travel agency ads.

If you have the time, or the inclination, there are some interesting options for travel between North America and Melbourne. These include flights via New Zealand, via the Pacific Islands and via Japan and other Asian countries. Council Travel, America's largest student travel organisation, has around 60 offices in the USA; its head office (☎ 800-226 8624) is at 205 E 42 St, New York, NY 10017. Call it for the office nearest you or visit its Web site at www.ciee.org. STA Travel (☎ 800-777 0112) has offices in Boston, Chicago, Miami, New York, Philadelphia, San Francisco and other major cities. Call the toll-free ☎ 800 number for office locations or visit its Web site at www.statravel.com.

From the US west coast, return low/high season fares start at US$845/1265, while fares from the east coast are more expensive, starting at around US$1180/1600. Return fares from Australia to the US start at A$1535/1640 to the west coast in the low/high season and A$1797/1895 to the east coast.

Travel CUTS (☎ 800-667 2887) is Canada's national student travel agency and has offices in all major cities. Its Web address is www.travelcuts.com. Fares out of Vancouver will be similar to those from the US west coast, while from Toronto return fares start at C$1880/2300 during the low/high season. Expect to pay around A$1550 for a low season return fare from Melbourne to Vancouver.

New Zealand

There is often much fare discounting on the popular New Zealand-Australia flights; shop around and you are likely to come up with a fairly good deal. Flight Centre (☎ 09-309 6171) has a large central office in

Auckland at National Bank Towers (corner of Queen and Darby Sts) and many branches throughout the country. STA Travel (☎ 09-309 0458) has its main office at 10 High St, Auckland, with other offices in Auckland as well as in Hamilton, Palmerston North, Wellington, Christchurch and Dunedin. The STA Web address is www.statravel.com.au. From Auckland standard return fares to Melbourne are around NZ$530, while fares from Melbourne to Auckland start at around A$449, depending on the time of year.

Asia

Although most Asian countries are now offering fairly competitive air fare deals, Bangkok, Singapore and Hong Kong are still the best places to shop around for discount tickets. Hong Kong's travel market can be unpredictable, but some excellent bargains are available if you are lucky. As Hong Kong–Australia flights are usually heavily booked, and Bangkok and Singapore flights are often part of the Europe-Australia route, plan ahead for both a seat and a reasonable fare.

Khao San Rd in Bangkok is the best place for finding budget fares. Bangkok has a number of excellent travel agents, but there are also some suspect ones; ask the advice of other travellers before handing over your cash. STA Travel (☎ 02-236 0262), at 33 Surawong Rd, is a good and reliable place to start.

In Singapore, STA Travel (☎ 737 7188) in the Orchard Parade Hotel, 1 Tanglin Rd, offers competitive discount fares for Asian destinations and beyond. Singapore, like Bangkok, has hundreds of travel agents, so you can compare prices. Chinatown Point shopping centre on New Bridge Rd has a good selection of travel agents.

Hong Kong has a number of excellent, reliable travel agencies and some not-so-reliable ones. A good way to check on a travel agent is to look it up in the phone book: fly-by-night operators don't usually stay around long enough to get listed. Many travellers use the Hong Kong Student Travel Bureau (☎ 2730 3269), 8th floor, Star House,

Tsimshatsui. You could also try Phoenix Services (☎ 2722 7378), 7th floor, Milton Mansion, 96 Nathan Rd, Tsimshatsui.

Shop around, but typical return fares to Melbourne start at around 32,900B from Bangkok, S$948 from Singapore and HK$7380 from Hong Kong. From Melbourne, fares to Asia vary according to the time of year you plan to travel and the availability of discount fares. Expect to pay around A$845 for a standard return fare to Hong Kong, A$773 return to Singapore and $966 return to Bangkok.

Africa
There are several direct flights between Perth and Harare (Zimbabwe) or Johannesburg (South Africa), with connections to/from Melbourne. Return fares between Melbourne and Harare or Johannesburg range from A$1700 to A$2095.

South African Airways and Air Zimbabwe fly from Nairobi (Kenya) to Mumbai and Delhi, with connections to Melbourne; return fares start at around A$2200. Other airlines that connect southern Africa and Australia include Malaysia Airlines (via Kuala Lumpur), Singapore Airlines (via Singapore) and Air Mauritius (via Mauritius).

South America
Two routes operate between South America and Australia. The Chile connection involves Lan Chile's Santiago-Tahiti flight (via Easter Island), which operates twice a week; from Tahiti you fly Qantas or another airline to Australia. Return fares start at around A$1950. Alternatively, Aerolineas Argentinas/Qantas flies from Buenos Aires to Melbourne (via Auckland); a low season return fare starting at around A$1660.

Other Parts of Australia
Regular flights connect Melbourne with all other major airports in Australia. Qantas Airways (☎ 13 1313 from anywhere in Australia) and Ansett Australia (☎ 13 1300) are the major domestic carriers. Their respective Web sites are at www.qantas.com.au and www.ansett.com.au. In mid-2000 UK-operated Virgin Atlantic and the Australian-owned airlines Spirit and Impulse were due to launch no-frills, and considerably cheaper, domestic air services between Melbourne, Sydney and Brisbane. The launch of these companies will inevitably impact upon the fares offered by both Qantas and Ansett.

All nonresident international travellers can get up to 30% discount on internal Qantas flights and 25% on Ansett flights. You simply present your international ticket when booking an internal flight. It seems there is no limit to the number of domestic flights you can take, it doesn't matter which airline you fly into Australia with, and it doesn't have to be on a return ticket. Note that the discount applies only to the full economy fare, so in many cases it will be cheaper to take advantage of other discounts offered. The best advice is to ring around and explore the options before you buy.

Within Victoria Because of the state's compact size, scheduled flights within Victoria are somewhat limited. Kendall Airlines, which you book through Ansett (☎ 13 1300), flies daily between Melbourne and Mildura ($183), Portland ($137) and Albury ($133). Southern Australia Airlines, which you book through Qantas (☎ 13 1313), also flies between Melbourne and Mildura for $183. Kendall and Southern Australia offer advance-purchase discounts on one-way and return fares. Several small airlines fly to other destinations.

Qantas subsidiaries, Eastern Australia Airlines and Southern Australia Airlines have commenced flights to the Victorian ski resort, Mt Hotham, from Sydney and Melbourne from late June to mid-September. The 36-seat planes operate return flights from Sydney to Mt Hotham on Fridays and Sundays (fares starting at $299), and return flights from Melbourne to Mt Hotham on Wednesdays, Fridays, Saturdays and Sundays (fares starting at $198).

BUS
Travelling by bus is the cheapest way to get around Australia, and you get to see more of the wide red-brown land than if you fly. But

don't forget that it's a big country – bus travel can be slow and tedious.

There is only one truly national bus network – Greyhound Pioneer Australia (☎ 13 2030 from anywhere in Australia). McCafferty's (☎ 13 1499) is Australia's next biggest operator, with services all along the east coast as well as the loop through the Centre from Adelaide, Alice Springs and Darwin to Townsville. There are a few smaller companies, such as Firefly (☎ 9670 7500), which operate discounted bus trips between Melbourne, Sydney and Adelaide.

You can book directly with the bus companies, although it's often worth checking with travel agents and fare brokers such as the Backpackers' Travel Centre (☎ 9654 8477), at Shop 19, Centre Place, off Flinders Lane.

There are basically two types of fares for bus travel – express fares and bus passes (ask the bus companies for more information). Students, backpackers (YHA and VIP card holders) and pensioners get discounts of at least 10% off most express fares and bus passes.

Note that the majority of bus services within country Victoria are operated by V/Line – see Within Victoria in the Train section following.

Alternative Bus Tours & Networks

If you're travelling between Melbourne and Adelaide, you'll miss some great countryside if you fast-track along the main highway. The Wayward Bus (☎ 1800-882 823) explores the natural attractions of the coastal route between Melbourne and Adelaide, stopping at Port Fairy and Beachport overnight. Take a look at Wayward's Web site at www.waywardbus.com to see what they offer you.

Oz Experience (☎ 1300-300 028) is basically a backpacker bus line. It has frequent bus services up and down the east coast and through central Australia to all the major destinations, with off-the-beaten-track detours. Contact the company for details on prices and schedules.

TRAIN

Australia's railway system is less comprehensive than its bus networks, and train services are less frequent and more expensive. However, interstate trains are now as fast or faster than buses, and in recent years the railways have cut their prices in an attempt to be more competitive with both bus fares and reduced air fares. Somewhat confusingly, the individual states run their own railway services – Victoria has V/Line (☎ 13 6196), Queensland has Queensland Rail, NSW has Countrylink and Western Australia has Westrail.

As the booking system is computerised, any station (other than those on metropolitan lines) can make a booking for any journey throughout the country. For reservations telephone Countrylink ☎ 13 2232 from anywhere in Australia; this will connect you to the nearest booking agent. Hours for this service vary slightly from state to state. In Victoria, the service is available from 7 am to 9 pm daily, in NSW 6.15 am to 10 pm.

Fares & Conditions

There are three standard fare levels for rail travel – economy, 1st class and sleeping berths, although sleeping berths aren't available on all trains. Ticket prices are set by V/Line, so you won't get better deals by shopping around. Depending on availability, a limited number of discounted fares are offered on most trains. These cut 10% to 40% off the standard fares, and if you book early or travel at off-peak times, you'll usually qualify for one of these cheaper fares. There are also half-price concession fares available to children under 16 years of age, secondary-school students and Australian tertiary students, but unfortunately there are no discounts for backpackers.

On interstate journeys you can make free stopovers – you have two months to complete your trip on a one-way ticket and six months on a return ticket.

There are no discounts for return travel – a return ticket is just double the price of a one-way ticket.

GETTING THERE & AWAY

Interstate Services & Fares

Interstate railway services operate between the capital cities. That means that while there are direct services from Melbourne to Sydney, if you want to go from Melbourne to Brisbane you have to go via Sydney, and if you want to go from Melbourne to Perth you have to go via Adelaide. Fares are also calculated on each sector; for example, to go from Melbourne to Brisbane you'll pay the Melbourne to Sydney fare *plus* the Sydney to Brisbane fare.

Countrylink runs daily XTP (express) trains between Melbourne and Sydney. The trip takes 10¾ hours and a standard economy/1st-class/1st-class sleeper fare is $104/145/240, although discounts of between 10% and 40% apply for advance bookings.

To get to Canberra from Melbourne by rail you need to take the daily Canberra Link, which involves a train journey to Wodonga on the Victoria-NSW border and then a bus from there. This takes about eight hours and costs $49/64.50 economy/1st class. The Canberra service must be booked through V/Line (☎ 13 6196).

The *Overland* operates between Melbourne and Adelaide each night except Wednesday and Saturday. The trip takes 12 hours and costs $64/199 economy/1st-class sleeper. There are also budget seats for $30, but you have to book in person at Melbourne's Spencer St train station (or at an Adelaide station). You can transport your car on the *Overland* for $149.

To get to Perth by rail from Melbourne you take the *Overland* to Adelaide and then the popular *Indian-Pacific* (which comes through Adelaide from Sydney). The Melbourne to Perth trip takes two days and three nights, and fares are $326 for an economy seat, $618/753 for a 'holiday fare' (economy/1st class seat to Adelaide, then sleeper to Perth) or $1069 for a 1st-class sleeper (all meals included).

For the 60-hour trip from Melbourne to Alice Springs, the *Ghan* runs a service every Wednesday. A one-way economy/'holiday fare'/1st-class sleeper fare is $270/528/895. On the way back to Melbourne, fares are slightly lower.

All Countrylink fares go up during the peak period from 1 September to 31 October.

Rail Passes There are a number of rail passes – available from major train stations, travel agents or the V/Line Travel Centre at 589 Collins St, Melbourne – that allow unlimited travel, but these passes are now only available to international visitors. To qualify you need to show your passport or return air ticket.

Within Victoria

Extensive train and bus services within country Victoria are operated by V/Line (☎ 13 6196). The major centres are serviced by trains, with buses filling in the gaps and doing the cross-country runs between towns.

On return tickets, V/Line offers special off-peak fares called Super Savers, which give you nearly a 30% discount. For 'inter-urban services' (generally shorter trips), Super Saver fares are available each weekday, although you mustn't arrive in Melbourne before 9.30 am or leave Melbourne between 4 and 6 pm. For 'inter-city services' (generally longer trips), Super Saver fares are available Tuesday, Wednesday or Thursday. V/Line's Victoria Pass, which is only available to international visitors, gives you seven days unlimited travel on V/Line trains and buses within the state for $75, or two weeks unlimited travel for $130.

From Melbourne, all long-distance trains exit the Spencer St train station, on the western side of the city centre. Long-distance buses operate out of the Spencer St coach terminal, 100m north of the train station.

Out of Melbourne, the principal train routes (in bold) and connecting bus services are as follows:

South-west to Geelong then to Warrnambool
A daily bus service, Bellarine Buslines (☎ 5248 2655), runs along the Great Ocean Rd from Geelong through Lorne ($11.20) and Apollo Bay ($18), with a connecting service to Warrnambool on Friday (also on Monday during summer).

North-west to Ballarat, Stawell, Horsham then Adelaide ($51) Buses connect from Stawell to Halls Gap in the Grampians (Gariwerd).

North through Bendigo to Swan Hill Buses continue from Bendigo to Echuca.

North to Shepparton and Cobram.

North to Albury-Wodonga Buses run from Wangaratta to Beechworth and Bright. Buses also run from Wodonga to Canberra. The train continues to Sydney.

East through Traralgon and Sale to Bairnsdale Buses connect from Bairnsdale to Lakes Entrance, Orbost, Cann River and Merimbula.

One-way economy fares are quoted throughout this book; 1st-class fares (available on trains only) are around 30% more than economy fares, and return fares are double the one-way fare.

CAR & MOTORCYCLE

The main road routes into Victoria are as follows: between Sydney and Melbourne you have a choice of either the Hume Hwy (870km, and freeway most of the way) or the coastal Princes Hwy (1039km, much longer and slower but a hell of a lot more scenic). There's a similar choice if you're travelling between Adelaide and Melbourne, with either the fairly direct Western Hwy (730km) or the slower Princes Hwy coastal route (894km), of which the section closest to Melbourne is known as the Great Ocean Rd.

If you're travelling between Brisbane and Melbourne, the quickest route is via the Newell Hwy (1890km).

See the Getting Around chapter for details of road rules, driving conditions and information on buying and renting vehicles.

BOAT

The *Spirit of Tasmania* (☎ 13 2010) car and passenger ferry operates regular services across Bass Strait between Melbourne and Davenport (Tasmania). There are dozens of different fares available; prices depend on the type of sleeping quarters and the time of year, and all include breakfast and dinner. Cheapest are the 'hostel fares' at $106/136 per person each way in the low/high season. The next level up costs around $156/181 for a two or four-berth cabin, with the most expensive option being $232/317 for a luxury suite. Return fares are just double the one-way fares, and high-season prices apply from 11 December to 23 January. Heavily discounted advance fares (up to 50% off) are sometimes available.

The *Spirit of Tasmania* takes a leisurely 14½ hours to cross Bass Strait, and leaves Station Pier in Port Melbourne at 7.30 pm each Monday, and 6 pm Wednesday and Friday. It returns to Melbourne from Devonport at 6 pm each Tuesday and Thursday, and 4 pm on Saturday.

For more information on other ways of getting to the Apple Isle, fly-drive packages etc, telephone or visit the Tasmanian Travel Centre (☎ 9206 7922, 1800-806 846) at 259 Collins St.

Crewing on Yachts

It is quite possible to make your way round the Australian coast, or even to/from other countries like New Zealand, Papua New Guinea or Indonesia, by hitching rides or crewing on yachts. Ask around at harbours, marinas or yacht clubs. It's often worth contacting the secretaries of sailing clubs and asking whether they have a notice board where people advertise for crews – some of the major Australian clubs even run waiting lists for people wanting to crew on yachts. Look under 'Clubs – Yacht' in the *Yellow Pages* telephone directory. It obviously helps if you're an experienced sailor, but some people are taken on as cooks (not very pleasant on a rolling yacht).

Getting Around

TO/FROM THE AIRPORT

Melbourne airport is at Tullamarine, 22km north-west of the city centre. It's a modern airport with a single terminal: Qantas at one end, Ansett at the other, international in the middle. There are two information desks at the airport: one on the ground floor in the international departure area and another upstairs next to the duty-free shops.

The Tullamarine Fwy runs from the airport almost into the city centre, finishing in North Melbourne. A taxi between the airport and city centre costs about $25.

Skybus (☎ 9662 9275) operates a 24-hour shuttle-bus service between the airport and the city centre, costing $10/4.50 for adults/children. Skybus has two main city terminals: Bay 30 at the Spencer St coach terminal, with departures every 30 minutes between 5 am and 10.45 pm daily, plus a midnight departure; and the Melbourne Transit Centre at 58 Franklin St, with departures about every 30 minutes between 7 am and 11 pm daily. Outside these times, the bus picks up from outside the Melbourne Town Hall on Swanston St at 10 minutes past the hour between 1.10 and 4.10 am. Buy your ticket from the driver; bookings are not usually necessary. You can take your bicycle on the Skybus, but the front wheel must be removed.

There is also a fairly frequent bus operated by Gull Airport Services (☎ 5222 4966) between the airport and Geelong, costing $20 one way. The Geelong terminus is at 45 McKillop St. Other airport buses operate services to the Mornington Peninsula and other outer areas. The airport information desks can provide travellers with details.

PUBLIC TRANSPORT

Melbourne's public transport system, the Met (☎ 13 1638), incorporates buses, trains and the famous trams, and operates as far as 20km out from the city centre. Trams are relatively frequent and a fun way to get around. Buses take routes where the trams

Gateway to Melbourne

The gateway to Melbourne project is DCM's (flavour-of-the-1990s) most abstract and symbolic structure to date. Looking something like a Suprematist painting pulled off the page, the gargantuan red and yellow beams appear to be about to collapse onto the freeway, making a drive under them an exciting if somewhat unsettling experience. The concept, we are told, was to create a symbolic archway and frame through which Melbourne could be seen in the distance as a dynamic, technologically advanced city. Of course this is all architect speak, and as impressive as the structure is (especially at night), nobody is fooled by the lofty concept that would have you thinking that you are about to drive into the world of *Bladerunner* instead of a city made up of tree-lined streets, shuffling trams and laidback locals.

don't go, while trains radiate from the city centre to the outer suburbs.

At the time of writing the Met was in the throws of privatisation, and although the sell-off has had little effect on services and pricing structures as yet, there is already talk of cutting the number of tram stops on certain routes. Melbourne's public transport infrastructure is one of the world's best; however, the previous Liberal government's emphasis on road-building and privatisation has placed enormous pressure on the system, and it could be too late for Labor to stop the rot.

For information on public transport, phone the Met Information Centre (☎ 13 1638), which operates from 7 am to 9 pm daily. The Met Shop, at 103 Elizabeth St in the city (open from 8.30 am to 5.15 pm weekdays, to 6 pm Friday and from 9 am to 1 pm Saturday), also has transport information and sells souvenirs and tickets. The shop also has a 'Discover Melbourne' kit. If you're in the city it's probably a better bet for information than the telephone service, which is usually busy. The few remaining manned train stations also have some information.

Ticketing

Melburnians and visitors alike are finding the new automatic ticketing system, known as Metcard, about as un-user-friendly as you can get (see Buying a Ticket later in this section). The same ticket allows you to travel on trams, trains and buses. The most common tickets are based on a specific period of travelling time – eg, two hours, one day, one week – and allow you unlimited travel during that period and within the relevant zone. You must validate your ticket in the validating machine when boarding a tram or bus or entering a train station platform (validation is used by Met to assess user statistics).

The metropolitan area is divided into three zones, and the price of tickets depends on which zone(s) you will be travelling in and across. Zone 1 covers the city and inner-suburban area, and most travellers won't venture beyond that unless they're going right out of town – on a trip to the Healesville Wildlife Sanctuary, for example, or down the Mornington Peninsula. The fares are as follows:

zones	2 hours	all day	weekly
1	$2.30	$4.40	$19.10
2 or 3	$1.70	$3.00	$13.10
1 & 2	$3.90	$7.10	$32.30
1, 2 & 3	$5.30	$9.50	$39.50

Monthly and yearly Met tickets are also available.

Note that if you buy a weekly, monthly or yearly zone 1 ticket, it also allows you unlimited travel in zones 1, 2 and 3 on weekends. If you're heading into the city by train from zone 2 or 3, you can get an off-peak ticket for use after 9.30 am which will take you into the city and then allow unlimited travel on trams and buses within the city area. Most services operate between 5.30 am

and midnight Monday to Saturday and from 8 am to 11 pm on Sunday.

There are also 'short trip' tickets ($1.50) which allow you to travel two sections on buses or trams in zone 1, or you can buy a 'short trip card' ($12.50) which gives you ten short trips. (There are numerous other deals, but let's try to keep this simple!)

Buying a Ticket You would think that buying a ticket should be the least of your worries – well, it's not. Many small businesses, such as newspaper kiosks and milk bars, sell most tickets but not short trip tickets. The machines on trams sell only short trip and two-hour tickets, and only take coins. Small machines at train stations sell many types of tickets but not short trips. Large machines at train stations take coins, some notes and some bank cash cards; small machines at stations take coins only. Are you still with me? Manned stations have booking offices that sell most tickets. On buses you can buy short trip, two-hour and all-day tickets from the driver using coins and notes.

As you can see, buying a ticket is a complicated business. To make matters worse, plain-clothed and uniformed inspectors will assume you are guilty of fare dodging before believing you're the victim of an unworkable system, and won't hesitate to give you an on-the-spot $100 fine. Call the Met feedback line on ☎ 1800-800 120 with any complaints or suggestions.

Tram

Melbourne's trundling trams are one of the city's most distinctive features, but you might need to exercise a little patience as they're not particularly speedy.

Tram routes cover the city and inner suburbs quite extensively. The majority of routes operate as back-and-forth shuttle services, with the city centre acting as the hub of the wheel and the tram routes as the spokes. This makes it a good system if you want to get to somewhere from the city centre, but not so good if you want to travel across from one suburb to another. All tram stops are numbered out from the city centre. Most trams are the traditional green and yellow, but some have been decorated by local artists, others are mobile billboards, and there is talk of a complete colour change with the trams' privatisation. For the total 'tram experience', the old W-class trams can't be beaten, but the modern trams are generally faster and more comfortable.

There are also 'light rail' services to some suburbs – these modern express trams are a sort of hybrid between a train and a tram.

Trams run along most routes about every six to eight minutes during peak hours and every 12 minutes at other times, but this could change with the privatisation of the Met system. Unfortunately, trams have to share the roads with cars and trucks, so the reality is they are often subject to delays. Services are less frequent on weekends and late at night.

Be extremely careful when getting on and off a tram: by law, cars are supposed to stop when a tram stops to pick up and drop off passengers, but that doesn't always happen.

See the Tram Tours section later in this chapter for details on the free City Circle tram service.

Train

Melbourne has an extensive train network that covers the city centre and suburban areas. The trains are generally faster and more convenient than trams or buses, but they don't go to many inner suburbs, eg, Fitzroy, Carlton, St Kilda or South Melbourne.

Flinders St Railway Station is the main suburban-line terminal. The famous clocks that sit above the entrance on the corner of Swanston and Flinders Sts indicate when the next train will be departing on each line. There's an information booth just inside the entrance.

Trains on most lines start at 5 am and finish at midnight and should run every ten minutes during peak hours, every 15 to 20 minutes at other times, and every 30 minutes after 7 pm on weekdays. They run every 30 minutes from 5 am to midnight on Saturday, while it's every 30 minutes from 7 am to 11.30 pm on Sunday. Of course, these are just rule-of-thumb times. In a perfect world (or if Mussolini were

transport minister) all of the above would be accurate. In reality, expect deviations, plus the odd strike.

The city service includes the underground City Loop which is a quick way to get from one side of town to the other. The stations on the loop are Parliament, Melbourne Central, Flagstaff, Spencer St and Flinders St.

Bicycles can be carried free on trains during off-peak times and weekends. During peak hours you'll need to buy a concession ticket for the bike.

Bus

Melbourne's privatised bus network is ancillary to the trains and trams – it fills in the gaps. Generally, buses continue from where the trains finish, or go to places, such as hospitals, universities, suburban shopping centres and the outer suburbs, not reached by other services. If you find you can't get somewhere by train or by tram, ring the Met – chances are they will have a bus going that way.

Disabled Travellers

Melbourne's excellent *Mobility Map* is available from tourist information booths in the Bourke St Mall and Rialto Towers, and from the Melbourne City Council's information desk (☎ 9658 8679) on the corner of Swanston and Little Collins Sts (ring and they will post one to you). An interactive version of the map, plus lots of other helpful information, can be found at the Web site www.accessmelbourne.vic.gov.au.

Victoria's Public Transport Corporation (PTC) publishes *Disability Services for Customers with Specific Needs* and provides accessible rail services on V/Line Sprinter trains to the major rural centres of Geelong, Ballarat, Bendigo, Seymour and Traralgon. Hoist-equipped buses then link other centres and also Adelaide (via Ballarat); contact V/Line (☎ 13 6196). All Melbourne trains on the Met's accessible suburban rail network carry a portable ramp in the driver's compartment. Just wait at the end of the platform where the front of the train will be.

See the Car Rental and Taxi sections for further information.

CAR

You can get around Melbourne and between the main country centres easily enough by train and bus, but many of Victoria's finest features – the national parks, the remote beaches, the mountain regions, the backroad country towns – are not readily accessible by public transport. So if you're planning to explore Victoria in intimate detail or just want to get off the beaten track, you'll need your own wheels – and for many visitors, that means buying or renting a car.

CityLink

Melbourne's CityLink tollway road system has two main links: the southern link, runs from the South-Eastern Fwy, from the Malvern section in the south-eastern suburbs, to Kings Way (on the southern edge of the city centre); the western link runs from the Calder Fwy intersection with the Tullamarine Fwy to the West Gate Fwy (on the western edge of the city centre). At the time of writing only the Tullamarine section was in operation.

The annoying thing about CityLink isn't the cost but the inconvenience. Tolls are 'collected' from a transponder in the car (an e-TAG), which you obtain after opening a CityLink account ($22.50 minimum, non-refundable). Motorists are allowed up to 12 day passes a year, which are the best option for visitors. To buy a day pass, you can either go to an Australia Post office (anywhere in Australia) or to another Melbourne outlet. Alternatively, you pay by credit card by telephoning CityLink (☎ 13 2629). Charges vary depending on which part of the network you wish to use. For example, to go to the airport, joining CityLink at Flemington Rd, costs $2.50. A day pass for the entire system when it is operational will cost $7. And if you don't get a pass you'll be fined around $100. Car hire companies have various options to cover toll charges. CityLink has a Web site at www.transurban.com.au and a customer centre at 67 Lorimer St, Southbank.

Car Rental

All the big car-rental firms operate in Melbourne. Avis (☎ 13 6333), Budget (☎ 13 2727), Hertz (☎ 13 3039) and Thrifty (☎ 1300-367 227) have desks at the airport, and you can find plenty of others in the city. Car-rental offices tend to be at the northern end of the city centre or in Carlton or North Melbourne.

The major companies all offer unlimited-kilometre rates in the city; in country areas it's a flat rate plus so many cents per kilometre. One-day hire rates are around $50 to $60 for a small car, $70 for a medium car or $90 for a big car – obviously, the longer the hire period, the cheaper the daily rate.

For disabled travellers Avis and Hertz can provide hand-controlled rental vehicles. Norden Transport Equipment (☎ 9793 1066) has a self-drive van which is equipped with a lift and is available for long- or short-term rentals.

Melbourne also has a number of budget operators, renting older vehicles at lower rates. Their costs and conditions vary widely, so it's worth making a few enquires before going for one firm over another. Be sure to ask about kilometre charges, whether rates include insurance, the excess, and so on. Beware of distance restrictions; many companies only allow you to travel within a certain distance of the city, typically 100km. Some companies won't rent a car to you at all if you're under 25; others may slap on a surcharge.

Some places worth trying are Delta (☎ 13 1390), which has branches around Melbourne, and Airport Rent-a-Car (☎ 1800-331 220): rates start at about $35 a day.

If you're after a real cheapie (around $30 a day) try one of the 'rent-a-wreck' operators, such as Rent-a-Bomb (☎ 9428 0088) in Richmond or Ugly Duckling Rent A Car (☎ 9525 4010) in St Kilda. The *Yellow Pages* lists lots of other firms under 'Car &/or Minibus Rental', including some reputable local operators who rent newer cars but don't have the nationwide network (and overheads) of the big operators.

4WD Renting a 4WD costs from around $85 a day for a Mitsubishi Challenger to around $140 a day for a Toyota Landcruiser (plus a hefty deposit which is returned if you

GETTING AROUND

do no damage to the vehicle). Companies in Melbourne with 4WDs for hire include Hertz (☎ 13 3039), Budget (☎ 13 2727), Thrifty (☎ 1300-367 227), Delta (☎ 13 1390) and Off Road Rentals (☎ 9543 7111).

Buying a Car

Shopping around for a used car involves much the same rules as anywhere. Firstly, used-car dealers in Melbourne are just like used-car dealers from Los Angeles to London – they'd sell their mothers into slavery if it turned a dollar. You'll generally get a car cheaper by buying privately through newspaper ads – try the *Age* classifieds on Wednesday or Saturday, or the weekly *Trading Post* – rather than through a car dealer, although if you buy through a dealer and spend more than $3000 you get a warranty of at least 3000km or two months.

In Australia third-party personal-injury insurance is always included in the vehicle registration cost, but you'd be wise to extend that to at least third-party property insurance as well – a minor collision with a Rolls Royce tends to be a surprisingly expensive mishap.

In Victoria it's compulsory for a car to have a safety check (Road Worthiness Certificate – RWC) before it can be registered in the new owner's name. Don't let yourself be talked into buying a vehicle without a RWC or registration – it almost always turns into a nightmare. Stamp duty has to be paid when you buy a car, and because this is based on the purchase price it's not unknown for buyer and seller to agree privately to understate the price. It's much easier to sell a car in the state in which it's registered, otherwise it has to be re-registered in the new state.

For a fee ($100, or $130 for nonmembers), the RACV (☎ 13 1955, www.racv.com.au) will check over a used car and report on its condition before you agree to purchase it. Most mechanics and garages offer a similar service. Arranging a mechanical test might seem like a hassle at the time, but it's a sensible investment that could save you a bundle of money and much heartache.

Royal Automobile Club of Victoria (RACV)

The RACV provides an emergency breakdown service, literature, excellent maps and detailed guides to accommodation. They can advise you on regulations you should be aware of and give general guidelines about buying a car. The RACV's head office (☎ 9790 2211) is at 550 Princes Hwy in Noble Park, although they also have two offices in the city centre – at 422 Little Collins St and at 360 Bourke St.

If you're a member of the AAA in the USA or the RAC or AA in the UK, you can use any of the RACV's facilities, but bring proof of membership.

Road Rules

In Australia, vehicles are driven on the left-hand side of the road. Although overseas licences are acceptable (preferably with photo-ID), an International Driving Permit – obtained from your home country – is preferred.

The speed limit in residential areas is 60km/h (changing to 50km/h in January 2001), rising to 75km/h or 80km/h on some main roads and dropping to 40km/h in specially designated areas such as school zones. On highways the speed limit is generally 100km/h (roughly 60 miles per hour), while on many freeways it rises to 110km/h.

Speed and red-light cameras operate throughout Victoria and police cars are equipped with radars for speed checks, so be warned.

The wearing of seat belts is compulsory, and small children must be belted into an approved safety seat. Motorcyclists must wear crash helmets at all times when riding.

Whatever you do, don't drink and drive – Victoria's blood-alcohol limit of 0.05% is strictly enforced by the police. Random breath-tests occur throughout the state and penalties are severe, including losing your licence and having to pay a heavy fine. Probationary and learner drivers must display, respectively, 'P' and 'L' plates and at all times maintain a blood-alcohol reading of zero.

Cars & Trams

Car drivers should treat Melbourne trams with caution – trams are about half the weight of an ocean liner and seldom come off second best in accidents. You can only overtake a tram on the left and must always stop behind a tram when it halts to drop off or collect passengers (except where there are central road 'islands' for passengers).

Melbourne has a notoriously confusing road rule, known as the 'hook turn', for getting trams through the city centre without being blocked by turning cars. To turn right at certain intersections, you have to pull over to the left on the actual intersection, wait until the light of the street you're turning into changes from red to green, then complete the turn. These intersections are identified by the black-and-white hook signs that hang down from the overhead cables. This manoeuvre can be most disconcerting for first-timers – stay calm, and observe a few locals before trying it yourself!

Parking

If you're lucky enough to find an on-street parking space in the city centre, the meters take $0.20, $1 and $2 coins. Check parking signs for restrictions and times, and watch out for clearway zones that operate during peak hours.

There are over 70 car parks in the city, and the Melbourne City Council produces a map-and-brochure guide to city parking – it's available from Melbourne Town Hall. Hourly rates vary depending on the car park's location, but you'll pay around $3 to $6 an hour or $12 to $25 a day during the week – less on weekends.

MOTORCYCLE

If you want to bring your own motorcycle into Australia you'll need a *carnet de passage*, and when you try to sell it here you'll get less than the market price because of bureaucratic problems in registering vehicles without Australian approval markings.

One option is hiring, though there aren't many places where you can do this and it often costs less to hire a car. Garner's Hire-Bikes (☎ 9326 8676) at 179 Peel St (on the

Public versus private transport with style

corner of Queensberry St) in North Melbourne has Victoria's biggest range of trail bikes and large road bikes for hire, with prices ranging from $90/180/450 per day/weekend/week for a Suzuki TS185 trail bike all the way up to $250/495/1120 for a Harley-Davidson Softail Custom; prices include insurance and unlimited kilometres. Victorian Motorcycle Hire & Sales (☎ 9817 3206), at 606 High St in East Kew, also has a wide range of bikes for rent, ranging from a Kawasaki ZR250 for $100 a day to a Honda CBR1000 for $150 a day.

An easier option might be a buy-back arrangement with a large motorcycle dealer – Elizabeth St near Franklin St in the city centre is a good hunting ground. They're keen to do business, and basic negotiating skills allied with a wad of cash (say, $4000) should secure a good second-hand bike with a written guarantee that they'll buy it back in good condition minus 25% after your three-month tour. Shop around.

See the earlier Car section for details of road rules etc.

TAXI

All taxis in Melbourne are yellow, irrespective of which company they're from, with a

GETTING AROUND

strip of chequered yellow and green running along their flanks. They also have large dome lights on their roofs that are lit up when they're available for hire.

There are plenty of taxi ranks in and around the city. The main ones in town are outside the major hotels, outside Flinders and Spencer St train stations, on the corner of William and Bourke Sts, on the corner of Elizabeth and Bourke Sts, in Lonsdale St outside Myer and outside Ansett in Franklin St.

Flagfall is $2.60, and the standard tariff is $0.96 per kilometre. There is a $1 charge for telephone bookings, another $1 charged for service between midnight and 6 am, and most cabs only take cash, American Express or Diners Card; many cabs also have Eftpos facilities. Tipping is not expected, but always appreciated.

If you want to book a taxi, the major companies include Silver Top (☎ 13 1008), Arrow (☎ 13 2211), Black Cabs (☎ 13 2227) and Embassy (☎ 13 1755). Specifically for disabled persons, Maxi Taxi can be booked through a central booking service (☎ 1300-354 050).

BICYCLE

Melbourne's a great city for cycling. It's reasonably flat, so you're not struggling up hills too often, and there are some great cycling routes throughout the metropolitan area. Two of the best routes are the bike path that runs around a section of Port Phillip Bay from Port Melbourne to Brighton, and the bike path that follows the Yarra River out of the city for more than 20km, passing through lovely parklands along the way. There are numerous other bicycle tracks, including those along the Maribyrnong River and the Merri Creek (see Cycling in the Things to See & Do chapter).

Discovering Melbourne's Bike Paths ($14.95) has excellent maps and descriptive routes of the city's bicycle paths. The *Melway Greater Melbourne* street directory is also a useful resource for cyclists. Note that bicycles can be taken on suburban trains for free during off-peak times. One note of caution: tram tracks are a major hazard for cyclists in Melbourne.

Every cyclist has their own 'wheel-stuck-in-tram-track' horror story.

Quite a few bike shops and companies have bikes for hire, and a good mountain bike, helmet and lock will cost about $20 to $30 a day. The following places are all worth trying: St Kilda Cycles (☎ 9534 3074), 11 Carlisle St, St Kilda; Cycle Science (☎ 9826 8877), 320 Toorak Rd, South Yarra; Bicycles for Hire (☎ 0412 616 633), below Princes Bridge on the south side of the Yarra; Borsari Cycles (☎ 9347 4100), 193 Lygon St, Carlton; and Christies Cycles (☎ 9818 4011), 80 Burwood Rd, Hawthorn.

WALKING

There are some wonderful walking areas in and around Melbourne. Some of the most popular city destinations include the Yarra River parklands, the Kings Domain, the Royal Botanic Gardens, Royal Park, Albert Park Lake and around Port Phillip Bay. See the Things to See & Do chapter for details of our suggested walking tour of the city centre as well as for details of other guided walks.

There are also plenty of great places just beyond the city outskirts, including the Dandenong Ranges, the Yarra Valley, the Brisbane Ranges National Park and Anakie Gorge, the You Yangs, Kinglake National Park and the Mornington Peninsula – particularly the Point Nepean National Park and Cape Schanck Coastal Park (see the Excursions chapter).

BOAT

Williamstown Bay & River Cruises (☎ 9688 4664) operates two ferry services across to Gem Pier in Williamstown; one from the city centre, the other from St Kilda. The *Williamstown Seeker* runs daily between Southgate and Williamstown, stopping at the casino, the Exhibition Centre and the Scienceworks museum. The one-way/return fare is $10/18.

The company also operates the *John Batman* ferry between St Kilda Pier and Williamstown, which runs year round on weekends and public holidays and costs $6/10. For details on departure times and other fares, call the above number or the recorded information number (☎ 9506 4144). The same company also operates a range of cruises.

Between October and May the restored 1933 steam tug *Wattle* (☎ 9328 2739) runs a ferry service on Sunday between Station Pier in Port Melbourne and Gem Pier in Williamstown. It leaves from Station Pier at 10.30 am, noon, 1.30 and 3 pm, and returns from Williamstown at 11.30 am, 1, 2.30 and 4 pm; the return fare costs $10 ($7 for children). Bookings are advised.

See the Excursions chapter for details of the ferry services between Sorrento, Portsea and Queenscliff.

ORGANISED TOURS

There's a huge array of tours on offer in and around Melbourne. The free *Melbourne Events* guide, available at tourist information centres, hotels and newsagents has an extensive section on tours. The Victoria Visitor Information Centre should be able to help if you're looking for something in particular.

City Bus Tours

Companies such as Australian Pacific, AAT King's and Down Under Day Tours run conventional city bus tours, as well as day trips to the most popular tourist destinations such as Sovereign Hill, Healesville Wildlife Sanctuary, Phillip Island and along the Great Ocean Road.

London Transport Bus Tours (☎ 9650 7000) also operates several popular double-decker bus tours around Melbourne. Their City Explorer does a continuous circuit around the city and inner suburbs, with 15 stops including the Royal Melbourne Zoo, the Queen Victoria Market, the Shrine of Remembrance and the Victorian Arts Centre. From November to April, the City Wanderer does a similar circuit around the inner-city area, as well as heading over the West Gate Bridge to the Scienceworks museum and the Melbourne Planetarium and Williamstown. One-day passes for either bus cost $22 for adults, $10 for children or $50 for a family of five. Tickets for both buses get you discounts on entry to various attractions, and you can get on and off all day from 10 am to 5 pm.

Tram Tours

In the city centre, the free City Circle trams travel on a fixed route along Flinders, Spring and Nicholson Sts to Victoria Parade and then back along Latrobe and Spencer Sts. Designed primarily for tourists, and passing many city sights along the way, the trams run between 10 am and 6 pm daily, every ten minutes or so. There are eight W-class trams operating on this route. Built in Melbourne between 1936 and 1956, they have all been refurbished and painted a distinctive deep burgundy and gold.

You can even dine on board a tram while taking a scenic night cruise around Melbourne's streets – see the boxed text 'Colonial Tramcar Restaurant' in the Places to Eat chapter.

River Cruises

Melbourne River Cruises (☎ 9629 7233) offers regular cruises along the Yarra River, departing every half-hour from Princes Walk (on the north bank of the river, east of Princes Bridge) and from Southgate. You can take a one-hour cruise either upstream or downstream ($15/8 for adults/children) or combine the two for a 2½-hour cruise ($27/14). Southgate River Tours (☎ 9682 5711) offers a daily one-hour steamboat cruise from Southgate up the river to Herring Island, some 3.5km away. The cost is $15/10 for adults/kids, including tea and coffee. There are also two-hour round-trip cruises to Williamstown ($18/9 return). Both cruises have a commentary, and bookings are essential.

PABLO GARCIA GASTAR

Cruising under steam on the river Yarra

Maribyrnong River Cruises (☎ 9689 6431) offers 2½-hour cruises up the Maribyrnong River to Avondale Heights, with a stopover at the interesting Living Museum of the West. The cruise costs $14/4 for adults/children. The company also offers one-hour cruises down to the West Gate Bridge and Docklands ($7/4); boats depart from the end of Wingfield St in Footscray.

You can also take a cruise to the penguin colony off St Kilda pier – see the St Kilda section of the Things to See & Do chapter for details.

Hot-Air Balloon

For those who can afford it, Balloon Sunrise (☎ 9427 7596, 41 Dover St, Richmond) will take you on an aerial tour of the city, complete with a (postflight) champagne breakfast. Tickets are either $225 or $285, and bookings are essential. For those who can't afford it, the balloons still make a wonderful sight crossing the city in the early morning.

Not quite wings of desire

Time waits for no-one...and nor do the trains!

Ned Kelly's armour

Vintage car rally, Albert Park

Floral clock, Queen Victoria Gardens

Hello possum!

Another sunny day in St Kilda

Luna Park's big wheel keeps on turning

Look into the eyes at Luna Park, St Kilda

The Palais Theatre, St Kilda

Things to See & Do

WALKING TOURS

The following walking tour shows how easy it is get around town via the city's historic arcades, laneways and less crowded streets, avoiding the busy thoroughfares. The sights of the following recommended city walk are confined to Map 2.

The walk begins on the corner of Flinders and Elizabeth Sts, opposite the city's public transport icon **Flinders St Railway Station**. Head east along Flinders St, turning left into Degraves St with its cafes and tiny shops. As you enter Centre Place note the beautiful **Majorca Building** on the corner of Flinders Lane, one of Melbourne's city-dwellers' most sought-after addresses. Follow **Centre Way** arcade through to leafy Collins St; this section of the famous street has retained much of its former glory thanks to classic 1930s buildings, such as **Lyric House, Kodak House** and **Newspaper House**.

Cross the street and enter the upmarket **Australia on Collins** shopping mall, taking the escalator to the 1st floor to exit into Little Collins St. Pop into the adjacent **Royal Arcade** to get an idea of what shopping malls were like in the 19th century. Built in 1869–70, the Royal is Melbourne's oldest arcade. Head back to Collins St by taking **Block Place**, a few steps to the left. This characterful alleyway is clustered with some of the city's most popular cafes and threads its way to the **Block Arcade**. The Block was built in the 1890s and is the city's grandest and most beautiful arcade – its mosaic floors, marble columns and detailed plasterwork are miraculously still intact. Turn left into Collins St and pop into the shop on the eastern corner of the arcade and take a look at its frescoed ceiling (a reminder of the Block Arcade's glory days).

Following Collins St to Swanston St you'll passing some fine boutiques, and on the corner is the glorious **Manchester Unity Building**, a 1930s Commercial Gothic Modern marvel. The **Melbourne Town Hall**, on the corner opposite, is a classic example of

gold-boom ostentation, and was the model for many a suburban town hall. The recently rescued **Regent Theatre** is on Collins St just beyond the former City Square and gargantuan Westin Hotel; if the doors are open, pop into the Regent to be dazzled by the ostentatious foyer.

Hidden behind the white classical facade of the adjacent **Baptist Church** is an 1845 structure, making the building the oldest Baptist church in Victoria. Say a prayer for the now defunct **Georges** department store, whose hallowed atmosphere, prestigious labels and luscious lattes are still sadly missed by many. The Russell St corner is watched over by **Scots** and **St Michael's Churches**, textbook examples of High Victorian architecture by the prolific Joseph Reed, who, in partnership with Frederick Barnes, appears to have built just about every 1860s building in the city.

The easternmost section of Collins St was once known as the 'Paris end' of the city, but today only the plane trees and the incredibly exclusive **Le Louvre** boutique are reminiscent of the City of Light. (See also the Collins Street section later in this chapter.)

Cross over to Macarthur St, diagonally to the left, passing the back garden of Parliament House, and walk along to **St Patrick's Cathedral**, a Gothic Revival masterpiece (for more detail see the East Melbourne section later in this chapter). Backtrack to Parliament Square to drop in for something refreshing at the luxurious **Park Hyatt** hotel-cum-1930s ocean liner. Loop around Albert St onto Lonsdale St and then into Little Bourke St for **Chinatown**. End the walk with a visit to the **Museum of Chinese Australian History** and some late-in-the-day yum cha.

Other Walking Tours

Melbourne's Golden Mile Heritage Trail is a self-guided tour starting at the Immigration Museum on Flinders St and winding its way through the city, ending at the Royal Exhibition Building. The walk takes about 2½ hours and is an excellent introduction to historical Melbourne and its heritage-listed buildings. A brochure costing $2 and gold-markers set into the footpath show you the way. The brochure can be purchased at the Victoria Visitor Information Centre in the town hall and at the Immigration Museum.

Around Melbourne City Walks (☎ 9562 0034) conducts informative and interesting walking tours of Melbourne's lanes, arcades, chapels, churches and cathedrals.

The tour lasts about two hours and costs $20 per person.

Aboriginal Heritage Walk (☎ 9252 2300) is a great way to learn about the customs, heritage and traditions of the area's original landowners, the local Bunurong and Woiwurrung people. The walk is within the Royal Botanic Gardens, which part of their ancestral land. The tour takes about 1½ hours and costs $10/7.50 for adults/children.

Another View Walking Trail is a self-guided tour to 17 sites of cultural significance around the inner city, exploring the relationship between Koories and settlers. The walking time is four to five hours; by using the free City Circle tram it is around 2½ hours. The brochure is available from the Victoria Visitor Information Centre.

Chinatown Heritage Walks (☎ 9662 2888) covers a visit to the Museum of Chinese Australian History and a guided walk through little Bourke St and its adjoining laneways. This is the oldest continuously Chinese quarter in Australia, dating back to 1854. The tour costs $15/8 for adults/children and takes about two hours.

The **Haunted Melbourne Ghost Tour** (☎ 9670 2585) is a spooky two-hour tour of over 40 of the city's haunted sites. The tour costs $20 and commences at 8 pm.

Market Tours & Tasting Trips

Food is something of an obsession for many Melburnians, and if you're interested in exploring behind the scenes there are a few good tours available.

Queen Victoria Market Tours (☎ 9320 5835, 9320 5822 on weekends) runs great two-hour tours around the market every Tuesday, Thursday, Friday and Saturday. You get to visit all sorts of different stalls, meet a fascinating bunch of characters and taste a variety of interesting goodies – great fun! **The Magical History Tour** starts at 10.30 am and costs $12, including morning tea. **The Foodies Dream Tour** starts at 10 am and costs $18 – it's great if you're specifically interested in food, and you get to try weird and wonderful things. Tours depart from the market's visitor centre, at 69 Victoria St, and bookings are essential.

Chocolate & Other Desserts Walk (☎ 9815 1228 or 0412 158 017) takes you to some of the city's best sugar hit locations, including Haigh's (chocolates) and Charmaine's (ice creams). But don't think you'll get off that easily; there is also a visit behind the scenes where you'll meet chefs and have demonstrations before finishing with afternoon tea at the Grand Hyatt. The tour runs from 2.30 to 4.30 pm each Saturday and costs $22. The same operator also has a **Coffee, Cafes and Chocolate Walk** from 10 am till noon Saturday, costing $22. Bookings are essential for both tours.

Art & About (☎ 0417 589 987) runs popular tours including an Arts City Backstage tour, held on the last Wednesday of every month, which takes you behind the scenes and into the rehearsal rooms and costume departments of the Australian Ballet, Opera Australia and the Victorian Arts Centre. Melbourne Treasures, held on the second Wednesday of every month, is a tour of the city's churches, cathedrals and public buildings. All tours cost $20 and it's advisable to book; call for details of other tours.

Melbourne Cemetery Tours (☎ 9890 9288) have been running for over 15 years. The tours change frequently, each concentrating on a particular area of the cemetery. Tours take two hours and cost $15 per person, refreshments included.

Queen Victoria Market – Foodies Dream Tour (☎ 9320 5835, 9320 5822 on weekends) is an exciting trip of the gastronomical kind. Sample the best and freshest the Queen Vic has to offer. Bookings are essential. For other food-oriented walking tours, see the boxed text 'Market Tours & Tasting Trips'.

Regent & Forum Theatres Tour (☎ 9820 0239) explores two of the city's most lavish theatres (originally built as cinemas). Bookings are essential.

TRAM TOURS

If you're tired of walking and following map directions buy yourself a zone 1 daily Met ticket and continue your exploration of Melbourne by tram. For $4.30, you can spend the entire day travelling around the city and inner suburbs by tram – a bargain, and a great way to get a feel for Melbourne. The same ticket will also let you use trains and buses in zone 1.

Try taking the No 96 tram (the light rail) heading south. From Bourke St Mall in the city, it crosses the river at Spencer St with the casino complex on the left and Exhibition Centre on the right, continues through the lovely old suburbs of South Melbourne, Albert Park (with the sports and aquatic centre, lake and grand prix track on the left), Middle Park and then onto Fitzroy St, The Esplanade, Luna Park and Acland St, St Kilda.

Melbourne's Aboriginal Places

Although more than 160 years have passed since Melbourne was colonised, traces of the area's Aboriginal past remain. For a different perspective on some of Melbourne's attractions, visit the following sites:

- **Yarra Park** is home not only to the Melbourne Cricket Ground, but also to two ancient trees whose trunks were scarred by the removal of their bark to build canoes. Incidentally, it is thought that a form of Australian rules football was played by Aborigines, using a possum-skin rather than the traditional pig's bladder as a ball.
- **Fitzroy Gardens** has a scarred tree that is not far from Captain Cook's Cottage.
- **Burnley Park**'s *corroboree* tree (now a stump) is a site of spiritual significance for the Wurundjeri people. The tree was a marker of clan territory, a site for meetings and formal corroborees. Other corroboree places include the sites of the Supreme Court, the Melbourne Town Hall and Emerald Hill (South Melbourne).
- **St Kilda Junction**'s corroboree tree is now surrounded by traffic and fumes, and is believed to be around 300 years old. The site was both a meeting area and a fringe camp used by survivors of white settlement. The area was bordered by wetlands, a great source of food. Today the wetlands form the basis of nearby Albert Park Lake.
- **Brighton**, an upmarket seaside suburb, is home to the Brighton midden, the largest in the Melbourne area. Middens are formed from layers of shells, bones and charcoal, and are evidence that the area was the site of a succession of Aboriginal camps.
- **Queen Victoria Market** is on the site of Melbourne's pioneer cemetery. Few visitors enjoying the market's vibrancy realise that buried beneath the numerous food stalls lie around 10,000 graves, which makes building renovations a tricky exercise. The section reserved for Aboriginal sites lies under sheds F to J, near Queen St.

Another popular tram ride is the No 8 from Swanston St south down St Kilda Rd. It travels beside the Kings Domain and through South Yarra and Toorak.

For details of the free City Circle tram, see the boxed text 'Free Melbourne' later in this chapter.

CITY CENTRE
Federation Square (Map 2)

Mooted as the city's new civic and cultural hub for the 21st century, Federation Square was still in the early stages of construction at the time of writing. Yet another controversial building project that's had its fair share of opposition, it will cover the area from the Yarra River to Flinders St, running between Swanston and Russell Sts.

The square will be comprised of a large civic plaza capable of holding up to 10,000 people, a 120m-long covered atrium, and the Museum of Australian Art (MAA), which will house the work of both indigenous and nonindigenous Australian artists, previously housed at the National Gallery of Victoria (NGV). Cinemedia will have a strong focus on cinema and multimedia, with the TV broadcasting station SBS also sharing the space. There will, of course, also be a reasonable smattering of cafes, restaurants and retail outlets.

The proposed completion of the project is May 2001, although this is subject to change.

Swanston Street (Map 2)

Running through the heart of the city, Swanston St was closed to cars early in 1992 to create Swanston Walk, an unsuccessful attempt to bring new life to a strip that had become decidedly seedy. Common sense prevailed, and in late 1999 Swanston Walk became a street once more, although it's only open to traffic after 7 pm. At the time of writing, the jury was still out as to exactly what the future of troubled Swanston St might be. Unfortunately, the stretch of Swanston between Flinders and Bourke Sts continues to be as unappealing as ever, with an excess of amusement dens and $2 trash troves. Despite this seediness, and the unfortunate construction of the Westin Hotel in

the city square (which has ruined the area's aspect), many of Swanston St's impressive old buildings remain. Look up!

On the corner of Swanston and Collins Sts, the **Manchester Unity Building** is a marvellous example of 1930s modern Gothic skyscraper style. Modelled on the Chicago Tribune building, it was one of architect Marcus Barlow's best works and was for a time the city's tallest building.

Melbourne Town Hall, opposite the Manchester Unity Building, was built between 1867–70, with the addition of the temple-like porticle in 1887. It's probably most famous for visits by British notables Queen Elizabeth II, who took tea there in 1954, and the Fab Four, who held court on the portico in front of thousands of screaming fans in 1964. It's amazing what a difference a decade can make! Ring ☎ 9658 9658 for information on the free tour of this celebrated building, which became the prototype for many a town hall built in the late 1880s.

Opposite Melbourne Town Hall, at No 113, is the **Capitol Theatre**, built in 1921–24. Local architect and writer Robin Boyd called the theatre 'possibly the finest picture theatre ever built anywhere'. The ceiling, designed by the team of Marion Mahony and her husband Walter Burley Griffin (the architects of Canberra), is a kaleidoscopic creation that glitters like illuminated crystals. Unfortunately, many of the theatre's original interior features are gone and the facade was demolished to make way for an arcade over 20 years ago. Until recently the theatre's future was dubious. However, in May 1999 the Capitol was purchased by RMIT (Royal Melbourne Institute of Technology) which is committed to a restoration program that will see the theatre returned to something like its original splendor. For information on events and open days phone ☎ 9925 1986.

Farther north, in the block between Little Lonsdale and Latrobe Sts, is the State Library of Victoria (see the following section).

The next block north along Swanston St is dominated by what local architect Dimity Reed once called 'a concrete building in the neo-Stalinist style of the 1960s' – the

Royal Melbourne Institute of Technology. Between 1991–94 the RMIT Building 8 was radically transformed with the addition of cheap-looking postmodernist facades.

On the corner of Swanston and Victoria Sts is the **Melbourne City Baths**, built in 1903 in the Edwardian baroque style. With the award-winning addition of a gymnasium and squash courts in 1980, the City Baths continue to be a great place to take a dip.

State Library of Victoria (Map 2)

The State Library, with its Classical Revival facade facing Swanston St, was built in various stages from 1854. When it was completed in 1913, the reinforced concrete dome over the octagonal **Reading Room** was the largest of its kind in the world. In 1871, Marcus Clarke wrote much of his *For the Term of His Natural Life* – an Australian masterpiece about transportation and the penal system – in this room. Like much of the city, however, this wonderfully tranquil public space is currently under re-furbishment and won't re-open until at least 2002.

The library's collection of more than a million books and other reference materials is notable for its coverage of the humanities and social sciences, as well as the arts, Australiana and rare books dating back to a 4000-year-old Mesopotamian tablet. The collection also includes the records of the ill-fated Burke & Wills expedition, and various interesting items are periodically displayed in glass cabinets.

Collins Street (Map 2)

Collins St is Melbourne's most elegant streetscape, although much of its original grandeur and history was lost during short-sighted periods of 'development'. Collins St has a fashionable end and a financial end. The west end (from Elizabeth St) is home to bankers and stockbrokers, while the east, or top end, is mostly five-star hotels and exclusive boutiques. The top end was once known as the 'Paris End' as it was lined with plane trees, grand buildings and street

LA TROBE PICTURE COLLECTION, STATE LIBRARY OF VICTORIA

Francois Cogne, *Collins Street (From Queen Street)*, 1864. Now lined with plane trees, Cogne depicts a more open Collins Street as it sweeps eastwards to the Treasury Building.

cafes. The trees remain (and are beautifully lit at night by fairy lights), but many of the finer buildings are now gone.

Between Russell and Swanston Sts are two of Melbourne's most historic churches: **Scots Church** (1873), at No 140, is built in the decorative Gothic style; adjacent is **St Michael's Church** (1866), the first church in Victoria to be built in the Lombardic Romanesque style. **Kay Craddock's Antiquarian Bookshop**, at No 156, is a marvellous place for book lovers. The **Athenaeum Theatre**, at No 188, dates back to 1886 and was recently refurbished. There's a general library on the 1st floor which is open to the public. Across the road, the **Regent Theatre** was one of the most lavish theatres of its kind when it was built in 1929 with the advent of the talkies. Destroyed by fire and then restored in 1945, the Regent had fallen into a state of disrepair by the 1990s. After a major restoration project beginning in 1994, the theatre re-opened in late 1996 and is now used mainly for blockbuster stage shows.

Just across Swanston St, **Australia on Collins** is a large shopping centre, with a spacious, well-planned layout and a good food court on the lower-ground floor.

The section of Collins St between Swanston and Elizabeth Sts contains some interesting examples for students of 1930s architecture. Some of the better buildings are the former **Wertheim's Lyric House**, at No 248, **Kodak House**, at No 252, and **Newspaper House**, at No 247 – an 1880s warehouse that received a new facade in 1932, complete with mosaic mural.

The **Block Arcade**, which runs between Collins and Elizabeth Sts, was built in 1891 and is a beautifully intact 19th-century shopping arcade. Its design was inspired by the Galleria Vittorio in Milan (although a lot smaller in scale) and features intricate mosaic-tiled floors, marble columns, Victorian window surrounds and magnificently detailed plasterwork on the upper walls. The arcade has been fully restored, and houses some fairly sedate specialist shops selling everything from lingerie, crystal and glass to teddy bears, chocolates and clothing. The old-fashioned **Hopetoun Tearooms** is the perfect spot to catch up with your grandmother over tea and asparagus rolls.

Nestled between the Block Arcade and Little Collins St, **Block Place** is a bustling lane filled with coffee shops, sidewalk tables and chairs and an endless stream of caffeine addicts (see Little Collins Street Area in Places to Eat).

The city's financial sector begins across Elizabeth St, but this area isn't all banks and brokers. At No 320 is **Henry Buck's**, a gentlemen's outfitter of distinction. It's a great place if you're in the market for classic menswear. At No 338, **Hardy Brothers** is one of Australia's most famous jewellers.

The financial sector also has some of Melbourne's best-preserved old buildings. The original facade of the **CBA Bank**, at No 333, was one of the most extreme examples of Classicism of its time, but unfortunately the bank decided to 'update' its image in 1939, and the new facade represents the austerity of between-the-wars architecture. The interior is another matter, and you can wander inside to enjoy the magnificent Baroque Revival domed foyer.

On the corner of Collins and Queen Sts the former **Melbourne Stock Exchange**, at No 376–80, the former **ES&A Bank**, at No 390, and what was originally the **National Mutual Life Building**, at No 389–99, are all fine examples of late 19th-century Revivalist Gothic architecture built during Melbourne's land-boom period.

The block between William and King Sts is a striking contrast of old and new. The Gothic facade of the three **Olderfleet buildings**, at No 471–77, has been well preserved, and **Le Meridien at Rialto**, at No 495, is an imaginative five-star hotel behind the facades of two marvellous old Venetian Gothic buildings, with the original cobbled laneway between them covered as an internal atrium. These older buildings are dwarfed by the soaring **Rialto Towers**, Melbourne's tallest building and at one time the tallest building in the Southern Hemisphere. The Rialto's most distinctive feature is the semi-reflective glass exterior which changes colour as the sun sets. (See also the following section.)

The former **McPherson's Pty Ltd Building**, at No 546–66, was built between 1934–97 and is a good example of the Streamlined Moderne, with its horizontal design and glass frontage.

Rialto Towers Observation Deck (Map 2)

This popular lookout is on the 55th floor of Melbourne's tallest building, the Rialto Towers on Collins St west. The lookout platform offers a spectacular 360° view of Melbourne's surrounds, and there's a cafe if you want to linger. It's open from 10 am to 10 pm daily; entry costs $7.50 and includes a free 20-minute video on the development of Melbourne.

Bourke Street (Map 2)

The area in and around the centre of Bourke St is home to the city's main department stores. The mall section between Swanston and Elizabeth Sts is closed to traffic, and pedestrians share the Bourke St Mall with an assortment of street performers, buskers and trams (beware of the latter!).

The north side of the mall is dominated by the frontages of the Myer and David Jones department stores, and the tower-topped **GPO** on the corner of Elizabeth St. This elaborate and elegant post office was built in stages, and if you look closely at the designs on the columns, you'll see that the three levels feature the classical Doric, Ionic and Corinthian forms respectively. On the other side of the mall, the **Royal Arcade** built in 1869–70 is Melbourne's oldest arcade, and like the later-built Block and Centreway Arcades was designed as a pedestrian-friendly response to the city's street grid. Lined with souvenir, travel, food and jewellery shops, look up and you'll see the fine detail of the original 19th-century arcade. At the Little Collins St end of the arcade, the tall figures of **Gog & Magog** stand guard. These mythological giants were modelled on the original figures in London's Guildhall, and have been striking the hour on the clock here since 1892.

The eastern end of Bourke Street, beyond the mall and the seedy Russell St corner, has some excellent cafes and restaurants, interesting book and music shops and mainstream cinemas.

Spring Street (Map 2)

At the eastern end of Collins St, beside the Treasury Gardens, the **Old Treasury Building** was built in 1858, and it is considered to be Melbourne's most elegant 19th-century building. The huge basement vaults were designed to hold much of the £200 million worth of gold that came from the Victorian goldfields. Incredibly, designer JJ Clark was a 19-year-old government draftsman; he went on to become one of the city's finest architects. Three permanent exhibitions are housed in the Old Treasury Building, and admission to all three costs $5/4/3 for an adult/senior/concession or child. The *Built on Gold* exhibition tells the story of Victoria's gold rushes and their legacy, and is presented in the building's former gold vaults; *Growing Up in the Old Treasury* and *Melbourne Then and Now* are equally impressive exhibitions.

At 103 Spring St, between Bourke and Little Collins Sts, the **Windsor Hotel** is a marvellous reminder of the 19th-century era. Built in 1883–84, it was extensively restored during the 1980s and is one of grandest historic hotels in the country. A visit to the Windsor should be on every traveller's agenda.

Opposite, the **Parliament House of Victoria** building was started in 1856, when two main chambers – the lower house (Legislative Assembly or House of Representatives) and the upper house (Legislative Council or Senate) – were built. The library was built in 1860 and Queen's Hall in 1879. The original plans included a dome over the entrance, which is still on the drawing board; the side facades were never completed to plan. Despite being incomplete, this structure is still the city's most impressive public building. Australia's first federal Parliament sat here from 1901 before moving to Canberra in 1927.

The interior is superb and well worth seeing – free half-hour tours through both houses and the library commence at 10 and

Changing Skylines

RICHARD I'ANSON

DCM, Melbourne Exhibition Centre

Although Melbourne has long been characterised by its remarkably intact Victorian architecture, radical changes have remoulded the city over the past decade. Fostered by the political and economic climate of the former Kennett government reign, and by a new desire for inner-city living, the city centre and its fringes have been transformed in recent years by a proliferation of new buildings and developments. The city has been energised by a resurgent architectural vigour, and a visit to Melbourne is no longer complete without marvelling at the new architectural offerings that suggest a city looking towards its future.

It is impossible to cover every new building of note, but some of the larger civic projects that have permanently marked the urban fabric are definitely worth a mention. Many of these are easily accessible on foot, and their viewing makes a pleasant city stroll; if you're wearing your soles thin, you can always get to most by tram.

A handful of firms are responsible for the bulk of the new work. They produce architecture that engages with current American and European trends, all the while addressing local concerns of context, as well as the scale and character that are particular to Melbourne. Among the largest of these projects is the **Crown Entertainment Complex** (1993–96), designed by Bates Smart and others (see also the section on Crown later in this chapter). Stretched along the western section of Southbank (Map 2), on the southern edge of the Yarra River, Crown utilises an array of materials and forms. As a multifunctional building it melds the 'glamour' required of a gaming complex with geometric forms clad in a variety of materials and colours – ranging from brass and zinc to polished pink sandstone. A departure from this homage to vice is the **Melbourne Exhibition Centre** (1996), a little farther to the west and designed by Denton Corker Marshall (DCM). Critiquing the traditions of exhibition halls, this building exaggerates and deforms the standard elements of column, wall, window and roof into a brilliant and elegant expression of technology, complemented by sensitive landscaping to the Yarra River.

Into the business heartland, and again designed by DCM, is **101 Collins Street** (1986–90; 1990, Johnson Burgee responsible for foyer and columns), soaring upward in the grandest of gestures to the skyscraper while carefully articulating the standard 'office box' into a far more interesting language. But if anything characterises the city's progression it is a new playfulness fostered largely by architect Nonda Katsalidis and his various partnerships. Katsalidis has defined the stretch of Latrobe St from the corner of Russell, with **No 170 Latrobe St**, west to the **Terrace Apartments** (1994) overlooking the Queen Victoria Market; this stretch is punctuated with the **Argus Centre** (1991) and **Republic Tower** (1998–2000), both between Elizabeth and William Sts. These buildings energise the city with a new appreciation of materials and a bold use of form not seen before in buildings of this size in Melbourne. With references in form to historical, maritime and coastal themes, these remarkable sculptures provide an amazing contrast in the architectural idiom of Melbourne. Katsalidis continues his urban themes into Richmond with the **Silo Residential Apartments** (1996). These former silos are converted into a sleek statement of steel and concrete, writing the site's industrial past into its residential present. The most recent addition to Katsalidis' influential flock is the **Ian Potter Museum of Art** (completed in 1998), on the eastern side of the University of Melbourne (Map 4). A fetishised parcel wrapped in zinc panels, the visceral qualities of this building are exposed where the cladding discontinues to reveal rusted steel panels, further enhancing the elegant yet powerful composition of the building. Anchored to the edge of the University of Melbourne precinct, this definitive building is complemented by its interior, which houses a worthwhile collection of art and hosts a fascinating program of temporary exhibitions (See the Carlton & Parkville section later in this chapter).

Farther south on Swanston St from the Ian Potter, the Royal Melbourne Institute of Technology (RMIT; Map 2) has become a repository for ground-breaking buildings. Perplexing and fascinating, Edmond & Corrigan's **Building 8** (1991–94) is a dizzying conglomeration of elements and colours that is as impressive as a scenographic element ob-

Nonda Katsalidis, Republic Tower

served from the west side of Swanston St as it is close up for its mosaic complexity. It speaks more of the city fabric than of a single building, signalling the pluralism of the city and choosing to reflect this rather than dwell on any single design element. Owing much to postmodern explorations into colour and layering, this building stands as a landmark in progression of architectural composition.

Adjacent to this and wearing a conspicuous shade of green is **Storey Hall** (1992–95), designed by Ashton Raggatt McDougall, with Allom Lovell Associates. It owes just a much to chaos theory for its faceted appearance as it does to the complexities of site and program. Challenging convention, the interior folds one space and surface into another, commenting on the appropriateness of tertiary-education institutions as sites for progressive architecture. This building is perhaps Melbourne's most sophisticated statement of dwelling in a high-tech, postindustrial society.

Stroll through the leafy Carlton Gardens and you'll see the enormous blade of DCM's new **Melbourne Museum** (1998–2000) slicing sharply through the tree tops from behind the Royal Exhibition Building (Map 3). A collection of skewed angles, smooth surfaces and fine details, this extensive and controversial building pushes the city edge farther into suburbia. With forms colliding, intersecting and projecting at various angles, the museum is an impressive sight. Held together by the regularity of a gridded structure over an inclined roof, this building intends to encompass the tension of its city–suburb site while affecting elegance though clean lines and a monumental scale.

The city's architectural resurgence is far from over, and the talent of local designers will undoubtedly take Melbourne farther into the new century. Keep your eyes to the skyline and your feet to the pavement to see where it's headed.

Nonda Katsalidis, Silo Apartments (upper levels)

Brett Moore

11 am, noon and 2, 3 and 3.45 pm each weekday when Parliament is in recess. Ask about the story behind the second ceremonial mace that went missing from the lower house in 1891 – rumour has it that it ended up in a brothel! The tour guide points out some fascinating design aspects and explains the symbolism underlying much of the ornamentation. Another way to see the houses is to visit when Parliament is sitting. The public galleries of both houses are open to the public; phone ☎ 9651 8568 to find out when Parliament is in session.

The small and pretty **gardens** behind Parliament House are open to the public, as are the **Parliament Gardens** to the north. The steps of Parliament House give great views of Bourke St, the Windsor Hotel and the elaborate facade of the restored **Princess Theatre**.

At the top of Spring St, the building of the **Royal Australasian College of Surgeons** stands alone, a marvellous and restrained example of 1930s Nordic Classicism. Unfortunately the building is not open to the public.

Chinatown (Map 2)

Little Bourke St has been the centre for the Chinese community in Melbourne since the days of the gold rush, and it's a fascinating walk along the section from Spring St to Swanston St.

This is the only area of continuous Chinese settlement in the country, as well as one of Melbourne's most intact 19th-century streetscapes. In the 1850s, the Chinese set up their shops alongside brothels, opium dens, boarding houses and herbalists. Nowadays the area is mainly occupied by restaurants and discount traders.

Built in 1888, the **Sum Kum Lee General Store** is a mix of baroque and mannerist styles. The building has been occupied by Chinese food and grocery vendors pretty much since it opened.

The **Po Hong Trading Company**, on the corner of Cohen Place, is famous for its huge assortment of Chinese knick-knacks. It is housed in the former Chinese Mission Hall, built in 1894 by a Chinese evangelist.

The **Museum of Chinese Australian History**, at 22 Cohen Place, was established in 1985 to document the history of Chinese people in Australia. The ground-floor gallery has a few artefacts on display and is the home of Dai Loong, the long Chinese dragon that comes out to party on Chinese New Year. On the 1st floor you'll find an audiovisual history and on the 2nd floor an exhibition gallery for the works of Chinese artists. It's open from 10 am to 4.30 pm daily (from noon Saturday) and admission is $5/3 for adults/children. The museum also conducts two-hour walking tours around Chinatown every morning; these cost $15, or $28 including lunch at a Chinatown restaurant. Phone ☎ 9662 2888 for bookings.

There are many well-preserved old buildings and warehouses in Little Bourke St and the narrow, cobbled lanes that run off it. Sunday-morning yum cha is very popular, and the busiest and most lively time to visit.

Old Melbourne Gaol (Map 2)

This gruesome old gaol and penal museum (☎ 9663 7228) is at the north end of Russell St. It was built of bluestone in 1841 and was used until 1929; in all, over 100 prisoners were hanged here. It's a dark, dank, spooky place. The museum displays include death masks and histories of noted bushrangers and convicts, Ned Kelly's armour, the very

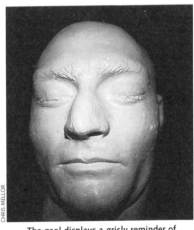

The gaol displays a grisly reminder of Austraila's most enigmatic hero, Ned Kelly.

CHRIS MELLOR

scaffold from which Ned took his fatal plunge and some fascinating records of early 'transported' convicts. The gaol is open from 9.30 am to 4.30 pm daily, and admission is $9/6/7/25 for an adult/child/concession/family. There are also tours of the gaol at 7.45 pm on Wednesday and Sunday (8.45 pm during daylight saving time), costing $15/8 for adults/children.

Immigration & Hellenic Antiquities Museums (Map 2)

In a country of immigrants you may well wonder why it's taken so long to realise a museum dedicated to the subject. The Immigration Museum (☎ 9927 2732) offers a sensitive and moving historic account that mixes display and audio in an almost dreamlike way. Housed in the Old Customs House (1858–70) on Flinders St, between William and Market Sts, the restored building alone is worth the visit; its most important space, the Long Room, is a magnificent piece of Renaissance Revival architecture. On the 2nd floor, the Hellenic Antiquities Museum has constantly changing displays from Greece.

Both museums are open from 10 am to 5 pm daily and admission is $7/3.50/5.50 for an adult/child/concession. There's also a cafe, and wheelchair access is from Market St.

Post Master Gallery (Map 2)

The Post Master Gallery, at 321 Exhibition St, has an outstanding collection of stamps and related subject matter of much interest to philatelists, collectors and kids alike. It has a regular program of exhibitions and is open from 10 am to 5 pm Tuesday to Friday, 12 pm to 5 pm Saturday to Monday.

Queen Victoria Market (Map 2)

On Victoria St, between Elizabeth and Peel Sts, the Queen Vic Market is one of Melbourne's most popular tourist attractions. A lively mix of Melburnians and visitors flock here to shop for the wide variety of produce and goods: fresh fruit and vegetables, meat, seafood, poultry, deli and bakery goods, clothing and general wares. Saved from demolition in the 1970s, the market has been

PABLO GARCIA GASTAR

Queen Vic Market – a must for the gourmand

on the site for more than 130 years and many of the sheds and buildings are registered by the National Trust.

It's open from 6 am to 2 pm Tuesday and Thursday, 6 am to 6 pm Friday, 6 am to 3 pm Saturday and from 9 am to 4 pm Sunday. On Sunday few produce stalls are open. See the boxed text 'Market Tours & Tasting Trips' earlier in this chapter for details of market tours.

Other Historic Buildings (Map 2)

Much of Melbourne's architectural history has been destroyed in the past to make way for some questionable building projects. Admittedly some might add to the shimmering night skyline, but that's about it. Attempts have been made to combine the past and present sympathetically – **Le Meridien** at Rialto (see Collins Street in earlier chapter) has been developed with a lot more success than the **Melbourne Central** shopping and office complex, on Latrobe St between of Melbourne Central is an old **shot tower**, built on the site in 1889. The shopping complex was built around the tower, which is now covered by a 20-storey-high, cone-shaped glass structure. Decide for yourself!

The city's other historic buildings are too numerous to mention here. However, some of the more notable include the simple Georgian **John Smith's House** (1848), at 300 Queen St; the massive structure of the **law courts** buildings (1874–84), on William St between Little Bourke and Lonsdale Sts; the **Old Royal Mint** (1872), on William St adjacent to the Flagstaff Gardens; and **St James' Old Cathedral** (1842), which was

Carry on at Your Convenience

In 1859, when Victorian Melbourne finally broached the then unmentionable subject of bodily functions, the city's first men's public urinal was built in Bourke St. Until then, the laneways and hidden nooks and crannies of 'Marvellous Smelbourne' (as the Sydney *Bulletin* dubbed the city) had been a free for all when the urgency of a rapidly expanding population had become pressing. Soon, elaborately designed one-man urinals, based on the French *pissoirs*, were dotted around the city (sadly, none of these remain). Unfortunately, these urinals were not connected to the sewerage system until the early 1890s, so the waste flowed freely down the street-channels and the stench continued.

As one might expect, prudish concerns also raged over certain nefarious goings on that may or may not have occurred in these establishments, leading to urinals being relocated to less sensitive surroundings. Between 1903 and 1918, two-, three- and four-person cast-iron urinals were built. Thankfully, many of these lovely old green structures remain and are still functional. An out-of-sight, out-of-mind approach led to the construction of several impressive underground toilets, which also heralded the inclusion of the city's first public toilet for ladies. Although much of the interior of these toilets has been altered over the years, a visit still has the aura of a welcome step back (and a few steps down) in time. Along with more recent additions, Melbourne boasts an assortment of clean, safe and historically fascinating public toilets. See for yourself!

Male and female underground toilets
- The corner Swanston and Collins Sts, next to the town hall. Built in 1914, this recently refurbished underground ladies', men's and baby-change toilet is tastefully decorated with halogen lighting, and has spotlessly clean facilities. The city's best.
- Outside the GPO on Elizabeth St. Built in 1910, these toilets have plenty of character and are well maintained.
- Opposite the Queen Victoria Market on Elizabeth St. Built in 1907, this toilet is very handily positioned.
- Gordon Reserve. A ladies' toilet built in 1939 in the historic Gordon Reserve.

Operating men's cast-iron urinals
- If you're in North Melbourne and in need, the gent's cast-iron toilet opposite the town hall, on the corner of Queensberry and Errol Sts, is a good, and intact, example of the four-person urinal.
- The corner of Exhibition and Flinders Sts
- Exhibition St, between Lonsdale and Little Lonsdale Sts
- The corner of Swanston and Lonsdale Sts
- The corner of Lonsdale and King Sts
- The corner of Nicholson and Albert Sts

From Victorian Values to Melbourne Now

For a room with a view, the floor-to-ceiling windows of the ladies' and gents' toilets on the 35th-floor of the Hotel Sofitel, 25 Collins St, frame fantastic views of Port Phillip Bay and the Melbourne Cricket Ground, stretching all the way to the Dandenong Ranges. You don't need to suffer from vertigo to go weak at the knees if you get too close to the edge.

As you can see, many of these old facilities are still in use today!

MICK WELDON

moved to its present site at 419 King St in 1913, and is Melbourne's oldest building.

Victoriana enthusiasts may also find some very small Melbourne structures of interest. Scattered around the city are a number of very fine cast-iron men's urinals (like French *pissoirs*) and underground toilets.

ARTS PRECINCT

This small area, on St Kilda Rd across the Yarra River from Flinders St Railway Station, is the high-culture heart of Melbourne. It contains the National Gallery of Victoria, Melbourne Concert Hall and theatres of the Victorian Arts Centre, Victorian College of the Arts and the CUB Malthouse theatres (Map 7).

National Gallery of Victoria (Map 2)

The NGV is closed for a complete refurbishment and is due to re-open in early 2002. Most of its Australian collection will move to the new **Museum of Australian Art** in Federation Square, which will open in early 2001. The controversial closure and planned renovation is yet another development in the gallery's troubled life. Designed by Sir Roy Grounds and constructed from bluestone and concrete, the stark, Brutalist facade with its moats and fountains has had many critics over the years. With only 5% of the collection on display at any one time, the addition of three new levels and an upgrade of the rest of the gallery is expected to increase the overall space by 35%.

Highlights from the gallery's collection are on display at the temporary **National Gallery of Victoria on Russell** in the State Library of Victoria. These impressive old rooms, recently vacated by the museum, were the NGV's original home from 1861 to 1968. But no matter how delightful the old building is, the temporary exhibition seems sadly lacking. The gallery is open from 10 am to 5 pm daily; entry is free.

Victorian Arts Centre (Map 2)

The Victorian Arts Centre is made up of two separate buildings – the Melbourne Concert Hall and the Theatres Building –

which are linked to each other and to the gallery by a series of landscaped walkways.

The **Melbourne Concert Hall**, the circular building closest to the Yarra, is the main performance venue for major artists and companies, and the base for the Melbourne Symphony Orchestra (MSO). Most of the hall is below ground, resting in Yarra mud so corrosive that a system of electrified cables is needed to prevent its deterioration. The **Theatres Building** is topped by the distinctive spire, underneath which are housed the State Theatre, the Playhouse and the George Fairfax Studio. The stylish interiors of both buildings are quite stunning and are well worth visiting in their own right, although you should try and see a performance at the centre. Both buildings feature works of prominent Australian artists, and in the Theatres Building the **Westpac Gallery** and the **Vic Walk Gallery** are free gallery spaces with changing exhibitions of contemporary works.

There are one-hour tours of the complex ($11.50) at noon and 2.30 pm each weekday and at 10.30 am and noon each Saturday. On Sundays you can visit the backstage at 12.15 pm ($12). Phone ☎ 9281 8198 for details, as backstage tours aren't always available. Children under 12 years are prohibited from the backstage area.

The **Performing Arts Museum** is at ground level in the Concert Hall, on the riverside. It's a small space that has changing exhibitions on all aspects of performing arts – it might be an exhibit on horror in the theatre or an even more terrifying display of rock musicians' outfits. Admission is free and the museum is open when the building is.

SOUTHBANK

South across the river from the city centre, the area known as Southbank is a former industrial area that was transformed in the early 1990s by the Southgate development. An arched footbridge crosses the Yarra River from the rear of Flinders St Railway Station, linking the city centre to the arts precinct and to the Southgate complex itself. Riverside walkways flank the river on both sides, where you once would have seen bellowing chimney stacks, saw-toothed roofs and the late-lamented Allen's Anticol neon sign.

The Southgate complex houses three levels of restaurants, cafes and bars, all of which enjoy a marvellous outlook over the city skyline and the river (see under Southgate in the Places to Eat chapter). There's also an international food hall, a shopping galleria with big-name boutiques, and a collection of specially commissioned sculptures and other artworks.

Crown Entertainment Complex (Map 2)

A little farther west down the Yarra, the Crown Entertainment Complex could be labelled with many an adjective, but subtlety most certainly wouldn't be one of them. The sprawling complex includes the enormous luxury Crown Towers Hotel and the Crown Casino, with over 300 tables and 2500 gaming machines open round the clock (see Gambling in the Entertainment chapter).

Thrown in for good measure, and all in the worst possible taste, are waterfalls and jets of fire, a giant cinema complex, a variety of nightclubs, a 900-seat showroom, a multitude of bars and restaurants, a designer-wear and specialist shopping complex and of course the obligatory Planet Hollywood.

A visit to the Crown Entertainment Complex feels a little like spending time in an international airport, when where you really want to be is on the connecting flight home.

Melbourne Aquarium (Map 2)

One of Melbourne's latest tourist attractions is the Melbourne Aquarium (☎ 9620 0999), on the corner of Queenswharf Rd and King St. Highlights are the floor-to-ceiling, ground-floor coral tank, the 360° fish-bowl viewing area and the 2.2 million litre oceanarium displaying the wonders of the deep. Not so impressive are the simulator deep-sea ride and overall feel of the place, which owe more to a trashy fun-fair aesthetic than to the beauty and mystery of the big blue. Great for the kids! Opening hours are 9 am to 9 pm daily during

January, 9 am to 6 pm daily for the rest of the year. Admission is $17.50/8.50/12.50/45 for adults/children/concessions/families.

Melbourne Exhibition Centre (Map 2)

Across Clarendon St, the Melbourne Exhibition Centre is in stark contrast to the casino complex. The designers, Denton Corker Marshall, have cloaked this huge exhibition space with their architectural vision of a brave new Melbourne. The trademark sharp angles, straight lines and thrusting blades are there, but the facade's true highlight are the giant letters perched on a sloping canopy spelling out the building's name against a background of sky. The building hosts trade exhibitions, having taken over the task from the Carlton Garden's Royal Exhibition Building.

Polly Woodside Maritime Museum (Map 2)

The Polly Woodside Maritime Museum (☎ 9699 9760) is on the riverfront, adjacent to the Melbourne Exhibition Centre. The *Polly Woodside*, an old iron-hulled, three-masted sailing ship, was built in Belfast in 1885, and spent the first part of her working life carrying coal and nitrate between Europe and South America. She made the rounding of Cape Horn 16 times before ending her career as a coal hulk. Bought by the National Trust in the 1970s, she has been lovingly restored by volunteers.

The *Polly Woodside* is now the centrepiece of a maritime museum park, sitting proudly in a dry dock. Other attractions are the historically listed **cargo sheds** – now an excellent museum housing relics, displays and film footage, a testament to the port's historical importance – and the **old pump** and **boiler house** used to operate the dry dock.

The ship and museum are open from 10 am to 5 pm daily and admission is $8/4 for adults/children.

Victorian Police Museum (Map 2)

Located at the Victoria police centre, 637 Flinders St (concourse level), this museum has a small but interesting collection of police history and paraphernalia. It has various displays, including one of the four original sets of the Kelly gang's armour. The museum is open from 10 am to 4 pm weekdays; entry is free.

Docklands (Map 2)

Originally a wetland and lagoon used by Koories as a hunting ground, the Docklands area is at the rear of Spencer St train station. It served primarily as the city's main industrial and docking area until the mid-1960s, when demand for larger berths to accommodate modern cargo vessels necessitated a move, leaving the Docklands a virtual wasteland. With its close proximity to the city centre, the Docklands area has become the focus of Melbourne's next big development boom. The new 52,000-seat **Colonial Stadium**, a sporting and entertainment venue, has already been completed, giving the city a plethora of sporting stadiums, but barely an art gallery to speak of!

There are also plans for a waterfront entertainment and retail precinct – with cinemas, restaurants, nightclubs, etc – residential apartments, office space, marinas and more entertainment venues. In a word, Docklands looks set to be Southbank many times over.

Thankfully, the planned Grollo Tower (which was to be the largest building in the world) has been shelved for the time being – let's hope for good. If you're interested in keeping abreast of the developments, the Docklands Web site is at www.docklands .vic.gov.au.

PARKS & GARDENS

Thanks to the foresight of the city's founders, Melbourne's formal grid plan is balanced by the array of excellent public parks and gardens that surround it.

Royal Botanic Gardens (Map 7)

Certainly the finest botanic gardens in Australia, and arguably among the finest in the world, these gardens form one of the best spots in Melbourne. There's nothing more genteel than a Devonshire tea by the lake on a Sunday afternoon. The beautifully laid out gardens are right beside the Yarra River; indeed, the river once ran right through the gardens, and the lakes are the remains of its curves, cut off when the river was straightened to lessen the annual flood damage.

There's a surprising amount of **wildlife** in the gardens, including water fowl, ducks, swans, cockatoos, rabbits and possums. A large contingent of fruit bats, usually found in the warmer climes of north Queensland, has taken up residence for the last 13 summers or more – look for them high in the trees of the fern gully. The bats (also known as 'flying foxes') are extremely noisy and an annoyance for the gardens' staff. But this is more than made up for by the uniquely gothic image of them flying over the horizon as the sun sets.

You can pick up guide-yourself leaflets at the park entrances; these leaflets change with the season and tell you what to look out for at the different times of year. There are various entrance gates around the gardens; the visitor centre is in the National Herbarium inside Gate F on Birdwood Ave. Free guided tours depart from the visitor centre at 10 and 11 am most days. During the summer months, the gardens play host to the **Moonlight Cinema** and **theatre performances** (see the Entertainment chapter for more details). The gardens are open from sunrise to sunset daily and admission is free. The tearooms and kiosk beside the lake are open from 9 am to 5 pm daily (to 4.30 pm in winter).

Kings Domain (Maps 2 & 7)

The Royal Botanic Gardens form a corner of the Kings Domain, a park containing the Shrine of Remembrance, Governor La Trobe's Cottage and the Sidney Myer Music Bowl. The domain is bordered by St Kilda Rd, Domain Rd, Anderson St and the Yarra River.

The whole park is encircled by **The Tan**, a 4km-long former horse-exercising track, now Melbourne's favourite venue for joggers. The track has an amusing variety of exercise points – 'a mixture of the Stations of the Cross and miniature golf', someone once said.

THINGS TO SEE & DO

Statues

Simpson and his loyal donkey are memorialised in bronze.

DAWN DELANEY

There are some fine statues throughout the city and its park-lands. Many of them commemorate significant figures in the history of Melbourne. Those that follow are just a few.

In the forecourt of the National Mutual building, 447 Collins St (Map 2), stand statues of the two founders of Melbourne, John Pascoe Fawkner and John Batman. Beside St Paul's Cathedral (Map 2) is Charles Gilbert's statue of a young Matthew Flinders, who, during his voyage of 1802–3, became the first person to circumnavigate Australia and chart its coast-line. The Burke & Wills Memorial in the City Square (Map 2) was Melbourne's first public monument, erected in 1865 to commemorate the tragic expedition that first crossed the con-tinent from south to north.

A fine statue of poet and horseman Adam Lindsay Gordon stands opposite the Windsor Hotel (Map 2) in Spring St. Gor-don shot himself on Brighton Beach in 1870 after reading a re-view of his most recent book of poetry. Near the Shrine of Remembrance (Map 7) is the statue of Simpson and his don-key. It was erected in memory of Private John Simpson Kirk-patrick for his bravery during the Allied Forces landing at Gallipoli in WWI, after he helped wounded soldiers from the front line. Kirkpatrick was killed less than a month after the landing, aged 22.

The Queen Victoria Monument (Map 2), in the Queen Victoria Gardens, shows the monarch ac-companied by four female figures which represent her birth, marriage, reign and death.

Beside St Kilda Rd stands the massive **Shrine of Remembrance** (Map 7), built as a memorial to Victorians killed in WWI. Its design is partly based on the Temple of Halicarnassus, one of the seven ancient wonders of the world, and it wasn't com-pleted until 1934. The memorial stone is in-scribed with the words:

This holy place commemorates Victoria's glori-ous dead. They gave their all, even life itself, that others may live in freedom and peace. Forget them not.

These words are heeded every Anzac Day, held on 25 April, when a dawn service at the shrine is attended by thousands, and also on Remembrance Day at the 11th hour of the 11th day of the 11th month – the time at which the Armistice of 1918 was declared. At this moment, a shaft of light shines through an opening in the ceiling to illumi-nate the Stone of Remembrance. The fore-

court, with its cenotaph and eternal flame, was built as a memorial to those who died in WWII, and several other war memorials surround the shrine.

It's worth climbing to the top as there are fine views from the balcony to the city, north along St Kilda Rd, and south-west towards the bay. The shrine is open from 10 am to 5 pm daily.

Across Birdwood Ave from the shrine is **Governor La Trobe's Cottage** (Map 7), the original Victorian government house sent out from the mother country in prefabri-cated form in 1840. It's open daily except Tuesday and Thursday, and admission is $2.

The cottage provides a dramatic contrast with the more imposing **Government House** (Map 7), where Victoria's governor resides. It's a copy of Queen Victoria's palace on England's Isle of Wight, and was built in 1872. There are guided tours on Monday, Wednesday and Saturday for $8 per person (no tours from mid-December to the end of January). You'll need to book tours on ☎ 9654 5528.

Near to La Trobe's humble cottage are the **Old Melbourne Observatory** (Map 7) and the **National Herbarium** (Map 7) at the main entrance to the Royal Botanic Gardens. The herbarium, was established by Baron von Mueller in 1853 as a centre for identifying plant specimens.

Across the road from the herbarium, on Dallas Brooks Drive, is the **Australian Centre for Contemporary Art** (ACCA; Map 7), for which you'll find details under Other Art Galleries later in this chapter. Near the city end of the park is the **Sidney Myer Music Bowl** (Map 2), a functional outdoor performance area in a natural amphitheatre. It's used for all manner of concerts in the summer months, and in winter it's turned into a skating rink.

The small section of park across St Kilda Rd from the Victorian Arts Centre is the **Queen Victoria Gardens** (Map 2), containing a memorial statue of the good queen herself, a statue of Edward VII astride his horse, and a huge floral clock, as well as several contemporary works of sculpture.

Fitzroy & Treasury Gardens (Maps 2 & 3)

The leafy Fitzroy Gardens divide the city centre from East Melbourne. With stately avenues lined with English elms, these gardens are a popular spot with wedding photographers – on Saturday afternoons there's a continuous procession of wedding cars pulling up for the participants to be snapped.

Governor La Trobe's nephew designed the original layout in 1857, which featured paths in the form of the Union Jack. James Sinclair, the first curator, was landscape gardener to Russian Tsar Nicholas I until the Crimean War cut short his sojourn. Sinclair amended and softened the original design, and the gardens are now a rambling blend of elm and cedar avenues, fern gullies, flower beds and lawns.

In the centre of the gardens are ferneries, fountains and a kiosk. By the kiosk is a miniature **Tudor village** (Map 3) and a **Fairy Tree**, the latter carved in 1932 by the writer

Ola Cohn. The painted carvings around the base of the tree depict fairies, pixies, kangaroos, possums and emus. In the northwest corner of the gardens is the **People's Pathway** (Map 2) – a circular path paved with individually engraved bricks.

Captain Cook's Cottage (Map 2) is actually the former Yorkshire home of the distinguished English navigator's parents. It was dismantled, shipped to Melbourne and reconstructed stone by stone in 1934. The cottage is furnished and decorated as it would have been around 1750, complete with handmade furniture and period fittings. There is an interesting exhibit on Cook's life and achievements during his great exploratory voyages of the southern hemisphere. The cottage is open from 9 am to 5 pm daily and admission is $3/1.50/7.50 for an adult/child/family.

Possums in the Park

Both the Fitzroy and Treasury Gardens have a large resident population of common ring-tail and common brush-tail possums. These possums are fairly tame and are used to being fed by people. The best time to turn up is at dusk, when they come out to feed for a couple of hours (especially in warmer weather). They have a preference for fruit.

KATE NOLAN

The nearby **Conservatory** (Map 2) was built in 1928 and contains glorious floral displays and a tropical-rainforest atmosphere.

The smaller Treasury Gardens (Map 2) is a popular lunch and barbecue spot. It contains a memorial to John F Kennedy and is the site of an outdoor art show, held as part of the annual Moomba Festival.

Other Parks & Gardens

The **Flagstaff Gardens** (Map 2), near the Queen Victoria Market, were first known as Burial Hill – it's where most of the early settlers ended up. Because the hill provided one of the best views of the bay, a signalling station was set up here – when a ship was sighted arriving from Britain, a flag was raised on the flagstaff to notify the settlers. Later, a cannon was added, and fired when the more important ships arrived. Once newspapers started publishing shipping information, the signalling service became redundant. These days, free lunchtime concerts are a frequent feature in the gardens, particularly in warmer weather.

The **Carlton Gardens** (Maps 2 & 3) surround the historic **Royal Exhibition Building** (☎ 9270 5000), a wonder of the southern hemisphere when it was built for the Great Exhibition of 1880. It is the world's oldest surviving 19th-century exhibition hall. It was used by the state Parliament for 27 years, while the Parliament House of Victoria was used by the National Legislature until Canberra's parliament house building was finally completed. It has been gradually restored to regain the appreciation it deserves, and at night the building is brilliantly lit in the same ceremonial manner as it formerly was.

ALONG THE YARRA RIVER

Melbourne's prime natural feature, the 'muddy' Yarra River, is the butt of countless jokes, although it is actually a surprisingly pleasant river. Despite being known as 'the river that flows upside down', it is simply muddy – not particularly dirty. The Yarra is slowly but surely becoming more of an attraction as new parks, walkways and buildings appear along its banks.

This hasn't always been the case. During the gold-rush period, the Yarra was everything from a water supply to an open drain. Raw sewage was emptied into the river until 1900, and industrial wastes from tanneries, soap works and, later, chemical companies were dumped into it as well. In recent years efforts have been made to clean up the river and beautify its surrounds.

There are some beautiful old bridges across the river, and the riverside boulevards provide delightful views of Melbourne by day or night. The Yarra Blvd follows the river in several sections from Richmond to Kew. Much like the Great Ocean Rd, the Yarra Blvd was a relief-work project of the Great Depression.

Boat cruises along the river depart from Princes Walk (below Princes Bridge) and from Southbank. A series of bike paths start from the city and follow the Yarra River; bikes can be hired from various places (see Bicycle in the Getting Around chapter).

Yarra Bend Park (Map 5)

North-east of the city centre, the Yarra River is bordered by the Yarra Bend parkland, much loved by runners, rowers, cyclists, picnickers and strollers. To get there, follow Johnston St through Collingwood and turn into the scenic drive of Yarra Blvd, or better still hire a bike and ride along the riverside bike paths – a leisurely 40-minute roll. By public transport, take tram No 42 from Collins St east along Victoria St to stop No 28, then walk up Walmer St and over the footbridge; or take bus No 201 or 203 from Flinders St Railway Station, both of which go up Studley Park Rd.

The park has large areas of natural bushland (not to mention two golf courses and numerous sports grounds) and there are some great walks. In parts of Studley Park you could be out in the bush; with the songs of bellbirds ringing through the trees and cockatoos screeching on the banks it's hard to believe the city's all around you. At the end of Boathouse Rd is the **Studley Park Boathouse** (☎ 9853 1972), open for lunch daily. These timber buildings on the riverbank date to the 1860s – there are also

Pack a picnic and paddle on the Yarra from Studley Park Boathouse.

boats and canoes available for hire. Kanes suspension bridge takes you across the river, from where it's about a 20-minute walk to Dights Falls at the confluence of the Yarra River and Merri Creek, with some great views along the way. You can also walk to the falls along the southern riverbank. On the way is the **Pioneer Memorial Cairn**, which commemorates Charles Grimes (the first European to discover the Yarra River, in 1803) and the first settlers to bring cattle from Sydney to Melbourne (in 1836).

Farther around the river, Fairfield Park is the site of the **Fairfield Amphitheatre**, a great open-air venue used for concerts and film screenings. The **Fairfield Park Boathouse & Tea Gardens** (☎ 9486 1501), on Fairfield Park Drive, is a restored early 20th-century boathouse with broad verandas and an outdoor garden restaurant. It's open from 9.30 am to 5.30 pm weekdays, 9.30 am to sunset weekends (from May to September it only opens on weekends).

YARRA PARK

Yarra Park is the large expanse of parkland to the south-east of the city centre. It contains the Melbourne Cricket Ground (MCG), the Melbourne Park National Tennis Centre, Olympic Park, the new Multi Purpose Venue and several other sports ovals and open fields.

Melbourne Cricket Ground (Map 3)

The MCG is the temple in which sports-mad Melburnians worship their heroes and heroines. There are sports stadiums and there are

sports stadiums, and the MCG is one of the world's great sporting venues, imbued with an indefinable combination of tradition and atmosphere. In 1858 the first game of Australian rules football was played where the MCG and its car parks now stand, and in 1877 the first test cricket match between Australia and England was played here. (For details of the footy and cricket, see Spectator Sports in the Entertainment chapter.) The MCG was also the central stadium for the 1956 Melbourne Olympics. In 1992 the Great Southern Stand was opened, providing spectators with a greatly improved standard of facilities.

The Melbourne Cricket Club (MCC), founded in 1838, manages the MCG and in return retains a section of the ground for the exclusive use of its members. The **Members' Pavilion** is the oldest stand and, if you're interested in sports, you can lose hours wandering through the pavilion's creaking corridors of sporting history. Its walls are lined with a collection of fascinating old sporting photos. The pavilion also houses the famous Long Room (members only!) and the MCC Cricket Library & Museum, which has thousands of items of sporting memorabilia, books, records and ancient equipment. The pavilion, library and museum are open from 10 am to 4 pm weekdays (except match days) and admission is free. Guided tours are also offered – see following section.

Australian Gallery of Sport & Olympic Museum (Map 3)

In front of the members' entrance to the MCG, near the corner of Jolimont St and Jolimont Terrace, is the Australian Gallery of Sport & Olympic Museum, dedicated to Australia's sporting passions. It has three levels: the foyer and souvenir shop are on the ground floor, the 1st floor houses special exhibitions and topical displays, and the 2nd floor houses the permanent collection, with 10 separate sporting sections and the Olympic Museum. It's open from 9.30 am to 4.30 pm daily; admission is $9.50/6/25 for adults/children/families (including a tour of both the MCG and the museum). Tours run on the hour between 10 am and 3 pm, although they may be curtailed on match days.

Melbourne Park National Tennis Centre (Map 3)

A footbridge links the Melbourne Park National Tennis Centre (formerly Flinders Park) with the MCG, crossing the Jolimont railway yards from the members' car park. The No 70 tram route has stops for both the MCG and Melbourne Park. Opened in 1988, the centre hosts the Australian Open Grand Slam championship each January, and is used as a basketball and concert venue. (For details of the tennis and basketball, see Spectator Sports in the Entertainment chapter.) Both the centre court (recently renamed the Rod Laver Arena) and the nearby new Multi Purpose Venue are covered with retractable roofs. The centre has five indoor and 23 outdoor courts available to the public (see Tennis in the Activities section later in this chapter).

EAST MELBOURNE (MAP 3)

East Melbourne is a small residential pocket of elegant Victorian town houses, historic mansions and tree-lined avenues. Clarendon, Hotham and Powlett Sts are all worth a wander if you're interested in seeing some of Melbourne's most impressive early residential architecture.

Tasma Terrace, in Parliament Place behind Parliament House, is a magnificent row of six attached Victorian terraces. Designed by Charles Webb, who designed the Windsor Hotel (see Spring St earlier this chapter), the three-storey grey-stuccoed terraces were built in 1879. The restrained cast-iron decoration is a feature of the buildings, which are owned by and house the office of the **National Trust**, an organisation dedicated to preserving Australia's heritage. It's worth visiting the office – it has a range of information on National Trust properties, and the interior of the reception office is a great example of Victoriana. The terrace next door has also been restored, and if you ask nicely they will show you the parlour and sitting room with its original Victorian furniture and artworks. The last terrace houses the

Victorian National Parks Association (☎ 9650 8296), a lobby group for conservation and the promotion of national parks. They also host regular bushwalks and nature walks in and around Melbourne. Ring the association for details.

St Patrick's Cathedral, behind Parliament House in Cathedral Place, is said to be one of the world's largest and finest examples of Gothic Revival architecture. Designed by William Wardell, it was begun in 1863 and built in stages until the spires and west portal were added in 1939. The imposing bluestone exterior is floodlit to great effect at night and is spectacular when viewed from Brunswick St to the north.

Diagonally across Gisborne St from the cathedral is the Eastern Hill Fire Station. The Old Fire Station building, on the corner of Gisborne St and Victoria Parade, was built in 1891. Its ground floor now houses the **Fire Services Museum of Victoria** (Map 2), which has a historic collection of

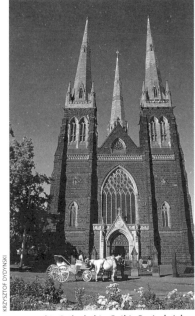

KRZYSZTOF DYDYNSKI

St Patrick's Cathedral in Gothic Revival style

fire-fighting equipment, including fire engines, helmets and uniforms, as well as medals and photographs. It is open from 9 am to 3 pm Friday, from 10 am to 4 pm Sunday; admission is $5/2 for adults/children. Facing Albert St, the unattractive facade of the newer building has been brightened up with a mural designed by Harold Freedman, who is also responsible for the murals at Spencer St train station and the Australian Gallery of Sport. The **mosaic mural** depicts the history and legends of fire.

The **WR Johnston Collection** (☎ 9416 2515) is a private museum of 18th-century decorative arts from England, displayed in the collector's former home, 'Fairhall', at 152 Hotham St. Tours are held weekdays and cost $12/6 adult/concession; ring in advance to book.

PARKVILLE & CARLTON

Up this end of town you'll find a cosmopolitan area that blends the intellectual with the gastronomic, the sporting with the cultural, and here you'll see some of the city's finest Victorian residential architecture.

In Parkville there are the University of Melbourne and the Royal Melbourne Zoo; in Carlton the Melbourne General Cemetery and some great restaurants in the Italian quarter around Lygon, Drummond and Rathdowne Sts.

Royal Park (Map 4)

Royal Park is a large expanse of open parkland that contains a number of sports ovals and open spaces, large netball and hockey stadiums, a public golf course and the Royal Melbourne Zoo. In the corner closest to the University of Melbourne is a garden of Australian native plants, and a little farther north, just south of MacArthur Rd, a **memorial cairn** marks the spot from which the Burke & Wills expedition set off in 1860 on its fateful crossing of the Australian interior.

Royal Melbourne Zoo (Map 4)

Melbourne's zoo is one of the city's most popular attractions, and deservedly so. Established in 1861, this is the oldest zoo in

Left or right? Meerkats looking for home.

DENNIS JONES

Australia and the third oldest in the world. In the 1850s, when Australia was considered a foreign place full of strange plants and animals, the Acclimatisation Society was formed for 'the introduction, acclimatisation and domestication of all innoxious animals, birds, fishes, insects and vegetables'. The society merged with the Zoological Society in 1861 and together they established the zoo on its present site.

Set in spacious, attractively landscaped gardens with broad strolling paths, the zoo's enclosures simulate the animals' natural habitats. The walkways pass through the enclosures – you walk through the bird aviary, cross a bridge over the lions' park, enter a tropical hothouse full of colourful butterflies and walk around the gorillas' very own rainforest. There's also a large collection of native animals in a native bush setting, a platypus aquarium, fur seals, lions and tigers, plenty of reptiles and lots more to see. You should allow at least half a day. There's also a good selection of not-too-tacky souvenirs, as well as quite a few snack bars and two bistros.

The zoo is open from 9 am to 5 pm daily and admission is $14/7/38 for adults/children/families. On Thursday to Sunday during January and February the zoo stays open until 7 pm, then jazz bands play until around 9.30 pm – see Jazz & Blues in the Entertainment chapter for details. To reach the zoo from the city, take tram No 55 or 56 from William St, or an Upfield line train to Royal Park train station (no trains on Sunday). You can also take a tram from Elizabeth St in the city up Royal Parade, then walk from the Walker St tram stop.

University of Melbourne (Map 4)

The University of Melbourne was established in 1853 and is well worth a visit. A wander around the campus will reveal an intriguing blend of original Gothic-style stone buildings and some incredibly unattractive brick blocks from more recent 'functionalist' periods of architecture. The college buildings, to the north of the campus, are particularly noteworthy for their fine architecture.

The grounds have open lawns and garden areas, and during semester there's always something going on. There are often bands playing in North Court (behind Union House), or you could sit in on a lecture, go book browsing in the Baillieu Library, inspect the rare plants in the System Garden (between the Botany and Agriculture & Forestry buildings) or visit one of several free galleries and museums.

The **Ian Potter Museum of Art** (formerly the Sir Ian Potter Gallery, which was close by) is housed in the newly built Nonda Katsalidis building on Swanston St, near the corner of Tin Alley. This art museum is home to the university's large collection of 19th- and 20th-century art, and it features regular exhibitions of contemporary art and a program of public lectures. It's open from 10 am to 5 pm Tuesday to Sunday (until 9 pm Thursday). There's also a Brunetti cafe on the ground floor.

The **University Gallery** in the former Physics building has a small but interesting collection of Australian art. On the Royal Parade side (next to the Conservatory of Music), the **Grainger Museum** is dedicated to the life and times of Percy Grainger (1882–1961), an eccentric composer who lived an extraordinary life and travelled the world collecting and recording folk music on an old Edison recording machine. Grainger set up the museum before his death, and it contains his collections, instruments, photos, costumes and other interesting personal effects. The museum is open from 10 am to 4 pm weekdays and admission is free.

The **Griffin Gallery** is also at the university; admission is free.

Melbourne Museum (Map 3)

The new Melbourne Museum is located directly opposite the old Royal Exhibition Building in the Carlton Gardens, and should never have been given planning permission. The buildings stand face to face like a couple of boxers squaring up for a fight; in an attempt to contrast the old with the new this does neither building any justice. It would have made much more sense to plonk the museum over on Southbank where an injection of culture is sorely needed. (See also the aside on contemporary architecture earlier in this chapter.)

The $550 million museum was in the later stages of completion at the time of writing, but should be in full swing by the time you read this. Along with the museum's impressive collection, the complex will include an Aboriginal centre, a children's museum, living forest gallery, major exhibition galleries (covering Australian society, indigenous cultures, wonders of the human mind and body, and science and technology), touring exhibition hall, 3D interactive theatre, study centre and a two-level retail outlet and three themed restaurants/cafes.

Lygon Street (Map 3)

Carlton is Melbourne's Italian quarter, and Lygon St its backbone. Many of the thousands of Italian immigrants who came to Melbourne after WWII settled in Carlton, and Lygon St became the focal point of their community.

Lygon St is the most highly 'developed' example of the multicultural evolution of Melbourne's inner suburbs. A fondness lingers for the older less glamorous version, but as they say, you can't stop progress. The developers moved in and with their out-with-the-old and in-with-the-new philosophy gave Lygon St a facelift that didn't necessarily improve its looks. Lygon St lost its off-beat appeal and the bohemian element moved on to Brunswick St, Fitzroy, and beyond.

But not all of the old Lygon St was lost. Among the restaurants and exclusive fashion boutiques, you'll still find a few of the old favourites: Readings bookstore is still there, albeit in a new shop; Tiamo and Jimmy Watson's have resisted the winds of change; you can still play pool at Johnny's Green Room; and La Mama, the tiny, experimental theatre started by Betty Burstall in 1967, is still going strong in Faraday St.

Lygon St is one of Melbourne's liveliest streets. Day and night it is filled with people promenading, dining, sipping cappuccinos, shopping and generally soaking up the atmosphere. Every October, Lygon St hosts the lively Lygon St Festa, a four-day food-and-fun street party.

Other Attractions

Drummond St and **Royal Parade** (Map 3) are two attractive and broad, tree-lined avenues containing outstanding examples of 19th-century residential architecture. Drummond St in particular, from Victoria St to Palmerston St, is one of the most impressive and intact Victorian streetscapes in the city. **Rathdowne St** (Map 3), north of Princes St, has a great little shopping area and some good cafes and restaurants. Head up to North Carlton and Brunswick (Sydney Rd and the top end of Lygon St) to see the less commercial face of this cosmopolitan area.

Princes Park (Map 4), to the north of Melbourne University, has a number of sports grounds, including the Carlton Football and Cricket Clubs' main ground and a 3.2km fun-and-fitness exercise circuit.

A visit to the **Melbourne General Cemetery**, next to Princes Park, is a sombre reminder that no matter how many laps of the fun-and-fitness circuit you do, you can't avoid the inevitable. The earliest gravestones date back to the 1850s, and the cemetery is a graphic and historic portrait of the diversity of countries from which people have come to settle in Australia. You can wander around at your own leisure, or for tours see Other Walking Tours earlier in this chapter.

FITZROY & COLLINGWOOD (MAPS 3 & 4)

Fitzroy (Map 3) is where Melbourne's bohemian subculture moved when the lights got too bright in Carlton. It's a great mixture of artistic, seedy, alternative and trendy elements, and one of Melbourne's most interesting suburbs to live in or to visit.

In Melbourne's early years Fitzroy was a prime residential area, and the suburb contains some fine terrace and row houses from the mid-Victorian era – the most notable of which is **Royal Terrace** (1854) on Nicholson St, opposite the Royal Exhibition Building. Later, the suburb became a high-density, working-class stronghold with a large migrant population. The central location and cosmopolitan atmosphere has since attracted students, artists and urban lifestylers, creating the lively blend that now exists.

Brunswick St is one of Melbourne's most vibrant and lively streets, and you shouldn't visit the city without coming here. The blocks on either side of the Johnston St intersection have a good selection of young designer and retro clothes shops, bookshops, galleries and of course a sea of cafes and restaurants – see the Places to Eat and Shopping chapters. An interesting cross section of people frequent Brunswick St, so don't be surprised to overhear conversations covering everything from the price of real estate to the pain involved in foreskin piercing. Prominent on the Brunswick St calendar is the carnivalesque street parade and party that marks the beginning of the two-week Fringe Arts Festival each September.

Johnston St (Map 3) is the centre of Melbourne's small but lively Spanish-speaking community, with its tapas bars, the Spanish Club and several Spanish delicatessens. It also hosts the annual Hispanic Community Festival each November.

Smith St (Map 3) forms the border between Fitzroy and Collingwood, and the village-like streetscape is a reminder of how Brunswick St used to be. Those eager to escape Brunswick St's growing commercialisation are heading over here, so everyone else is sure to soon follow. Smith St not only has a great assortment of food stores,

Brunswick Street, the heart of vibrant Fitzroy

bookshops, pubs and restaurants, but it sells the best takeaway spanokopita in town (visit Melissa's Coffee Lounge, near the corner of Peel St).

Head up Brunswick St across Alexandra Parade into **North Fitzroy** (Map 4), where there are a few interesting and quirky shops to explore, more historic buildings, the Edinburgh Gardens and one or two good pubs in which to enjoy an ale. The **Fitzroy Swimming Pool**, on Alexandra Parade between Brunswick and Smith Sts, is open year round (see the boxed text 'A Bigger Splash' later in this chapter).

The baths were saved from closure by a huge community campaign; a similar campaign some years earlier couldn't prevent the freeway eating up the once-pretty Alexandra Parade and cutting North Fitzroy from Fitzroy proper. In a history of destruction, Melbourne slums were demolished to make way for the ugly public housing towers that dominate the skyline. It's said that planners drove around the inner suburbs, deciding on demolition sites without even getting out of their cars.

RICHMOND (MAPS 5 & 6)

There is still evidence in Swan St of Richmond's Greek Australian past, but the Vietnamese community has really transformed **Victoria St**, between Church and Hoddle Sts, into an exciting strip known as 'Little Saigon' (see the Places to Eat chapter).

The suburb is another centre for Victorian architecture, much of it restored or in the process of restoration. With Richmond's working-class roots, many of the houses are small workers' cottages and terraces, although the Richmond Hill area (between Lennox, Church and Swan Sts and Bridge Rd) has some impressive old mansions.

Bridge Rd and **Swan St** are a mish-mash of cafes, restaurants and shops where many Australian fashion labels sell their seconds and rejects. **Dimmey's** department store, at 140 Swan St, is an old-fashioned and chaotic wonderland of junk and bargains, and one of the cheapest and most bizarre places to buy just about anything.

Turn the corner south into Church St from Swan St to find a shopping experience at the opposite extreme to Dimmey's. **Dutton**

(Map 6) is half car dealer and half car museum. Nothing costs much under $100,000 and price tags over $250,000, for particularly fine examples of Italian exotica, are not at all unusual. It even sells racing cars from time to time. Oddly enough the cafe here, Cafe Veloce, is inexpensive.

In the adjacent suburb of Burnley, alongside the Yarra River, you'll find the **Burnley Golf Course** (Map 6), the Burnley Horticultural College and the **Burnley Park** off Yarra Blvd, laid out with lovely lawns, lily ponds and exotic trees.

SOUTH YARRA & TOORAK

South Yarra and Toorak are on what's commonly referred to as the 'right side of the river' – the high-society side of town. South Yarra is a bustling, trendy and very style-conscious suburb – the kind of place where avid readers of *Vogue Living* will feel very much at home.

Farther west, Toorak is the poshest suburb in Melbourne and home to the city's most wealthy home-owners (or at least its most ostentatious). Toorak doesn't hold much interest for travellers, although it can

be interesting to drive along the tree-lined streets looking at palatial homes. Sadly, a number of these are being bought and bull-dozed to be replaced by rows of fake Georgian townhouses. St Georges and Grange Rds are where you'll see some of the biggest mansions in the country.

While you're in South Yarra, visit **Como** at 16 Como Ave, one of Australia's finest colonial mansions (see the boxed aside, 'Historic Houses', on the previous page).

Toorak Road (Map 6)

Toorak Rd forms the main artery through both suburbs, and is one of Australia's classiest shopping streets, frequented by those well-known Toorak matrons in their Porsches, Mercedes Benzes and Range Rovers (known as 'Toorak Tractors').

The main shopping area in South Yarra is along Toorak Rd, in the stretch between Punt Rd and Chapel St. Here you'll find dozens of exclusive fashion boutiques, as well as specialist shops, cafes and restaurants, some great bookshops – such as Black Mask, Readings and Mary Martin's – and the Longford Cinema.

Historic Houses

Como and Rippon Lea, two of Melbourne's most magnificent early homesteads, are open to the public and well worth a visit. If you're particularly interested in Victoria's heritage, the National Trust, 4 Parliament Place, publishes a brochure that gives details of other historic properties throughout the state that are open to the public.

Como (Map 6; ☎ 9827 2500) overlooks the Yarra River from Como Park in South Yarra, and was built between 1840 and 1859 when Aboriginal rites and feasts were still held on the riverbank. The home, which is set in extensive grounds, has been faithfully restored and furnished and is operated by the National Trust. Como is open from 10 am to 5 pm daily and admission is $9.50/6.50/5/20 for an adult/student/child/family. You can get here on tram No 8 from Swanston St in the city – get off at stop No 30 on Toorak Rd and walk down Como Ave.

Rippon Lea (Map 9; ☎ 9523 6095) is at 192 Hotham St, Elsternwick, close to St Kilda. It's another fine old mansion with elegant gardens inhabited by peacocks. Rippon Lea is open from 10 am to 5 pm daily and admission is $9/6/5/20 for an adult/student/child/family. The tearoom is open between 11 am and 4 pm on weekends only. The easiest way to get there is to take a Sandringham line train to Ripponlea train station, from where it's a five-minute walk to the property.

Labassa (Map 9; ☎ 9509 6596), at 2 Manor Grove in Caulfield, is an elaborate French Renaissance-style, two-storey mansion noted for its richly detailed interior. It's well worth seeing, but is only open from 10.30 am to 4.30 pm on the last Sunday of each month. Admission is $7/5/18 for an adult/child/family.

The **Como Centre**, on the corner of Toorak Rd and Chapel St, is a sleek and stylish commercial development that houses upmarket boutiques and shops, offices, cafes, the Como Cinemas and the five-star Como Hotel.

At the St Kilda Rd end (west) of Toorak Rd stands the copper-domed **Hebrew Synagogue**, built in 1930. On the south side of Toorak Rd between Punt Rd and St Kilda Rd is **Fawkner Park**, an attractive and spacious park with large expanses of grass, tree-lined paths, tennis courts and various sports ovals. It's a great spot for a stroll or a picnic or perhaps to kick a football.

At the Toorak end (east) of Toorak Rd is the smaller and more exclusive group of shops and arcades known as **The Village**, between Wallace Ave and Grange Rd. The Village is the local convenience shopping area for some of Melbourne's wealthiest citizens – don't expect any bargains, but this is a great spot for window-shopping and people-watching.

Chapel Street (Map 6)

Chapel St is one of Melbourne's major and most diverse retail centres. The South Yarra end (north), between Toorak and Commercial Rds, is a stylish centre for retail fashion, and is virtually wall-to-wall clothing boutiques (with a healthy sprinkling of bars and cafes). If you want to see fashion, this is where you'll see it – in the shop windows, sitting outside the cafes and walking the street.

The **Jam Factory**, at No 500, produced mountains of the stuff from the late 19th century until the early 1970s. In its new incarnation it has become an aesthetic disaster of a shopping and entertainment complex, with only the shell of the building remaining. The interior has been redeveloped in a glitzy tribute to Hollywood-meets-Disneyland style, with an eight-screen cinema complex, giant models of screen idols and movie monsters, cafes and restaurants. The Jam Factory's only saving grace is the book-browsing offered by the huge Borders bookstore.

PRAHRAN (MAPS 6 & 7)

Surrounded by the more affluent neighbouring suburbs of South Yarra, Toorak and Armadale, Prahran is a blend of small Victorian workers' cottages, narrow, leafy streets and high-rise, government-subsidised flats for low-income earners. This area is populated by people from a broad range of ethnic backgrounds and is enlivened by a variety of cultural influences.

It has some lively streets, the most notable being Chapel St. Prahran's sector of Chapel St stretches south from Malvern Rd (the eastbound continuation of Commercial Rd) to Dandenong Rd, and is more diverse and less fashion-conscious than the South Yarra sector. The very good **Prahran Market** (Map 6) is just around the corner from Chapel St on Commercial Rd. See Prahran in the Places to Eat chapter for further details.

Commercial Rd (Maps 6 & 7) is something of a focal centre for Melbourne's gay and lesbian community, and has a diverse collection of nightclubs, bars, pubs, bookshops and cafes.

PABLO GARCIA GASTAR

Chapel St – a stronghold of consumer culture

Malvern Rd (Map 6) is another interesting shopping precinct, with a large number of antique shops and clothes boutiques. In Essex St, off Malvern Rd, you'll find the **Prahran Aquatic Centre** (Map 6) and beside it the popular **Skatebowl**, a council-run skateboarding centre with a large concrete bowl and metal ramp.

Running off Chapel St from Prahran Town Hall, **Greville St** (Map 6) has always seen itself as the area's shopping alternative, with an interesting collection of retro, grunge and designer clothing shops, bookstores, gift shops and some good bars and cafes. See the Shopping chapter for more details on Prahran's shops and market.

ST KILDA (MAP 9)

St Kilda is one of Melbourne's liveliest and most cosmopolitan areas, a fact jointly attributable to its seaside location and its chequered history.

In Melbourne's early days, St Kilda was something of a seaside resort, the fashionable spot for those wanting to escape the increasingly grimy and crowded city. Horse trams, and later cable trams, ran along St Kilda Rd carrying day-trippers, and by 1857 the railway line to St Kilda was completed. During the gold-rush period, many wealthier citizens built mansions in St Kilda, and Fitzroy St became one of the city's most gracious boulevards. Hotels were built, dance halls opened and sea baths and fun parks catered to the crowds – St Kilda was *the* place to go in search of fun and entertainment.

As things became more hectic, the wealthy folk moved on to the more exclusive areas such as Toorak. With the economic collapse of the 1890s, St Kilda's status began to decline. Flats were built and the mansions were demolished or divided up, and by the 1960s and 1970s St Kilda had a reputation as a seedy centre for drugs and prostitution. The suburb's decadent image of faded glory (and cheap rent) attracted a diverse mixture of immigrants and refugees, bohemians and down-and-outers.

In recent years, St Kilda has undergone an image upgrade. It has returned to the forefront of Melbourne's fashionable suburbs, the place it occupied more than a century ago, but with a few characteristic differences. Its appeal is now a mix of the old and the rejuvenated, the ethnic and the artistic, the stylish and the casual. St Kilda is a place of extremes – backpacker hostels and fine-dining restaurants, classy cafes and cheap takeaways, seaside strolls and Sunday traffic jams. Despite its improved image, however, some elements of its seedy past remain, and it can still be somewhat perilous to wander the streets late at night, particularly for women.

Of interest here is the historic **corroboree tree**, a 300-year-old Aboriginal ceremonial tree located between the Junction Oval and the intersection of Queens and St Kilda Rds. The **St Kilda Botanical Gardens** were first planted in 1859 and have recently been upgraded and improved. They feature a garden conservatory and the Alister Clarke Memorial Garden (a bed of roses). The gardens are tucked away off Blessington St, not far from the bottom end of Acland St, and are well worth searching out.

The *St Kilda Heritage Walk* brochure, with 22 historic points of interest, is available from the town hall on the corner of St Kilda Rd and Carlisle St. The walk concentrates on the foreshore and Esplanade area. Another interesting walk is to explore the St Kilda Hill area where some of the oldest and grandest buildings remain.

The **National Theatre** (☎ 9534 0221), a great old theatre on the corner of Barkly and Carlisle Sts, houses a ballet and drama school and stages a wide variety of productions – you'll need to ring to find out what's on.

If you follow **Carlisle St** across St Kilda Rd and into St Kilda East, you'll find some great Jewish food shops, bakeries and European delicatessens. Carlisle St is much less trendy than the bayside areas, and the shops are generally less expensive.

The **Jewish Museum of Australia** (☎ 9534 0083), at 26 Alma Rd, is a dynamic and fascinating museum with interactive displays relating to Jewish history and culture since the beginning of European settlement in Australia. The museum also hosts regular exhibitions and lectures. It's open from 10 am to 4 pm Tuesday to Thursday, 11 am to 5 pm Sunday, and entry is $5/3/13 for adults/children/families.

The St Kilda Festival, held on the second weekend in February, is a great showcase for local artists, musicians and writers, and features street parties, parades, concerts, readings and lots more. Acland St is closed to traffic and filled with food stalls and entertainment, and in Fitzroy St the restaurants put their tables on the footpath for alfresco dining. The finale of the festival weekend is a music concert and fireworks display over the beach.

Fitzroy Street

Fitzroy St, along with the rest of St Kilda, has to a large extent cleaned up its image from its seedier days. Although some of the more undesirable elements of the street still remain around the Grey St intersection, the growing number of bars, restaurants and cafes have made Fitzroy St one of Melbourne's most popular places to eat and drink.

Acland Street

The section of Acland St between Carlisle and Barkly Sts is famed for its continental cake shops, delicatessens, and older-style central European cafes and restaurants, such as Scheherezade. This part of Acland St became a centre for the wave of Jewish and European refugees who settled in the area during Hitler's rise to power and after WWII. Although fading, their influence and presence can still be felt among the restaurants, cafes, bars, bookshops and giftshops that have turned this once sedate street into a bustling strip where at weekends in particular pavement space is hard to find.

North of Carlisle St, Acland St is mostly residential all the way to Fitzroy St. The grand old two-storey mansion at 26 Acland St has been converted into the Linden–St Kilda Arts Centre. Registered by the National Trust, the building houses a contemporary art gallery, artists' studios, workshops and performance spaces. Linden is open from 1 to 6 pm Tuesday to Sunday; admission is free.

No 14 Acland St is the home of the excellent Theatreworks, a local fringe theatre company (see under Theatre in the Entertainment chapter).

Seaside St Kilda

St Kilda's foreshore has undergone the same rejuvenation as the rest of the suburb. The beaches have been cleaned up and topped up with sand, the foreshore parks landscaped and bike paths built. The sight of boats and yachts moored in the lee of the breakwater, the Canary Island palm trees planted along the foreshore and people promenading along the pier are all familiar sights. Two of St Kilda's most popular restaurants are superbly located in converted foreshore buildings: the stylish seafood restaurant Donovans was once a bathing pavilion, and the Stokehouse was originally an Edwardian teahouse.

The St Kilda Pier and breakwater are a favourite spot for strollers, who often reward themselves with a cappuccino, snack or lunch at the kiosk, a restored late 19th-century tearoom at the junction of the pier. On weekends and public holidays ferries run from the pier across the bay to Williamstown (see under Boat in the Getting Around chapter). Bicycles can be hired at the pier in summer. From the pier, you can also take a boat cruise with Penguin Waters Cruises (☎ 0412 311 922) to see a local penguin colony. The 1½-hour cruise departs from St Kilda daily at sunset, costing $30. The price includes an on-board barbecue.

On the foreshore south of the pier, the site of the former St Kilda Baths is currently undergoing a major and somewhat controversial redevelopment that will transform St Kilda's foreshore when it is completed – hopefully for the better. The new complex will house a 25m saltwater swimming pool, treatment baths, spas, a high-tech gym and health centre, shops, cafes, bars and restaurants.

The famous laughing face and Moorish twin-towers entrance of Luna Park on the lower Esplanade has been a symbol of St Kilda since 1912. Built by the same company that built the first Luna Park on Coney Island in 1903, this historic amusement park has some great attractions, including the heritage-listed roller coaster (the only roller coaster of its kind operating in the world) and a beautifully crafted carousel (built by the Philadelphia Toboggan Company and the only one of its kind to leave American shores). There are also dodgems, a Ferris wheel and ghost train. Admission is free to wander and look around; it costs $2 to $3 for most rides and you can buy multiple-ticket booklets at discounted prices. Luna Park is open from 7 to 11 pm Friday, 1 to 11 pm Saturday and 1 pm till dusk Sunday. During public and school holidays it's open from 11 am to 5 pm Monday to Thursday, 11 am to 11 pm Friday and Saturday. Ring the recorded information number (☎ 1902-240 112) for details.

The **Palais Theatre**, across the road, was built in 1927. At the time it was one of the largest and best picture palaces in Australia, seating over 3000. It's still a great venue for a wide variety of live performances.

Built in 1880, the **Esplanade Hotel** on the Upper Esplanade is the musical heart and soul of St Kilda, and perhaps the best-known pub in Melbourne. The actress Sarah Bernhardt stayed here back in 1891. Today the 'Espy' is much loved by St Kilda's locals, with its free live bands, comedy nights, good food and grungy atmosphere, but due to its prime location and run-down state its future is constantly under threat by developers who want to 'redevelop' it (ie, renovate it to look like every other renovated pub in town). See the Entertainment chapter for more detail on the Espy.

The **Esplanade Art & Craft Market**, every Sunday along the Upper Esplanade, features a huge range of open-air stalls selling a great variety of arts, crafts, gifts and souvenirs.

PORT MELBOURNE (MAP 7)

Only recently has Port Melbourne begun to feel the full force of the gentrification that has swept the inner suburbs. Factories, semi-industrial buildings and many of its small Victorian workers' cottages have been transformed, renovated or restored.

Bay St, the continuation of City Rd, is the area's main street, and runs all the way down to the bay. There are many historic

Inner-suburban beaches skirt Port Phillip Bay.

veranda-fronted terrace buildings of heritage character, and the street has a 'village' feel about it, with a good range of shops and some great pubs.

Station Pier is Melbourne's major passenger shipping terminal and the departure point for ferries to/from Tasmania. It also has good views of the city, old-fashioned kiosks and a Greek restaurant.

SOUTH MELBOURNE (MAP 7)

South Melbourne had humble beginnings as a shanty town of canvas and bark huts on the swampy lands south of the Yarra. The area was originally called Emerald Hill, after the grassy knoll of high ground that stood above the muddy flatlands. Nowadays, South Melbourne is an interesting inner-city suburb with a rich architectural and cultural heritage and quite a few sights worth seeing.

Clarendon St is the main street, running through the heart of South Melbourne from Spencer St in the city to Albert Park Lake. In the central shopping section, many of the original Victorian shopfronts have been restored and refitted with verandas, and you'll find all sorts of shops and quite a few pubs (the survivors from the days when the area boasted a pub on every corner).

Emerald Hill, between Clarendon, Park, Cecil and Dorcas Sts, was the first area built upon and is now a heritage conservation area. It has some fine old mansions and terrace houses, and the impressive restored **South Melbourne Town Hall** on Bank St. The **South Melbourne Market**, which dates to 1867, is on the corner of Cecil and Coventry Sts.

The **Victorian Tapestry Workshop** (☎ 9699 7885), at 260 Park St, produces large-scale tapestries, which are the collaborative work of skilled weavers and contemporary artists. At the workshop you'll be able to see the creation of what's said to be 'one of Western civilisation's oldest and richest art forms', and some pieces are available for sale. The workshop is open to the public from 10 am to 4 pm weekdays (entry $3), and tours run at 2 pm every Wednesday and at 11 am Thursday ($5). You need to ring and book a tour.

The **Chinese Joss House** (1856), 76 Raglan St, is said to be one of the finest Chinese temples outside China. It was built by the Sze Yup Society as a place of worship for the Chinese who came to Melbourne during the gold rush. The Joss House open from 9 am to 4 pm daily except Friday.

At 399 Coventry St is a set of three **portable iron houses** that have been preserved by the National Trust. These houses were prefabricated in England and erected here during the heady gold-rush days of 1853. Many early colonial dwellings were prefabs, and this set is one of the few remaining examples. The houses are open to the public from 1 to 4 pm Sunday (2 to 4 pm during daylight saving time).

ALBERT PARK (MAP 7)

Wedged between South Melbourne and the bay, Albert Park is a small 'village' suburb populated by an interesting blend of migrants, young families and the upwardly mobile. A large percentage of its Victorian terrace houses and cottages have been renovated, and the suburb is a popular spot for

beach-goers in summer and cafe-lovers at any time of the year.

On **Bridport St**, between Montague and Merton Sts, is a small but lively shopping area, with many food and clothing shops. Here you'll find some excellent and stylish cafes and delicatessens, a few exclusive speciality shops and boutiques, and the Avenue Bookstore. Just north of the shopping centre is the lovely **St Vincent Place**, a formal Victorian garden surrounded by beautiful terrace houses.

In summer, crowds of sun-lovers flock to Albert Park's beaches, especially to those around the **Kerford Rd Pier**. It's a great spot to slap on the sunscreen and observe Aussie beach etiquette in action.

Albert Park Lake is a 2.5km-long artificial lake surrounded by parkland, sports ovals, a golf-course and other recreation areas. The lake circuit is popular with strollers, runners and cyclists, and the sight of dozens of small yachts sailing across the lake on a sunny Saturday is one of Melbourne's trademark images. There are several restaurants and bars around the lake where you can sit and enjoy the views. The road around the lake was used as an international motor-racing circuit in the 1950s, and since 1996 the revamped track has been the venue for the **Australian Formula One Grand Prix** – see Spectator Sports in the Entertainment chapter for more details.

WILLIAMSTOWN (MAP 8)

Back in 1837, two new townships were laid out simultaneously at the top of Port Phillip Bay – Melbourne as the main settlement and Williamstown as the seaport. With the advantage of the natural harbour of Hobsons Bay, Williamstown thrived and government services such as customs and immigration were based here. Many early buildings were built from locally quarried bluestone and the township quickly took on an air of permanence.

When the Yarra River was deepened and the Port of Melbourne developed in the 1880s, Williamstown became a secondary port. Tucked away in a corner of the bay, it was bypassed and forgotten for years.

Williamstown has been rediscovered and is experiencing a renaissance, especially on weekends when crowds of day-trippers take ferry rides across the bay to enjoy the historic seaside atmosphere. **Nelson Place**, which follows the foreshore and winds around the docklands and shipyards, was patriotically named after British Navy Admiral Horatio Nelson. Nelson Place is lined with historic buildings, many of them registered by the National Trust, while the yacht clubs, marinas, boat builders and chandleries along the waterfront add to the maritime flavour. Williamstown's other attractions include restaurants and cafes, some good pubs and bars, art and craft galleries and interesting speciality shops.

The Williamstown Information Centre (☎ 9397 3791) on the Commonwealth Reserve, between Nelson Place and the waterfront, opens from 11 am to 3.30 pm on weekdays and until 5 pm on weekends. A **craft market** is held on the reserve on the third Sunday of each month. The reserve is also the main site for the Williamstown Summer Festival, held in late January.

Moored at Gem Pier is the **HMAS** *Castlemaine*, a WWII minesweeper that was built at Williamstown in 1941 and has been converted into a maritime museum. It is staffed by volunteers from the Maritime Trust of Australia and contains nautical exhibits and memorabilia. You can visit from noon to 5 pm weekends and admission is $4/2 for adults/children. **Cruises** around the harbour on the *Little Gem* leave from the pier on weekends and cost $5.

The *Enterprise* (☎ 9397 3477) is a timber replica of the ship that carried founding father John Pascoe Fawkner to the settlement. Weekend one-hour sails leave from Gem Pier at noon, 2 and 4 pm Saturday, noon and 4 pm Sunday ($15/5/35 for adults/children/families).

The **Historical Society Museum**, in the old Mechanics Institute building (1860) at 5 Electra St, has displays of maritime history, model ships, antique furniture and some strange relics including a spring-loaded fly-disturber. The museum is open from 2 to 5 pm Sunday; admission is $3.

Williamstown Railway Museum (☎ 9397 7412), operated by the Australian Railway Historical Society, is open from noon to 5 pm on weekends and public holidays, noon to 4 pm on Wednesdays during school holidays. It's a good spot for kids and rail enthusiasts, with a fine collection of old steam locomotives, wagons, carriages and old photos, and mini-steam-train rides for kids. It's part of the Newport Rail Workshops on Champion Rd in North Williamstown, and is close to the North Williamstown train station. Admission is $5/2.50 for adults/children.

On the corner of Nelson Place and Syme St, the **Customs Wharf** houses an interesting collection of arts and crafts and speciality shops. It's open from 11 am to 6 pm daily and entry costs $1. On the corner of Osborne and Giffard Sts, the small but lovely **Williamstown Botanic Gardens** are also worth a visit.

North along the Strand at **Parson's Marina**, Williamstown Boat Hire (☎ 9397 7312) hires out boats for fishing and cruising for around $25 an hour (with a two-hour minimum). It also hires tackle and sells bait.

The excellent **Scienceworks** and the **Melbourne Planetarium** are housed together just north of Williamstown in Spotswood (see Other Museums later).

Williamstown Beach, on the southern side of the peninsula, is a pleasant place for a swim. From Nelson Place walk down Cole St.

Getting There & Away

From the city centre Williamstown is about a 10-minute drive across the West Gate Bridge or a short train ride away (take either a Williamstown line train or a Werribee line train and change at Newport). You can also get there on the double-decker City Wanderer tour bus (see Organised Tours in the Getting Around chapter). Ferries link Williamstown with St Kilda and the city centre (see the Getting Around chapter).

A good bicycle path follows the foreshore reserve from the Timeball Tower and runs all the way to the West Gate Bridge, passing the Scienceworks museum. An interesting

SIMON BRACKEN

Fish and chips at Williamstown, under the covetous gaze of seagulls.

option for cyclists wanting to get from the city side across to Scienceworks and Williamstown is by a punt (☎ 0419 999 458) which ferries people across the Yarra River from under the West Gate Bridge. The punt operates between 10 am and 5 pm on weekends and costs $3/5 one way/return.

OTHER ART GALLERIES

Melbourne has dozens of art galleries that are open to the public. The magazine *Art Almanac*, a monthly guide to all city and regional galleries, is available from most galleries for $2.

At 7 Templestowe Rd in the suburb of Bulleen, the **Museum of Modern Art at Heide** (☎ 9850 1500) is on the site of the former home of the late John and Sunday Reed, under whose patronage the likes of Sir Sidney Nolan, John Perceval, Joy Hester, Albert Tucker and Arthur Boyd created a new movement in the Australian art world. Known as 'Heide', the gallery has an impressive collection of 20th-century Australian art. The main gallery space shows special exhibitions of works curated from other collections; the more intimate Reed gallery shows works from the Heide collection as well as from elsewhere. The sprawling park is an informal combination of

native and European trees, with a carefully tended **kitchen garden** and scattered sculpture gardens running right down to the banks of the Yarra. The museum is open from 10 am to 5 pm Tuesday to Friday, noon to 5 pm weekends and public holidays. Admission varies from show to show. Heide is signposted off the Eastern Fwy. Otherwise, bus No 203 goes to Bulleen from the city, and the Yarra bike path passes close by.

Montsalvat Gallery (☎ 9439 8771) is on Hillcrest Ave in Eltham, the mud-brick and alternative lifestyle suburb 26km north-east of the city. This artists' colony was established by Justus Jorgensen in the 1930s when the suburb was all hills and bush. Montsalvat features and sells the works of a variety of artists and craftspeople, and there's an eclectic collection of rustic stone and mud-brick buildings to explore. As well as hosting the Montsalvat Jazz Festival each January and the National Poetry Festival each December, Montsalvat is open to visitors from 9 am to 5 pm daily. Admission is $5/2.50 for adults/children, and it's about a 2km walk from Eltham train station.

The **Australian Centre for Contemporary Art** (Map 7; ☎ 9654 6422), on Dallas Brooks Drive across the road from the main entrance to the Royal Botanic Gardens, is well worth a visit, with regular exhibitions of cutting-edge contemporary art. Commonly known as ACCA, it also hosts lectures, screenings and other events, and welcomes visitors. It's open from 11 am to 5 pm Tuesday to Friday, 2 to 5 pm weekends; entry is free.

The top (east) end of Flinders Lane (Map 2) in the city is something of an enclave for art lovers, and there are plenty of interesting galleries here. The work of Aboriginal artists can be seen at **Gallery Gabrielle Pizzi** (☎ 9654 2944), at No 141, and the **Aboriginal Art Galleries of Australia** (☎ 9654 2516), at No 31. The **Alcaston Gallery**, at 2 Collins St, is another excellent gallery at which to see contemporary Aboriginal work.

Also in Flinders Lane are the **Robert Lindsay Gallery** (☎ 9654 2133) and **Span** (☎ 9650 0589), both at No 45; the **Chapungu Gallery** (☎ 9654 0299), at No 67, which specialises in sculpture; the **Flinders Lane Gallery** (☎ 9654 3332), at No 137–39; **Anna Schwartz Gallery** (☎ 9654 6131), at No 185; and **Tolarno** (☎ 9654 6000), at No 289.

Fitzroy has some good galleries, including the **Sutton Gallery** (Map 3; ☎ 9416 0727), at 254 Brunswick St; **Dianne Tanzer** (Map 2; ☎ 9416 3956) 108–10 Gertrude St; and **Roar Studios** (Map 2; ☎ 9419 9975), at 115 Brunswick St.

In Richmond (Map 5) there is the **William Mora Gallery**, at 60 Tanner St; **Niagara** (☎ 9429 3666), at 245 Punt Rd; and **Christine Abrahams Gallery** (☎ 9428 6099), at 27 Gipps St.

OTHER MUSEUMS

The Scienceworks museum and the Melbourne Planetarium are both under the same roof at 2 Booker St in Spotswood, in the shadow of the West Gate Bridge. **Scienceworks** (Map 1; ☎ 9392 4819) was built on the site of the Spotswood pumping station, Melbourne's first sewerage works, and incorporates the historic old buildings. The museum has a huge and fascinating array of interactive displays: you can spend hours wandering around inspecting old machines, poking buttons and pulling levers, and learning all sorts of weird facts and figures. Scienceworks is open from 10 am to 4.30 pm daily. It's very popular with school groups and can get pretty crowded; the quietest times are weekday afternoons during school terms and Saturday mornings – Sunday is hectic. Admission is $8/4 for adults/children. The museum is a 10-minute signposted walk from Spotswood train station down Hudsons Rd.

The **Melbourne Planetarium** (Map 1; ☎ 9392 4800) re-creates the night sky on a 15m domed ceiling using a computer and projection system. In the comfort of a reclining chair you can take a journey through the universe, where no man has gone before. Sessions commence hourly from 11 am to 3 pm. Tickets cost $13/7/19 for an adult/child/family (including entry to Scienceworks).

You'll find the **Jewish Holocaust Museum** (Map 9; ☎ 9528 1985) at 13 Selwyn St, Elsternwick, close to Elsternwick train station and Rippon Lea. It's a small but detailed museum with pictorial displays, documents and various items from the Nazi death camps of WWII. It tells a grim story, but one that must be told – the museum guides are survivors of the camps. School groups visit the museum daily, and it's open to the public from 10 am to 2 pm Monday to Thursday, 11 am to 3 pm Sunday. There is no entry fee (but donations are welcome).

Schwerkolt's Cottage is on Deep Creek Rd, about 500m from the corner of Maroondah Hwy and Deep Creek Rd in Mitcham (about 30km east of the city). Built in the 1860s and turned into a museum in the late 1960s, it has several period-style buildings containing plenty of artefacts from Melbourne's past. It's open on weekends and public holidays, and admission is $2/1.50 for adults/children. The cottage isn't far from Heatherdale train station.

Out at Moorabbin airport in Cheltenham, the **Moorabbin Air Museum** has a collection of old aircraft, including a number from WWII. It's open from 10 am to 5 pm daily.

The **Victoria Racing Museum** at Caulfield Racecourse has a collection of horse-racing memorabilia. It is open from 10 am to 4 pm Tuesday and Thursday, 11 am to 4.30 pm race days.

The **Living Museum of the West** is set in the wetlands and parkland of **Pipemakers Park** (Map 1) in Maribyrnong. This is a unique 'eco-museum', with display boards and photos documenting the heritage of the western suburbs. You can reach the museum by cruising up the Maribyrnong River (see the River Cruises section in the Getting Around chapter).

BEACHES

Melbourne has some fairly good beaches close to the city. Although there's no surf in the bay and the water can look a little murky, especially after high winds and rain, it's reasonably clean and fine for swimming.

Heading south from the city, Albert Park, Middle Park and St Kilda are the most popular city beaches. Farther around the bay are **Elwood**, **Brighton** and **Sandringham beaches**, which are all quite pleasant. Next is **Half Moon Bay,** which, for a city beach, is very good indeed, as is nearby **Black**

Rock. Farther around the bay there are some excellent beaches, particularly around **Mt Eliza** and **Mt Martha**.

On the west side of the city, **Williamstown** has a lovely beach that is worth visiting for a summer dip.

If you want to go surfing or see spectacular and remote ocean beaches, the Mornington and Bellarine Peninsulas, both a little over an hour's drive from the city, are the places to head for – see the Excursions chapter for more details.

ACTIVITIES
Billiards, Pool & Snooker

There are lots of dim, smoky pool venues around the city and inner suburbs, many with full-sized tables. Popular places include King's Pool, at 256 King St; the Cue, at 277 Brunswick St, Fitzroy; the Red Triangle, at 110a Argyle St, Fitzroy; the fabled Johnny's Green Room, at 194 Faraday St, Carlton; and Masters, at 150 Barkly St, St

---

Free Melbourne

Experiencing some of the things that Melbourne has to offer needn't cost you anything. Most of Melbourne's parks and gardens are free to visit, including the Royal Botanic Gardens, St Kilda Botanic Gardens and the System Garden at the University of Melbourne.

You can take a tour of the Parliament House of Victoria, or if you're interested in seeing how the legal system operates you can sit in on a court case. The law courts are on William St, between Lonsdale and Little Bourke Sts. A free tour of the Melbourne Town Hall can be arranged by phoning ☎ 9658 9658.

There are lots of free art galleries in the city, including the National Gallery of Victoria on Russell (though you'll have to pay to view the special exhibitions), and the Australian Centre for Contemporary Art (ACCA). In the State Library of Victoria, the municipal libraries or the universities you can book-browse and read. Or you could try taking a tour of Melbourne's major cathedrals, such as St Patrick's or St Paul's.

If you want to do something energetic, you can crew a racing yacht on the weekend (see the Sailing section later in this chapter); or if you want to sample an Australian rules footy game, the gates are opened at three-quarter time (around 4 pm) and you can see the last quarter for free.

Entry to the Shrine of Remembrance is free and its balcony offers excellent views of the city. A wander through the Melbourne General Cemetery in Carlton provides some interesting genealogical insights into Melbourne families. Visit any of Melbourne's markets to see what's on offer and to simply soak up the atmosphere.

The free City Circle tram, with its recorded commentary of sights along the way, is a great way to see the city and get your bearings. The tram is painted a dark wine colour and travels along Flinders St, turns onto Spring St, down Lonsdale to Spencer and back to Flinders St. You can jump on and off at any stop.

Kilda. The Victorian Billiards and Snooker Club (☎ 9388 1947) is at 203 Sydney Rd in Brunswick.

As well as designated pool halls, you'll find that many pubs will often have at least one table usually – half-sized.

In-Line Skating

In-line skating (also known as rollerblading, although Rollerblade is a brand name) is booming in Melbourne. The best tracks are those around Port Phillip Bay, particularly from Port Melbourne south through St Kilda to Brighton. You can hire gear from places like Rock 'n' Roll 'n' Skate Hire (☎ 9525 3434), at 11 Fitzroy St in St Kilda; Apache Junction Skate Hire (☎ 9534 4006), at 16 Marine Parade, St Kilda; and Albert Park In-Line Skates (☎ 9645 9099), at 179 Victoria Ave in Albert Park. Blades and accessories will cost around $8 for an hour (less for subsequent hours) or $25 for 24 hours.

Beachfront skating under the summer sun.

Cycling

Parks Victoria and Bicycle Victoria have an excellent series of free maps covering bike rides around Melbourne. The series includes the Main Yarra Trail (38km), off which runs the Merri Creek Trail (19km); the Outer Circle Trail; the Maribyrnong River Trail (22km) and the western beaches. You can pick up the maps at the Victoria Visitor Information Centre in the Melbourne Town Hall. At least 20 other long, urban cycle paths exist and all are marked in *Discovering Melbourne's Bike Paths* and the *Melway*; the city also has a growing network of on-road bike lanes. For more information on cycling contact Bicycle Victoria (☎ 9328 3000), and see the Bicycle section in the Getting Around chapter for details on bike hire.

Golf

Melbourne's sandbelt courses, such as Royal Melbourne, Victoria, Huntingdale and Kingston Heath, are world famous. It's tough to get a round at these members' courses, but there are also plenty of public courses on which anyone can play. You will need to book if you're going to play on a weekend. Green fees cost around $12 to $20 for 18 holes, and most courses have clubs and buggies for hire. Some good public courses close to town include Royal Park (Map 4; ☎ 9387 3585) in Parkville near the zoo, Yarra Bend (Map 5; ☎ 9481 3729) in Fairfield, Albert Park (Map 7; ☎ 9510 5588) next to Albert Park Lake. Yarra Bend is the best of these.

Running

Melbourne has some great routes for runners. One of the favourites is the Tan track around the Royal Botanic Gardens. The bicycle tracks beside the Yarra and around the bay also offer good running, but watch out for cyclists. Albert Park Lake is another favourite, especially on Saturday when the sailboats are racing.

Melbourne's premier annual running event, the Melbourne Marathon, is held each October. Other major runs include the 5km and 10km women-only Sussan Classic each March/April, and the 8km Run to the MCG in April/May. For details of fun runs, check the events calendar in the *Australian Runner* magazine or ring the publisher on ☎ 9819 9225.

Tennis & Squash

Tennis-court hire generally costs between $10 and $20 an hour. Weekend rates are often higher, and for floodlit or indoor courts you may well have to pay between $20 and $25 an hour.

Except in January during the Australian Open, the public can hire one of the 23 outdoor and five indoor courts of the Melbourne Park National Tennis Centre (Map 3; ☎ 9286 1244) on Batman Ave. Other tennis centres near town include the Albert Reserve Tennis Centre (Map 7; ☎ 9510 3311), on the corner of St Kilda Rd and Hanna St in South Melbourne; the South Yarra Tennis Centre (Map 7; ☎ 9820 0611), in Fawkner Park on Toorak Rd; and the East Melbourne Tennis Centre (Map 3; ☎ 9417 6511), in Powlett Reserve, on the corner of Simpson and Albert Sts.

Squash courts cost around $12 to $18 an hour. There are courts in the city at the Melbourne City Baths (Map 2; ☎ 9663 5888). For courts in other areas, check the *Yellow Pages* phone book.

Ice Skating

Every year from April until October, the Sidney Myer Music Bowl (Map 2) in Kings Domain, next to the Royal Botanic Gardens, operates as an ice-skating rink. Skating costs around $8 an hour. Call ☎ 9281 8360 for details.

Canoeing

The Yarra River offers canoeists a variety of water from tranquil, flat stretches to rapids of about grade three (classified 'difficult' and requiring some paddling technique). The best sections of river are in the upper reaches from Warburton to the lower reaches of Fitzsimons Lane, Templestowe. The lower reaches are still scenic, offering respite from the city, but they consist mostly of flat water.

Popular sections for those in kayaks and Canadians (open canoes) are Homestead to Wittons Reserve, Pound Bend including the tunnel (medium-water level and experienced paddlers only) and Fitzsimons Lane to Finns Reserve in Templestowe. In the lower reaches there's a canoe recreation area around Dights Falls.

Adventure Tag Along Tours (☎ 9761 8445) offer a range of safe and environmentally friendly tours, including canoeing and kayaking.

For more a more sedate form of canoeing, from either the Studley Park or Fairfield Park Boathouse, see the earlier section on Yarra Bend Park.

Fishing & Boating

You can fish in the Yarra and Maribyrnong Rivers, but you're better off heading down to the bay and hooking a few snapper from a pier – try the Port Melbourne, Albert Park or St Kilda pier. Tackle shops, such as the Complete Angler, at 19 McKillop St in the city, are good places to seek advice on all things fishy.

Boats can be hired for fishing on the bay, but the conditions can be deceptively treacherous. Don't go out unless you're sure of the weather. Try Williamstown Boat Hire (☎ 9397 7312), at Parson's Marina in Williamstown – the same people operate Southgate Boat Hire, with motor boats for cruising along the Yarra River. Another good boatshed is the long-established Keefers Boat Hire (☎ 9589 3917) in Beaumaris, about 30 minutes drive south-east from the city.

Navigating Port Phillip Bay under sail.

A Bigger Splash

A hot day in the middle of summer or a cold day in the middle of winter – either way, the luxury of taking a dip in an indoor or outdoor pool is yours. Like the beach, swimming pools have a culture all of their own and no two pools are alike. Here's a list of some of the best and what they have to offer.

Melbourne City Baths (Map 2; ☎ 9663 5888), on the corner of Swanston and Victoria Sts, has a 25m indoor pool plus a gym, spas, saunas and squash courts. The facilities are open from 6 am to 10 pm weekdays, 8 am to 6 pm weekends. A swim, spa and sauna costs $6.50.

Melbourne Sports & Aquatic Centre (Map 7; ☎ 9926 1555) is the new sports complex in the parklands of Albert Park Lake. It's a great place for a swim, with a 75m-long lap pool and several other pools, including a wave pool and an indoor water-slide. It's open from 6 am to 10 pm weekdays, 7 am to 8 pm weekends. Entry costs $4/3 for adults/children.

Prahran Aquatic Centre (Map 6; ☎ 9522 3248), 41 Essex Street, is a 50m heated pool surrounded by gardens and with piped music above water and below. It's one of the city's finest outdoor pools, and there is also a good cafe on the premises. The centre is open seasonally, from October to May, and admission is $3/2/1.30 for adults/students/children.

North Melbourne Pool (Map 3; ☎ 9329 2885), 1 Macaulay Rd, has a 25m swimming pool, a learner pool and a baby and toddler pool – all outdoors and all heated. The big attraction during the summer months is an evening lazing in the pool watching a movie projected onto a giant screen. It's open daily from the end of October to the end of April, and admission is $2.70/2 for adults/children.

Harold Holt Memorial Swimming Centre (Map 1; ☎ 9824 8800), 9 High St, Glen Iris, has both a newly renovated indoor pool and a 50m heated outdoor pool open daily, year round. There is also a high-diving platform and a shaded grassy area. Admission is $3/1.90 for adults/children.

Fitzroy Swimming Pool (Map 4; ☎ 9417 6493), Alexandra Parade, was saved from demolition a few years back, given an overhaul and has never looked back since. All types come here to escape the baking-hot Fitzroy streets. As well as the main pool, there is a learner and toddler pool. Yoga classes are also on offer most evenings. The pool is open daily, year round, and admission is $3.10/1 for adults/children.

Sailing

With about 20 yacht clubs around the shores of Port Phillip Bay, yachting is one of Melbourne's most popular passions. Races and regattas are held most weekends, and the bay is a memorable sight when it's sprinkled with hundreds of colourful sails and spinnakers. Conditions can change radically and without warning, making sailing on the bay a challenging and sometimes dangerous pursuit.

Many yacht clubs welcome visitors to volunteer as crew on racing boats. Phone the race secretary at one of the major clubs if you're keen. The big four are:

Hobson's Bay Yacht Club (☎ 9397 6393), Williamstown
Royal Melbourne Yacht Squadron (☎ 9534 0227), St Kilda

Royal Brighton Yacht Club (☎ 9592 3092)
Sandringham Yacht Club (☎ 9598 7444)

For more leisurely sailing, boats can be hired from the Jolly Roger School of Sailing (☎ 9690 5862) at Albert Park Lake.

If you'd rather be a spectator, head to the Royal Melbourne at St Kilda on the weekends. You can watch the boats preparing to race and see them start and finish from out on the breakwater. Williamstown is also a good spot for spectators.

Melbourne's two main ocean races are the Melbourne to Devonport and Melbourne to Hobart races, held annually between Christmas and New Year. The Melbourne to Hobart goes around Tasmania's wild west coast, unlike the more famous Sydney to Hobart which runs down the east coast.

THINGS TO SEE & DO

Surfing

The closest surf beaches to Melbourne are on the Mornington and the Bellarine Peninsulas (Map 10), both about an hour's drive from the city. **Bells Beach**, on the Great Ocean Road near Torquay, is recognised as a world-class surfing beach. See the Excursions chapter.

Windsurfing/Sailboarding

Close to the city, both Elwood and Middle Park beaches are designated sailboarding areas. Repeat Performance Sailboards (☎ 9525 6475), at 87 Ormond Rd in Elwood, hires out good boards starting at around $45 a day or $75 for a weekend.

COURSES

The Council of Adult Education (Map 2; ☎ 9652 0611), or CAE, is at 256 Flinders St in the city. It runs a wide variety of courses suited to travellers. Courses cover everything from languages, literature, the visual arts and music to computer studies, cooking, history and philosophy. Prices vary according to the number of sessions per course, which can run from one day up to eight weeks. The courses guide can be obtained by calling CAE or visiting the centre.

The Foreign Language Bookshop (☎ 9654 2883), at 259 Collins St in the city, has a great range of language books and courses. Its noticeboard advertises courses and tutors.

Places to Stay

Melbourne offers a wide range of accommodation options, ranging from backpacker hostels, pubs and motels to B&Bs and guesthouses, serviced apartments and deluxe hotels. Once you've decided what you're looking for, the tricky part is deciding which area to stay in. The city centre is convenient and close to theatres, museums, sporting venues and the train and bus terminals. The alternative is to stay in one of the inner suburbs that are mostly only a short tram ride from the action, can be a little quieter, and have much to offer in their own right.

Accommodation can be booked directly, or you can make reservations through Tourism Victoria (☎ 13 2842), in the Melbourne Town Hall on the corner of Swanston and Little Collins Sts. The more expensive hotels can be booked through travel agents, who might get a better rate than you can by booking directly. Many places are also bookable via email and Web sites.

Note that during major festivals and events accommodation in Melbourne is often very scarce, and you need to make reservations well in advance. This is especially the case during the Formula One Grand Prix, at which time you can also expect prices to rise substantially, even at the backpacker hostels.

CAMPING & CARAVAN PARKS

Melbourne has a few caravan and camping parks in the metropolitan area, although none are very close to the centre and most are in unattractive areas. An exception is the *Hobsons Bay Caravan Park* (Map 8; ☎ 9397 2395, 158 Kororoit Creek Rd, Williamstown). It's still a long way from the city centre (about 15km), but Williamstown is a pleasant little bayside suburb with a distinct personality (see the Things to See & Do chapter). Sites cost $15 and cabins are $45/50 a single/double. The caravan park is about 2km west of Williamstown's shopping centre and 2.5km west of the bayfront.

The closest place to the city is *Melbourne Holiday Park* (Map 4; ☎ 9354 3533, 265 Elizabeth St, Coburg East), 10km north of the city. Camping costs $18 for two, cabins from $51 to $55 with en suite.

HOSTELS

There are backpacker hostels in the city centre and most of the inner suburbs, the city and St Kilda being the most popular areas. Competition between hostels is fierce in winter but it can be difficult to find a bed in the better places over summer. Several of the larger hostels have courtesy buses that do pick-ups from the bus and train terminals.

The prices listed are only an indication, except at the YHA hostels where prices are fixed. You can expect to pay a little less in winter and a little more in summer.

City Centre (Map 2)

The city has some good hostels, which have the advantage of being central and close to the train station and bus depots. *Stork Hotel* (☎ 9663 6237), close to the Franklin St bus terminal and Queen Victoria Market, is a friendly old pub downstairs with budget accommodation upstairs. The rooms are small, simple and brightly coloured with polished floors, and facilities include a laundry and adjoining cafe-restaurant with a good range of inexpensive meals. The owners organise various live music and theme nights. Single and double rooms cost $39 and $49, and triples are $19 per person.

Farther down Elizabeth St, at No 441, *Toad Hall* (☎ 9600 9010, ❸ toadhall .hotel@bigpond.com) is quiet, stylish and well equipped, with a pleasant courtyard and off-street parking. A bed in a four- or six-bed dorm is $25, single rooms are $50 and double and twin rooms are $60. We have had a few reports about unfriendly and unco-operative staff, but we're prepared to put that down to a bad hair day!

Close to the Franklin St bus terminal, the very large *Hotel Bakpak* (☎ 9329 7525, *melbourne@hotelbakpak.com, 167 Franklin St)* offers just about everything a backpacker could ask for – from the basement bar and small cinema to a rooftop entertainment area with great city views. There's also a resource centre, which assists in finding short- or long-term work. Free airport pickup is also available. Dorms range from $16 to $20, doubles are $50.

The *Exford Hostel (☎ 9663 2697, 199 Russell St)* is a cheerful and well set-up hostel in the top section of an old pub. Costs range from $13 in a 10-bed dorm to $17 in a four-bed dorm; twins and doubles are $42.

The *City Centre Private Hotel (☎ 9654 5401, 22 Little Collins St)* is clean and reasonably quiet. All rooms have shared bathroom and there's a TV lounge and kitchen on each floor. Backpackers pay $17 in a three- or four-bed room and doubles are $35; serviced singles/doubles are $35/50.

Flinders Station Hotel (☎ 9620 5100, fax 9620 5101, 35 Elizabeth St) is, as the name suggests, only a stone's throw from Flinders St Railway Station. It's a well-run backpacker hostel with basic but clean four- to eight-bed dorms for $16, twins and doubles $55, or $80 with en suite. The big plus is the 24-hour Coles Express supermarket just across the road.

North Melbourne (Maps 2, 3, & 4)

Melbourne's two YHA hostels are in North Melbourne, north-west of the city centre, and they both offer discounts for a four-day stay or longer. From the airport you can ask the Skybus driver to drop you at the North Melbourne hostels. Bookings can be made on the YHA Web site (www.yha.com.au).

The YHA showpiece is *Queensberry Hill Hostel (☎ 9329 8599, @ queensberryhill@ yhavic.org.au, 78 Howard St)*. This huge, 348-bed hostel has excellent facilities, including modern bathrooms, a state-of-the-art kitchen, a rooftop patio with barbecues and 360° views of the city, and a security car park. Four-, six- or eight-bed dorms cost $17 to $18; singles/doubles and twins with shared facilities are $45/55, or with en suite $50/70. There are also family rooms, en suite

rooms and a self-contained apartment. A breakfast and dinner service is available, and office hours are 7.30 am to 10.30 pm, although there is 24-hour access once you have checked in. Catch tram No 55 from William St and get off at stop No 14, or take any tram north up Elizabeth St to stop No 13.

Chapman Gardens YHA Hostel (☎ 9328 3595, @ chapman@yhavic.org.au, 76 Chapman St) is smaller, older and a little more intimate than Queensberry Hill. A bed in a dorm here costs $17, twin share $18 per person and $44 for a double room ($2 more for nonmembers). From Elizabeth St in the city, take tram No 50 or 57 along Flemington Rd and get off at stop No 19, then walk down Abbotsford St. Chapman St is the first street on the left.

Both YHA hostels have good noticeboards if you're looking for people to travel with, for cheap airline tickets or for general information. There are a number of very good tours operating out of the hostels.

Opposite the Queen Victoria Market, *Global Backpackers (☎ 9328 3728, fax 9329 3728)*, at 238 Victoria St, is friendly, clean and offers plenty of information on budget tours and things to see and do around Melbourne. Single rooms are $28/150 a day/week, double and twin are $40/200 and dorm rooms $16/80.

Fitzroy (Map 3)

The Nunnery (☎ 9419 8637, 116 Nicholson St) is well located on the fringe of the city. One of the best budget accommodation options in Melbourne, it's a converted Victorian building with comfortable lounges, good facilities and a friendly atmosphere. The rooms are small but clean and centrally heated. Costs range from $18 in a 12-bed dorm to $20 in a three-bed dorm; singles are $40, twins and doubles $40 to $60. Take tram No 96, heading east along Bourke St, and get off at stop No 13.

Richmond (Map 5)

Richmond Hill Hotel (☎ 9428 6501, @ richmondhill@ozemail.com.au, 353 Church St) is a large Victorian-era building with spacious living areas, clean rooms and a variety of accommodation options. Dorm beds cost about $18 a night, singles/twins are $37/47, and there's a B&B section with good single/double rooms at $64/74; doubles with en suites are $95.

St Kilda (Map 9)

St Kilda is one of Melbourne's most interesting and cosmopolitan suburbs. It's close to the bay and has a good range of budget accommodation, as well as plenty of restaurants and entertainment. From Swanston St in the city, tram No 16 will take you down St Kilda Rd to Fitzroy St, or you can take the faster lightrail service, No 96 from Spencer and Bourke Sts, to the old St Kilda train station and along Fitzroy and Acland Sts.

More like a boutique hotel than a hostel, the facilities at the *Olembia Guesthouse* (☎ 9537 1412, ✉ stay@olembia.com.au, 96 Barkly St) are very good and include a cosy guest lounge, a dining room, courtyard and off-street parking. The rooms are quite small but they are clean and comfortable, and all have hand basins and central heating. Dorm beds cost $18, singles $40 and twins and doubles $54. You should book ahead.

The *St Kilda Coffee Palace* (☎ 9534 5283, fax 9593 9166, ✉ backpaca@ ozemail.com.au, 24 Grey St) is large and spacious, with its own cafe and a modern kitchen. There is also an on-site travel agency, work centre and Internet access. Dorms range from $12 to $15, singles are $25 and doubles are $32.

Middle Park & South Melbourne (Map 7)

Well located between Albert Park Lake and St Kilda, the *Middle Park Hotel* (☎ 9690 1882, fax 9645 8928) is a popular pub in a bayside shopping centre on the corner of Canterbury Rd and Armstrong St. The upstairs rooms are basic but clean and cost $17 in a four- or six-bed dorm, $25 in a twin share and $50 in a double (all with shared bathrooms, kitchen and lounge). Guests are served $5 meals in the downstairs bar.

Next to the South Melbourne market, within walking distance of Southgate and close to both lightrail and tram lines, *Nomad's Market Inn* (☎ 1800-241 445, ✉ mktinn@netspace.net.au, 115 Cecil St) is not really in the centre of things but it's still very well located. This pleasant hostel is a converted pub and charges around $17 in dorm rooms and $45 in a double; breakfast is included.

BUDGET HOTELS & GUESTHOUSES

Moving up a level from the backpacker hostels, there are some good budget options in and around the city centre, including small hotels, guesthouses, units and apartments.

City Centre (Map 2)

The hotels along Spencer St are convenient for the bus and train terminals, and only a walk or short tram ride to the heart of the city. Admittedly it's a rather depressing end of town, but it's on the up with the new Docklands redevelopment just behind Spencer St station in full swing.

The *Terrace Pacific Inn* (☎ 9621 3333, 16 Spencer St) is a modern budget hotel with smallish rooms with en suites starting at $124 a double. The tariff includes a light breakfast. The *Hotel Enterprise on the Yarra* (☎ 9629 6991, 44 Spencer St) is a reasonable hotel with budget singles/doubles starting at $79/109 with en suites. At No 66, the *Batman's Hill Hotel* (Map 2; ☎ 9614 6344) has doubles with en suite at $150.

The *Hotel Y* (☎ 9329 5188, ✉ melb@ ywca.org.au, 489 Elizabeth St), close to the Franklin St bus terminal, is an award-winning budget hotel run by the YWCA. It has simple four-bed bunkrooms costing $25, single/double/triple rooms at $70/80/90 and deluxe rooms at $90/100/110. The 'Y' has good facilities, including a budget cafe and communal kitchen and laundry. At the time of writing it was in the process of adding a gym and pool.

The *Victoria Hotel* (☎ 9653 0441, fax 9650 9678, 215 Little Collins St) is a Melbourne institution. It's brilliantly located, surrounded by elite designer retail outlets and some great restaurants and bars. Budget rooms with shared facilities cost $45/60 for a single/double, standard rooms with en suite and TV are $85/124, and executive rooms are $140 for both singles and doubles.

The *Welcome Hotel* (☎ 9639 0555, fax 9639 1179, ✉ welcome@allseasons.com.au, 265–81 Little Bourke St) is right in the heart of Melbourne's shopping district. This well-run tourist hotel has modern rooms with kitchenettes from $125.

South Yarra (Maps 6 & 7)

Tram No 8 from Swanston St in the city takes you along Toorak Rd to the chic suburb of South Yarra.

If it's character you're after, the *West End Private Hotel* (☎ 9866 5375, 76 Toorak Rd W) is a charming but slightly worn old mansion offering B&B with clean singles/ doubles at $45/60 (weekly rates available).

Farther east is the huge *Claremont Accommodation* (☎ 9826 8000, 189 Toorak Rd), an airy guesthouse offering rooms with shared bathroom starting at $46/58, including breakfast. The rooms are bright, with polished-timber floors, heating and modern communal facilities.

Albert Park & St Kilda (Maps 7 & 9)

St Kilda's signature collection of old boarding houses and private hotels has largely gone up market, creating a shortage of budget places other than backpacker hostels.

The *Hotel Victoria* (☎ 9690 3666, 123 Beaconsfield Pde) has a great position overlooking the bay. The impressively restored and elegant hotel dates back to 1888, and has a front bar, a bistro and a rather grand formal dining room. Double rooms start at around $90, suites with views of the bay at $150.

Opposite St Kilda beach, *Warwick Beachside* (☎ 9525 4800, ✉ julia@warwickbeachside.com.au, 363 Beaconsfield Pde) is a large complex of 1950s-style holiday flats. They're not glamorous, but they're quite well equipped, with a laundry and off-street parking. Prices range from $55 to $70 for single rooms, $55 to $85 for

doubles, and $55 to $85 for a studio (for up to three people).

MOTELS
City Centre (Map 2)

There are several motels in or near the city. *City Square Motel* (☎ 9654 7011, fax 9650 7107, 67 Swanston St) has fairly basic rooms, but is right in the centre of town, with singles/doubles starting at $85/95.

At the top end of town, a good choice is *City Limits Motel* (☎ 9662 2544, 20–22 Little Bourke St) in the heart of the theatre district and close to Chinatown. Apartment-style accommodation with kitchenettes starts at $110, plus $10/20 for each extra child/adult (the price includes a light breakfast).

Astoria Motel (☎ 9670 6801, 288 Spencer St) is close to the train station and has its own restaurant. Renovated rooms with en suites cost $84/86 for singles/ doubles. Nearby, the *Flagstaff City Motor Inn* (☎ 9329 5788, 45 Dudley St) charges $90/100 for rooms with en suites.

East Melbourne (Map 3)

George Powlett Lodge (☎ 9419 9488, fax 9419 0806, ✉ bookings@georgepowlett .com.au), on the corner of George and Powlett Sts, has rooms with en suites starting at $93/100; each extra person is $15 and all rooms have cooking facilities. There is also undercover parking. *Treasury Motor Lodge* (☎ 9417 5281, ✉ treasury@ozemail .com, 179 Powlett St) has fairly simple rooms with en suites, some with cooking facilities and off-street parking, for $105 for singles and doubles (each extra person is $10, or $13 with cooking facilities).

North Melbourne (Map 3)

The *Marco Polo Inn* (☎ 9329 1788, 9329 9950, on the corner of Flemington Rd and Harker St, is a friendly and unpretentious motel offering plenty of facilities: restaurant and cocktail bar, swimming pool and sauna and in-house videos. Single/double rooms are $98/108 and family suites $178.

The *Arden Motel* (☎ 9329 7211, fax 9329 5574, 15 Arden St) is in a quiet setting and all rooms have TVs, fridges and microwaves.

Places to Stay – Bed & Breakfast 99

Singles, doubles and twins are $77 and family rooms start at $94, breakfast included.

Carlton & Parkville (Maps 2, 3 & 4)

The **Downtowner on Lygon** (☎ 9663 5555, 66 Lygon St) has motel-style units starting at $129 and an on-site restaurant. Farther up Lygon St, right in the heart of the action, is **Lygon Lodge Motel** (☎ 9663 6633, 220 Lygon St) with twin, double and triple rooms all costing $99.

There is a string of motels along Royal Parade. Trams trundle up this tree-lined avenue past the University of Melbourne and Princes and Royal Parks.

Elizabeth Tower Motel (☎ 9347 9211) is on the corner of Royal Parade and Grattan St, opposite the university. This multilevel motel has its own restaurant and bar, and rooms start at $125. Farther north, the budget **Ramada Inn** (☎ 9380 8131, 539 Royal Pde) has singles/doubles for $94/99. **Princes Park Motor Inn** (☎ 9388 1000), on the corner of Royal Parade and Park St, has clean and pleasant rooms for $103/108.

South Yarra (Maps 6 & 7)

The well-situated **Hotel Saville** (☎ 9867 2755, fax 9820 9726, ✉ info@saville .com.au, 5 Commercial Rd) is a seven-storey octagonal building with smallish motel-style rooms ranging from $108 to $115 a double, plus its own bar and restaurant.

The **St James Motel** (☎ 9866 4455, fax 9820 4059, 35 Darling St) is an older motel with decent-sized but slightly worn double rooms at $75.

The **Albany Motel** (☎ 9866 4485, fax 9820 9419, ✉ albany@connexus.net.au), on the corner of Toorak Rd and Millswyn St, is opposite Fawkner Park and close to the Royal Botanic Gardens. Motel-style rooms cost $80/85 for a single/double and spacious period-style rooms cost up to $110/120.

St Kilda & South Melbourne (Maps 7 & 9)

St Kilda has plenty of motels, but some of them are fairly dodgy. The more respectable places include the **Cosmopolitan Motor Inn** (☎ 9534 0781, fax 9534 8262, 6 Carlisle St), which has a cafe-bar, rooms with kitchenettes, executive suites and serviced apartments. Prices range from $109 to $145 for both singles and doubles; apartments cost around $145, with rates changing according to the length of stay. The **Cabana Court Motel** (☎ 9534 0771, fax 9525 3484, 46 Park St) is only a hop, step and a jump to the beach, and has self-contained units from $85 to $95.

Another reasonably good option is the **Crest International Hotel/Motel** (☎ 9537 1788, fax 9534 0609, 47 Barkly St), a larger motel that incorporates a conference centre, restaurant and bar. All rooms range from $85 to $99.

Charnwood Motor Inn (☎ 9525 4199, 3 Charnwood Rd), on the east side of St Kilda Rd, is a good motel in a quiet suburban street within walking distance of Fitzroy St. Single/double rooms start at $65/70. **City Park Motel** (☎ 9686 0000, 308 Kings Way) is a 1970s-style motel on an extremely busy road, with singles/doubles starting at $110.

BED & BREAKFAST
East Melbourne (Map 5)

East Melbourne has a residential feel to it with its tree-lined streets and grand old Victorian terrace houses. The city is a pleasant walk away through the Fitzroy and Treasury Gardens. The **Georgian Court Guesthouse** (☎ 9419 6353, 21 George St) is an elegant and cosy B&B with doubles at $75, $95 with an en suite; prices include a buffet breakfast.

Albert Park & St Kilda (Maps 7 & 9)

The **Avoca** (☎ 9696 9090, fax 9696 9092, 98 Victoria Ave) is a lovely old double-storey terrace home set in a leafy avenue running down to the bay. The period-style rooms all have TVs, fridges and either en suites or private bathrooms. Singles cost $110 to $120, doubles $130 to $140.

Opposite the beach, **Robinsons by the Sea** (☎ 9534 2683, ✉ wendyr@alphalink .com.au, 335 Beaconsfield Pde) is an elegant and impressive Victorian-era terrace house. It has five comfortable double en suite rooms ranging from $130 to $170.

Victoria House B&B (☎ *9525 4512, fax 9525 3024, 57 Mary St*) is a very comfortable and well set-up Victorian home with three double rooms, one of which has its own kitchen. Friendly, with pleasant gardens and an attractive courtyard, it's good value with singles and doubles ranging from $100 to $110.

Caulfield (Map 9)

If you're a horse-racing aficionado, you might be interested in *Lord Lodge B&B* (☎ *9572 3969, 30 Booran Rd*). It's adjacent to the Caulfield Racecourse, about 15km south-east of the city centre, and attached to Colin Little's famous racing stables. An impressive historic home, it has three guest rooms, each named after a famous race-horse from the stables. Double rooms range from $115 to $150.

Williamstown (Map 8)

Williamstown is mainly thought of as a day-trip destination, but if you want to stay overnight in this historical and pleasant bayside suburb there are a few good B&Bs. *Hickenbotham House* (☎ *9397 2949, 2 Ferguson St*) is an 1862 two-storey home close to shops and restaurants; single/double rooms cost $80/100. Australian short-story writer Hal Porter wrote 'The Paper Chase' here while he was teaching in Williamstown.

Heathville House (☎ *9397 5959, 171 Aitken St*) is close to the waterfront and offers period-style accommodation in a comfortable late 19th-century house. Rooms are $80/115.

BOUTIQUE HOTELS
City Centre (Map 2)

Located in the heart of the city, *Hotel Causeway* (☎ *9660 8888, fax 9660 8877, @ reservations@causeway.com.au, 275 Little Collins St*) is close to restaurants, cafes, fashion boutiques and entertainment venues. Suitable for business and leisure travellers, the Causeway boasts excellent facilities including stylish and well-appointed rooms, nonsmoking floors, a gymnasium, a business

centre and a roof terrace. Rooms range from $190 to $280.

East Melbourne & Fitzroy (Map 3)

Magnolia Court Boutique Hotel (☎ *9419 4222, fax 9416 0841, @ info@magnolia-court.com.au, 101 Powlett St*) is a bright and friendly small hotel with two wings. The older section, formerly a ladies' finishing college, dates to 1862, and while the rooms in the new wing are of a good standard, they don't quite have the same charm. Standard singles/doubles are $113/117, superior rooms are $145 for both singles and doubles and two-room suites with cooking facilities are $165. The best option is the cute but tiny two-room Victorian cottage with its own kitchen at $165. The hotel has a breakfast room and garden courtyard.

King Boutique Accommodation (☎ *9417 1113, @ kingaccomm@bigpond.com, 122 Nicholson St*), directly across the street from the Carlton Gardens, is an impressive mansion that has been cleverly transformed into a hotel. The two bedrooms on the first floor have their own marble bathrooms, while the attic room has an en suite. Rooms start at $130.

South Yarra & Toorak (Maps 6 & 7)

The lovely *Tilba* (☎ *9867 8844, fax 9867 6567*), on the corner of Toorak Rd and Domain St, is a small, elegant hotel that has been lovingly restored in gracious Victorian style. Stepping inside is like taking a trip back in time – the 15 suites all feature old iron bedheads, leadlights and decorative plasterwork. Tariffs range from $140 to $195 a double, depending on the size of the room. We highly recommend this place.

Toorak Manor (☎ *1800-062 689, fax 9824 2830, 220 Williams Rd*) is another excellent boutique hotel. Set in lovely gardens, the gracious historic mansion has been impressively converted, with 12 comfortable period-style rooms with en suites, cosy lounges and reading rooms. Tariffs range from $145 to $185 a night. Toorak Manor is a short walk from Hawksburn train station.

St Kilda (Map 9)

Situated in the heart of busy Fitzroy St, *Hotel Tolarno* (☎ 9537 0200, fax 9534 7800, @ mail@htltolarno.com.au) is emblematic of late 1990s Melbourne style – 1950s and 1960s retro furnishings blend perfectly with modern appliances and design. The en suite rooms and family suites are all individually styled and range in price from $100 to $235.

Accommodation at *The Prince* (☎ 9536 1111, fax 9536 1100, @ thedesk@theprince .com.au) is part of the stylish refurbishment of the old Prince of Wales hotel, which includes the Mink Bar, Circa restaurant and Il Fornaio Cafe. The design is simple and sparse, and incorporates natural timbers and quality furnishings and fittings. Rooms and suites range from $250 to $450.

APARTMENT-HOTELS & SERVICED APARTMENTS

Melbourne has an ever-expanding range of apartment-style hotels and serviced apartments. Whether you're a high-flying executive in need of conference accommodation or a family looking for a bit more space there are plenty of good options in the city and inner suburbs. More spacious than regular hotels, with their own kitchen and laundry facilities, this style of accommodation can be better value and more comfortable than an equivalently priced hotel, especially for people travelling in a group.

City Centre (Map 2)

Mansion on Bourke (☎ 9631 0400, fax 9631 0500, @ mansions@bigpond.com, 151–63 Bourke St) offers state-of-the-art serviced-apartment living. The studios, one and two-bedroom apartments and deluxe apartments are stylish, with a nod to contemporary living. Each has separate kitchen and living areas, business facilities, including voice mail, fax and modem, and all bathrooms have a spa. There are also meeting-room facilities and a gymnasium, and there is an Italian-style restaurant on the ground floor. Prices range from $160 for a studio and $230 for one- and two-bedroom apartments to $250 for a two-bedroom deluxe suite.

The *Manhattan Serviced Apartments* (☎ 1800-681 900, fax 9820 1000, 57 Flinders Lane) is one of a group of four serviced-apartment complexes run by the same company. Each has a slightly different theme, and as you've probably guessed by the name, the Manhattan is open plan with high ceilings and plenty of designer chic. The gymnasium, spa, and business and conference facilities are well suited to the corporate clientele. One-bedroom apartments are $190, two-bedrooms are $230 and three-bedrooms are $290.

Another very good self-contained option in the city is *Oakford Gordon Place* (☎ 1800-818 236, fax 9639 1537, @ res.ogt@oakford.com, 24 Little Bourke St). In a historic setting and built around a garden courtyard where an enormous palm tree is close to bursting through the glass roof, the 59 stylish apartments are very popular and cater well to both corporate and leisure travellers. Singles and doubles in studios cost $145, one-bedroom apartments are $160, two-bedroom apartments are $210 and split-level suites are $300.

Punt Hill Serviced Apartments (☎ 1800-331 529, fax 9650 4409, @ info@ punthill-apartments.com.au, 267 Flinders Lane) is another company with a few locations in the inner city. The apartments are a little more conservative than the more design-conscious options. Facilities include fully equipped kitchens and separate living areas, en suite bathrooms and a guest laundry service. Prices range from $180 to $200 for one- and two-bedroom apartments, and extra beds can be added for $10.

Fairfax House Guest Lodgings (☎ 9642 1333, fax 9642 4607, 392 Little Collins St) is run by the Quest Lodging group. The one-, two- and three-bedroom apartments have good facilities, including kitchens, laundries and colour TVs, and are serviced daily. Although very centrally located, this five-storey Victorian-era building is on the quiet side of Little Collins St. Prices start at $170 per night for a one-bedroom apartment.

The *Pacific International Apartments* (☎ 9664 2000, fax 9663 1977, @ paclitt3@ pacificint.com.au, 318 Little Bourke St) occupies a lovely old heritage building right in the heart of the city. The four-star serviced apartments are comfortable and well equipped for both business and leisure travellers. Prices range from $135 to $180 for a double.

East Melbourne (Maps 3 & 6)

East Melbourne's serviced apartments are more modest and economical than those in the city centre. *East Melbourne Apartment Hotel* (☎ 9412 2555, fax 9412 2567, @ emah@blaze.net.au, 25 Hotham St) is a stylish block of 1940s flats converted into 38 studio apartments, with good facilities and kitchenettes. Prices range from $125 to $150 for singles, doubles and twin share.

Eastern Townhouses (☎ 9418 6666, fax 9415 1502, @ townhouse@brd.com.au, 90 Albert St) is a refurbished complex of studio units with very good facilities for $105 singles and doubles. The nearby *Albert Heights Serviced Apartments* (☎ 1800-800 117, fax 9419 9517, @ enq@ albertheights.com.au, 83 Albert St) is a comfortable motel-style block with a central garden area and small outdoor pool. Apartments cost around $125 for a double or twin, plus $15 per extra person.

North Melbourne (Map 3)

The *City Gardens Apartments* (☎ 9320 6600, 335 Abbotsford St) has 128 comfortable self-contained units on a busy street but in a pleasant courtyard setting. The one-, two- and three-bedroom units range from $130 to $225 a night.

Fitzroy (Map 2)

Fitzroy is fairly light on in terms of accommodation, but a good option is the *Royal Gardens Apartments* (☎ 9419 9888, fax 9416 0451, @ book@royalgardens.com.au, Royal Lane), well located in a quiet street only a block from the Royal Exhibition Building and the new Melbourne Museum, and close to Brunswick St. The 76 spacious and stylish apartments are built around a landscaped courtyard with a swimming pool, and cost $165/210/270 for one-/two-/ three-bedroom apartments.

Metropole Hotel Apartments (☎ 9411 8100, fax 9411 8200, @ Metropole@ bigpond.com.au, 44 Brunswick St) is a new development catering to both business and leisure travellers. The self-catered apartments and hotel-style studios each have a TV, microwave and dishwasher, as well as facilities for business guests. Prices range from $140 for a studio room to $170 to $215 for apartments. Executive apartments range from $205 to $340.

South Yarra (Maps 6 & 7)

South Yarra is the serviced-apartment capital of Melbourne. Most are blocks of flats from the 1950s and 1960s that have been refurbished, some better than others. Note that quite a few companies manage multiple blocks of apartments.

One of the best options here is the reasonably tasteful *South Yarra Hill Suites* (☎ 9868 8222, fax 9820 1742, @ syhs@ bigpond.com.au, 14 Murphy St), a five-star apartment-style hotel in a quiet, leafy street close to Toorak Rd. The hotel has 24-hour reception, a heated pool, spa and sauna. Well-equipped one-bedroom apartments start at $180 and two-bedroom apartments at $245.

A couple of more affordable options with good facilities are the motel-style *Darling Towers* (☎ 9867 5200, fax 9866 8215, @ requests@darlingtowers.com.au, 32 Darling St), which has good one-bedroom flats from $70, and the *Manor House Apartments* (☎ 9867 1266, fax 9867 4613, @ info@ manorhouse.com, 23 Avoca St), with well-equipped studios starting at $85.

St Kilda (Map 9)

Barkly Quest Lodgings (☎ 9525 5000, fax 9525 3618, 180 Barkly St) has 26 one-bedroom apartments costing $105 per night for two people or $135 for four (two on a fold-up couch). They're on a busy street, but the apartments are well renovated and fully equipped. The same company runs the *Redan Quest Inn Apartments* (☎ 9529 7595, 25 Redan St), in a quieter and more suburban part of St Kilda. Here studio apartments with kitchenettes start at $75 per night.

Queens Road (Map 7)

A good option in this area is the *Oakford Fairways* (☎ 9820 8544, 32 Queens Rd), an Art Deco-style apartment block opposite Albert Park's golf course and lake. These executive apartments have a tennis court, a pool and leafy landscaped grounds. One-bedroom apartments start at $110, two bedrooms at $130.

Port Melbourne (Map 7)

Near the top of the bay, the *Station Pier Condominiums* (☎ 9647 9666, **e** sails@stationpiercondos.com.au, 15 Beach St) has 54 modern and spacious apartments separated by landscaped gardens and boardwalks. It also has a pool and sauna, tennis court, conference facilities and a stylish bar and restaurant, with live jazz sessions on Sunday afternoons. One-bedroom apartments start at $160 a night, two-bedroom at $185.

MID-RANGE HOTELS

Most four-star hotels are located in the city centre. Since the hotels are used largely by business travellers, weekends tend to be a lot quieter so there are often good weekend packages on offer. These vary seasonally, so have a good look around. Note that it's extremely difficult to fix a standard price on the major hotels as rates seem to fluctuate wildly.

City Centre (Map 2)

Close to the Treasury Gardens, the MCG and the theatre district, *Hotel Lindrum* (☎ 9668 1111, fax 9668 1199, 26 Flinders Lane) occupies a lovely old building that's been renovated into an intimate and tastefully designed hotel with restaurant and bar. A pleasant change from the large chain hotels, the Lindrum suits both corporate and leisure travellers. Doubles start at $230.

The sharp lines and stylised designer interiors of the once ultra-modern *Adelphi Hotel* (☎ 9650 2709, 187 Flinders Lane) are looking rather dated of late. For a small hotel the Adelphi has a good range of facilities, including an excellent basement restaurant, great rooftop bar with views of the city, and of course the famous glass-bottomed open-air swimming pool, which extends over the street. Standard rooms are $250, deluxe rooms $270 and executive suites $450.

The *Savoy Park Plaza* (☎ 9622 8888, fax 9622 8877, **e** savoypp@werple.mira.net.au, 630 Little Collins St) was built in the 1920s and later became a police academy. It has been refurbished in period style and has a contemporary Art-Deco feel. Rooms start at around $200 and suites at $350.

Only a walk across the river to Southbank, the *Centra Melbourne on the Yarra* (☎ 9629 5111, fax 9629 5624, **e** mail@melbourne.centra.com.au), on the corner of Flinders and Spencer Sts, is a modern four-star hotel with rooms starting at $190.

Hotel Grand Chancellor (☎ 9663 3161, fax 9662 3479, 131 Lonsdale St) is comfortable and close to the theatre district and Chinatown. Double rooms range from $185 to $230. *Novotel Melbourne on Collins* (☎ 9650 5800, fax 9650 7100, 270 Collins St) is right in the heart of the city, and has rooms starting at $220.

North Melbourne & Carlton (Map 3)

Chifley on Flemington (☎ 9329 9344, fax 9328 4807, 5–17 Flemington Rd) is surprisingly quiet as the rooms are set back from the hotel reception area, running off a leafy cobbled courtyard. Facilities include a courtyard cafe, bar with open fireplace, a restaurant, pool, sauna and gymnasium. Rooms and suites range from $140 to $280.

At 701 Swanston St, the *Rydges Carlton* (☎ 9347 7811, **e** reservations_carlton@rydges.com) is a five-storey hotel built in 1970. It's comfortable and well run, and facilities include a restaurant, bar and rooftop spa and sauna. Rooms start at $120.

Richmond (Map 5)

Rydges Riverwalk Hotel (☎ 9246 1200, fax 9246 1222, **e** reservations_riverwalk@rydges.com, 649 Bridge Rd) is an impressive four-star hotel adjacent to the Yarra River. Many of the rooms have river views, and as the name suggests the opportunity is there for a stroll along the Yarra's banks. Prices start at $220 for a courtyard room, $240 for a studio or riverview room (with a kitchenette) and $280 for a two-bedroom apartment. The hotel also has two on-site restaurants.

St Kilda (Map 9)

The modern high-rise *Novotel St Kilda* (☎ *9525 5522, fax 9525 4805,* ✆ *tom@ novotelbay.com.au, 14–16 The Esplanade)* is anything but in keeping with the feel of the suburb. However, the position is excellent and the front rooms have great views of the bay. Rooms are $180 for a single or double and $220 for a triple.

Queens & St Kilda Roads (Map 7)

While most of the hotels along this stretch cater to corporate travellers, it can still be a good part of town to stay in.

Centra St Kilda Rd (☎ *9209 9888),* on the corner of Park St and St Kilda Rd, is an older hotel that has been fully refurbished. The front rooms have great views of the Shrine of Remembrance and parklands opposite. Rates vary depending on the time of the week and season, ranging between $105 and $140 for a single or double.

The modern and stylish *Eden on the Park* (☎ *9820 2222, 6 Queens Rd)* has 132 well-appointed and comfortable rooms. Standard rooms start at $175 and the suites, which have great views over the lake and parklands, range from $220 to $260. The *Carlton Crest Hotel* (☎ *9529 4300, 65 Queens Rd)* is a large tourist hotel with 385 rooms. Doubles range from $135 to $195.

Around the corner is the *Parkroyal on St Kilda Road* (☎ *9529 8888, 562 St Kilda Rd)*, a flashy four-star hotel with rooms starting at $200.

TOP-END HOTELS

As with mid-range hotels, most of Melbourne's five-star hotels are in the city centre, and offer good weekend packages.

City Centre (Map 2)

Entering the foyer of the *Park Hyatt* (☎ *9224 1234, fax 9224 1200,* ✆ *phmelbourne@ hyatt.com.au, 1 Parliament Square)* is like finding yourself on an Art-Deco ocean liner.

The finest marble, glass and wood panelling combine to create an opulence unmatched in any other hotel in the city. Sound over the top? It is! But this is only the beginning. Other features include an excellent French bistro-style restaurant, a ballroom, banquet rooms, cigar lounge, tennis court, gymnasium and 25m lap pool – which is not to forget the 216 spacious guest rooms and 24 suites. Weekend packages cost around $350 per night with breakfast, and you can expect to pay anything from $380 upwards for a room at any other time. Suites range upwards from $500.

They call the *Windsor Hotel* (☎ *9633 6000, fax 9633 6001, 103 Spring St)* Melbourne's 'Grand Lady', and she is indisputably the matriarch of Melbourne's hotels. There are other hotels more opulent, more luxurious and with better facilities, but there are some things you can't manufacture and a grand sense of history is one of them. Built in 1883–84 and restored during the 1980s, the Windsor is the epitome of old-world elegance. Beyond the top-hatted doorman, the foyer is all marble and mahogany, shaded lamps and potted palms. Rooms cost from $285 to $450, and the suites, which have accommodated everyone from the Duke of Windsor to Rudolf Nureyev, range from $410 to $1200.

The *All Seasons Premier Grand Hotel* (☎ *9611 4567, fax 9611 4655,* ✆ *grand@ allseasons.com.au, 33 Spencer St)* occupies part of the old Victorian Railways administration buildings. The sheer scale of the structure is daunting. The rooms, originally offices, have such high ceilings that loft-style

Melbourne's elegant old Windsor Hotel

mezzanines have been added to some of them. Thankfully much of the interior has been restored, and the new additions aren't too obtrusive. The overall design is open-plan, yet quite in keeping with the original. Rooms range from $200 to $225 for a one-bedroom suite and $280 to $360 for a two-bedroom.

The heritage-listed *Duxton Hotel* (☎ 9250 1888, fax 9250 1877, **e** duxtonmelbourne@ global.net.au, 328 Finders St) is another classic example of Melbourne's architectural history. Built in 1913 as the Commercial Travellers Club, much of the hotel has been restored to its original splendour. Rich, dark timber panelling and ornate touches are a feature throughout the public areas. Club rooms on the heritage floor have great period features, such as ornate ceilings, leadlight windows and columns. Prices range from $265 to $600 for suites and club rooms are $245.

The *Grand Hyatt Melbourne* (☎ 9657 1234, 9650 3491, **e** melbourne@hyatt .com.au, 123 Collins St) is the largest of the modern hotels, with 580 luxuriously appointed rooms. It features a cavernous foyer chiselled from Italian marble, as well as a pool, spa, sauna, gymnasium and rooftop tennis court. Rooms start at $295 and the suites at $500.

Hotel Sofitel (☎ 9653 0000, 25 Collins St) is another excellent five-star hotel at the top end of Collins St. The hotel's 365 rooms occupy the 30th to 49th floors of one of the twin towers of Collins Place, and the uninterrupted views are excellent. Rooms start at $260, suites at $325.

Fronted by the historic and elaborate Venetian facades of two buildings dating to 1891, *Le Meridien at Rialto Melbourne* (☎ 9620 9111, fax 9614 1219, 495 Collins St) boasts individually styled rooms overlooking an enclosed central atrium that covers the original cobbled laneway between the two buildings. This laneway now houses stylish bars, cafes and restaurants. Rooms start at $265, suites at $445.

Rockman's Regency Hotel (☎ 9662 3900), on the corner of Exhibition and Lonsdale Sts, prides itself on providing the level of personal service that only a small

hotel can, and is particularly popular with visiting celebrities. The rooms are spacious and tastefully decorated, and the hotel is close to the main theatres and Chinatown. Rooms start at $210, suites at $250.

The recently refurbished *Mercure Hotel Melbourne* (☎ 9205 9999, fax 9205 9905, 13 Spring St, **e** mercuremelbourne@bigpond .com.au) is comfortable, stylish and well-located, close to the Melbourne Cricket Ground (MCG), Tennis Centre and theatre district. Standard rooms cost $144 per night and deluxe rooms $166.

Part of the enormous Crown Entertainment Complex on the southern bank of the Yarra, *Crown Towers Hotel* (☎ 9292 6666, fax 9292 6299, **e** hotelreservations@ crownltd.com.au) has all the glam and glitz you would expect from Disney for adults. If money is no object and you're here to gamble you'll love it. Prices start at around $450 for a room, $600 for suites.

Southgate (Map 2)

Overlooking the Yarra and Flinders St station, the elaborately decorated and impressive *Sheraton Towers Southgate* (☎ 9696 3100, 1 Brown St, South Melbourne) is close to Southgate's restaurants and cafes, the Victorian Arts Centre, the National Gallery of Victoria, the Botanic Gardens and the Crown casino complex. The recently refurbished rooms start at $280 and suites range from $650 up to $2000 for the Royal Suite.

East Melbourne (Map 3)

The *Melbourne Hilton on the Park* (☎ 9419 2000, fax 9419 2001, **e** melbhilt@ozemail .com, 192 Wellington Pde) is a very pleasant 10-minute stroll from the city and is close to the MCG. The Hilton has been extensively refurbished and has rooms starting at $240 and suites at around $400.

South Yarra (Map 6)

Hotel Como (☎ 9824 0400, fax 9824 1263), on Chapel St near the corner of Toorak Rd, is an all-suite hotel with a huge variety of rooms (some with Japanese gardens!). The mood is civilised without being aloof, the design is subtle and distinctive, and the 107 suites are very stylish. There's also a pool, spa, sauna and gym, and room-service meals from the adjacent Maxim's, a renowned local restaurant. Suites range from $480 to $1180, weekend packages start at $270.

GAY & LESBIAN ACCOMMODATION

The Laird (Map 5; ☎ 9417 2832, 149 Gipps St, Collingwood), one block east of Hoddle St, is an old pub that has been converted into a gay men's bar and nightclub. Upstairs there are pub-style rooms (shared bathroom) and a self-contained flat. Across the road, the quieter *Norwood Guesthouse* has three rooms costing $65 to $75, including breakfast.

More upmarket is *163 Drummond St (Map 3; ☎ 9663 3081, 163 Drummond St, Carlton)*, a stylishly restored B&B with small single rooms starting at $45 and doubles with shared bathroom at $70.

Palm Court B&B (Map 5; ☎ 9427 7365, 283 Punt Rd, Richmond) is a restored two-storey Victorian terrace house with four double rooms, two bathrooms, a guest lounge and a pleasant barbecue courtyard. Tariffs are $50 to $60 for singles, $80 to $90 for doubles; breakfast included.

The *Star Hotel (Map 5; ☎ 9417 2696, 176 Hoddle St, Collingwood)* is a popular gay and lesbian hotel with single/double rooms starting at $50/$60.

If you're looking to stay longer, you'll find accommodation notices in *MSO* and *Brother Sister*, as well as on notice boards in many cafes and bookshops.

DISABLED ACCOMMODATION

Wheelchair accessible accommodation in Melbourne is at best limited and expensive, being provided primarily by four- and five-star hotels. Canberra-based National Information Communication Awareness Network (NICAN; ☎ 1800-806 769) has a database of wheelchair-accessible accommodation. *Queensberry Hill Hostel (Map 3; ☎ 9329 8599, ✆ queensberryhill@yhavic.org.au, 78 Howard St)* has an accessible bathroom on each of its four floors.

The Victorian Disabled Motorists Association (☎ 9386 0413) has two accessible motel units at Coburg, north of the city. The *Novotel St Kilda (Map 9; ☎ 9525 5522, fax 9525 4805, ✆ tom@novotelbay.com.au, 14–16 The Esplanade)* is a good, but not cheap, option with five wheelchair-accessible rooms.

Another option is to contact Travellers Aid Disability Access Service (☎ 9654 7690), which helps people with disabilities find accommodation.

Places to Eat

Melbourne's reputation as cuisine capital of Australia continues to be a contentious and hotly debated issue. Certainly, there is a unique style and sophistication that makes eating here a very Melbourne experience. The sheer volume of cafes and restaurants, and the pace with which things change, ensures that Melbourne's food watchers have to be constantly on their toes.

The European (especially Italian) influence remains as strong as ever, and is most evident in the vibrant cafe scene that dominates the city and inner suburbs. The culinary mix of European, Mediterranean and Asian flavours, the abundance of fresh local produce and the stable of imaginative chefs has resulted in a style of cooking now commonly known as 'modern Australian'.

CITY CENTRE (MAP 2)
Chinatown Area

The area in and around Chinatown, which follows Little Bourke St from Spring St to Swanston St, continues to be one of the city's most popular places to eat. As you would expect, Chinese and Asian restaurants predominate here, but delve a little deeper and you can also choose from Greek, Indian, Japanese and modern Australian. Part of the

> ## Highlights
>
> - Breakfast in the urbane atmosphere of Block Place
> - Coffee at Caffé e Cucina in upbeat Chapel St
> - Sunday-morning yum cha in Chinatown
> - Split-level fine dining at the theatrical and thoroughly entertaining Radii
> - Fish and chips on St Kilda foreshore while fighting off the seagulls

fun is just wandering around and soaking up the atmosphere, and there's always somewhere new to be found in the narrow cobbled lanes that run off Little Bourke St.

Starting from the top end of Little Bourke St, **Kri Kri** (☎ *9639 3444, 39 Little Bourke St*) is a stylish, friendly and inexpensive Greek restaurant, with a great choice for vegetarians. Share with friends a selection of small dishes washed down with a bottle of icy-cold retsina. **Shark Fin Inn** (☎ *9662 2681, 50 Little Bourke St*) is a very popular Chinese restaurant, with a good menu and exceptional service. If you're after the house

Legend Has It – Melbourne's Cafe Culture

When it opened in 1956 at 239 Bourke St, the Legend Café was an instant success. This thoroughly modern-looking cafe, complete with wall murals and stylish lighting, was a hang-out for students, theatre types, artists and a community of European emigres homesick for the cafe culture they had left behind. The Legend's Italian-based menu featured minestrone, toasted sandwiches, risotto, spaghetti, gelato, cappuccino and espresso coffee – items that continue to be the mainstays of many of Melbourne's cafes. The Legend may be gone but her presence can be felt throughout the city and inner suburbs, where the sheer abundance of cafes is more than matched by a public who want to visit them.

Everybody has their favourite haunt, but a few places worth searching out are: Caffé e Cucina, at 581 Chapel St, South Yarra; Degraves Espresso Bar, at 23 Degraves St in the city; C&B, in Block Place in the city; Wall Two 80, at the rear of 280 Carlisle St, East St Kilda; Babka Bakery Cafe, at 358 Brunswick St, Fitzroy; the Continental Cafe, at 132a–34 Greville St, Prahran; and the Richmond Hill Cafe & Larder, at 48–50 Bridge Rd, Richmond.

Colonial Tramcar Restaurant

Melbourne's most popular attractions include its trams and restaurants, but when some oddball came up with the idea of combining the two, most people thought it was a weird gimmick that would never last. Well, several years down the track (sorry!) the *Colonial Tramcar Restaurant (☎ 9696 4000)* is still a huge success with both visitors and locals – a great novelty idea backed up with good food and service. You can dine in comfort while taking a scenic evening tram cruise around Melbourne's streets.

There are two sittings: early dinner is from 5.45 to 7.15 pm and costs $55 a head, which includes three courses and all drinks; late dinner is from 8.30 to 11.30 pm and is $80 ($90 on Friday and Saturday), which includes five courses and all drinks. The converted 1920s tram even has specially built stabilisers so you don't have to worry about sharp corners. The tram leaves from Southbank Boulevard beside the National Gallery of Victoria and heads down St Kilda Rd, along The Esplanade to Acland St and back.

Dine on board Melbourne's *Colonial Tramcar Restaurant.*

PATRICK HORTON

speciality – you've guessed it, shark-fin soup ($16) – you need to order 24 hours in advance. Nearby, *Kuni's (☎ 9663 7243, 56 Little Bourke St)* serves simple Japanese food with the occasional hint of Italian. Mains cost between $8 and $20. Directly opposite, the *Bamboo House (☎ 9662 1565, 47 Little Bourke St)* is a mix of Cantonese and Sichuan, with mains starting at around $18. The slick black walls, banquet tables and bamboo-shaded windows are a plus.

It's impossible not to be intrigued by a place called *Madam Fang (☎ 9663 3199, 27–29 Crossley St)*. The menu is an adventurous and successful cross-breed where miyaki ($15), a selection of contrasting hors d'oeuvres, including curried chicken, and raw salmon wrapped in bok choy, sit comfortably alongside a hearty paella ($19). A short walk across the city grid *Marchetti's Latin (☎ 9662 1985, 55 Lonsdale St)* is elegant and romantic with a reputation as one of the best Italian restaurants in town.

On the corner of Little Bourke and Exhibition Sts, *CBD (☎ 9662 3151)* is big, modern and brash, but great for an inexpensive après-theatre pizza, pasta and drink. Back on the trail and light years away, the *Flower Drum (☎ 9662 3655, 17 Market Lane)* is Melbourne's best known Chinese restaurant, and a Chinatown institution. Exquisite food, professional staff and sumptuous decor make it a must, regardless of the expense. On the other side of Little Bourke St, tiny *Yamato (☎ 9663 1706, 28 Corrs Lane)* is perfect if you like Japanese food at a reasonable price and don't mind a tight squeeze.

Mask of China (☎ 9662 2116, 117 Little Bourke St) is another excellent and well-established restaurant, with mains in the $20 to $30 price range. Farther down, and across Russell St, *Fortuna Village (☎ 9663 3044, 253 Little Bourke St)* is particularly famous for its Peking duck, but you could order any of the reasonably priced dishes and have your tastebuds zinging. *Gaylord (☎ 9663 3980, 4 Tattersalls Lane)* has a good variety of mainly north Indian dishes, with a reasonable choice for vegetarians. The award-wining noorani kebab ($9) and the fish masala ($12) are highly recommended.

PLACES TO EAT

Bourke Street Area

At 159 Spring St, **Stella** (☎ 9639 1555) is a relaxed yet stylish affair with cushion-scattered bench-seating and rendered ochre walls. The food is imaginative modern Australian with a wine list and delectable desserts to match. Next door, the **European** (☎ 9654 0811) is long, dark and very European (even the wines). Standards are high, and at $14 to $18 for a main, prices are reasonable. **Pellegrini's** (66 Bourke St) is the classic Melbourne espresso bar with a reputation built over decades. It's uncomfortable, the food's as rudimentary Italian as you'll get and the coffee's OK. So who's complaining, we love it anyway!

Part restaurant, bar and produce store, **Becco** (☎ 9663 3000, 11–25 Crossley St) is not only big on style but continues to be one of the city centre's most popular Italian restaurants. **Nudel Bar** (76 Bourke St) serves an assortment of noodle dishes covering everything from macaroni cheese ($12.50) to mee goreng ($12.50) in a frenetic setting.

Chandeliers and murals depicting Florentine life imbue **Grossi Florentino** (☎ 9662 1811, 80 Bourke St) with a romantic air matched by a menu offering some of the best Italian food in town. At the same address, **Grossi Florentino Cellar Bar** is dark, intimate and more affordable: a great place to have a really good bowl of inexpensive pasta ($10) and a glass of ripe chianti. After a friendly welcome at **Ito Japanese Noodle Cafe** (☎ 9663 2788), on the corner of Market Lane and Bourke St, slip into an American diner-style booth and make your choice from the wide and varied menu. Mains range from around $7 to $25.

Hanabishi (☎ 9670 1167, 187 King St), in the heart of the city's legal precinct, is renowned for its exquisitely presented Japanese food. Bento boxes (around $30) and sets are the best way to sample a range of delicacies. A little farther north, **Sud** (☎ 9670 8451, 219 King St) makes elegance and style look easy in both its setting and market-fresh food. Whole sardines ($12.90) and rosemary and garlic roasted potatoes ($7.50) are favourites.

Little Collins Street Area

Narrow, more intimate and with less traffic congestion than busy Bourke St, Little Collins St is tailor-made for the influx of

Pellegrini's – a true Melbourne institution

cafes and bars that have sprung up here in recent times.

Bistro 1 (☎ 9654 3343, 126 Little Collins St) is all mood and style, with the added extra that it does French-bistro cooking very well. Delicious starters ($10 to $12), mains ($18 to $24) and desserts ($10 to $12) are all matched with a suggestion for an accompanying glass of wine.

The theatrically Italian **Il Bàcaro** (☎ 9654 6778, 168–70 Little Collins St) is one of the best, with its distinctly modern (Melbourne) style and simply delicious food. The unabashedly arrogant waiters (hand-picked for petulance) may have moved on since the restaurant changed management, but thankfully everything else remains.

The very popular **Hairy Canary** (☎ 9654 2471, 212 Little Collins St) is a frenetic mix of drinkers and diners enjoying the Mediterranean fare. The long, low-ceilinged room just about guarantees a noisy night with friends – as opposed to an intimate dinner for two.

Tony Starr's Kitten Club (☎ 9650 2448, Level 1, 267 Little Collins St) melds food and live jazz in a relaxed setting where you can choose from tables and chairs or comfy lounges to enjoy your thyme-marinated chicken breast with cinnamon-roasted pear, rocket and mascarpone ($16.50) from the modern Australian menu.

Laurent Patisserie (306 Little Collins St) is in stark contrast to the tiny enclave of cafes across the road. A spacious old bank building renovated to include an extra floor and grand swirling staircase, it's one of the best patisseries in town.

Running between Little Collins St and the Block Arcade (Map 2), Block Place has been transformed from a quiet laneway into a busy strip of sidewalk cafes with an atmosphere more in keeping with Barcelona than downtown Melbourne. At No 30, **Cafe Cortille** (☎ 9650 1564) is one of the best, great for lunch or a coffee and really coming alive in the evening. Risotto ($13.50) is a popular favourite from its contemporary Italian menu. **Cafe Segovia** (☎ 9650 2373, 33 Block Place) was here long before a hole in the wall could constitute a cafe. The

The best place on the Block for a caffeine fix

largest space on the block, and popular from sunrise to sunset, it's a great spot to sample modern Australian cooking in a mock-Cubist-meets-1950s setting. For the best coffee in Block Place head for tiny **C&B**, at Shop No 43.

Tucked away in a cobble-stoned laneway, **Syracuse** (☎ 9670 1777, 23 Bank Place) is *the* place in the city for delicious tapas, excellent wines and European ambience.

Collins Street Area

The top of Collins St is still referred to as the 'Paris end' of town, but sadly the comparison, which was made in the 1950s when trees and beautiful buildings lined the street, no longer applies. Today, only the trees are intact.

In Collins Place (Map 2), under the shadow of the twin towers that dominate the street, **Kenzan** (☎ 9654 8933, Collins Place, 45 Collins St) maintains its reputation as one of the best Japanese restaurants in the city. Great sushi and sashimi mains are $19 to $26, and divine sukiyaki ($47) prepared at your table make it an excellent choice.

Great for either breakfast, lunch, dinner or a drink, **Il Solito Posto** (☎ 9654 4466, 113 Collins St) is a popular basement Italian bar and restaurant with a warm ambience. Nearby, **Italy 1** (☎ 9654 4430, 27 George Pde) is intimate and stylish; the perfect setting to get up close and personal over some excellent Italian food. At *Box* (☎ *9663 0411, 189 Collins St)* award-wining architecture and adventurous modern-Australian cuisine are features of this long and very narrow restaurant-cafe. Mains cost from $25 to $27. Across the road, *Café d'Orsay* (☎ *9654 6498, 184 Collins St)* is safer territory for the palette, with a leaning towards Italian (fet-tuccine with smoked salmon, tomatoes and olives is $13.50). If you're after something on the run, the *Hyatt Food Court*, part of the Grand Hyatt Hotel complex, has a good range of reasonably priced food stalls in spa-cious surroundings.

Flinders Lane

A little like a toy-town version of New York's SoHo, Flinders Lane is gallery cen-tral for the contemporary art scene. Plenty of cafes and bars are sprouting up in the ad-jacent laneways to meet the demand of a crowd waiting for the happening to happen.

Langton's (☎ *9663 0222, 61 Flinders Lane)* has an ultra-modern decor, a great wine list and a big-name chef whose open kitchen pumps out modern French-Australian dishes such as crépinette of pheasant with ginger quince and cinnamon-infused jus ($25); reservations are essential. *Ezard at adelphi* (☎ *9639 6811, 187 Flinders Lane)* occupies the long and low-ceilinged basement of the Adelphi Hotel, and the cool grey tones and white linen give the place a very neutral but classy look. Fish and poultry predominate in the Asian- and European-influenced menu, with mains between $23 and $28.

Ristorante Roberto (☎ *9650 3399, 31 Russell St)* is a slice of formal Italian style in a Melbourne basement. Sit back in one of the comfortable red leather booths and enjoy the attentive service and fine Italian food. *Degraves Espresso Bar* (*23 Degraves St)* spills out onto the quiet pedestrian thor-oughfare between Flinders St and Flinders Lane, and offers a great view of the historic Majorca Building, the most attractive apart-ment block in the city. Panini ($5.50) is a justifiable favourite here, but there are al-ways a few reasonably priced mains.

Centre Place (*the* classic Melbourne laneway) is on the opposite side of Flinders

Lane from Degraves St and becomes a cov-ered arcade as it runs through to Collins St. Note the fantastic Art-Nouveau-style, wrought-iron lighting overhead that is also a feature of Degraves St. *Ten*, at No 12, is a tiny noodle bar with great sushi ($1.50 a piece) and stir-fried noodles in a box ($6.50 to $7.50). A few doors along and upstairs at No 20, *Hell's Kitchen* takes its name from the infamous New York precinct. This ex-cellent cafe-bar is a great but smoky place for lunch, a light dinner or a drink.

Other Areas

At No 122 Russell St, popular *Pizza Napoli* is perfectly positioned for grabbing a pizza or a plate of pasta before heading off to a city cinema.

Lounge, upstairs at 243 Swanston St, is a roomy and relaxed cafe and club with pool tables and a balcony, with sausages, stir-fries, satays and salads from $7 to $10.

One of the cheapest places in town, *Gopal's* at 139 Swanston St is a vegetarian cafe run by the Hare Krishna sect. Open for lunch and dinner, the food is surprisingly good, especially considering the price: a meal here will set you back about $8.

Lonsdale St between Russell and Swanston Sts is Melbourne's small Greek enclave, with cafes, restaurants, cake shops and gift shops. *Stalactites*, on the corner of Lonsdale and Russell Sts, is a Greek restau-rant best known for its bizarre stalactite decor and the fact that it's open 24 hours. Farther along Lonsdale St, *Tsindos the Greek* is also good value, and has live *bouzouki* music on Thursday, Friday and Saturday nights. At No 195, *Antipodes* (☎ *9663 4706)* brings a little bit of Mel-bourne style to the strip with its simple de-sign and modern Greek cooking.

Back on Swanston St at No 321, *Don Don Japanese Restaurant* is great for sushi boxes and noodles on the run with mains from $4 to $7. Honest, simple and very pop-ular, Don Don is a real find.

As well as being the home of Melbourne's outdoor adventure shops, Hardware Lane is a very attractive and popular cafe strip, es-pecially popular at lunch time. *Campari*

PLACES TO EAT

Bistro (☎ 9670 3813, 25 Hardware Lane) is one of the best. There's plenty on offer, but try the buffet ($4 to $17) which offers a great selection and is value for money. At No 37, *Fresh Express* is a great place for a quick and healthy bite to eat. A hearty soup with bread will cost around $6, and the smoothies are excellent. *Relax Dine Unwine* (☎ 9600 3803), at No 54, is admittedly a daft name, but it's a good spot on a summer evening when the sounds of live jazz fill the lane. The food here is a culinary mixed bag, incorporating Asian and Italian dishes.

Marchetti's Tuscan Grill (☎ 9670 6612, 401 Little Bourke St) serves up excellent pasta, seafood and meat dishes in a large and spacious basement setting.

At 1 Parliament Square at the top of the city, in the luxurious surrounds of the Park Hyatt, *Radii* (☎ 9224 1211) is as good as it

Fine Dining

Nothing quite matches a night of fine dining, and in Melbourne the choices are as varied as they are many. Here are just a few worth dressing up for. Prices given are an approximate cost of a three-course meal for one person, excluding drinks.

Langton's (Map 2; ☎ 9663 0222, 61 Flinders Lane) seems right at home below street level in Melbourne's commercial gallery district. Here Chef Phillipe Mouchel adds a touch of Australian flavour to his modern French cooking style, and the restaurant has an excellent wine list ($55).

Il Bàcaro (Map 2; ☎ 9654 6778, 168–70 Little Collins St) is as good as it gets. It's a hybrid of Fellini's *La Dolce Vita* and the best Italian food in town ($50).

Flower Drum (Map 2; ☎ 9662 3655, 17 Market Lane) is one of Melbourne's most famous and stylish Chinese restaurants, where the experience far out-weighs the price ($85).

Walter's Wine Bar (Map 2; ☎ 9690 9211, Upper Level, Southgate) has the big three covered: a great view across the Yarra to the city, a fine modern Australian menu and an excellent wine list ($50).

Radii (Map 2; ☎ 9224 1211, Park Hyatt, 1 Parliament Sq, East Melbourne), with its split levels, giant open kitchen, over-the-top interior and sumptuous Modern European food, is a dining experience not to be missed ($60).

Est est est (Map 7; ☎ 9682 5688, 440 Clarendon St, South Melbourne) is fine dining at its best. The simple but elegant interior, delicious European cooking and wonderful wine list make this one a must ($70).

Pomme (Map 7; ☎ 9820 9606, 37 Toorak Rd, South Yarra) is the brainchild of Brit chef Jeremy Strode, who brings a great deal of flair to his modern French-style cooking ($75).

Crack your way through a carapace.

Jacques Reymond (Map 6; ☎ 9525 2178, 78 Williams Rd, Windsor), set in a grand historic mansion in Windsor, is famous for its exquisite modern Australian food, impeccable service and unbeatable setting ($80).

Circa The Prince (Map 9; ☎ 9536 1122, 2 Acland St, St Kilda) combines modern French cooking with a cool design sense to create one of the best restaurants in town ($85).

Donovans (Map 9; ☎ 9534 8221, 40 Jacka Blvd, St Kilda) overlooks the bay from the St Kilda foreshore. The wonderful location is complimented by excellent meat and seafood dishes and an impressive wine list ($55).

Cafe culture bursting at the seams

Bustling Brunswick Street, Fitzroy

CUB Malthouse, South Melbourne

Chinatown, Little Bourke Street

Chinese dragon

Brunswick Street parade, Fitzroy

Just another day at the office for the St Kilda Festival

gets. Celebrity chef Paul Wilson whips up exquisite contemporary cuisine in his open kitchen. Damn the expense, just go!

Each of the city's three major department stores – Myer, David Jones and Daimaru – has an excellent food emporium with a wide selection of goods to choose from. Particularly worth searching out is the *Daimaru Sushi Bar*, at level one in Melbourne Central – the omelettes, sushi boxes and udon soups are excellent.

SOUTHGATE (MAP 2)

Since opening in the early 1990s, the Southgate development at Southbank, on the southern side of the Yarra River, has quickly become a popular Melbourne eating spot. With great views over the river and the city skyline, it's also close to galleries, theatres and the gardens of King's Domain. There are plenty of bars, cafes and restaurants to choose from, most of which have outdoor terraces and balconies suitable for alfresco dining in the warmer weather.

On the upper level, *Walter's Wine Bar* (☎ 9690 9211) blends culinary flair, professional service and a justifiably famous wine list. How can you go wrong with oysters with avocado salsa ($15 for a half dozen), snapper with salad ($25) and mango tarte tatin ($10.50), accompanied by a delicious dessert wine? *Red Emperor* (☎ 9699 4170), with its grand sense of occasion, panoramic views and vibrant Cantonese and Beijing cuisine, has brought Chinatown to Southgate. Yum cha here might cost a little more than most, but it's definitely up there with the best. Mains cost anything between $15 and $56.

On the mid-level the elegant style of *Mecca* (☎ 9682 2999) is matched by the quality of its modern-Australian menu. Crispy-skinned garfish ($13) and spiced lamb cutlets on couscous ($21) are just a sample of what Mecca has to offer. As impressive as the Italian bistro *Scusa Mi* (☎ 9699 4111) might be, the level of service can spiral downwards from arrogant. However, the chef's signature dish, roast duckling ($28.50), and the creamy panna cotta ($9.50) should save the day. Much more affordable, the loud and hugely popular *Blue Train Cafe* (☎ 9696 0111)

serves breakfasts, pasta and risotto, wood-fired oven pizza, salads and more, with mains costing between $6 and $10.

On ground level, Mediterranean meets Asian at *Blakes* (☎ 9699 4100) – one of the best and most popular modern Australian restaurants in Southgate. Steamed coral trout with a sautée of Asian greens ($24) is a good example of the blend. *Bistro Vite* (☎ 9690 9271) serves French bistro-style food with a contemporary edge in an easy-going, relaxed atmosphere. The complimentary fresh bread and basil pesto is a nice touch. The house speciality is bouillabaisse ($19.50), along with classic desserts such as crème brûlée and chocolate mousse ($7.50).

The centre of the ground floor is taken up by the *Wharf Food Market*, where a mix and match of reasonably priced international food stalls offer something for everyone.

CROWN ENTERTAINMENT COMPLEX (MAP 2)

Farther west along the Yarra from Southgate, *Crown Entertainment Complex* has a few good restaurants. *Silks* (☎ 9292 6888, Level 1, Crown Towers) serves top-of-the-range Cantonese food at top-of-the-range prices. If the Mongolian tent in the centre of the room used as a pre-dinner drinks bar sounds good to you, then you'll love Silks.

As big as a palace, *Cecconi's* (☎ 9292 6887, ground level, Crown Complex) is potentially an organisational nightmare. Thankfully, a sure hand at the helm keeps the show running smoothly, and the steady flow of quality modern Italian dishes just keeps on coming.

The safest bet at Crown is the *Automatic Cafe* (☎ 9690 8500, Ground Level, Crown Complex), serving up everything from bacon and eggs ($5.90) to wood-fired pizza, calzone and Turkish pide ($7 to $10).

NORTH & WEST MELBOURNE (MAPS 2 & 3)

This area, close to the Queen Victoria Market and home to the YHA hostels, might lack the glamour and popularity of some other inner suburbs, but there are some great places to eat in these relatively quiet

PLACES TO EAT

and community-minded semi-industrial Victorian suburbs.

The deli section of the Queen Victoria Market (via the Therry St entrance) has a few reasonably priced food stalls selling everything from frankfurters to focaccia and coffee.

If you're a vego in need of a protein hit, then the **White Lotus Vegetarian Restaurant**, at 185 Victoria St, is the place for you. There's plenty of tofu, as well as a few mock-meat dishes, which might not be to a strict vegetarian's liking. Soups start at $4.50 and main dishes range from $8 to $14.

Maria's Trattoria (☎ 9329 9016, 122 Peel St) is a North Melbourne institution, and seems to have been going for as long as we can remember. It's a simple, family-style Italian trattoria, with dishes ranging from pasta to meat and seafood ($7 to $12). Be careful not to over-order, as servings are on the large side.

Back on Victoria St and part of a very successful Melbourne pizza chain, **La Porchetta**, at No 302, is large, noisy and always packed. The pizza is surprisingly good with a nice thin base and plenty of topping. Prices range from $4.40 for a small to $6 for a large pizza.

Don Camillo's, at No 215, is a couple of blocks up from Victoria Market, and one of the finest examples of the city's 1950s Italian cafe-restaurants. The terrazzo floor was one of the first to be laid in Melbourne. Pictures of footy stars (many of whom pop in) cover the walls. Breakfast includes toasted sandwiches and eggs any style ($5 to $9), while lunch is traditional Italian: soup, pasta, seafood and meat dishes ($8 to $14). Don's is open for dinner on Thursday and Friday evenings.

Two doors up, the **Traveller's Cafe** is a good choice for those with a small budget and a big appetite. Breakfast ranges from healthy muesli with dried fruit and yogurt to bacon and eggs ($4 to $7). Main meals include soup of the day ($5), nachos, risotto and a variety of pasta dishes priced from $7 to $9. The cafe is closed on Saturday.

Farther west along Victoria St at No 305, **Warung Agus** is a cosy and simple two-room restaurant that serves great Balinese food, with mains from $10 to $13.

Amiconi (☎ 9328 3710, 359 Victoria St) is a traditional little Italian bistro that has been a local favourite for years, so you'll probably have to book. Across the road at No 488, the **Peppermint Lounge Cafe** is a good spot for breakfast or lunch.

A little off the beaten track, **Akita** (☎ 9326 5766), on the corner of Courtney and Blackwood Sts, is one of the best Japanese restaurants in town, with mains from $17 to $19.

CARLTON (MAP 3)
Lygon Street

In the days when Anglo-Saxon Melbourne was largely devoid of other cultural influences, Lygon St was affectionately thought of as the city's multicultural centre, with its fascinating blend of cosmopolitan immigrants and bohemian university students. But, progress being progress, eventually the Italian tailors and small shopkeepers moved out and the developers and entrepreneurs moved in. Nowadays, Lygon St is no longer considered a trend-setter in Melbourne's restaurant scene, although some of the long-running places are still worth a visit.

Tram Nos 1 and 21, which run along Swanston St, will take you to Lygon St from the city centre, or if you feel like walking, it's a very pleasant stroll north up Russell St.

The stretch of Lygon St from the top of the city up to Grattan St is choc-a-block with Italian restaurants. The competition to get punters onto seats is fierce, and the sycophantic spruikers trying their best to do so has made this stretch of Lygon St a fairly unattractive tourist trap. Having said that, this is pretty much what you'd expect in Italian cities like Venice or Florence, so you could say it has a touch of authenticity about it.

For something different, **Lemongrass Thai** (☎ 9662 2244, 176 Lygon St) combines ancient royal Thai recipes with immaculate presentation and good service, earning it a reputation as one of the best Thai restaurants in the city. Mains cost between $17 and $30. At No 257, the **University Cafe** and **Universita Bar Restaurant**

(☎ 9347 2142) have been Carlton institutions since the 1950s, with unforgettable coffee in the street-level cafe and classic Italian dining in the restaurant upstairs.

Farther north at No 303, **Tiamo** *(☎ 9347 5759)* has been around forever and is as reliable as it is authentic. This old-fashioned Italian bistro keeps its prices low, which accounts for its popularity with Melbourne University students who love its good coffee and breakfasts, its hearty minestrone ($5) and tasty pasta from around $8. This end of Lygon St also has some good gelati bars and coffee and cake shops.

At No 333, **Jimmy Watson's Wine Bar Restaurant** *(☎ 9347 3985)* is legendary among wine lovers, and offers an extensive and varied list of wines ($12 to $200 per bottle) as well as excellent European cuisine in the stylish upstairs restaurant. Across the road, **Trotters** *(☎ 9347 5657)* at No 400 is another popular little bistro, serving good breakfasts and hearty Italian fare in the $7 to $12 range.

Just off Lygon St, **Shakahari** *(☎ 9347 3848, 201 Faraday St)* has been one of Melbourne's favourite vegetarian restaurants for over 20 years. Shakahari's Asian-influenced menu blends fresh and seasonal ingredients to create imaginative, delicious dishes. **Brunetti** *(☎ 9347 2801)*, opposite at 198 Faraday St, is both an Italian trattoria and pasticceria/gelateria, with great coffee and cake, pasta, mains and desserts.

Elgin Street

At No 118 Elgin St, **Jakarta** *(☎ 9349 3881)* is a restaurant that specialises in Indonesian-style seafood, with main courses ranging from $16 to $20. Across the road at No 109, **Abla's** *(☎ 9347 0006)* is synonymous with Lebanese food at its very best. Everything on the menu, from the dips ($3.50 each) to a great choice of mains ($13 to $15), is wonderfully flavoursome.

At No 162 **Toofey's Seafood Restaurant** *(☎ 9347 9838)* prides itself on serving the best and freshest seafood available – and with exceptional dishes such as the seafood risotto ($27), Atlantic salmon ($28) and yellow fin tuna ($27), we must agree.

Smoke Signals

Many a dining experience has been ruined not by the setting or the quality of the food but by someone at the next table lighting up. In Melbourne, nonsmokers have had little choice when it comes to a smoke-free dining environment. Although some restaurants have an allotted smoke-free area (which in many cases amounts to little more than a token few tables, or a policy of no smoking until a certain hour), in general Melbourne has been very much in favour of the smoker. With ongoing research into passive smoking and evidence to suggest that, contrary to popular belief, businesses have benefited from a nonsmoking policy, the state government will impose new laws with a complete smoking ban in cafes and restaurants by July 2001.

The end of the ashtray's humble life as we know it?

FITZROY & COLLINGWOOD (MAPS 3 & 4)
Brunswick Street

Somewhat usurped by Fitzroy St (St Kilda) as the city's happening restaurant strip, Brunswick St continues to be as popular and diverse as ever. And with so much to choose from, don't be surprised if you end up not being able to see the wood for the trees. The

PLACES TO EAT

listings below are a good indication of the variety and range on offer and should help you to see things a little more clearly.

Most of the action is up around Johnston St, but there are quite a few interesting places down the city end near Gertrude St. *De Los Santos* (☎ 9417 1567, 175 Brunswick St) is a casual Spanish-influenced restaurant where a selection of tapas, paella, and other dishes priced from $9 to $16 can be enjoyed sitting on the comfy sofa in front of the log fire.

A little farther north at No 252, the *Black Cat Cafe* is classic homey mix-and-match of 1950s tables and chairs, relaxed atmosphere and simple snack menu. Most dishes are under $6, making it a great spot to hang out without damaging the finances.

In complete contrast, *Guernica* (☎ 9416 0969), at No 257, is intimate and stylish with a reputation for subtle and inventive dishes in the modern-Australian style, with mains from $18 to $23. Three doors up at No 263, *Mao's Restaurant* serves very good, inexpensive Chinese-inspired dishes such as spicy calamari ($5.50) and Hunan chicken hotpot ($9.90). The long-running *Sala Thai Restaurant* (☎ 9417 4929), at No 266, brings a little calm to Brunswick St with its quality Thai dishes, low lighting and unhurried service (mains $10 to $15). *Thai Thani*, at No 293, is another good option for Thai food.

At No 302, *Bistro Inferno* (☎ 9416 0953) has long been a favourite for its original and subtly spiced dishes, and it's a lot less pricey than most restaurants serving food of this quality, with mains between $11 and $18.

On the corner of Johnston St, *Cafe Provincial* (☎ 9417 2228) is an old pub-cum-restaurant decorated in the distressed style. It's large, noisy and very popular, and the Italian bistro-style food is of a high standard and reasonably priced. Next door, on Johnston St, the *Ruby Cafe & Bar* is popular for its Malay/Indian home-style cooking and distinctive deep red interior with huge satin lanterns. *Marios Cafe*, at 303 Brunswick St, continues to be one of the most popular Italian cafes in the area, with good coffee, excellent breakfasts and main meals. Adjacent, and a few doors up, *Piraeus Blues* covers

most of the traditional Greek favourites as well as a few lesser-known dishes, with mains between $15 and $20.

Always busy, the *Brunswick Street Noodle Palace*, at No 328, offers a good choice of tasty Asian noodle dishes for under $11. *Babka Bakery Cafe*, at No 358, is not only a welcome relief from the usual Brunswick St style, it's also one of the best cafe-bakeries in the area. The bakery is renowned for its breads and pastries, and the pristine cafe produces a wonderful variety of sandwiches and Russian-influenced dishes.

At No 366, *Joe's Garage* has a central bar, with benches and stools on one side and a large dining area on the other. It's a friendly place with a lively atmosphere, and serves up breakfasts, focaccia and salad, pasta, risotto and other mains.

On the corner of Rose St, the cavernous *Vegie Bar* offers a wide range of value-for-money vegetarian meals for under $9. A couple of blocks north on the Westgarth St corner, *Retro Cafe* has high ceilings and a 1950s decor. The Retro is equally popular for a laid back weekend breakfast or a meal from its selection of Asian and European dishes.

Just over Alexandra Parade, *Rubira's* (☎ 9489 1974, 5 Rae St), at the back of the old Jika Jika Hotel, is a real gem – some of the city's best seafood can be consumed in this unassuming and unfussy restaurant. Farther north at 533 Brunswick St, *Matteo's Ristorante* (☎ 9481 1177) is fine dining indeed, with its antique chairs, starched linen, impeccable service, impressive wine list and outstanding modern Italian-Australian cuisine. Mains begin around $23.

The *Moroccan Soup Bar* (☎ 9482 4240, 183 Georges Rd) serves up a great selection of North African vegetarian dishes in marvellously Maghreb surroundings. The delicious and authentic flavours of marinated vegetables and an assortment of dips are followed by couscous, tajine or a bake, with mains from around $8 to $10.

Johnston Street

The stretch of Johnston St between Brunswick and Nicholson Sts is Melbourne's Spanish quarter. The demand for tapas has

Places to Eat – Richmond 117

faded of late and places have started to close, but a couple of old stalwarts remain.

Hogar Español, at 59 Johnston St, is a simple bar and restaurant. For something more atmospheric, the **Carmen Bar** (☎ 9417 4794), at No 74, is a hectic and down-to-earth restaurant with authentic Spanish food and live flamenco and Spanish guitar from Thursday to Saturday nights. At No 95, the huge and bellowing **Bull Ring** is part Spanish restaurant, part tapas bar, part nightclub.

Gertrude Street

Farther south, Gertrude St has an interesting collection of galleries, art suppliers, costume designers and antique shops, as well as a few good places to eat. **Growlers**, at No 153, is a local favourite serving fresh and inventive Mod Oz food, with mains from $11 to $18. At No 193, **Arcadia** is a popular cafe with plenty of retro charm and an eclectic selection of inexpensive dishes, while at No 199 the very straightforward **Macedonia** does chargrilled meats, goulash and other Balkan specialities at reasonable prices.

Smith Street

Forming the border between Fitzroy and Collingwood, Smith St lacks the razzamatazz of Brunswick St, but it has a nice down-beat alternative quality, and still hasn't lost the community spirit that has all but disappeared from Brunswick St.

The **Smith St Bar & Bistro** (☎ 9417 2869, 14 Smith St) is a very pleasant and stylish bar-restaurant. There's a front bar with snacks, a spacious lounge area with couches and an open fire, and an elegant dining room with French/Italian mains in the $14 to $18 range. At No 99, **Planet Afrik** serves up an interesting assortment of West African dishes served on bare wooden tables, in a huge high-ceilinged building that doubles as a venue for African music and dance performances.

Farther north at No 117, **Vegetarian Orgasm** is a friendly vegie cafe by day and a cosy candle-lit restaurant by night. There is plenty of choice for vegetarians, vegans and those with food allergies. At 129, **Cafe Coco** is a relaxed and popular cafe with good breakfasts and a variety of main

dishes with some scope for vegetarians. On the corner of Peel St, the **Grace Darling Hotel** is a great pub with cheap bar snacks and an excellent restaurant.

At 275 Smith St, the **Soul Food Cafe** is a popular vegan cafe serving salads and hot foods for under $10; there's an organic grocer next door.

Mamma Vittoria, at No 343, serves simple Italian dishes using fresh quality produce in a setting best described as a tribute to the mamma herself, with a mosaic portrait on the front of the building and copies of her collection of recipes available at the door. Mains Range from $12 to $17.50.

At No 376 is the **Robbie Burns Hotel**. Don't be fooled by the distinctly nondescript look of this pub, inside you'll find, incongruously enough, that they serve the best paella in town – the huge dish for two is $14 per person.

RICHMOND (MAP 5)
Victoria Street

Walk down Victoria St and you'll soon realise why this area has become known as 'Little Saigon'. Melbourne's growing Vietnamese community has transformed what was once a dull and colourless traffic route into a fascinating, bustling commercial centre. The stretch of Victoria St between Hoddle and Church Sts is lined with Asian supermarkets and grocers, butchers and fishmongers, discount stores selling Asian goods, and dozens of bargain-priced Vietnamese restaurants.

If you're coming by car, note that parking spaces are at a premium. Otherwise, tram No 42 or 109 from Collins St in the city will get you there.

Don't expect vogue decor in the restaurants, but the food will be fresh, cheap and authentic, and the service lightning fast and friendly. You can have a huge, steaming bowl of soup that will be a meal in itself for around $6, and main courses generally cost between $6 and $12, so you can afford to be adventurous.

One of the original, and still one of the most popular places, is **Thy Thy 1** (142 Victoria St), hidden away up a narrow, uninviting

The Price is Right

You don't have to push the funds to the maximum in an attempt to savour the best of Melbourne's cuisine. Some of the best and freshest dishes can cost no more than a few dollars, and the city is crammed with excellent options for the budget conscious. Here's just a few worth searching out.

Don Don Japanese Restaurant *(Map 2; 321 Swanston St)* is small, informal and pulls in a mixed crowd with its sushi boxes starting at $3.50 and noodle dishes from $5 to $7. **Kri Kri** *(Map 2; 39 Little Bourke St)* can be great value for a group. Share a mix of authentic Greek dishes at around $6 to $10 a pop, with a great selection for vegetarians. The Hare-Krishna run **Gopal's** *(Map 2; 139 Swanston St)* is another vegetarian option with very good Indian dishes. A meal here will only cost you about $8. **Ten** *(Map 2; 12 Centre Place)* is a hole-in-the-wall noodle shop with sushi for $1.50 a piece and delicious stir-fried noodles in a box for $6.50 to $7.50. **Sheni's Curries** *(Map 2; Shop 16, 161 Collins St)*, which you enter from Russell St, specialises mainly in Sri Lankan food with a smattering of South Indian dishes, and nothing is over $7. **Cafe Baloo's** *(Map 3; 260 Russell St)* offers a cheap 'n' cheerful mix of Italian and Indian food.

The Vegie Bar *(Map 3; 380 Brunswick St)* in Fitzroy is as popular as it is good. The wide range of hearty vegetarian dishes (generous in size) are well worth the price, with nothing over $8.50.

Visit any of the Vietnamese restaurants in Victoria St (Map 5), between Hoddle and Church Sts, in Richmond, and you are guaranteed fresh and delicious dishes at great prices. Over on Bridge Rd at No 430–32, the **Thai Oriental Cafe** *(Map 5)* has very fresh and very tasty Thai dishes from around $6 to $10.

Bala's *(Map 9; 1d Shakespeare Grove)* in St Kilda has a great mix of Indian and Thai snacks from $1.50 to $3.00 and main meals from $7 to $12.

set of stairs. This no-frills place is dirt cheap, but the food is fresh and excellent. The same people have a slightly more up-market place called **Thy Thy 2** down the road at No 116. Try the pork, chicken, prawn or vegetable spring rolls – 10 for $5, complete with mint and lettuce leaves for do-it-yourself construction.

Vao Doi, at No 120, is another good place to try, as is *Victoria* across the road at No 311. The menu here also offers Thai and Chinese food – and no, you can't eat those big fish in the tank up the back, they bring the owners good luck! *Tran Tran*, at No 76, is also popular.

Farther along at No 397, *Minh Tan III* is a bit more upmarket than most other places, and specialises in seafood. Mains cost from $10 to $15, with banquets around $22. At the city end of Victoria St, at No 66, *Tho Tho* is a cavernous, noisy but stylish bar-restaurant that fills up quickly most nights. Mains range from $7 to $12.

Only a slight detour from Victoria St, the *Carringbush Hotel* (☎ 9417 2918, 228 Langridge St, Abbotsford) is another old pub gone to pastures new. The excellent and reasonably priced modern-Australian food in an Aussie pub setting ensures that you should book in advance. Mains range from $12 to $20.

Swan Street

Richmond's Swan St, in the block east of Church St, has a small selection of Greek restaurants, all reasonably priced and with similar menus: an assortment of dips, such as tzatziki and taramasalata with pitta bread, souvlaki and sausages, sardines and calamari, stuffed peppers and moussaka – all the usual favourites. To get here from the city, take tram No 70 from Flinders St, across from the station, to the corner of Swan and Church Sts.

Elatos Greek Tavern (☎ 9428 5683, 213 Swan St) is one of the best in the area, with seafood a standout. Mains cost between $13 and $17. Across the road, the tiny *Salona* is also popular and a little cheaper. At No 258 *Nikita's Greek Tavern* (☎ 9428

9544) is another favourite, with live music on Saturday evenings.

Back-tracking down Swan St, the brightly painted **Mexicali Rose** *(☎ 9429 5550, 103 Swan St)* looks even brighter after a couple of frozen margaritas, and the menu offers a little more than the standard taco fare.

Bridge Road Area

Running parallel with and lying between Swan and Victoria Sts, Bridge Rd is slowly but surely making its presence felt on the culinary map. Take tram No 48 or 75 from Flinders St in the city.

Starting at the city end of Bridge Rd, **Chilli Padi**, at No18, serves authentic Malaysian food in an elegant setting. Noodle and vegetable dishes cost from $8 with other mains from $13 to $18.

At Nos 48–50, **Richmond Hill Cafe & Larder** *(☎ 9421 2808)* does everything extremely well. In this large, open, comfortable space, the breakfasts, lunches and evening dishes all have the touch of the simplicity and style you would expect from a place identified with celebrity chef Stephanie Alexander.

At 78 Bridge Rd, the **Tofu Shop** is an enduringly popular vegetarian cafe. It can be a tight squeeze at lunch time, and you might have to stand in line, but the healthy and hearty food is well worth the wait.

Across the road at No 61, the famed **Vlado's** *(☎ 9428 5833)* has a reputation for serving the best steaks in the country, and if you're into meat, followed by meat, and maybe more meat, you'll be more than happy to pay over $50 for the set menu.

Spargo's Sidewalk Cafe Bar *(☎ 9428 2656)*, at No 288, is another old pub that's been given the renovation treatment. It's not the most relaxing of places, with the sidewalk tables being the most sought-after location, but the wood-fired oven pizza is popular and there are a few good mains and desserts. A few doors up at No 314, **Groove Train** is a large restaurant-bar in retro style. It has comfy armchairs and sofa seating at the front, and a slightly more formal area at the back. It's great for either a drink and a lounge or a wood-fired pizza.

Farther up Bridge Rd at No 338, **Djakarta** *(☎ 9428 7086)* somehow manages to mix 1950s camp kitsch, rich dark colours and soothing lighting with fine Indonesian cuisine and friendly, professional service. It might sound strange, but it's a perfect balance. A stroll to the restrooms through the grotto-like-back garden is yet another pleasant surprise.

The **Curry Club Cafe**, at No 396, serves both traditional and modern Indian (often over-spiced) dishes in a postmodern Indian setting and incredibly noisy atmosphere. The **Thai Oriental Cafe**, at No 430–32, is as popular a takeaway as it is a cheap and cheerful Thai cafe, with unbeatable flavours at unbeatable prices (mains $6 to $10).

Kanzaman *(☎ 9429 3402)*, at No 458, serves Lebanese food that is almost upstaged by the large and fantastically moody interior. Expertly crafted wall murals and velvet drapes make this a must-see show.

Off bridge Rd at 64 Lennox St is the **All Nations Hotel** *(☎ 9428 5612)*. It's a little difficult to get to because of a series of one-way streets, but make the effort and you'll be rewarded with some of the best pub food in town. It's an original, honest and friendly pub, the sort of place everyone wishes they had as a local (if it wasn't so popular). It's open for lunch from noon to 3 pm daily and for dinner 6.30 to 9 pm Wednesday to Friday. Main meals range from $11 to $19.

SOUTH YARRA (MAPS 6 & 7)

Most of South Yarra's places to eat are along Toorak Rd and Chapel St. The No 8 tram heading south from the city will get you there.

Shopping is the main pastime here, with eating coming a close second. Foodwise, no particular cuisine dominates. Variety is the key, although being one of Melbourne's more affluent areas there aren't too many cheapies. Still, you'll find some honest Italian bistros, some good places to take lunch and rest your weary shopping feet, and dozens of cafes and restaurants ranging from the simple to the extravagant.

PLACES TO EAT

Toorak Road

Starting from the Punt Rd end, take a walk down to the Botanical Gardens to the **Observatory Cafe** on Birdwood Ave, beside the Melbourne Observatory. It's a tranquil spot for coffee and cake or lunch with a crisp white wine.

Back in the throng of things, **France-Soir** (☎ 9866 8569, 11 Toorak Rd) is a very stylish French brasserie with a reputation for being one of the best in town. A wide variety of classic French dishes are on offer, with mains from $18 to $24.

Pomme (☎ 9820 9606), at No 37, is fine dining in a modern setting to match. Dishes such as terrine of duck and pistachio served with a confit of gizzards ($17.50) and fillet of wild barramundi with crushed kipfler potatoes ($29) give you some idea of what Pomme is about.

On the other side of Toorak Rd, pop into the dainty **Frenchy's**, at No 76, for a coffee and one of its sublime French pastries (about $3). Next door at No 74 is the popular **Barolo's**, a narrow bistro with a warm feel and a pleasant rear courtyard. It has pasta for $11.50 to $16.50 and more expensive Italian-style mains. If your pocket isn't quite that deep, head down to **La Porchetta**, at No 93, for one of the best-value pizzas in town (from $5.50 to $8), with other mains under $13.50.

Next door, **Da Noi** (☎ 9866 5975, 95 Toorak Rd) is a tiny restaurant with an exciting Sardinian menu, with mains $17.50 to $29. Da Noi has a comprehensive selection of wines and is well worth a visit.

The wood-lined **Tamani Bistro** (156 Toorak Rd) and nearby **Pinocchio's** at No 152 are popular, cheap Italian restaurants in the casual-rustic mode. Pinocchio's is essentially a pizzeria, while Tamani is a more general bistro.

Over the hill and across the railway line is **Pieroni** (☎ 9827 7833, 172 Toorak Rd), a cavernous Italian bar-restaurant. Next door, highly acclaimed **Chinois** (☎ 9826 3388, 176 Toorak Rd) is a restaurant specialising in innovative East-meets-West cuisine. The lunch special is $22.50 for three courses plus a glass of wine, and the a la carte menu offers mains from $25 to $36.

A block east of the Chapel St intersection there's the strange spectacle of several almost identical Italian bistros, side by side, each fronted by a sun terrace with umbrella-shaded tables. All are popular, but for the record, the wood-lined **Davinci's** (304 Toorak Rd) is the cheapest and its immediate neighbour, **Vecchio Trastevere** the most expensive.

Chapel Street

Although there's a glut of cafes, bars and restaurants nestled in among the fashion boutiques between Toorak and Commercial Rds, the area is a little lacking in originality. Still, it's a good spot to refuel and soak up the Chapel St side show.

At No 581, **Caffé e Cucina** (☎ 9827 6076) brought a whole new approach and style to Melbourne's cafe culture. It has now been unashamedly plagiarised, but is as yet unmatched. Everything from the food and wine to interior decor in this small, dimly lit restaurant is close to perfection, although at times the waiters can be on the ridiculous side of arrogant. Next door at No 583, the **Greek Deli & Taverna** (☎ 9827 3734) shares the footpath with its famous neighbour, and the tastes, smells and sounds of Greece hold up well in this atmospheric taverna. Mains cost between $15 and $22.

A bit farther south, the friendly **Chapelli's**, at No 571, is a bar-restaurant with reasonable food, and most importantly, it's open round the clock. Right next door is **Kanpai**, a popular little Japanese restaurant with a pleasant atmosphere and some good-value dishes. Sushi starts at $3, teriyaki at $11.50.

Across the road at No 560, **Zampelli's Cafe Greco** is a sparse bar-restaurant with Greek-inspired food and red-leather booth seating. A very popular local favourite, **La Lucciola**, at No 487, is a long-running and reasonably priced Italian bistro with a good range of tried and tested dishes. **Kazbar** (☎ 9826 6442), opposite at No 481, is a very friendly and relaxed cafe-bar, great for a drink and a bite between shopping bouts.

Close to Commercial Rd, **The Argo** (☎ 9867 3344, 64 Argo St) is worth searching out in the maze of one-way streets. You can choose from the noisy bar-bistro where pizza and pasta are on offer, or relax in the more refined ambience of the restaurant, which offers excellent modern-Australian fare. Bookings are essential.

PRAHRAN (MAP 6)
Commercial Road
& Chapel Street

Commercial Rd is the border between South Yarra and Prahran. The Prahran Market (actually in South Yarra), is a terrific place to shop, with some of the best fresh fruit and vegetables, seafood and deli items this side of the city. Within the market complex there are a couple of reasonable places to lunch or snack, including the huge *Let's Eat*, which is part produce store and part food hall covering a range of cuisines. This stretch of Commercial Rd is something of a centre for Melbourne's gay and lesbian community (see that section of the Entertainment chapter), and down past the market there's a string of popular cafes and restaurants.

Near the market, at No 209 Commercial Rd, *Sweet Basil* is a good Thai place with noodle and curry dishes for around $13. Opposite the market, the *Blue Elephant Cafe*, at No 194, is a two-level cafe-restaurant with breakfasts starting at $5, pasta and pizza at $10.50, and other mains from $12.50 to $19.50. Nearby at No 176, *Chinta Ria* serves good Malaysian meals, ranging from $8 to $15, accompanied by a soundtrack of jazz and soul music. *Cafe 151*, at No 151, and *Alternative*, at No 149, are both stylish licensed cafes, while *Sandgropers*, at No 133, is a friendly cafe with a wide variety of dishes at reasonable prices.

East of Chapel St *Jacques Reymond* (☎ 9525 2178, *78 Williams Rd*) has few rivals in the best Australian restaurant category. Dining out at this grand Victorian mansion is an occasion for which you will pay not much less than the average weekly wage, but sometimes money shouldn't get in the way of a good night out. An evening of sumptuous modern-Australian cooking is one of them – treat yourself.

One of the best on Chapel St, *Blue Bar* (☎ 9529 6499, *330 Chapel St*) has an electric blue lightbox as its only signage, and

can easily be missed. An understated theme continues throughout this stylish bar, designed by the Six Degrees team who is responsible for Meyer Place and the Public Office. Japanese and seafood dishes are popular, but the menu also serves vegetarians as well. Farther down at No 218, the *Globe Cafe* is a local favourite with plenty of interesting mains on offer, good coffee and a great choice of cakes. Mains range from $9.50 to $14.

With its exotic and intimate interior and great food, *Patee Thai*, at No 135, is the best Thai restaurant in the area. Here the mains are $12 to $15, and there's a budget version of Patee Thai at Revolver (see Alternative Clubs in the Entertainment chapter).

If you're looking for good food and good value at this end of Chapel St during the day, try the licensed and unmistakably hued *Cafe Orange*, at No 126, where simple, tasty food and plenty of good tunes are a cure for the night that's been and a prerequisite for the night to come.

Wild Rice on Chapel (☎ 9533 8655, *159 Chapel St*) is a stylish, well-run macrobiotic-based vegan and vegetarian restaurant, serving clean and flavoursome food. The seasonal menu is more adventurous and extensive than that of the St Kilda branch. Mains cost between $11.50 and $14, and there is a selection of organic beers and wines.

Greville Street

Greville St, which runs off Chapel St beside the Prahran Town Hall, seems to be an ever-changing mishmash of young designer and retro clothing boutiques, bookstores, music shops, restaurants and cafes.

The licensed *Continental Cafe* (☎ 9510 2788, *132a–34 Greville St*) serves great breakfasts all day, but the mains are just as good ($9 to $18.50) in this very popular and stylish cafe-bar; the live music venue upstairs has dinner-and-show deals (see the Alternative Clubs section in the Entertainment chapter).

Across the street at No 143, the *Greville Bar* blends soft jazz tunes, dark wood interiors and an interesting modern-Australian menu, to create an atmosphere perfectly

Where to Find the Best

Rather than settle for second best, here are tips that money can't buy!

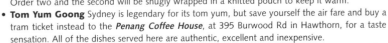

SIMON BRACKEN

- **Caffè Latte** For consistency and attention to detail, *Wall Two 80*, at the rear of 280 Carlisle St, Balaclava, gets it right every time. Perfect strength and perfect temperature will have you ordering a second within minutes.
- **Boiled Eggs** Without any hesitation, *Richmond Hill Cafe & Larder*, at 48–50 Bridge Rd, comes out on top every time – they know a badly boiled egg will ruin your day. Order two and the second will be snugly wrapped in a knitted pouch to keep it warm.
- **Tom Yum Goong** Sydney is legendary for its tom yum, but save yourself the air fare and buy a tram ticket instead to the *Penang Coffee House*, at 395 Burwood Rd in Hawthorn, for a taste sensation. All of the dishes served here are authentic, excellent and inexpensive.
- **Pizza by the Slice** For Roman-style pizza with a great choice of toppings, St Kilda's *cafe a taglio*, at 157 Fitzroy S,t is the best in town.
- **Martini** Dress up and drop into the *Gin Palace* in a laneway at 190 Little Collins St, where Manhattan comes to Melbourne and Luis Buñuel's martini recipe will have you tripping the light fantastic.
- **Fish and Chips** For fish and chips by the seaside, you can't go wrong at St Kilda's *Acland Seafood & Sushi*, at 92 Acland St, and *Clams Fast Fish*, at 141 Acland St.
- **Spanakopita** Any Melburnian in the know heads down to *Melissa's Coffee Lounge*, at 118 Smith St in Collingwood, where the delicious spanakopita disappears as quickly as it comes out of the oven.
- **Kosher Snacks** As well as its famous bagels, blintzes and latkes, many more mouth-watering delicacies can be found at *Glick's Cakes and Bagels*, 330a Carlisle St, Balaclava.
- **Sourdough Bread** Join the queue at *Firebrand Sourdough Bakery*, 69 Glen Eira Rd, Ripponlea, where the 'staff of life' comes organic, chemical-free and way too good to miss.
- **Chocolates** Head down to the Block Arcade, where *Haigh's* have been dealing in the finest milk and dark chocolates for decades.

suited to an intimate table for two. For something on the run, pop into the *trés* sceney *Candy Bar*, at No 162, for delicious snacks, drinks and a chat. For those wishing to linger a while, DJs are playing most nights, making this a great place for an impromptu boogie.

ST KILDA (MAP 9)

Established as a beach resort for the wealthy, St Kilda became home to Russian and Polish emigres in the 1940s. In the 1970s, artists, musicians, refugees from the suburbs and a colourful mix of seedy low-life flocked here to take advantage of the raffish atmosphere and cheap rental accommodation, transforming the suburb yet again. In the 1990s St Kilda was discovered by the caffè latte crowd, with focaccia becoming more popular than mozza ball soup, and chicken Kiev making way for spaghetti pesto. A dingy flat became a 'studio apartment' and real estate prices hit the roof. The transformation is now virtually complete, and even Luna Park has been given a face lift.

Fitzroy and Acland Sts are where the majority of cafes and restaurants are to be found, and there are also some good places down by the sea.

PLACES TO EAT

Fitzroy Street

Fitzroy St was once the domain of junkies and prostitutes, and the only other reason to visit the suburb was to grab a cheap pasta or pizza at Leo's Spaghetti Bar. There's still a lot of money passing hands here, but these days it's mostly diners parting with their cash. Gentrification happened quickly after the first few restaurateurs were brave enough to take the risk. The frenzy of development that followed has seen Fitzroy St become one of the best and most popular eating spots in the city.

The beach end of Fitzroy St is an obstacle course of busy cafes and sidewalk tables and chairs. In the commotion, blink and you'll miss the place you're looking for. Starting from this end, *One Fitzroy Street Restaurant* (☎ 9593 8800) has postcard views of the bay and street from the first-floor restaurant. Quality seafood and beef dishes are favourites, with mains $18 to $26. A few doors up, *Madame Joe Joe* (☎ 9534 000, 9 Fitzroy St) is a yardstick for style and subtlety. The soaring ceilings, leadlight frontage and, best of all, the gorgeous modern-Australian cuisine make it a must. A standout in quality, the tiny *Superbo* (☎ 9534 7332, 19 Fitzroy St) produces a mix of European-style dishes from $9 to $20 that keep it up there with the best.

Cafe Barcelona (☎ 9525 4244, 25 Fitzroy St) veers somewhat from the traditional Spanish menu – some dishes work and some don't – but the original wood-panelling and simple design make it a great place to eat. On the corner of Fitzroy and Acland Sts, *circa, The Prince* (☎ 9536 1122, 2 Acland St) burst onto the scene with a flurry of ooohs and aaahs. The exceptional modern French cuisine, served in a setting worthy of the best in fine dining, ensures that the adjectives (and maybe a few expletives when the bill arrives) will continue to flow for some time to come. Next door (on Acland St), *Il Fornaio* is a large concrete car park shell transformed into one of the best Italian bakery-cafes in the city.

Café di Stasio (☎ 9525 3999, 31a Fitzroy St) was one of the first restaurants on Fitzroy St, and is still one of the best. Classic Italian food and cosy sophistication make it an occasion worth the cost. With complete indifference to the changing face of Fitzroy St, *Leo's Spaghetti Bar* (55 Fitzroy St) maintains its position as a St Kilda icon, and the reasonably priced Italian dishes are on a suitably large scale.

Across the street, *Tolarno Bistro* (☎ 9525 5477, 42 Fitzroy St) is famous for its hamburgers ($7.50) and its gregarious TV chef Ian Hewitson. There is a choice of hearty seafood and meat dishes costing $13 to $20.

Back on the busy side of the street, *97* (☎ 9525 5922, 97 Fitzroy St) is a small cafe serving Mediterranean-style food with mains from $9 to $20. *Chichio's*, at No 109, is a popular and inexpensive Italian cafe – big with backpackers and the budget conscious.

On the corner of Fitzroy and Grey Sts, the once grand George Hotel stood tattered and torn for years. The vast potential wasn't lost on the local restaurateur who has transformed this ailing giant into one of the most popular bar-restaurants around. *The George Melbourne Wine Room* (☎ 9525 5599, 125 Fitzroy St) is a welcome respite from the noisy front bar (where excellent bar meals are available). The splendid wine list and excellent menu of modern Italian-Australian dishes (mains $22 to $28) are just two reasons for the wine room's well-deserved popularity.

At the city end of Fitzroy St, *cafe a taglio* at No 157 is the best place in the city for pizza served up by the slice. The choice of toppings include mushroom and gorgonzola, mozzarella and parmesan, and the delicious potato and leek – all at around $3.50 to $4.50 a slice. Next door, *Cleopatra's* (☎ 9525 4222) dishes up great Lebanese food, including an excellent felafel and superb cardamom-flavoured coffee.

Acland Street Area

Acland St is renowned for its fine European delicatessens and cake shops, and the traditional Sunday promenade has always included a spell of gloating at window displays where an impossibly delicious selection of delights tempt even the most resolved of wills.

On the corner of Acland and Fawkner Sts, a couple of European-style places have stood the test of time. *Spuntino* is a relaxed Italian cafe serving focaccia, pasta, antipasto etc, while two doors up, at No 54, the *Dog's Bar* was the first cafe-bar in the area and continues to be one of the most popular, although the distressed paint finish is looking a little too much like the real thing. You can choose from tapas-style snacks with a drink at the bar, or a meal from the Italian-influenced menu, with mains $7 to $15.

Just off Acland St, the *Galleon Cafe (9 Carlisle St)* began its life as a hangout for St Kilda's alternative residents. For years it has fuelled the juices of the creative community with simple and inexpensive cafe-style food. It's still inexpensive and the menu has changed only slightly to include a few more evening dishes such as Atlantic salmon with bok choy and mashed potatoes ($12.50). Not too far away, near the corner of Inkerman and Barkly Sts, *Luxe (☎ 9534 0255, 13 Inkerman St)* might seem a little cold and industrial in the design department, but don't be put off – the modern French cooking is as exciting as it is affordable in this award-winning restaurant, with mains ranging from $16.50 to $20.

Wall Two 80, across Brighton Rd at 280 Carlisle St, is as fantastic as it is simple. This renovated kosher butcher's shop-cum-local cafe serves one of the best coffees in the city, and the basic menu of toasted pide with assorted fillings ensures that everything happens at speed.

Back on Acland St at No 94, *Chinta Ria (☎ 9525 4664)* mixes fine Malaysian food with the sounds and images of jazz and soul. Judging by its popularity (you will need to book), it's a marriage that seems to work. Main meals are $8.50 to $16.50. Farther up at No 6 Acland St, *Chinta Blues* is more suited to the fan of the 12-bar format.

Across the road in Shakespeare Grove, *Bala's* is an excellent and inexpensive eat-in or takeaway cafe specialising in Thai, Malaysian and Indian dishes.

Scheherezade (99 Acland St) and the *Blue Danube (107 Acland St)* are a reminder that St Kilda is a suburb with a central European past. Hearty dishes such as Russian borscht, Hungarian goulash, cabbage rolls and gefilte fish are as popular as ever with the old-timers in these refreshingly low-key restaurants.

At No 130, *Cicciolina* is a small, cosy and very popular Italian bistro. Deep-fried oysters ($9.50) and delicious risotto with shiitake mushrooms and black truffle oil ($15.50) are just a couple of the dishes that make it well worth the visit. *Veludo (☎ 9534 4456, 175 Acland St)* is both an upstairs restaurant and a dark neo-1950s downstairs bar, which serves less-expensive meals. Unlike the bar, the restaurant is light and open with a fantastic view over Acland St, offering fine dining in a relaxed setting. Mains are between $18 and $25. A few doors up at No 189, the *189 Espresso Bar* is a small and very popular re-fuelling spot for the St Kilda set. It's worth pushing your way in for a good coffee, snacks and light meals.

On the corner of Acland and Barkly Sts, *Big Mouth* is a small downstairs cafe-bar with a sprawling upstairs restaurant, both with reasonably priced meals. At 211 Barkly St, *Wild Rice* makes great use of a tiny space – don't miss the dreamy courtyard garden. The simple menu is based on macrobiotic principles and hits the spot for vegetarians and carnivores alike, with a selection of organic snacks, savoury pies, bakes and casseroles. Around the corner, the popular and even smaller *Rasa's Vegie Bar (5 Blessington St)* has been pumping out vegetarian rice balls, tofu and lentil burgers, stir-fries and curries since the beginning of time.

Seaside St Kilda

Right on the foreshore, *The Stokehouse (☎ 9525 5555, 30 Jacka Blvd)* has the location that everyone dreams about. The upstairs restaurant affords wonderful views of the bay and the menu combines classic French cuisine with spicy Asian flavours. Downstairs, the atmosphere is loud and frenetic and the menu a lot simpler with antipasto, burgers, fish and chips, and gourmet pizza, all from around $10 to $17.

PLACES TO EAT

Nearby, ***Donovans*** *(☎ 9534 8221, 40 Jacka Blvd)* has an equally good beachside position. The upmarket beach-house atmosphere, complete with log fire, is complimented by excellent meat and seafood dishes and a very good wine list. Mains are between \$14 and \$30.

ALBERT PARK (MAP 7)

If you're in Albert Park with an appetite, just follow the No 1 tram line, which runs down to the beach. Most of the area's eateries are along this route.

Vic Ave Pasta & Wine *(135 Victoria Ave)* is a bustling Italian bistro with a rear courtyard. Farther along, ***99 East*** *(☎ 9686 8199, 99 Victoria Ave)* successfully combines a diverse array of flavours in a series of mainly Asian-influenced dishes – with mains from \$10 to \$15. ***Misuzu's***, at No 7, is a small and extremely popular 'village-style' Japanese cafe, with a menu that takes a pleasant stroll away from more traditional Japanese fare.

With its wide footpaths and classic Victorian architecture, Albert Park is a pleasant and relaxed spot with a thriving cafe scene. There are some excellent places around Bridport St and Victoria Ave in the strip known as Dundas Place. On Bridport Rd, the ***Albert Park Deli***, ***Villagio Deli*** and ***Dundas & Faussett*** all serve good coffee, cooked breakfasts, focaccia, filled croissants, salads, pasta and home-made cakes. You can eat in, take it away or enjoy the view from a sidewalk table.

Ricardo's Trattoria *(☎ 9699 5536, 99 Dundas Place)* is a smart and popular open-fronted little Italian bistro serving traditional Italian dishes, with mains starting at \$19.

Heading towards Middle Park, ***Le Petit Cafe*** at 40–42 Armstrong St is an unassuming little place serving simple but delicious French cafe food.

SOUTH MELBOURNE (MAP 7)

Home to the South Melbourne produce market, advertising agencies and video production houses, this historic suburb has plenty of good cafes and restaurants. Park and Clarendon Sts are the most popular areas.

Kobe Japanese Restaurant *(☎ 6990 2692)*, at 179 Clarendon St, is a simple Japanese restaurant with good main meals in the \$14 to \$18 range. Farther up at ***est est est*** *(☎ 9682 5688, 440 Clarendon St)*, husband and wife celebrity chefs team up to provide an exquisite display of culinary flair – if fine dining is your passion, then this is just about the finest.

The ***Limerick Arms***, on the corner of Clarendon and Park Sts, is a revamped pub with a pleasant courtyard restaurant, and bar meals for around \$10. At 254 Park St, ***The Near East Restaurant*** *(☎ 9699 1900)* offers a good range of quality South-East Asian dishes, with the emphasis on fresh ingredients. Mains cost from \$15 to \$20.

Formerly the Centenary Hotel, ***O'Connell's*** *(☎ 9699 9600, 193 Montague St)* is an extremely popular bar and bistro where celebrity chef Greg Malouf's exciting mix of Middle East/Mediterranean cooking has the punters lining up at the door. Mains cost between \$22 and \$26.

The ***Isthmus of Kra*** *(☎ 9690 3688, 50 Park St)* is one of Melbourne's best and most elegant Asian restaurants. Delicious southern Thai dishes with a Malaysian influence cost between \$13 and \$21, and banquets (four or more people) are \$30 to \$45 – you'll need to book.

WILLIAMSTOWN (MAP 8)

Williamstown has an abundance of cafes and restaurants, most of them spread along Nelson Place. The influx of day-trippers and weekend visitors gives Williamstown the feeling of a smaller and more manageable version of St Kilda.

Aquis Cafe & Restaurant *(☎ 9397 2377, 231 Nelson Place)* has a stylish cafe-bar downstairs and an even more impressive restaurant upstairs. The open balcony is a great spot to enjoy the modern European-style cooking and the cool sea breeze. Mains cost between \$15 and \$20.

Hobson's Choice Foods *(213 Nelson Place)* is an extremely popular street-front cafe with everything from pies and brioches to breakfasts, sandwiches and vegetarian meals. Nearby at No 203, ***Scuttlebutt Cafe***

is 1950s-style and friendly with reasonably priced snacks and meals. Next door, ***Docks of Williamstown*** is sparsely decorated inside and on a sunny day most of the action takes place at the busy sidewalk tables. The menu is international with a wide range of seafood and meat dishes. The lunch specials board is also worth a look.

The next stretch of Nelson Place, west of the Cole St roundabout, also has a few good places. ***Atomic Bar*** has a good cafe downstairs and a billiards club upstairs. Near the Syme St corner, ***Sam's Boatshed*** is built around an old sailing ship with a menu consisting of pasta and wood-fired pizza.

On the southern side of the peninsula overlooking the sandy Williamstown Beach is ***Siren's*** (☎ *9397 7811)*, on The Esplanade. It's a converted bathing pavilion that incorporates a smart bar and bistro, an open-air, timber-decked area and an elegant restaurant with a leaning towards Mediterranean flavours.

The Strand (☎ *9397 7474)*, on the corner of The Strand and Ferguson St, is stylish, simple and ultra-modern, with a small bar, an open-air courtyard and good views over the bay. The menu is predominantly seafood, with main courses in the $15 to $30 range. There's an upmarket ***fish and chippy*** next door.

Another good option is ***The Anchorage*** (☎ *9397 6270)*, half a kilometre north along The Strand at No 34. This former boat shed sits over the water and has a cosy maritime feel, with timber decking, fishing nets hanging from the roof and a wonderful outlook across the bay to the city skyline. Seafood is a speciality, with main courses costing around $23.

Entertainment

Melbourne has a thriving nightlife, a lively cultural scene and some great bars and nightclubs. The city offers everything from stand-up comedy and live music in a crowded pub to opera at the Melbourne Concert Hall or a play at one of its dozens of theatres.

The best source of 'what's on' information is the *Entertainment Guide (EG)*, published every Friday in the *Age* newspaper. *Beat* and *Inpress* are free music and entertainment magazines, each with reviews, interviews and a comprehensive gig guide. They're available from pubs, cafes and venues.

Ticketmaster is the main booking agency for theatre, concerts, sports and other events. For inquiries ring ☎ 9645 7970 or ☎ 13 6100. To make credit-card bookings for sporting events call ☎ 13 6122; for theatre and arts events call ☎ 13 6166. The telephone service operates from 9 am to 9 pm Monday to Saturday, 9 am to 5 pm Sunday. Besides taking bookings by phone, Ticketmaster has outlets in places such as Myer, major theatres and shopping centres.

If you're after cheap tickets, visit the Half-Tix (Map 2; ☎ 9650 9420) booth in the Bourke St Mall, which sells half-price tickets to shows and concerts on the day of the performance. There are usually some great bargains going, but make sure you find out where you'll be sitting, as obviously they don't sell the best seats in the house at half-price. Half-Tix opens from 10 am to 2 pm Monday and Saturday, 11 am to 6 pm Tuesday to Thursday, and 11 am to 6.30 pm Friday. Cash payments only.

PUBS & LIVE MUSIC VENUES

For the bigger local and international acts, Melbourne's main live music venues are the National Tennis Centre (Map 2), the Melbourne Concert Hall at the Victorian Arts Centre (Map 2), Festival Hall (Map 2), the Forum Theatre (Map 2) and the Palais Theatre (Map 9). Some (mainly classical) concerts are held at the outdoor Sidney Myer Music Bowl (Map 2) in Kings Domain.

Melbourne is widely acknowledged as the country's rock capital, and has long enjoyed a thriving pub-rock scene where internationally successful bands such as AC/DC, INXS and Nick Cave & the Bad Seeds took their first tentative steps towards becoming part of rock's rich tapestry. There's still plenty around but in recent times the pub-rock scene has taken a bit of a nose dive, with beer swilling and the bump and grind of hard-assed rock'n'roll making way for a tab of E, electronic live acts and DJ sounds. This cultural change has resulted in pubs either attempting to cross over and cater to both markets, or giving up operating as live venues altogether. Overseas trends suggest that the swing back to bands and beer is likely.

To find out who's playing what and where, look in the *EG*, *Beat* or *Inpress*, or listen to the gig guides on FM radio stations such as 3RRR (102.7) and 3PBS (106.7), both of which are excellent independent radio stations.

Pubs

The HiFi Bar & Ballroom (Map 2; ☎ 9654 7617), at 125 Swanston St in the city, is a popular venue where more successful home-grown acts such as the Screaming Jets perform. Also in the city, on the corner of Queensberry and Elizabeth Sts, *Arthouse (Map 3; ☎ 9347 3917)*, at the Royal Artillery Hotel, is the place to head if you're

ENTERTAINMENT

into death metal and the occasional poetry or country night.

In St Kilda, the legendary *Esplanade Hotel (Map 9; ☎ 9534 0211, 11 Upper Esplanade)* has free live bands every night and on Sunday afternoon. It's also a good place to just sit back with a beer and watch the sun set over the pier, or have a meal in the Espy Kitchen out the back. *The Prince (Map 9; ☎ 9536 1166, 29 Fitzroy St)* in St Kilda has been given a bit of a face lift and is no longer its seedy former self. The *Greyhound Hotel (Map 9; ☎ 9534 4189)*, on the corner of Carlisle St and Brighton Rd, is small, sweaty and as authentic as you'll get, with bands most nights.

On the corner of Brunswick and Kerr Sts, the *Evelyn Hotel (Map 3; ☎ 9419 5500)* has gone a little bit upmarket, but is still one of Fitzroy's major band venues. Across the road at 376 Brunswick St, the grungy *Punters Club (Map 3; ☎ 9417 3006)* has bands most nights. The *Builders Arms (Map 3; ☎ 9419 0818)*, at 211 Gertrude St, is another good Fitzroy watering hole. Just down the road in Collingwood, the *Tote (Map 3; ☎ 9419 5320, 71 Johnston St)* is a popular pub with a good mix of cheap live music.

Richmond used to be something of an enclave for rock pubs, but these days only the *Corner Hotel (Map 5; ☎ 9427 7300, 57 Swan St)* manages to hold its own. In North Melbourne, there's the laidback *Town Hall Hotel (Map 3; ☎ 9328 1983)*, at 33 Errol St, and *The Keeper's Arms (☎ 9329 7081, 351 Queensberry St)* where sporting fans, particularly the soccer-crazy, can swill a pint while watching live telecasts and video replays.

Folk & Acoustic Music

If you're into more mellow music, the *EG* has an 'Acoustic & Folk' listing. One of the main venues is the *Dan O'Connell Hotel (Map 4; ☎ 9347 1502)*, at 225 Canning St in Carlton. As a measure of its Irishness, it claims to sell more Irish whisky than Scotch. Another popular Irish pub is *Molly Bloom's Hotel (Map 7; ☎ 9646 2681)*, on the corner of Bay and Rouse Sts in Port Melbourne, which has traditional Irish folk music seven nights a week.

Jazz & Blues

There are some great jazz joints in the city centre. Hidden down a narrow lane off Little Lonsdale St (between Exhibition and Russell Sts), *Bennetts Lane (Map 2; ☎ 9663 2856)* is a quintessential dim, smoke-filled jazz venue, and it's well worth searching out. It's open every night except Tuesday until around 1 am, and until 3 or 4 am on weekends.

Dizzy's Jazz Bar (☎ 9428 1233, 90 Swan St, Richmond) occupies the National Trust-listed old post office building. Large and spacious with a good bar, Dizzy's is a great spot to blow your horn. Opens from 8 pm Thursday to Saturday; music is from 9 pm.

Ruby Red (☎ 9662 1544), at 11 Drewery Lane (near the corner of Swanston and Lonsdale Sts), is an old warehouse with a dimly lit bar, a restaurant and a small stage. It has live jazz, soul, R&B and blues from Tuesday to Saturday nights – you'll need to book if you're coming for dinner. *Purple Emerald Lounge Bar (Map 2; ☎ 9650 7753)*, at 191 Flinders Lane, is spacious and relaxed, with jazz, funk, Latin and soul acts.

Quite a few pubs also have good jazz and blues sessions on certain nights – check the gig guide in the *EG*. Places worth trying include *Spleen Central (Map 2; ☎ 9650 2400)* at 41 Bourke St in the city; *Limerick Arms (Map 7; ☎ 9690 0995)* in South Melbourne; the cosy *Commercial Hotel (☎ 9689 9354)*, 238 Whitehall St in Yarraville; the *Rainbow Hotel (Map 3; ☎ 9419 4193)*, 27 St David St in Fitzroy; the *Grace Darling Hotel (Map 3; ☎ 9416 0055)*, on the corner of Smith and Peel Sts in Collingwood; and the *Emerald Hotel (Map 7; ☎ 9690 4719)*, 415 Clarendon St in South Melbourne.

During January and February, the Royal Melbourne Zoo in Parkville has an extremely popular 'Zoo Twilights' season of open-air sessions, with jazz or big bands performing from 7 to 9.30 pm on Thursday, Friday, Saturday and Sunday nights. Call the recorded information line (☎ 9285 9333) for details.

NIGHTCLUBS

Melbourne's club scene is a diverse and mixed bag, and what's here today might be gone tomorrow. Clubs range from barn-sized

asket cases

Cooking up a storm at Melbourne Food & Wine Festival

Asian snacks

poilt for choice at Prahran Market

Aboriginal river float, Moomba Festival

Melbourne International Festival

discos, where anyone is welcome, to the small and more exclusive places where you stand a good chance of a knock-back at the door. Cover charges range from $5 to $15, although some places don't charge at all.

Most places have certain dress standards, but it's generally at the discretion of the door staff to decide whether or not you are dressed for the occasion.

Mainstream Clubs

The city centre is home to most of Melbourne's mainstream clubs, and the *Metro* *(Map 2; ☎ 9663 4288)* at 20 Bourke St is the best of them. It's an enormous club with eight bars on three levels, and plenty of variety on offer.

King St in the city is a well-known but less than recommendable club hot spot. There is a cluster of places here, including *Inflation (Map 2; ☎ 9614 6122)* at No 60.

Just outside the city centre, the *Chevron (Map 7; ☎ 9510 1281)*, at 519 St Kilda Rd, has been around forever. It's a huge place with a mixture of DJs and live bands, a cocktail bar and cheap drink deals. Nearby, the *Dome Nightclub (Map 7; ☎ 9529 8966, 19 Commercial Rd)* has four bars and a great choice of sounds with everything from Asian dance nights to house and retro.

Billboard, at 170 Russell St, the *Mercury Lounge*, at the casino, *Silvers*, at 45 Toorak Rd, and the long-running *Chasers (Map 6)*, at 386 Chapel St in Prahran, are other mainstream clubs.

Heaven (Map 7; ☎ 9696 2777) at the Carousel, an upmarket bar and restaurant overlooking Albert Park Lake from Aughtie Drive, has dance, house and techno nights.

Alternative Clubs

Melbourne has a vibrant alternative club scene. Some bars also double as clubs, and most venues play host to a variety of styles. The best way to keep up with what's happening is to check the alternative club pages in the entertainment papers.

In the city, *Lounge (Map 2; ☎ 9663 2916)*, upstairs at 243 Swanston St, was first in with the retro style and it's still a popular venue featuring everything from

Latin rhythms and soul grooves to techno (Wednesday) and hip-hop. *Velour (Map 2; ☎ 9663 5589)*, at 121 Flinders Lane, is a long dark club-bar with a touch of kitsch and plenty of variety in the DJ sounds. *Club 383 (Map 2; ☎ 9670 6575)*, at 383 Lonsdale St, is a popular haunt for fans of retro and indie pop. The *Up Top Cocktail Lounge (Map 2; ☎ 9663 8990)*, upstairs at 163 Russell St, looks like a hangout for beatniks and cool cats with its 1950s style and feel. Drinkers and dancers are well catered for here with a good bar and mix of DJs and styles. At 169 Exhibition St, *Club UK (☎ 9663 2075)* is for homesick lovers of all things Brit pop (if only they had a Supergrass night!).

The *Continental Cafe (Map 6; ☎ 9510 2788)*, above the restaurant of the same name at 132a–34 Greville St in Prahran, is a relaxed and sophisticated cabaret-style venue with a choice of dinner-and-show deals from $35 to $55, or standing-room-only from $15 to $20.

Revolver (Map 6; ☎ 9521 5985, 229 Chapel St) is a popular venue with a young crowd, art-covered walls and a packed program featuring DJs, bands, film nights and spoken word. The cavernous space includes a lounge area and the very good and inexpensive Patee Thai restaurant.

Dream (Map 3; ☎ 9349 1924), at 229 Queensberry St in Carlton, is one of the best alternative venues, covering everything from gothic on Friday to indie/alternative on Saturday.

In Fitzroy, the *Night Cat (Map 3; ☎ 9417 0090)* at 141 Johnston St is a large, comfortable space with a great atmosphere, skewwhiff 1950s decor (a Melbourne trademark) and jazz, soul and contemporary bands. The *Laundry (Map 3; ☎ 9419 6115, 50 Johnston St)* happily mixes everything from live music and DJs to film and gay and lesbian nights.

BARS

Melbourne's pub scene has been dissipated over the last few years with the invasion of gambling machines in pubs. What were once lively hubs where friends could get

The ABC of nocturnal pursuits

together have become alienating gambling dens frequented by what appear to be the living dead. In reaction to this, a new underground movement of bars and clubs has appeared in the heart of the city and the inner suburbs. What was initially born out of necessity is now a Melburnian obsession, and the thriving scene has fast become an important part of the city's cultural landscape. Hidden at the top of a dark staircase or lost in a laneway, this instinctive, human and altogether individualistic approach is very much in keeping with the character of the city, in stark contrast to the corporate greed and monster developments that have been so prevalent in recent times. With an ingenious use of design, clever utilisation of often limited space and a fascination with a 1950s to 1970s retro look, the new wave of bars has created an aesthetic that is quite unique to Melbourne.

City Centre

In Little Collins St, the *Gin Palace (Map 2; ☎ 9654 0553)*, at No 190, is the transmutation of a side alley basement into a sophisticated, dimly lit and beautifully furnished New York-style cocktail bar. One killer martini and you're away. The *Hairy Canary (Map 2; ☎ 9654 2471)*, at No 212, is long and low ceilinged with a bright and breezy atmosphere that gets more frenetic as the evening progresses. It's as popular an eating spot as it is a bar.

Tony Starr's Kitten Club (Map 2; ☎ 9650 2448), upstairs at No 267, mixes 1950s and 1970s moderne style as successfully as it does its cocktails. Terrific atmosphere and a good menu.

The *Purple Emerald Lounge Bar (Map 2; ☎ 9650 7753, 191 Flinders Lane)* has the luxury of being long and spacious, and the ubiquitous 1970s lounge chairs and light fittings make an appearance. As the night gets into full swing so does the dancing and live acts, with everything from funk, acid, Latin and jazz.

Downstairs at 55 Elizabeth St, *e:fifty five (Map 2; ☎ 9620 3899)* is a cosy Internet lounge and bar with comfy sofas and chairs that melds the 1950s with modern technology making it a great spot to have a beer and get connected.

Meyer Place (Map 2; ☎ 9650 8609, 20 Meyer Place) paved the way for many a Melbourne bar with its disparate mix of design elements. It's small and dark with a partially stripped ceiling, shag-pile and velvet-curtained walls, beer on tap and a simple drinks list.

Spleen Central (Map 2; ☎ 9650 2400, 41 Bourke St) has a grungy retro atmosphere, with plenty of couches and armchairs on which to lounge. Like Meyer Place nearby, Spleen is a good bar to have a drink and relax with friends.

Misty (Map 2; ☎ 9663 9202, 3–5 Hosier Lane) is how a bar in the year 2000 might have been visualised through the eyes of an early 1970s movie set designer. Turns out he would have been right. Can get very crowded and high on the decibel count as the evening progresses.

Scubar (Map 2; ☎ 9670 2400, 389 Lonsdale St) feels like you've walked into a nuclear bunker that's been renovated by a mad collector of retro junk. Features include a fish tank, waterwall, leopard-skin pool table and a very cute little dance floor.

Troika (Map 2; ☎ 9663 5461, 106 Little Lonsdale St) brings a bit of collage to the bar scene, with plenty of artworks dotted around to catch the eye.

Vis (Map 2; ☎ 9662 9995, 245 Swanston St) is located below Lounge and owned by the same people. The stylish decor and warm atmosphere make it a good spot for a quiet drink or a meal.

Rue Bebelons (Map 2; ☎ 9663 1700, 267 Little Lonsdale St) is a small cafe-bar that's popular with a mainly student crowd. It doesn't take too many bodies to fill this place, but the relaxed atmosphere is conducive to having a quiet chat over a coffee or drink .

The Melbourne Supper Club (Map 2; ☎ 9654 6300, 1st floor, 161 Spring St) is reminiscent of an English gentlemen's club, the idea being that you throw yourself onto a leather lounge or armchair and wait for the table service to arrive. A great place to enjoy a terrific bottle of wine and a light supper with friends.

Other Areas

There are some great bars in the inner suburbs well worth searching out. The *Public Office (Map 2; ☎ 9321 6500, 100 Adderley St)* is a little removed from the thick of things, but it's a great spot for a drink. On the top floor of an old building overlooking Docklands and the railway yards, it offers a quite unusual view of Melbourne. Another bar worth trying is the very tasty *Blue Bar (Map 6; ☎ 9529 6499)*, at 330 Chapel St in Prahran (see the Places to Eat chapter).

With its dim lighting, ornate furniture and gold-and-vermilion flocked wallpaper, *Yelza (Map 3; ☎ 9416 3977, 245 Gertrude St, Fitzroy)* is baroque style incarnate. You'll find that the garden bar is also good during the balmy months. *The George Lane Bar (Map 9; ☎ 9534 8822, 127 Fitzroy St, St Kilda)* is a sparse and stylish bar tucked away behind the George Hotel.

A few other great bars worth visiting include the *Globe Back Bar (Map 6; ☎ 9510 8693)*, at 218 Chapel St, Prahran, and in St Kilda *Mink (Map 9; ☎ 9536 1199)*, at 2b Acland St, *Glow Bar (☎ 9593 9000)*, at 140

Acland St, and the long and skinny *Veludo (Map 9; ☎ 9534 4456)*, at 175 Acland St.

GAY & LESBIAN VENUES

The following venues are specifically for gays and lesbians, but most venues in the new generation of bars and nightclubs are 'gay friendly'.

Commercial Rd around the Prahran Market is Melbourne's 'gay precinct', and here you'll find the popular *Market Hotel (Map 6; ☎ 9826 0933, 143 Commercial Rd)*, which is open from 9 pm until late Thursday to Saturday and from 5 pm until late Sunday, and which attracts a mixed crowd. There's plenty of dance-floor action and drag shows. The *Exchange Hotel (Map 6; ☎ 9867 5144)*, at No 119, is a popular spot.

Collingwood has some good men's venues. *The Peel Hotel (Map 3; ☎ 9419 4762)*, on the corner of Peel and Wellington Sts, is one of the best known and most popular. DJs big on trance, house and garage music keep the dance floor the centre of attention. *The Laird (Map 5; ☎ 9417 2832)* at 149 Gipps St is a gay men's pub catering to an older leather crowd, with pool tables, a beer garden and theme nights.

Also in Collingwood, the *Glasshouse Hotel (Map 5; ☎ 9419 4748)*, on the corner of Gipps and Rokeby Sts, is a mainly women's pub. It has entertainment nightly, including drag, bingo, pool competitions and karaoke.

Sunday Prince (aka *Homosexuelle*), upstairs at Prince (Map 9) in St Kilda, from 5 until 8 pm on Sunday, attracts an eclectic and eccentric crowd. Saturday nights, from 11 pm until very late, you'll find *Freakazoid* at the back of the Chevron (Map 7).

CINEMA

Melbourne has plenty of mainstream cinemas playing latest releases, although if you've come from the US or Europe they might be last year's latest. The main chains are Village, Hoyts and Greater Union, and the main group of city cinemas can be found around the intersection of Bourke and Russell Sts. Tickets cost around $9.50 during the day, around $11.50 at night. Check

SIMON BRACKEN

Moody nights at Myer Place

ENTERTAINMENT

the *EG* in Friday's *Age* or other newspapers for screenings and times.

Melbourne also has an excellent collection of independent cinemas that feature arthouse, classic and alternative films, although it can be difficult to find much variety when it comes to the classics, other than the re-cut and the re-issued type. However, *Cinémathèque* has screenings at Cinemedia *(☎ 9650 2562, Lower Plaza, 1 Macarthur St, East Melbourne)* at Treasury Theatre, formerly the State Film Theatre, 7 pm every Wednesday night.

Independent cinemas include the not-to-be-missed Art Deco nostalgia of the *Astor (Map 9; ☎ 9510 1414)* on the corner of Chapel St and Dandenong Rd in Prahran, with double features every night (and great ice creams!). Other good alternative cinemas include the ever-expanding *Cinema Nova (Map 3; ☎ 9347 5331)*, at 380 Lygon St in Carlton; the *Kino (☎ 9650 2100)*, in Collins Place (Map 2), at 45 Collins St in the city; the *Longford (Map 7; ☎ 9867 2700)*, at 59 Toorak Rd in South Yarra; the twin *George Cinemas (Map 9; ☎ 9534 6922)*, at 133 Fitzroy St in St Kilda; the *Lumiere (Map 2; ☎ 9639 1055)*, at 108 Lonsdale St in the city; the *Trak (☎ 9827 9333)*, at 445 Toorak Rd in Toorak; and *Cinema Europa (☎ 9827 2440)*, in the Jam Factory (Map 6) on Chapel St.

The *Chinatown Cinema (☎ 9662 3465)*, at 200 Bourke St in the city centre, screens Chinese films.

Open-Air Cinema

During the summer months, the wonderful open-air **Moonlight Cinema** (☎ 9427 1311) in the Royal Botanic Gardens screens classic, arthouse and cult films, commencing sundown. Tickets cost $12/8 for adults/children. Bookings are handled by Ticketmaster (☎ 13 6100) and tickets can be bought at the gate from 7.30 pm onwards – entry is through Gate F on Birdwood Ave. BYO rug, picnic basket and wine! For screening details ring (☎ 1900-933 8990) or check out the Web Site at www.moonlight.com.au.

The cinemas at the universities also have interesting and inexpensive nonmainstream screenings. The closest to the city centre are the *Union Theatre (☎ 9344 6976)* at the University of Melbourne (Map 4) and the *Union (☎ 9660 3713)* at RMIT (Map 2).

Melbourne's *IMAX Theatre (Map 3; ☎ 9663 5454)* is part of the new museum complex near the Royal Exhibition Building in the Carlton Gardens. As is the norm with IMAX, you can expect a huge spectacle on a grand scale. Great for kids both big and small.

THEATRE

The *Victorian Arts Centre (Map 2; ☎ 9281 8000)* on St Kilda Rd is Melbourne's major venue for the performing arts. Flanked by the Yarra River on one side and the National Gallery of Victoria on the other, the complex houses the Melbourne Concert Hall and three theatres – the State Theatre, the Playhouse and the George Fairfax Studio.

If you're in Melbourne during the summer months watch out for the excellent open-air theatre productions staged in the Royal Botanic Gardens. See the *EG* listings or ring Ticketmaster for details.

Theatre Companies

The *Melbourne Theatre Company (MTC; ☎ 9684 4500)* is Melbourne's major theatrical company, with performances at the Victorian Arts Centre. The MTC stages around 15 productions each year, ranging from contemporary and modern (including many new Australian works) to Shakespearean and other classics.

Melbourne has a number of other major theatre companies. *Handspan Visual Theatre (☎ 9645 5331)* performs at various theatres. This group is Australia's foremost puppet-theatre company. Their work has a strong visual element, using effects such as shadow screens and animation, and their strength is children's theatre.

La Mama's Theatre (Map 3; ☎ 9347 6948) is at 205 Faraday St, Carlton. Historically significant to Melbourne's theatre scene, this tiny, intimate forum produces new Australian works and experimental

theatre, and has a reputation for developing emerging playwrights

Playbox *(Map 7; ☎ 9685 5111)* is located at the CUB Malthouse Theatre, at 113 Sturt St, South Melbourne. This outstanding company stages predominantly Australian works by established and new playwrights.

Theatreworks *(Map 9; ☎ 9534 3399, 14 Acland St)* combines community theatre and storytelling with diverse and innovative productions.

Melbourne's other major theatres venues include:

Athenaeum Theatre (Map 2; ☎ 9650 1500) 188 Collins St, Melbourne
Comedy Theatre (Map 2; ☎ 9242 1000) 240 Exhibition St, Melbourne
National Theatre (Map 9; ☎ 9534 0221) cnr Barkly and Carlisle Sts, St Kilda (once the home of Melbourne opera, now a popular community venue)
Princess Theatre (Map 2; ☎ 9299 9800) 163 Spring St, Melbourne (venue for musicals)
Regent Theatre (Map 2; ☎ 9299 9500) 191 Collins St, Melbourne (venue for musicals)
Universal Theatre (Map 3; ☎ 9482 5633) 13 Victoria St, Fitzroy (off-beat productions from comedy to narrative)

Melbourne also has such a huge amateur and fringe-theatre circuit that the magazine *Stage Whispers* is devoted solely to fringe and amateur news (see that magazine or the *EG* for listings of current productions).

The opulent facade of the Princess Theatre

COMEDY

Melbourne prides itself on being the home of Australian comedy, although its ability to laugh at itself was brought into question when American comedian Jerry Seinfeld suggested that Melbourne was the anus of the world (well, geographically speaking, at least).

Barry Humphries is without doubt the city's most famous and most brilliant comedian. His sardonic wit and playfully derisive jibes at his homeland are not always played just for laughs. For a fascinating and hilarious insight into growing up in mid-20th century Melbourne, Humphries' autobiography *More Please* is a must.

A very healthy stand-up comedy circuit has developed over the last couple of decades in Melbourne, and since 1987 the International Comedy Festival has been held in the city each April. During the festival the city becomes a giant venue, with local comedians joining forces with international acts (including many from the famous Edinburgh Festival) to perform in pubs, clubs, theatres and on the city streets.

Melbourne has a few regular comedy venues and nightspots where stand-up comics stand or fall. Look in the *EG* for weekly gigs.

The **Comedy Club** *(Map 3; ☎ 9348 1622)*, at 380 Lygon St in Carlton, is a good cabaret-style comedy venue with regular shows. The **Prince Patrick Hotel** *(☎ 9419 4917)*, at 135 Victoria Parade in Collingwood, is another old stager in the comedy scene. Other stand-up venues include the **Waiting Room** *(☎ 9534 0211)*, in the Esplanade Hotel's (Map 9) Gershwin Room, on the Upper Esplanade, St Kilda; the **Star & Garter** *(☎ 9690 5062)*, at 70 Nelson Rd, South Melbourne, which has comedy on Thursday nights; and **Edward's Tavern** *(☎ 9510 9897)*, 211 High St, Prahran, with comedy every second Monday night.

POETRY READINGS

Some of Australia's best young poets (and some of the older ones) read their poetry at **La Mama** *(Map 3; ☎ 9347 6948, 205 Faraday St, Carlton)* at 8 pm on the first Monday of most months.

Several pubs and other venues have regular performance poetry sessions, and newcomers are usually welcome to listen or even perform their own work. Venues include the **Dan O'Connell Hotel** (Map 4; 9347 1502), at 225 Canning St in Carlton; the **Empress Hotel** (Map 4; 9489 8605), at 714 Nicholson St in North Fitzroy; the **Evelyn Hotel** (Map 3; 9419 5500), on the corner of Brunswick and Kerr Sts in Fitzroy; **Lounge** (Map 2; 9663 2916), in Swanston St in the city; and the **Arthouse** (Map 3; 9347 3917), on the corner of Queensberry and Elizabeth Sts. Check the 'Readings' listing in the EG for more details.

GAMBLING

Gambling swept through Melbourne like a plague during the 1990s, leaving a trail of financial devastation and cultural destruction in its wake. That might sound like a puritanical and hysterical over-reaction, but the architects of Melbourne's so-called 'casino-led recovery' definitely have a lot to answer for.

First came the introduction of poker machines. Seemingly overnight, hundreds of pubs and clubs were converted into nauseously identical 'gaming rooms' – live-music venues, restaurants and bars had to make way for the pokies, and instead of bands, bistros and conversation, pubs were filled with people sitting moronically feeding money into coin slots, watching lemons spin round and round.

Then in 1993 Melbourne got its own casino. Flooded on a daily basis with thousands of people wanting to shed their excess cash, the casino has quickly become an extremely effective tool for the redistribution of wealth – the rich get richer, while the poor pour money they don't have into the casino's coffers. And as the casino thrives, hundreds of other local businesses – restaurants, retailers, theatres etc – claim to be suffering as a direct result. Meanwhile, the churches and welfare groups are left to try to clean up the social destruction.

Melbourne's massive **Crown Casino** (Map 2) dominates the south bank of the Yarra, and is open 24 hours a day.

SPECTATOR SPORT

Australians in general, and Melburnians in particular, are fanatical supporters of sport, especially when it comes to watching it. The two biggest events on the sporting calendar are a horse race and a game of Australian rules football!

Melbourne Cup & Spring Racing Carnival

Horse racing takes place in Melbourne throughout the year – at Flemington, Caulfield, Moonee Valley and Sandown – but spring is when the culture of racing is at its most colourful and frenetic.

The Melbourne Cup, one of the world's greatest horse races, is the feature event of Melbourne's Spring Racing Carnival, which runs through October and finishes with the Melbourne Cup early in November. The carnival's major races are the Cox Plate, the Caulfield Cup, the Dalgety, the Mackinnon Stakes and the holy grail itself, the Melbourne Cup. Apart from these races, Derby Day and Oaks Day feature prominently on the spring racing calendar.

The two-mile (3.2km) Melbourne Cup, which is always run on the first Tuesday of November at Flemington Racecourse, was first run in 1861. The Cup brings the whole of Australia to a standstill for the three or so minutes during which the race is run. Cup day is a public holiday in the Melbourne metropolitan area, but people all over the country are affected by Melbourne's spring racing fever. Serious punters and fashion-conscious racegoers pack the grandstand and lawns of the Victoria Racing Club's beautiful Flemington Racecourse. The city's once-a-year betters make their choice or organise Cup syndicates with friends, and the race is watched or listened to on TVs and radios in pubs, clubs, TAB betting shops and houses right across the land.

Tickets for reserved seats in the Lawn Stand can be booked through Ticketmaster (☎ 13 6122) and cost around $75. If you've not booked, you can just front up on the day and buy a general admission ticket for around $25.

The Footy

Without a doubt, Australian rules football – otherwise known as 'the footy' – is the major drawcard, with games at the Melbourne Cricket Ground (MCG; Map 3) regularly pulling crowds of 50,000 to 80,000. If you're here between April and September you should try to see a match, as much for the crowds as for the game. The sheer energy of the barracking at a big game is exhilarating. Despite the fervour, crowd violence is almost unknown.

The Australian Football League (AFL) runs the nationwide competition, and while there are teams based in Perth, Adelaide, Sydney and Brisbane, Melbourne is still considered the game's stronghold. It's also the place where Aussie rules football was created: on 7 August 1858, the first game was played between Melbourne Grammar and Scotch College on the very spot where the MCG and its car parks now stand. The playing field was a rough 1.5km-long paddock, and each team had 40 players. There was no result after the first day, so the teams met on the following two Saturdays, at the end of which the game was declared a draw. Since then the footy rules have been (slightly) refined.

Being the shrine of Aussie rules, the MCG is still widely regarded as the best place to see a match, although the opening of the new Colonial Stadium (Map 2) in Docklands, which boasts a retractable roof and state-of-the-art facilities, looks set to poach many events from the MCG's sporting and entertainment calender.

Tickets can be bought at the ground for most games, and entry costs $13.50/7.50/2 for adults/concessions/kids under 14 (and you'll need another few dollars for the obligatory pie and a beer). Reserved seats can be booked (this might be necessary at big games) through an agency such as Ticketmaster for $23.50.

Cricket

The MCG (Map 3) is one of the world's great sports stadiums. For any cricket fan, or general sports fanatic, a visit to the MCG is not only compulsory but something of a

Winners & Losers

It's virtually impossible to say a bad word about the Aussie rules Grand Final, the highlight of Melbourne's sporting calender. Trying to tell a Melburnian you're not interested in the footy is like trying to tell a lemming not to throw itself off a cliff. If you find yourself in the city on this, the most important day of the year, just give in to the mayhem. Pick a team, buy a scarf, wave a flag, have a beer, watch the match on TV, celebrate with the winners and commiserate with the losers. Come Sunday, the madness will be over for another year.

pilgrimage. During the summer, international test matches, one-day internationals and the Pura Milk Cup (formerly the Sheffield Shield, the national cricket competition) are all played here. General admission to international matches is around $26 and reserved seats start at around $32, with finals costing more.

Motor Sports

Melbourne hosts both the Australian Formula One Grand Prix and the Australian round of the World 500cc Motorcycle Grand Prix. The Formula One takes place in Albert

Sit back and relax!

PHIL WEYMOUTH

ENTERTAINMENT

Park (Map 7) in March, and the motorcycles race at Phillip Island (Map 10) in October. Tickets for the Formula One Grand Prix cost around $33 to $80 for a day ticket, $135 to $270 for a 4-day ticket and $290 to $480 for a grandstand ticket. Tickets can be bought through Ticketmaster (☎ 13 6100) or the Grand Prix hotline (☎ 13 1641). For drag racing, head out to Calder Thunderdome, just outside the city on the Calder Fwy.

Tennis

For two weeks each January the Melbourne Park National Tennis Centre (Map 2), on Batman Ave (south-east of the city centre), hosts the Australian Open tennis championships. Top players from around the world come to compete in the year's first of the big four Grand Slam tournaments. Tickets are available through Ticketek (☎ 13 2849) and range from about $25 for early rounds to $90 for finals.

Basketball

Basketball became hugely popular in the 1990s when the frenzy of advertising and marketing reached saturation point. National Basketball League games are of a high standard and draw large crowds, the main venue being Melbourne Park National Tennis Centre (Map 2). The season runs from October to March, and tickets are

around $15 to $20 and can be booked through Ticketek (☎ 13 2849).

Soccer

Soccer has always had a strong fan base in Melbourne, with the Italian and Croatian communities being particularly avid followers of the game. Interest has been strengthened in recent years with the overseas success of home-grown players and the continued improvement of the national side. The national soccer league season, which includes four Melbourne teams, commences in October and finishes in May. For details on home matches and venues contact the Victorian Soccer Federation (☎ 9682 9666).

Rugby

Rugby union has been slow to catch on in Melbourne, but despite this the MCG attracts enormous crowds to international matches.

Rugby league, on the other hand, has made a huge impact on Melbourne's sport-mad public. Melbourne Storm – the only Melbourne side in the national league – won the Grand Final in 1999 after competing in the league for only a couple of years, heralding wild celebrations that were evidence of the game's meteoric rise in popularity.

April to September is the season for both codes. Melbourne Storm's home matches are played at Olympic Park.

Shopping

Melburnians' love of shopping is as great as their passion to eat, and discussion on both topics can be a heart-felt affair. The closure of the revamped Georges department store in 1999 was a classic example. The epitome of style and sophistication, Georges was the Titanic of Australian department stores, with cafes, a restaurant and four floors of shopping elegance. The news of its demise rocked the city's shopping fraternity, who were shocked to discover that Melbourne's shoppers (unlike New York's and London's) didn't have the spending power to sustain a store of Georges' calibre and price tags.

Shopping in Melbourne continues to be a highlight for many visitors. A thorough investigation into the city's shopping possibilities requires a fair amount of inner-suburb hopping, so use your feet in the city and tram it to the suburbs. It's impossible to cover every great option on offer; this list covers a wide range and will get you to the shopping hot-spots, giving a good indication of what you can expect to find there.

CITY CENTRE (MAP 2)
Department Stores

Standing side by side, Myer and David Jones dominate much of the Bourke St Mall.

Myer (☎ 9661 1111) stretches from the mall back to Lonsdale St, and its fare covers everything from cosmetics, jewellery, homewares and food to ladies' and men's fashion and a comprehensive sporting emporium. David Jones (DJs; ☎ 9643 2222) has stores on both sides of the mall and covers the same range of goods but is just that little bit more upmarket; DJs has a particularly good food department.

At 30 Lonsdale St, in the Melbourne Central shopping complex, Daimaru (☎ 9922 1100) is an expensive Japanese store with a range of ladies' and men's fashion labels, cosmetics, homewares and a food hall.

Shopping Radar

City Centre The masses hit the mall for the department stores, while the style-conscious make a bee-line for Collins and Little Collins Sts, the old arcades and hidden laneways.

Fitzroy This is the suburb where style wars are waged in cafes, bookshops, speciality shops and, most of all, on the street.

Prahran Home to Greville St and the refreshingly downbeat end of Chapel St, Prahran is where all things retro are washed ashore.

Richmond Here designer-label factory outlets rub shoulders with an authentic slice of Asia.

South Yarra The beautiful and the damned share the pavement where designer chic and cafe culture meld into one.

St Kilda Weekend revellers, beach bums and cutting-edge fashion groupies take to St Kilda's bookshops, clothing stores, cafes and delicatessens.

Clothing & Jewellery

Collins Street Le Louvre (☎ 9654 7641) resides at the top of Collins St at No 74, but in reality is beyond most of us. Behind the couturier's classic and enigmatic facade, the rich and famous are measured up for the likes of Westwood, Givenchy, Lagerfeld and Galliano. Cosi Ipanema (☎ 9650 1364), at No 123, is great for a $400 shirt and a gander through the hallowed collections of the likes of Dolce & Gabbana, Issey Miyake and Gaultier. The sparse but opulent former banking chambers at 161 Collins St house the excellent New Zealand designer labels Zambesi (☎ 9654 4299), Helen Cherry and Workshop (☎ 9639 5589). Other imported labels to choose from here include Helmut Lang, Nom D and Martin Margiela.

If you're after the Aussie bushranger look, RM Williams (☎ 9662 9126), at No 180, is the place for a no-nonsense Driza-bone (an

The Big Store

Russian-born Jews Simcha and Elcon Baevski left poverty and persecution behind when they fled Russia for Australia in the late 1890s. After working as hawkers tramping around country and rural Victoria with their fabrics, clothing, buttons and thread, the brothers took advantage of the possibilities offered by their adopted country. In 1900 Simcha (by this time calling himself Sidney Myer) and his brother opened a small drapery store in Bendigo. The novelty of being able to walk around the store looking at and touching the goods, rather than having to stare at them from over a counter, proved extremely popular. In 1911 Sidney Myer employed architects HW and FB Tompkins to design his new Bourke St store, based on San Francisco's Emporium. This was the beginning of a huge business empire that was to shape the future of shopping in Melbourne.

CHRIS MELLOR

oilskin stockman's coat), trousers, boots, Akubra hats and more. The Polo Ralph Lauren (☎ 9654 0374) store, at No 181, is the first of its kind in Australia, and the atmosphere is suitably rarefied in keeping with this stylish and upmarket leisurewear label. Farther down Collins St, the Sportsgirl Complex (☎ 9650 6755), at No 234, and Australia on Collins (☎ 9650 4355), at No 260, are large mall arcades with ladies' and men's fashion, homewares, gift shops and inexpensive food courts.

Little Collins Street This street is a hot spot for men's and women's designer clothing, as well as for modern and antique jewellery. At No 324, Klepners (☎ 9650 2659) has been dealing in traditional antique jewellery since 1889. Across the street, Ina Barry Gold & Silversmith (☎ 9650 3355), at Shop 36 Block Place, displays a love of amber in her uniquely modern designs. Nearby, Love It (☎ 9654 1226), at Shop 22, Royal Arcade, could be dangerous for the impulse buyer, with its wonderful range of contemporary jewellery incorporating semiprecious stones.

At 279 Little Collins St, Scanlan & Theodore (☎ 9650 6195) continues to be one of the city's finest designers of quality women's clothing. Howey Place is a hub for such fashion, where names like Stellini, Andrea Yasmin, Saba, La Bella Donna, Alan-

nah Hill and Jacqui Fernandes rub shoulders. Farther up the hill Calibre (☎ 9654 8826), at Shop 3, 182 Little Collins St, is very much for the beautiful young men among us, with a fine collection of neat-fitting shirts, pants and jackets, as well as name imports such as Dolce & Gabbana, Hudson and Vivienne Westwood. Nearby, Roy (☎ 9654 9951) is a must for men, offering a nonconformist and odd mix of street and designer wear. Opposite at No 185, e.g.etal (☎ 9663 4334) has a great selection of contemporary jewellery by local designers. Next door you'll find AG (☎ 9663 6488), a Melbourne-based menswear designer label with a great line in suits. Victoria Triantafyllou (☎ 9639 7668), at No 171, and Victoria Loftus (☎ 9662 9779), at No 173, specialise in elegant evening wear for women, while Verve (☎ 9639 5886), at No 177, is part cafe, part women's fashion store, where you can sweat over your dog-eared credit cards while sipping your caffè latte.

Outdoor & Workwear

The best place to shop for quality outdoor gear is around the intersection of Hardware Lane and Little Bourke St. In Hardware Lane you'll find Auski (☎ 9670 1767) at No 9, and the Melbourne Ski Centre (☎ 9670 2855) at No 17. In Little Bourke St, Patagonia (☎ 9642 2266) is at No 370, Platypus Outdoors (☎ 9602 4303) is at No 385,

Bogong Equipment (☎ 9600 0599) is at No 374 and Snowgum (☎ 9670 1177) is around the corner at 366 Lonsdale St.

Australia produces some of the world's best surfing equipment and surf/streetwear. A couple of places worth visiting are the Melbourne Surf Shop (☎ 9654 8403) in the Tivoli Arcade, at 249 Bourke St, and Surf Dive 'N' Ski (☎ 9650 1039), at 213 Bourke St.

Sam Bear (☎ 9663 2191), at 225 Russell St, is a great place to go for tough, durable work clothing and footwear. Brands such as Blundstone and Redback for boots, and King Gee and Hard Yakka for shirts and pants are popular for both work and casual wear. It's also a good place for camping and walking gear, woollen hats and warm socks.

Akubra hats are incredibly popular with travellers and an essential item during the summer months. Good city hat shops include City Hatters (☎ 9614 3294), beside the main entrance to Flinders St Railway Station at 211 Flinders St, and Top Hatters (☎ 9650 2063), at Shop 19, 259 Collins St.

Books, Maps & Stationery

With its curved and sloping shop design, Page One (☎ 9654 3886), at 179 Collins St, is famed for its fine selection of art, architecture and graphic design titles. Of similar note are Architext (☎ 9650 3474), at 41 Exhibition St, and Art Salon (☎ 9662 2918), at 5 Crossley St. Farther down Collins St, at No 259 in the Centre Way Arcade, Tafts the Pen People (☎ 9654 7993) have been experts at putting the right pen in the right hand since 1906. At basement level in the arcade, the Foreign Language Bookshop (☎ 9654 2883) covers everything from travel guides, language kits and dictionaries to foreign-language novels and air-freighted newspapers.

Around the corner at 107 Elizabeth St, Officeworks (☎ 9670 1644) is spread over two floors and caters to your every office and stationery need. The ABC Bookshop (☎ 9626 1167, Shop 26 Galleria Shopping Plaza, 385 Bourke St) specialises in ABC TV and radio-related books, tapes, videos and merchandising. For things that go bump in the night try the spooky Haunted Bookshop (☎ 9670 2585, 15 McKillop St) for a cornucopia of the paranormal. A couple of blocks across town at 372 Little Bourke St, Map Land (☎ 9670 4383) is the place to be if you're lost on the lonely planet. Back on track, Deans Art (☎ 9602 2184), at 369 Lonsdale St, can equip everyone from budding watercolourist to the master in oils with its extensive range of art supplies.

At the top of Bourke St, Mary Martin Bookshop Cafe (☎ 9663 9633), at No 108, the Hill of Content (☎ 9662 9472) bookshop, at No 86, and the small but excellent Paperback Bookshop (☎ 9662 1396), at No 60, make this a great area to browse and buy.

Records & CDs

Large mainstream music stores in the city include Sanity (☎ 9654 5833) and HMV (☎ 9654 8533), in the Bourke St Mall, and JB Hi-Fi, at 289 Elizabeth St – *the* place for discounted CDs and tapes.

Interesting independent stores around town include Gaslight (☎ 9650 9009), at 85 Bourke St (open nightly till late); Missing Link (☎ 9654 5507), at 262 Flinders Lane; and Au Go Go (☎ 9670 0677), at 349 Little Bourke St. Discurio (☎ 9600 1488), at 105 Elizabeth St, stocks a wide range of classical, jazz, blues and folk recordings.

Aboriginal Art

Although prices for Aboriginal artworks are way out of reach for the average traveller, more affordable art-and-craft works on sale include prints, baskets, small carvings, decorated boomerangs, didgeridoos, music sticks etc, and the work of Aboriginal craft cooperatives. See Other Art Galleries in the Things to See & Do chapter for galleries specialising in Aboriginal art.

In the city centre, the following places offer a wide range of bark paintings, didgeridoos and other handicrafts from all over the country: the Aboriginal Gallery of Dreamings (☎ 9650 7291), 73–77 Bourke St; Aboriginal Creations (☎ 9662 9400), Shop 3, 50 Bourke St; AustraLias Indigenous Creations (☎ 9650 0855), Shop 5, 108 Bourke St; and Aboriginal Handcrafts (☎ 9650 4712), 130 Little Collins St.

Crafts & Souvenirs

Australian souvenirs are available from dozens of places around town. In the city, places worth checking out include the Australiana General Store, at Shop 32, Collins Place, and Monds Gifts & Souvenirs Store (☎ 9650 1739), at 133 Swanston St.

The opal is Australia's national gemstone, and opals and opal jewellery are popular souvenirs. Gem and opal stores in town include Andrew Cody Opals (☎ 9654 5533), on the 1st floor at 119 Swanston St; Bentine Gems, on Level 2, Grand Hyatt Shopping Court; Altmann & Cherny, at 120 Exhibition St; and John H Mules (☎ 9650 3566), at 110 Exhibition St.

Specialist Stores

The Anti-Cancer Council Shop (☎ 9642 3801) at 115 Elizabeth St is the place to get sun smart with sunglasses, sun creams, hats, children's cossies and more. Further up Elizabeth St at No 211, Bernard's Magic Shop (☎ 9670 9270) runs the gamut from fart cushions to blood capsules, along with more sophisticated tricks for the less childish prankster.

Hearns Hobbies (☎ 9614 3603), at 295 Flinders St, is a great place for kids and adults alike with a vast array of hobby pursuits – plastic kits, model trains, balsawood and modelling accessories, to mention just a few.

Genki (☎ 9650 6366) can be found at Shop 5 in the small and lovely Cathedral Arcade, 37 Swanston St. Here designer clothing and some rather eccentric footwear share the tiny space with cutesy Japanese toys and accessories.

Markets & Produce Stores

The Queen Victoria Market, on the corner of Victoria and Elizabeth Sts, is Melbourne's best and most famous produce market, not only for the diversity of its produce, but also for the bustling atmosphere and historic setting. The market is open from 6 am to 2 pm Tuesday and Thursday, 6 am to 6 pm Friday, 6 am to 3 pm Saturday and from 9 am to 4 pm Sunday. On Sunday most of the fruit, vegetable, meat

and fish stalls are closed, replaced by vendors selling jewellery, clothes, souvenirs, antiques and bric-a-brac. (See the Things to See & Do chapter for details of walking tours of the market.)

As well as being a fine restaurant, Becco (☎ 9663 3000), at 11–25 Crossley St, specialises in quality, but pricey, fruit and veg, seafood, meat, pasta, bread and deli products – handy for those staying in serviced accommodation. Coles Express (☎ 9654 3830), at 2 Elizabeth St, is open 24 hours – perfect for night owls and city dwellers alike.

The Sunday market at the Victorian Arts Centre starts at 10 am and has arts and crafts from around the state. For those willing to venture farther into suburbia, the Sunday morning trash-and-treasure market held in Camberwell's huge shopping car park is well worth the tram fare (Nos 70 and 75 heading east from Flinders St Railway Station).

SOUTHGATE & CROWN ENTERTAINMENT COMPLEX (MAP 2)

There's plenty of choice for shoppers over this side of the river, but essentially Southgate is just another mall without much atmosphere. Crown can boast outlets for some of the world's top designers – Prada, Armani, Versace and DKNY – in a showy but totally uninspiring setting.

FITZROY & COLLINGWOOD (MAP 3)
Clothing & Jewellery

Dangerfield (☎ 9416 2032), at No 289, is great for streetwear and club clobber. Douglas & Hope (☎ 9417 0662), around the corner at 80 Johnston St, is a small but lovely shop selling women's designer clothing and – for something different – gorgeous quilts. Back on Brunswick St, at No 362, A Jewellery Store Named Desire (☎ 9415 9915) is a tempting mix of stylish designs and glittery surprises. At No 348, the Ministry of Style (☎ 9419 4952) sells streetwear at full volume. If you have a hankering for New Zealand designer wear, try Chroma (☎ 9486 0032), at No 415. Retro clothing stores appear and disappear at this end of Brunswick St as quickly as the fashions do, so there's no point listing them. See for yourself!

Stephen Davies (☎ 9419 6296), at 65 Gertrude St, is the man to see if you're in need of a pair of classic but stylish men's or women's shoes made to order. If you're a burly bloke with a penchant for the Priscilla look, drag yourself down to It's My World (☎ 9415 9776) at 197 Gertrude St for the best range in clothing for the cross-dresser.

At 78 Smith St, Vegan Wares (☎ 9417 0230) is an exciting store for those who don't want to wear dead animals on their feet but like a bit of style. Excellent, durable and well-made shoes (and bags) should finally put an end to that tired old argument 'but you wear leather shoes, how can you be a vegetarian!' Farther up at No 321, DNA Concepts (☎ 9419 7083) has a great selection of rave and streetwear clothing, jewellery and accessories.

Bookshops

The Brunswick St Bookstore (☎ 9416 1030), at 305 Brunswick St, is a friendly and informal store with a wide range of art and literature titles. Farther up at No 330, Polyester Books (☎ 9419 4961) specialises in the things that other bookstores don't, including underground literature, erotica and adult comics. At No 379, Grub Street Bookshop (☎ 9417 3117) is an excellent secondhand bookstore with an especially good section on Irish history and literature.

Records & CDs

Polyester Records (☎ 9419 5137), at 387 Brunswick St, is great for grunge, while Sister Ray (☎ 9417 3576), at No 260, covers a wider range and also has a selection of books.

Specialist Stores

At the rear of 230 Brunswick St (enter via St David St), Juggleart (☎ 9417 7772) is the perfect place to pick up some gear before you run away to join the circus. Tea Too (☎ 9417 3722), at No 340, has a huge and varied selection of teas for sale in an otherwise coffee-dominated suburb. At 24 Smith

St, Maison de Tunisie (☎ 9416 1385) is a tiny shop specialising in all things North African, including ceramics, homewares, foods and bath products.

Markets & Produce Stores

Simon Johnson (☎ 9486 9456), at 12–14 St David St, is a must for lovers of gourmet foods, deli items, ingredients and accessories. Nothing here comes cheap, except the free coffee while you browse, but you may be tempted nevertheless.

CARLTON (MAP 3)

Lygon St is an old-fashioned, veranda-covered shopping strip that is home to high-street chains such as Sportsgirl and Country Road, various Italian delicatessens and one of Melbourne's most popular bookshops, Readings (☎ 9347 6633), at No 309. Readings has three other stores located in Hawthorn, Malvern and South Yarra. The Lygon St branch hosts up to two literary events and readings per week, when local and international authors get up and show us what they're made of. Events programs can be picked up at any Readings store.

RICHMOND (MAP 5)
Clothing & Jewellery

Shoppers flock to Bridge Rd and Swan St between Punt Rd and Church St, where a plethora of factory outlets and seconds stores specialise in designer labels such as Jag, Trent Nathan, Sportsgirl, Kamikaze, Country Road, Fiorelli, Aquila Shoes and more. Exentrix (☎ 9428 7771), at 307 Bridge Rd, has a good selection of samples and first runs by young designers.

Victoria St, in the stretch between Church and Hoddle Sts, is known as Little Saigon, and you'll see why when you go there: Vietnamese restaurants, Chinese herbalists, produce stores, fish stalls and gift shops all jostle for position.

SOUTH YARRA (MAP 6)

For years Chapel St has had a reputation as Melbourne's style strip – it's where designers such as Scanlan & Theodore set up their first retail outlet – and it's still one of the most popular hang-outs for the fashion and style makers, watchers and wearers.

Clothing & Jewellery

Chapel St is chock-a-block with clothing stores and cafes, as well as retail chain stores such as Sportsgirl, Jigsaw, General Pants and Atelier.

Country Road (☎ 9824 0133), on the corner of Chapel St and Toorak Rd, stocks a range of conservative but stylish men's and women's clothing, shoes and accessories as well as a small selection of homewares.

Collette Dinnigan (☎ 9827 2111), at No 553, is the darling of Australian fashion, and every waif wants to squeeze into her detailed and fragile garments. At No 509, Christopher Graf (☎ 9826 4711) pushes the boundaries of taste with its cartoon interior and exaggerated design. The women's clothing isn't quite as loud, but it's strong enough to take a little style and a lot of courage to wear it. Mooks (☎ 9827 9961), at No 491, makes dressing down a lot easier than dressing up, with a good line in casual streetwear and accessories.

The Body Beautiful

Stressed out and in need of pampering? Reflexology, shiatsu massage, acupuncture, aromatherapy or simply a relaxing spa are just a few of the therapies Melburnians (both male and female) can choose as an antidote to the strains of modern city life. The holistic approach is just as popular for those in search of a glowing skin, with everything from seaweed wraps and plant therapy to hydrating facials and scalp massage on the menu. For the business person wishing to look and feel their best when clinching that all-important deal, or the traveller run ragged while trying to enjoy a holiday, here's a few places worth a visit. But remember, beauty doesn't come cheap!

- **Geisha** (☎ 9663 5544, 1st floor, 285 Little Collins St) Hair, health and massage are all on offer at Geisha, with a range of Japanese-influenced packages covering the lot.
- **Balnae Aroma Spa** (☎ 9654 2455, Level 5, Australia on Collins, 260 Collins St) Balnae offers soothing and gentle spas, body mud wraps, executive massages and beauty therapy treatments.
- **Aveda** (☎ 9654 2217, Shop 318, Australia on Collins, 260 Collins St) Environmentally friendly and big on holistics, there's a wealth of plant and flower based products here to treat both body and mind. A range of facial and body treatments are also available.
- **Jurlique** (☎ 9827 8719, 433 Chapel St, South Yarra) Jurlique has a wealth of excellent skin-care products and essential oils (all organically and biodynamically produced in South Australia); it also provides a range of facials, massages and aromatherapy treatments.
- **Klein's Perfumery** (☎ 9416 1221, 313 Brunswick St, Fitzroy) This is the perfect one stop shop where you'll find the best range of products to liven up your looks and leave you smelling sensational. Blooms, L'occitane, Aesop, Jurlique, Ambre and Klein's own range are all stocked here.
- **The Japanese Bath House** (☎ 9419 0268, 59 Cromwell St, Collingwood) If you're all shopped out, treat yourself to a soothing soak and a sauna at this traditional bath house. Shiatsu massage is available here, and bookings are essential for all visits.
- **Man, What a Fuss** (☎ 9642 3860, 5 McKillop St) For hair treatments, massages, facials, manicures and pedicures, Man leaves no stone unturned in an attempt to get the guys looking their best.
- **Vince & Dom Hairdressing** (☎ 9663 1335, 98 Little Bourke St) For an inexpensive trim or short back and sides by a traditional barber, blokes should head to the heart of Chinatown. Here Vince and Dom proudly display ageing photos of past victims, including David McCalum and Melbourne's own Barry Humphries.
- **Hepburn Spa Resort** (☎ 5348 2034). Farther afield, Hepburn Springs is famous for its rejuvenating spas. There's plenty of therapies on offer at the Hepburn Springs Resort (see the Excursions chapter).

Bookshops

At 500 Chapel St in the Jam Factory, Borders (☎ 9824 2299) is the first of the huge American bookstore chains to hit Australia, and was seen as a threat to independent bookstores when it opened. As well as books, magazines, CDs and videos there is also a licensed cafe and kids' play area.

Records & CDs

Mighty Music (☎ 9827 4753), at 497 Chapel St, has a good selection of local and imported CDs and vinyl that covers alternative and dance. Sanity (☎ 9827 9866), in the Jam Factory, is for everything mainstream.

Specialist Stores

Made in Japan (☎ 9827 6243), at 533 Chapel St, is an expensive nod in the direction of the east with a selection of Japanese furniture and homewares.

Dinosaur Designs (☎ 9827 2600), at 562 Chapel St, combines the translucency of resin with bright colours and strong, almost primitive designs to create a unique range of homewares and contemporary jewellery.

PRAHRAN (MAP 6)
Clothing & Jewellery

Greville St is where new blood, such as Lush (☎ 9525 0166), at No 116, keeps the retro theme alive. Next door, Fool (☎ 9521 4909) adds contrast with its happy logo, bright colours and quirky line in designer streetwear. Stussy (☎ 9529 7788), at No 111, Dangerfield Boys, at No 140, and Revival Clothing at, No 148, are also worth a look. Around the corner at No 2 Grattan St, Route 66 (☎ 9529 4659) is still a favourite with its trademark range of retro 1950s clothing and accessories. As Greville St is in a constant state of flux, too much listing can be hazardous at the best of times. Enough already!

Shoe Craft (☎ 9510 9993), at 221 High St, is for lovers of the high heel, with a terrific range in shoes, boots and seamed stockings to match.

Mortisha's (☎ 9533 6255), the haunt of Melbourne's original Gothic gal, has moved shop to 47 Chapel St, Windsor. Her sumptuous ladies' and gents' clothing and assorted paraphernalia is perfect when arranging to meet with the dark lord.

Bookshops

Kill City (☎ 9510 6661), at 126 Greville St, has the best in soft to hardboiled crime fiction. Across the street at No 115, Andrew Isles Natural History Bookshop (☎ 9510 5750) deals in new and second-hand titles on, you guessed it, natural history. The Greville Street Bookstore (☎ 9510 3531) is a well-stocked and friendly store covering art, design, music and literature.

The Printed Image Bookshop (☎ 9521 1244), at 232 Chapel St, stocks a comprehensive range of new and second-hand photography books, postcards and posters. Hares & Hyenas (☎ 9824 0110), at 135 Commercial Rd, specialises in gay and lesbian literature and critical writing. You can pick up free weekly street papers here, which will have listings of clubs, bars and events in the gay and lesbian scene.

Records & CDs

Rhythm and Soul Records (☎ 9510 8244), 128 Greville St, has a range of house, club, funk and soul on both CD and vinyl, and knows precisely how many beats per minute make for a good groove. Greville Records (☎ 9510 3012), at No 152, covers the alternative and independent scene.

Markets & Produce Stores

Prahran Market on Commercial Rd opens on Tuesday, Thursday, Friday and Saturday, and offers a great range of vegetables, seafood, meat and delicatessen items. The small Greville St arts, crafts and second-hand market starts at around noon on Sundays and is the perfect place to recover from Saturday night.

Dan Murphy's Cellars (☎ 9497 3388), at 282 Chapel St, has a fantastic range of Australian and imported wines at unbeatable prices in a cavern-sized Victorian-era building. The Chapel St Bazaar (☎ 9529 1727), at No 217–23, is a large indoor market with a mostly affordable range of antiques, bric-a-brac, antique and retro clothing, jewellery and more.

ST KILDA (MAP 9)

The area around Acland and Barkly Sts has an assortment of retro and designer clothing stores, book and gift shops.

Clothing & Jewellery

Barkly St is a heady mix of retro and designer wear. Frocks and Slacks (☎ 9537 2337), at No 186, and Do It Baby, at No 186a, both do a good line in mainly 1960s and 1970s retro clothing. Zimmerman (☎ 9537 1900), at No 188b, is an elegant designer label for women. At No 188c, Shrew (☎ 9534 7337) stocks quality women's designer labels, including Elene Ambé, Milk and Brave. Rich, at No 194–96, is a local label with a fine range of stylish women's and men's clothing, cut from quality Italian fabric.

Bookshops

At No 112 Acland St, Cosmos Books & Music (☎ 9525 3852) is an excellent store, with a huge range of modern fiction titles, psychology, cooking and gardening, and a reasonable selection of CDs. Farther up at No 160, Metropolis (☎ 9525 4866) covers photography, fashion, the arts and travel in a large and airy shop – perfect for browsing.

Specialist Stores

Urban Attitude (☎ 9525 5977), at 125 Acland St, has as many slopes and curves as it has unusual gifts. It's difficult to choose between the amazing flexible vases, the inflatable palm trees, the great range of Alessi designs, Alfex watches, Mimco handbags and much more.

House of Balscheit (☎ 9593 8744), at 1–3 Inkerman St, is an interior design company that doubles as a retail outlet for new and retro furnishings of 1950s to 1970s style.

Markets & Produce Stores

The Esplanade Art & Craft Market operates every Sunday from the Upper Esplanade. Stall holders sell has a wide range of art, handcrafts and jewellery.

Royal Arcade, just one of Melbourne's 19th-century gems

One too many!

Tasty treats

scream, you scream...

Beam me up, Scotty

Melbourne goes mall at Southbank

Melbourne Central

Glitz 'n' glam on Chapel Street, South Yarra

Excursions

If you have time during your stay, leave the city behind for a while and explore the areas surrounding Melbourne (Map 10). You have plenty to choose from: the beaches and coastal townships of the Mornington and Bellarine Peninsulas; the forests, gardens and bushwalks of the Dandenong Ranges; the wilds of the Kinglake National Park; the wineries of the Macedon Ranges, Yarra Valley, Mornington Peninsula and the Geelong area; the Healesville Sanctuary in the scenic Yarra Valley; the stunning natural features of the Great Ocean Road; and of course the more famous tourist attractions, such as the Penguin Parade at Phillip Island and the historic gold-mining township of Sovereign Hill in Ballarat.

Note that many of these places are popular holiday destinations, so if you're planning to stay overnight you should try to book accommodation in advance, especially during the Christmas holiday season, Easter and other school holidays.

This chapter recommends some of the best day or overnight trips from Melbourne, but it gives only an introductory coverage to the areas mentioned. For more details on these places and the rest of the state, see Lonely Planet's *Victoria* guide.

South-West of Melbourne

MELBOURNE TO GEELONG
It's a one-hour drive down the Princes Fwy (M1) to Geelong. You leave Melbourne via the soaring West Gate Bridge, with fine views of the city, and there are a few interesting detours along the way.

Werribee Park Mansion & Zoo
Signposted off the freeway about 30 minutes from Melbourne is Werribee Park, with its zoological park and the huge Italianate Werribee Park Mansion (☎ 9741 2444),

which was built between 1874 and 1877. The flamboyant building is surrounded by formal gardens, including picnic and barbecue areas and the **State Rose Garden**, with 3000 plants forming the shape of a giant Tudor rose. Entry to the garden is free, but admission to the mansion is $10/5 for adults/children (under five years free). The mansion is open from 10 am to 3.45 pm weekdays and 10 am to 4.45 pm weekends and during summer.

The adjacent **Open Range Zoo** (☎ 9731 9600) is a 200-hectare free-range park with African herbivores – zebra, giraffe, hippo, rhinoceros etc – in an incongruous Australian bush setting. Entry to the zoo costs $14.50/7.20/39 for an adult/child/family and includes a safari bus tour (50 minutes). The tours depart hourly between 10.30 am and 3.30 pm weekdays, every 20 minutes on weekends and during holidays.

Met trains run to Werribee train station (zone 1 & 2 Met ticket), and an infrequent bus service (six buses on weekdays, three on Saturday, none on Sunday) runs the 5km between the station and the park – ring the Met for details (☎ 13 1638).

RAAF Museum
Near Werribee is the RAAF Museum (☎ 9256 1300), at the RAAF base at Point Cook. Displays include an exhibit on the

WWI German ace Baron von Richtofen, and the museum's collection of 20 aircraft ranging from a 1916 Morris Farman Shorthorn to a 1970 F4 Phantom. Seven of the vintage planes still fly, and the resident aces use them for air shows. The museum is open from 10 am to 3 pm Tuesday to Friday, until 5 pm on weekends; admission is free.

You Yangs Forest Reserve

Another worthwhile detour off the Princes Fwy is the You Yangs, a picturesque little range of volcanic hills. Ecologically, the park is quite degraded, but a climb up **Flinders Peak**, gives fine views down to Geelong and the coast. Matthew Flinders scrambled to the top in 1802.

GEELONG

pop 176,000

Geelong, Victoria's largest provincial city, sits on the shores of Corio Bay. For most Victorians, the word 'Geelong' conjures up Australian Football League football and Ford: the city is the home of the Cats and a major car factory. For many Melburnians, Geelong means being stuck in traffic en route to the surf coast. If this seems a good reason to give the city a miss, think again. Central Geelong is a historic and attractive bayside city, with fine parks and gardens, some impressive museums and galleries, good restaurants, modern shopping and recreational facilities, and a lively nightlife.

Information

The Geelong & Great Ocean Road Visitor Information Centre (☎ 5275 5797, 1800-620 888) is on the Princes Hwy about 7km north of the town centre. You'll see it on the left as you come in from Melbourne.

There are also tourist offices in the National Wool Museum (☎ 5222 2900), on Moorabool St, and in the Market Square shopping centre (☎ 5222 6126). Visit the Web site at www.greatoceanrd.org.au for information about the west coast.

Things to See & Do

Geelong has more than 100 National Trust-classified buildings, many of them open to the public. **The Heights**, 140 Aphrasia St, is a quaint weatherboard home with some original furnishings. It's open between 11 am and 4.30 pm Wednesday to Sunday; entry costs $5/3/14 for an adult/child/family. **Barwon Grange** in Fernleigh St, Newtown, is a classified neo-Gothic homestead that's open from 11 am to 4.30 pm on Wednesday and weekends; entry costs $4/2.50/10. **Corio Villa**, overlooking Eastern Beach, is another historic old home with a tale to tell. It's privately owned, so you'll have to be satisfied with a view from the outside.

The **National Wool Museum** (1872), on the corner of Brougham and Moorabool Sts, is Geelong's main tourist attraction. Housed in the historic bluestone wool store, this excellent museum details the history of one of Australia's major industries. The museum is open from 9.30 am to 5 pm daily; admission costs $7/3.50/18 for an adult/child/family.

Geelong Naval & Maritime Museum in Swinburne St, North Geelong, is open from 10 am to 4 pm daily, except Tuesday and Thursday; admission is $2/0.50/4 for an adult/child/family. The **Geelong Art Gallery**, on Little Malop St, has a good collection of early Australian and contemporary art; it's open from 10 am to 5 pm weekdays, 1 to 5 pm weekends, and entry is $3 (free on Monday). For theatre lovers, the **Geelong Performing Arts Centre**, opposite the art gallery, has just had a $2 million face-lift; some of the best Australian theatre companies perform here.

The **Ford Discovery Centre**, on the corner of Gheringhap and Brougham Sts, takes both a historical and contemporary look at the Ford motor industry using interactive displays and exhibits. It's open from 10 am to 5 pm Wednesday to Monday; admission is $6/3/15 for an adult/child/family.

Only a short walk from the city centre, **Eastern Beach** has had a major face-lift, with the restored pools and promenade part of a multimillion-dollar renovation. A new restaurant and cafe are situated in the restored pavilion, and the Cunningham Pier restaurant complex with city views is a popular spot. The well-maintained **Geelong**

Botanic Gardens and Eastern Park are also popular attractions for visitors.

For wineries around Geelong, see the boxed text 'Vineyards Around Melbourne' later in this chapter.

Places to Stay

There are several caravan and camping parks across the Barwon River in Barrabool Rd, Belmont – not too far from the town centre and Eastern Beach. The *Riverglen Caravan Park (☎ 5243 5505, 75 Barrabool Rd)* has a range of two-bedroom cottages for $65 and spa cabins for $80, all with TV, kitchen and en suite facilities (each extra person is $10). A budget option on Geelong's outskirts is *St Albans Backpackers (☎ 5248 1229)*, on Homestead Drive in Whittington. Set on a historic horse-stud property, it has bunks for $17 and one double for $34.

The *Eastern Sands Motel (☎ 5221 5577, 1 Bellerine St)* is very centrally located, only a block from Eastern Beach. Singles range from $75 to $84, doubles from $85 to $94.

Pevensey House 1892 (☎ 5224 2810, 17 Pevensey Cres) is a beautifully restored heritage-listed mansion close to the Botanical Gardens. Antique furnishings abound in this excellent B&B, where doubles cost $140. The *All Seasons Ambassador Hotel (☎ 5221 6844)*, on the corner of Gheringhap and Myers Sts, has views of Corio Bay and an on-site restaurant, cafe, bar, pool, spa and sauna. All rooms have spa bath and in-house movies. Standard rooms have a queen-size bed and cost $165; executive suites cost $185.

Getting There & Away

V/Line trains (☎ 13 6196) run a frequent service between Melbourne and Geelong; the trip takes about an hour and economy costs $8.60/17.20 one way/return (off-peak Super Saver is $12 return). Two to three trains each day continue from Geelong to Warrnambool ($24.50) and to Ballarat ($9.20).

There is no V/Line bus service from Melbourne to Geelong, but from Geelong the Great Ocean Rd is well served, with services to Torquay ($4.50), Lorne ($11.20) and

Apollo Bay ($18) operating three times daily (twice on weekends).

McHarry's Bus Lines (☎ 5223 2111) operates the Bellarine Transit bus service with frequent buses from Geelong to Barwon Heads and Ocean Grove (both $3.60), Queenscliff and Point Lonsdale (both $5.55).

BELLARINE PENINSULA

Beyond Geelong the Bellarine Peninsula is a twin to the Mornington Peninsula, forming the western side of the entrance to Port Phillip Bay. This is a popular holiday region and boating venue. Queenscliff is a fashionable and historic seaside resort with up-market guesthouses, grand old hotels and good cafes and restaurants. Farther west, Ocean Grove and Barwon Heads have excellent ocean beaches and are popular resorts during the summer months.

See the Geelong section for details of bus services to the peninsula. A car and passenger ferry also operates daily between Queenscliff and Sorrento – see the Mornington Peninsula Getting There & Away section for details.

Queenscliff

Queenscliff was originally established as a settlement for the sea pilots, whose job it was to steer ships through the treacherous Port Phillip Heads. They weren't always successful – the coast along here is littered with the wrecks of ships that didn't make it.

During the gold rush, Queenscliff was favoured by diggers who had struck it rich, and by the 1880s the town was fashionably known as the 'Queen of the South'. A cluster of fine and extravagant buildings were erected to accommodate the visiting hordes, many of which remain to give the town its historic character.

In recent years Queenscliff has been 're-discovered' as a popular holiday destination, with many of the grand old buildings now restored into guesthouses and upmarket hotels.

Things to See & Do The most impressive buildings are along Gellibrand St, where you'll find the Ozone Hotel, Mietta's Queenscliff Hotel, Lathamstowe and a row of old **pilots' cottages** dating back to 1853. Hesse St, the main street, also has some great buildings, in particular the **Vue Grand Hotel** with its ornate and opulent interior.

Fort Queenscliff was built to protect Melbourne from the perceived threat of Russian invasion during the Crimean War. There are guided tours of the military museum, magazine, cells and Black Lighthouse at 1 and 3 pm on weekends and public holidays ($4/2 for adults/children) and at 1.30 pm weekdays ($5/2).

The **Bellarine Peninsula Railway** (☎ 5258 2069) is run by local rail enthusiasts, and a steam train does the 1¾-hour return Queenscliff-Drysdale run at 11 am and 2.30 pm each Sunday for $12/8 for adults/kids. It also operates Tuesday, Thursday and Saturday during school holidays.

The peninsula is a popular diving and snorkelling location. The Queenscliff Dive Centre (☎ 5258 1188) and Dive Experience (☎ 5258 4058) run diving courses and hire out equipment. Bikes can be hired from 'Mr Queenscliff' (☎ 5258 3403) near the pier. A recommended excursion is to take the steam train to Drysdale and cycle back – it's downhill all the way.

There are quite a few interesting galleries and craft and antique shops in Hesse and Hobson Sts. The **Queenscliff Historical Centre**, on Hesse St, displays various old relics from the town's past and is open from 2 to 4 pm daily.

The **Marine Discovery Centre** (☎ 5258 3344) on Weeroona Parade (the educational unit of the Institute of Marine Sciences) offers an excellent series of trips and programs focusing on the hidden wonders of the bay. Its trips include 'snorkelling with the seals' (about $40), two-hour canoe trips ($12), marine biology tours, rock-pool rambles and lots more – ring to find out what's on.

Next door, the **Queenscliff Maritime Museum** is open on weekends and daily during school holidays. Admission costs $4/1.50 for adults/children.

Places to Stay Queenscliff has four camping and caravan parks. The simple *Queenscliff Recreation Reserve* (☎ 5258 1765) on

Mercer St is the most central, and has sites from $16.50 to $25.

The town has quite a few charming and historic guesthouses. The friendly *Queenscliff Inn* (☎ 5258 4600, 55 Hesse St) has a relaxing old-world ambience, with B&B from $50 for singles and $75 to $90 for doubles. It also has a few budget rooms for travellers, ranging from $15 to $25.

Athelstane House (☎ 1800-170 180, 4 Hobson St) has B&B accommodation starting at $150, while the elegant *Maytone by the Sea* (☎ 5258 4059), on the corner of The Esplanade and Stevens St, does B&B Sunday to Thursday for $100 a double; weekend rates (Friday/Saturday or Saturday/Sunday) are $250 a double B&B.

At 16 Gellibrand St, the National Trust-classified *Mietta's Queenscliff Hotel* (☎ 5258 1066) is renowned for its fine food and gracious Victorian-era accommodation. Dinner, B&B packages range from $110 to $190 per person – prices depend on when you come.

Built in 1881 and later converted into a hotel, the *Ozone Hotel* (☎ 1800-804 753, 42 Gellibrand St) has retained much of its old-world charm. B&B costs $150 Sunday to Friday and $285 on Saturday. The opulent *Vue Grand Hotel* (☎ 5258 1544, 46 Hesse St) is the place to splurge, with en suite rooms, an indoor heated pool and spa, billiard room and gymnasium. From Sunday to Friday a double room with a three-course dinner and breakfast the following morning costs $295; on Saturday night it's $330. Double/single B&B costs $210/125 Sunday to Friday.

Point Lonsdale

About 5km west of Queenscliff, Point Lonsdale is a laid-back little coastal town centred around its **lighthouse**, built in 1902 to help guide ships through the Heads and into the bay. The Rip is the turbulent passage of water leading into the bay; it is rated as one of the most dangerous seaways in the world. **The Rip View Lookout** is one vantage point from which you can watch freighters and other vessels negotiating the waterway – **Point Lonsdale Pier** is another.

Around the Bay in a Day

One of the best ways to appreciate Melbourne's bayside location is to circumnavigate Port Phillip Bay, making use of the ferry services between Queenscliff and Sorrento. It's an easy day trip by car (about 200km), but you could make it a two-day trip, staying overnight on either the Bellarine Peninsula or the Mornington Peninsula. You could also do it by public transport or bicycle.

Going anticlockwise from Melbourne, the first highlight is the view from the West Gate Bridge, with the city skyscrapers behind you, the industrial areas to the west and the bay stretching south to the horizon. It's a quick 70km down the freeway to Geelong, a small city built on the wealth of Western District wool – its National Wool Museum is worth seeing. Look carefully for the road that takes you the 30km to Queenscliff: although it's signposted it's easy to miss. There are two ferry services between Queenscliff and Sorrento (see the Mornington Peninsula Getting There & Away section of this chapter). Book your ticket then look around the town, particularly the old fort and the grand old hotels.

You can see Port Phillip Heads from the ferry, but it gives them a fairly wide berth to avoid the dangerous current known as 'The Rip'. You might see dolphins frolicking round the bow of the boat, and lots of sea birds around Mud Island and the unfinished island fortress called Pope's Eye. The ferry runs parallel to the coast past Portsea, and you'll have a good view of the luxury cliff-top houses which overlook the bay. As the boat comes in, the Sorrento beachfront is particularly attractive with its tall pine trees and old-fashioned bandstand rotunda.

There's wonderful coastal scenery on the southern tip of the Mornington Peninsula, on both the Bass Strait side and the bay side, and especially in the Point Nepean National Park. You can't see the city from here during the day, but at night it's like a string of diamonds across the water. Heading back towards the bright lights, you can take the Nepean Hwy, which follows the coast, or the freeway which runs further inland. Take the more leisurely coastal route if you want to find out about urban sprawl – from Frankston to the city it's over 40km of nonstop suburbia.

The foreshore around the headland is a marine wonderland at low tide, when an array of rock pools and caverns become natural aquariums – bring a pair of swimming goggles.

Point Lonsdale has two rocky beaches, the calmer bay beach and the surf beach, the latter of which is patrolled by a life-saving club over summer. The town's **cemetery** has the graves of early pioneers, pilots, lighthouse keepers and shipwreck victims.

Places to Stay The council-run *Royal Caravan Park* (☎ 5258 1765), on the foreshore, opens between December and Easter. *The Terminus B&B & Lighthouse Resort* (☎ 5258 1142, 31 Point Lonsdale Rd) is a cosy guesthouse with a tennis court, pool and guest lounges. The four refurbished rooms with bathrooms cost from $130 to $190 a double for B&B, smaller rooms are $90 a double and more spacious doubles are $110.

Ocean Grove

It might not be the prettiest of towns but Ocean Grove is on the ocean side of the peninsula, and the area around the surf life-saving club is very popular with surfers. There is good scuba diving off the rocky ledges of the bluff, and farther out there are wrecks of ships which failed to make the tricky entrance to Port Phillip Bay. Some of the wrecks are accessible to divers.

The **Ocean Grove Nature Reserve**, on Grubb Rd to the north of town, is a large area of natural bushland with 11km of marked walking tracks and lots of native flora and fauna. The 143-hectare reserve is conserved and managed by a staff of volunteers.

Barwon Heads

Barwon Heads is a smaller, quieter and prettier resort 4km west of Ocean Grove, at the mouth of the Barwon River. Since the popular TV series *Seachange* was filmed here, a steadily increasing number of fans make the pilgrimage to Barwon heads. It has sheltered river beaches, surf beaches around the headland – **Thirteenth Beach** is one of the best – and the magnificent **Barwon Heads Golf Club** (☎ 5254 2302), set among rolling coastal hills and sand dunes with inspirational ocean views. It's open to the public most days, but the green fees are a not-so-inspirational $50!

Places to Stay The *Barwon Heads Park (☎ 5254 1115)* on the foreshore has good camp sites, cabins and cottages. *Honnington on Bridge (☎ 5254 2234)* is a comfortable B&B close to the beach, with doubles for $110.

Torquay

Torquay is one of the most popular surfing and summer resorts on the coast, and the capital of Australia's booming surfing industry. The town itself is no oil painting, but it has a great range of beaches that cater for everyone from paddlers to world champion surfers.

The Visitor Information Centre (☎ 5261 4219) is in the same building as Surfworld Australia and is open from 9 am to 5 pm weekdays, 10 am to 4 pm weekends.

Things to See & Do The excellent **Surfworld Australia Surfing Museum** (☎ 5261 4606), Surfcoast Plaza, has everything from the Australian Surfing Hall of Fame to a wave-making tank. It's open from 9 am to 5 pm weekdays and 10 am to 4 pm weekends, and entry is $6/4/16 for adults/children/families. You can also hire surfing gear here or book surfing lessons with the Westcoast Surf School (☎ 5261 2241).

The beach is the reason most people come to Torquay. **Fishermans Beach** is protected from the ocean swells, making it popular with families. The **Front Beach** is ringed by Norfolk Pines and sloping lawns, while the **Back Beach** is patrolled by members of the life-saving club during summer. The sandy beaches at **Jan Juc** are more exposed to the ocean swells. A couple of kilometres farther south-west, the **Bells Beach Recreation Reserve** is famous for its powerful waves.

The Bells Surfing Classic, held annually at Easter, attracts the world's top professional surfers and thousands of spectators over the five days of the contest.

Tiger Moth World Adventure Park (☎ 5261 5100), 5km north-east of Torquay on Blackgate Rd, has an aviation museum, daily air shows, and lots of entertainment for the kids. It's open from 10 am to 5 pm daily and costs $7/6/25 for an adult/child/family. There are also joy flights in vintage Tiger Moths that start at $80, or six people can fly to the Twelve Apostles for $70 per person.

The **Surf Coast Walk** follows the coastline from Jan Juc to Airey's Inlet. The full distance takes about 11 hours, but can be done in stages. The Surf Coast Touring Map, available from tourist offices in Geelong and along the coast, has this walk marked on it.

Places to Stay Torquay has four caravan parks, but over summer and Easter the town is flooded with campers and it can be hard to find a site. The *Torquay Public Reserve (☎ 5261 2496)*, the *Zeally Bay Caravan Park (☎ 5261 2400)* and the *Bernell Caravan Park (☎ 5261 2493)* all have sites, vans and cabins.

Potter's Inn B&B (☎ 5261 4131, 40 Bristol Rd) is a nice alternative with singles/doubles starting at $60/85, including breakfast. The *Ocean Road Retreat (☎ 5261 2971)*, on the corner of Sunset Strip and Bells Blvd, is set on two acres of bushland overlooking a lake – it really is a retreat. There's a choice of a small cottage for $120 and spa suites for $150; each option includes a cooked breakfast.

GREAT OCEAN ROAD

The Great Ocean Rd, running between Anglesea and Warrnambool, is one of the world's most spectacular coastal routes. The road takes you on a journey of dramatic contrasts around the Shipwreck Coast – lush rainforests, sheer and ragged cliffs, idyllic sandy beaches, mountains and forests of towering eucalypts, intriguing rock formations, some great state and national parks and charming seaside settlements.

EXCURSIONS

Things to See & Do

Anglesea is famous for its sheer cliffs and the scenic **Anglesea Golf Club** (☎ 5263 1582), which is as much home to a large population of kangaroos, grazing indifferently on the fairways and greens, as it is to the golfers who pay $20 for the privilege.

Aireys Inlet is an interesting little town, popular with people who find Lorne just a little too much to take. There are some great beaches and excellent bushwalks through the nearby Angahook-Lorne State Park.

The **Angahook-Lorne State Park** covers 22,000 hectares of coast and hinterland between Aireys Inlet and Kennett River. The park has cool-temperate rainforests, bluegum forests, cascades and numerous well-signposted walking tracks. The park has an abundance of wildlife, and seven designated camping areas.

Lorne is the most fashionable and popular town along this stretch of coast, attracting a mix of holiday-makers, weekenders and surfers with its great beaches, bush-walks, cafes and restaurants and wide range of accommodation. Despite the summer madness, with traffic jams leading into town and a dearth of available accommodation, Lorne has managed to retain much of its charm and appeal.

Perhaps the most spectacular section of the Great Ocean Rd is between Lorne and Apollo Bay, where the contrast of the ocean on one side and the forests and mountains of the **Otway Ranges** on the other is breathtaking. The Otways are an area of great natural beauty with scenic drives, walking trails, waterfalls and tiny hillside townships.

The pretty fishing town of **Apollo Bay** is a popular summer beach resort. It's also a little more relaxed than Lorne, and, in addition to all the fishing folk, quite a few artists and musicians live in and around the town.

The **Otway National Park**, at the southernmost tip of this coast, is another natural wonderland, while farther west is the small and beautiful **Melba Gully State Park**.

To visit the most famous section of this spectacular coastal area, you really need to take a good few days to journey beyond Apollo Bay. Take Lonely Planet's *Victoria* guide to help you on your way.

Places to Stay

Anglesea The *Anglesea Family Caravan Park* (☎ 5263 1583) has sites ranging from $15 to $20 and cabins and cottages starting at $45. On the main road, *Debonair Motel & Guesthouse* (☎ 5263 1440) has cosy, period-style rooms and motel-style units. B&B is from $85 to $95 a double in the guesthouse and starts at $75 a double in a motel unit. At the southern end of town, the attractive *Roadnight Cottages* (☎ 5263 1820) provide good, self-contained accommodation for $100 to $130 a night for up to four people.

Aireys Inlet The friendly *Bush to Beach B&B* (☎ 5289 6538, 43 Anderson St), a cedar cottage in a bushy setting, has guestrooms and doubles starting at $90. The owner also offers good guided walks. The impressive *Lighthouse Keeper's Cottages* (☎ 5289 6306) offers self-contained accommodation for $140 to $165 a double.

Standing watch at Cape Otway, near Apollo Bay

EXCURSIONS

EXCURSIONS

Lorne The Lorne Foreshore Committee (☎ 5289 1382) manages five good caravan and camping reserves in and around Lorne, for which you'll need to book in advance. The excellent **Great Ocean Road Cottages & Backpackers** (☎ 5289 1070), in a leafy hillside setting in Erskine Ave, has bunks starting at $16 and attractive timber cottages that sleep up to six people and range from $95 to $175 a night.

Erskine House (☎ 5289 1185), in landscaped grounds on the beachfront, is a 1930s guesthouse with old-fashioned rooms ranging from $95 to $165 a double, including breakfast. The romantic **Allenvale Cottages** (☎ 5289 1450) are in an idyllic setting, with tariffs ranging from $95 to $125 a night.

Lorne to Apollo Bay In Wye River, the cosy **Rookery Nook Hotel** (☎ 5289 0240) has simple motel units overlooking a pretty bay for $50/100 a single/double.

About 10km farther south-west, **Whitecrest Holiday Resort** (☎ 5237 0228) has modern apartments from $95 to $145 per double weekdays. At weekends the minimum booking of two nights includes one dinner in the restaurant and two breakfasts, starting at $445 a double.

At Skenes Creek, just before Apollo Bay, the wonderful **Chris' Restaurant & Villas at Beacon Point** (☎ 5237 6411) has spectacular cliff-top views. It has luxurious two-bedroom villas starting at $180 a night weekdays, and a two-night minimum stay at weekends for $220 per double per night. The restaurant offers one of Victoria's finest dining experiences (book well in advance).

Apollo Bay The **Pisces Caravan Resort** (☎ 5237 6749) has powered sites from $17 to $30 for two, and standard cabins from $40 to $70. The modern **Lighthouse Keepers Inn** (☎ 5237 6278, 175 Great Ocean Rd), north of the town centre, has units with ocean views from $70 to $110 a double. The elegant **Greenacres** (☎ 5237 6309) has an excellent bar and restaurant, with B&B ranging from $55 to $180 a double.

North-West of Melbourne

DAYLESFORD & HEPBURN SPRINGS

Set among the scenic hills, lakes and forests of the central highlands, the delightful historic twin towns of Daylesford and Hepburn Springs are enjoying a booming revival as the 'spa centre of Victoria'. Melburnians love this area and use it as a retreat from the urban rat race. It also has a thriving gay and lesbian scene.

The Daylesford Tourist Information Centre (☎ 5348 1339) is on Vincent St, next to the post office.

Things to See & Do

The best route from Melbourne to Daylesford is via the **Wombat State Forest**. The areas around the towns of Blackwood and Trentham are well worth exploring via the 50km scenic **Wombat Forest Drive**.

The nearby **Lerderderg Gorge** has some great walks. Just west of Blackwood, the lovely **Garden of St Erth** has four hectares of shaded lawns and stone paths, fragrant flower beds and dappled pools. It's open from 10 am to 4 pm daily.

North of Blackwood, **Katteminga Lodge** (☎ 5424 1415) is a horse-riding ranch where rides start at $15 an hour. It also offers accommodation in self-contained units, starting at $75 a double.

The health-giving properties of the area's mineral springs were known before gold was discovered here, and by the 1870s Daylesford was a popular health resort, attracting droves of fashionable Melburnians. The current trend towards healthy lifestyles has prompted a revival of interest in the area. The **Hepburn Spa Resort** (☎ 5348 2034) in the Mineral Springs Reserve is an impressive relaxation and rejuvenation centre, with a wide range of services including heated spas, plunge pools, flotation tanks, massages and saunas. Daylesford and Hepburn Springs also boast masseurs, craft and antique shops, gardens, galleries, excellent cafes and restaurants, and dozens of charming guesthouses, cottages and B&Bs.

Daylesford's most popular attraction is the **Convent Gallery**, a huge 19th-century convent brilliantly converted into an art and craft gallery and set in lovely gardens. It's open from 10 am to 6 pm daily and entry is $3.

Also worth a visit are the lovely **Wombat Hill Botanic Gardens**, **Lake Daylesford** and **Jubilee Lake**, the **Historical Society Museum** and the **Central Highlands Tourist Railway** (☎ 5348 3503). There are also some wonderful **walking trails** in the region.

Places to Stay

Daylesford and Hepburn Springs have a wide range of accommodation, although budget options are somewhat limited.

In Daylesford, the *Jubilee Lake Caravan Park* (☎ 5348 2186) and *Victoria Caravan Park* (☎ 5348 3821) have camp sites and vans. In Hepburn Springs, *Continental House* (☎ 5348 2005, 9 Lone Pine Ave) is an old rambling alternative guesthouse with a vegan cafe; beds range from $12 to $20 a night (bring your own linen). A little more expensive, the *Springs Hotel* (☎ 5348 2202, 124 Main Rd) has good rooms starting at $55/65 a single/double.

If you're not on a tight budget there's a fine selection of guesthouses and B&Bs to choose from. Double rooms generally start at $120 or more a night. Places worth trying in Daylesford include the smoke-free *Ambleside B&B* (☎ 5348 2691, 15 Leggatt St) overlooking Lake Daylesford and with plenty of olde-worlde charm. The rooms are all en suite and cost $100 for singles and $145 to $195 for doubles (ask for a lakeview room and you might strike it lucky). *Pendower House* (☎ 5348 1535, 10 Bridport St) is a beautifully restored Victorian-era home. Doubles range from $130 to $160 during the week, with weekend packages starting at $335. The *Lake House* (☎ 5348 3329), in King St, shares with the wonderful restaurant of the same name, and overlooks Lake Daylesford. Rates, including dinner and breakfast, vary depending on the view, with doubles ranging from $330 to $465, and a weekend package from $750 to $900.

In Hepburn Springs, try *Villa Parma* (☎ 5348 3512), set in a cottage garden and crammed with antiques and plenty of character. The three guestrooms share one bathroom, and here B&B costs from $120 to $160. Overlooking the Mineral Springs Reserve, *Mooltan Guesthouse* (☎ 5348 3555) has weekend packages (two nights accommodation with breakfasts and a three-course dinner Saturday evening) starting at $170/250 for singles/doubles; during the week B&B is $50/75. The *Genoa Spa Villas and Spa Country House* (☎ 5348 1151, 28 Main Rd) offers every luxury under the sun, with two-night packages starting at $330 weekdays and $420 on weekends.

For something completely different, *Shizuka Ryokan* (☎ 5348 2030), on Lakeside Drive, brings some Japanese flavour to the springs. The less-is-more principle applies here, so lovers of minimalism will enjoy the *tatami* matting, private Japanese garden and *shoji* screens. The price is more than minimal, however, with weekend packages starting at $550 a double.

If you're looking for something self-contained, the helpful Daylesford Cottage Directory (☎ 5348 1255, ✉ daylecot@netconnect.com.au) manages more than 50 cottages in the area. Check out its Web site at http://daylecot.spacountry.net.au.

Getting There & Away

You'll need to catch the train from Melbourne to Woodend, from where V/Line (☎ 13 6196) runs buses to Daylesford ($4.30). Melbourne to Daylesford takes two hours, and an economy/1st-class fare is $12.20/15.60.

BALLARAT

pop 65,000

When gold was discovered near Ballarat in 1851, the rush was on and thousands of diggers flooded into the area. Ballarat's alluvial goldfields were but the tip of the golden iceberg, and when deep-shaft mines were sunk incredibly rich quartz reefs were struck. The mines were worked until the end of WWI, and about 28% of the gold unearthed in Victoria came from Ballarat.

Ballarat eventually grew into a major provincial town and it has a wealth of gracious Victorian architecture, a reminder of the prosperity of the gold-rush era. The town's major attraction is Sovereign Hill, but there are plenty of other points of interest in and around Ballarat, and you could easily spend a few days or more here.

The Ballarat Visitor Information Centre (☎ 5332 2694) is in the centre of town at 39 Sturt St.

Things to See & Do

Lydiard St is considered one of the country's best and most intact architectural examples of a Victorian-era streetscape. The excellent Ballarat Fine Art Gallery is one of the country's best provincial galleries; it's open from 10.30 am to 5 pm daily and entry is $4/2/1 for adults/students/kids. Farther north, Lake Wendouree is edged by the Ballarat Botanic Gardens. Also of interest are the Eureka Stockade Centre, the Ballarat Wildlife Park and Kryal Castle. The colourful Begonia Festival in early March is a great spectacle.

Ballarat's main tourist attraction is Sovereign Hill, a fascinating re-creation of a gold-mining township of the 1860s. It is probably the best attraction of its type in the country, and has won numerous awards – allow at least half a day for a visit. It's a living-history museum, with shops and businesses in the period style and staffed by people in period costume. There's an old mineshaft, lots of old mining equipment, and visitors can pan for gold in the stream. Sovereign Hill is open from 10 am to 5 pm daily and admission is $20.50/15/10/55 for adults/

The new Eureka Stockade Centre

students/kids/families – expensive, but well worth it. The same ticket gets you into the nearby Gold Museum, which has imaginative displays and samples from all the old mining areas in the Ballarat region.

Places to Stay

There are half a dozen caravan parks in town. The **Sovereign Hill Lodge YHA** (☎ 5333 3409) has bunk rooms starting at $16 for members ($19 for nonmembers), budget rooms for $46 and en suite doubles at $98.

George Hotel (☎ 5333 4866, 27 Lydiard St N) has single/double rooms starting at $35/50 ($50/65 for an en suite). The elegantly restored **Craig's Royal Hotel** (☎ 5331 1377, 10 Lydiard St S) is a lovely old hotel right in the centre of Ballarat. There is a variety to choose from, with budget rooms at $40, en suite rooms at $70 to $90 and suites at $120 to $160.

For excellent B&B try the **Ballarat Heritage Homestay Cottages** (☎ 5332 8296), which operates five historic cottages dotted around Ballarat. Each cottage combines period furnishings and modern amenities, and all are smoke-free. A two-night weekend package ranges between $250 and $320 for two people; for one night midweek the rate ranges between $120 and $150 for two.

Getting There & Away

V/Line trains and buses run regularly from Melbourne to Ballarat. The 1¾-hour trip costs $13.80/19.40 economy/1st class.

Sovereign Hill is 3km from the station, but a direct bus meets the 8.50 am train, or you can take a local bus or a taxi – station staff will direct you to the bus stop.

MACEDON RANGES & HANGING ROCK

The Calder Hwy takes you north-west from Melbourne towards Bendigo. The route itself isn't terribly exciting, but there are quite a few pleasant surprises not far off the beaten highway.

For a more scenic route, take the Tullamarine Fwy from central Melbourne and follow the Bendigo signs. North of Tullamarine airport, **Gellibrand Hill Park** is a flora and fauna reserve, popular with walkers, cyclists and bird-watchers. Just beyond the outskirts of Melbourne you come to the turn-off to the pretty and little-known **Organ Pipes National Park**, which has a visitor centre, picnic spots and walking trails. This park features some fascinating geological structures – hexagonal basalt columns that look like giant organ pipes and form a natural outdoor amphitheatre.

Some 5km east of the highway in the satellite town of Sunbury are two of Victoria's most historic wineries: **Goona Warra** and **Craiglee**, both of which were built and originally planted in the 1860s. Back on the highway and 11km farther on is a turn-off to the historic and pretty township of **Gisborne**, a former coach stop on the goldfields route.

Dromkeen Homestead Children's Literature Museum (☎ 5428 6799) is 10km east of Gisborne, in Riddells Creek. It has a works-in-progress gallery, original sketches from Australian classics, such as *The Magic Pudding, Blinky Bill* and *Snugglepot &*

Basalt columns at Organ Pipes National Park

Cuddlepie, and gardens with barbecue facilities. It's opens from 9 am to 5 pm weekdays, noon to 4 pm Sundays (entry is free).

Mt Macedon

Just north of Gisborne you can turn off the Calder Hwy and head through the small town of Macedon to Mt Macedon, a 1013m-high extinct volcano. Over the years many of Melbourne's wealthiest families have built summer homes up here, surrounded by glorious exotic gardens. There are several tearooms, restaurants and a pub on the mountain.

The 'scenic route' up Mt Macedon Rd takes you up and over the mountain, past the beautiful mansions and into some pretty countryside beyond. At the summit of Mt Macedon is a **memorial cross** and **lookout** point. Beyond the summit, the turn-off to the left leads to Woodend, or you can go straight on to Hanging Rock. The nearby **Camel's Hump** is popular with rock climbers.

A 10-minute drive west of Mt Macedon on Shannon's Rd, the **Barringo Wildlife Reserve** (☎ 5426 1680) has emus, kangaroos, peacocks and deer running free. Across the road, Barringo Valley Trail Rides (☎ 5426 1778) offers horse rides through the area's scenic valleys and forests.

Places to Stay *The Mountain Inn* (☎ *5426 1755, 694 Main Rd)*, an English-style inn, has double rooms ranging from $75 to $99 on weekends, a bit less during the week. The inn also serves good bistro meals. The period *Horley B&B* (☎ *5426 2448)* on the slopes of Mt Macedon has comfortable doubles starting at $100.

Woodend

Woodend is an attractive little commuter town nestled on the fringes of the Black Forest. In the gold-rush days, bushrangers roamed the forest, robbing travellers en route to the goldfields.

Keatings Country Hotel (☎ *5427 2510)*, on the main street, is an old-style pub with rooms at $20 per person mid-week, $25 on weekends. The *Bentinck Country House* (☎ *5427 2944, 1 Carlisle St)* is a charming

English-style guesthouse with a cottage set in landscaped gardens. B&B starts at $135/160 for singles/doubles in the cottage; $165/195 in the main guesthouse.

Hanging Rock

The Hanging Rock Reserve (☎ 5427 0295) is 10km north-east of Woodend. Hanging Rock was made famous by Joan Lindsay's novel and the subsequent Peter Weir film *Picnic at Hanging Rock*, about the unsolved disappearance of a group of schoolgirls. The rock is a sacred site for men of the Wurundjeri Aboriginal tribe, and it has a strangely haunting atmosphere. Formed from solidified lava and eroded over time to its present bizarre shape, it was once a refuge for bushrangers, including the notorious Mad Dan Morgan. It's a popular spot for a picnic and there are walking tracks and good lookouts with superb views from higher up. The ranger's office and tearooms are near the entrance, and admission to the reserve is $7 per car.

Getting There & Away V/Line trains will take you as far as Woodend ($8.60), from where a taxi (☎ 5427 2641) to Hanging Rock costs about $11.

North-East of Melbourne

YARRA VALLEY

The Yarra Valley is not far beyond the north-eastern outskirts of Melbourne. It is a place of great natural beauty and is well worth exploring. This is an excellent area for bicycle tours or bushwalks, and there are dozens of fine wineries to visit as well as the very good Healesville Wildlife Sanctuary.

The Yarra Valley Visitor Information Centre (☎ 5962 2600) is at 127 Maroondah Hwy in Healesville. The Department of Natural Resources & Environment (NRE) has plenty of information about the area

---

Vineyards Around Melbourne

Geelong Region

In the 19th-century Geelong was one of Victoria's major wine-growing districts, and the area is particularly known for its outstanding pinot noir and cabernet sauvignon wines.

Today there are a dozen or so small wineries in the region. They include the **Idyll Vineyard & Winery**, at 265 Ballan Rd in Moorabool, and the tiny **Asher Vineyard**, at 360 Goldsworthy Rd in Lovely Banks (both about 8km north of Geelong); the rustic **Mt Anakie Winery** and **Staughton Vale Vineyard** (both in Anakie, about 37km north); **Tarcoola Estate**, on Spillers Rd in Lethbridge (32km northwest); the **Mt Duneed Winery** on Feehans Rd in Mt Duneed (10km south); and the **Prince Albert Vineyard** on Lemins Rd in Waurn Ponds (12km south-west).

There are also several wineries on the Bellarine Peninsula: **Kilgour Estate** and **Scotchman's Hill Vineyard** are both off the road between Drysdale and Portarlington, and on weekends you can also visit the historic **Spray Farm Estate** near Portarlington – ring Scotchman's Hill (☎ 5251 3176) to check opening hours for Spray Farm Estate. For further information and brochures contact the Geelong & Great Ocean Rd tourist information line on ☎ 1800-620 888.

Macedon

Despite its proximity to Melbourne, the Macedon wine region is one of Victoria's best kept secrets. This is a great area for leisurely tours and exploration, with a dozen or so small and picturesque wineries scattered around an often rugged and spectacular countryside.

The area's altitude favours cool-climate varieties such as chardonnay and pinot noir, and the sparkling 'Macedon' wine is a regional speciality. Brochures, maps and guides to the region's wineries are available from local information centres and all wineries.

and maps, which are available from the Outdoor Information Centre, 8 Nicholson St, East Melbourne.

Healesville Wildlife Sanctuary

The Healesville Wildlife Sanctuary (☎ 5962 4022) is one of the best places to see Australian native fauna. The sanctuary is in a natural bushland setting, with a circular walking track and boardwalk which takes you through a series of spacious enclosures, aviaries, wetlands and display houses. The sanctuary's residents include wallabies, kangaroos, wombats, dingoes, lyrebirds, Tasmanian devils, bats, platypuses, koalas, eagles, snakes and lizards. There are regular demonstrations, such as bird-of-prey feeds and snake shows. Some enclosures – eg, the platypus enclosure – are only open at certain times of the day, so ring ahead to avoid being disappointed.

The sanctuary is open from 9 am to 5 pm daily, and admission is $14.50/10.80/7.20 for adults/students/children.

Other Attractions

The **Warrandyte State Park**, one of the few remaining areas of natural bush in the metropolitan area, is just 24km north-east of the city. Walking and cycling tracks are well marked, there are picnic and barbecue areas, native animals and birds and an abundance of native wildflowers in the spring. Although it's a part of suburban Melbourne, Warrandyte has the feel of a country village. Artists and craftspeople have always been attracted to the area, and there are quite a few galleries and potteries dotted throughout the hills. One of the best ways to explore the river and park is in a canoe; several local operators hire out canoes and equipment and organise canoeing trips.

A couple of kilometres north of Yarra Glen, **Gulf Station** (☎ 9730 1286) is a National Trust-classified farm dating to the 1850s. The farm remained in the same family until recent times, and little has changed over the years. With the old slab-timber farmhouse, barns, stables and slaughterhouse, the

---

Vineyards Around Melbourne

Yarra Valley

The Yarra Valley is one of Australia's most respected wine-growing regions, with more than 30 wineries scattered among these beautiful hills and valleys. The region is particularly noted for its pinot noir, chardonnay, cabernet sauvignon and sparkling 'methode champenoise' wines. Wineries that are open daily include **Domaine Chandon**, **Lilydale Vineyards**, **De Bortoli**, **Fergusson's**, **Coldstream Hills**, **Kellybrook**, **St Hubert's** and **Yarra Burn**. Many of the wineries charge a $2 to $5 tasting fee, which is refundable if you buy a bottle.

Mornington Peninsula

In the last decade the Mornington Peninsula has blossomed into one of Victoria's prime wine-producing regions. Wedged between the two bays, the peninsula's fertile soils, temperate climate and rolling hills have become home to vineyards that produce consistently good wines. Wines from this area, however, tend to be relatively expensive due to the high cost of real estate at such close proximity to Melbourne. The region is particularly noted for its pinot noir, but also produces good shiraz and chardonnay.

There are dozens of wineries, mostly in the elevated central area around Red Hill and Main Ridge. Most of these are small-level producers, and many are individually run. More than 20 of the wineries are open to the public on weekends, and those open daily include **Dromana Estate**, **Hann's Creek Estate**, **Hickinbotham of Dromana**, **Main Ridge Estate**, **Red Hill Estate**, **Stonier's Winery at Merricks**, the **Briars Vineyard** and **T'Gallant** at Darling Park.

A map and brochure is available from information centres and from the wineries themselves, or you can contact the Mornington Peninsula Vigneron's Association on ☎ 5989 2377.

original implements and the replanted sustenance gardens and orchards, Gulf Station gives an interesting insight into 19th-century farm life. It's open from 10 am to 4 pm Wednesday to Sunday and on public holidays, and admission is $7/4/18 for adults/children/families.

Much of the valley's early history relates to the timber industry. More timber passed through Yarra Junction than any town in the world, except for Seattle in the USA. Evidence of the old mills, timber tramlines and charcoal plants can still be found throughout the forests.

Powelltown, 16km south-east of Yarra Junction, was a busy timber town during the 19th century. A series of excellent forest walks now follow the old timber tramlines and tunnels that were built to transport the timber to the railway line. Walks include the Reid's Tramline Walk, the Ada Tree Walk (past a 300-year-old, 76m-high mountain ash) and the Seven Acre Rock Walk. The two-day, 36-km **Walk into History** track takes you all the way to Warburton. The Parks Victoria/NRE office (☎ 5964 7088) in Woori Yallock has further information.

There are also some great scenic drives. The Warburton-Healesville-Marysville triangle takes you through some great countryside, eg, along the **Reefton Spur** between Marysville and Warburton. There are several different routes and plenty of great off-the-beaten-track spots to explore. Both the Acheron Way and Woods Point Rd are excellent drives along good gravel roads.

In Yarra Junction, the interesting **Upper Yarra Historical Museum** is open from 1.30 to 5 pm Sunday and public holidays, and entry is $2.

Warburton is a pretty little town set in a lush, green valley by the river, with rising hills on both sides. This area was a popular health retreat last century, when droves of city folk came to Warburton's guesthouses to breathe the fresh mountain air. The township still has a sleepy charm to it. It's a short drive from Warburton up to **Mt Donna Buang**, which, during winter, is capped with the closest snow to Melbourne.

The **Centenary Trail** follows the old Lilydale to Warburton railway line from Woori Yallock to Warburton, and offers good cycling and walking.

The **Yellingbo State Fauna Reserve**, to the south of Woori Yallock on the Warburton Hwy, is the last remaining refuge of the rare helmeted honeyeater.

Places to Stay

Ashgrove Caravan Park (☎ 5962 4398) is 4km south-east of the centre of Healesville and close to the sanctuary. Camp sites start at $13 and on-site cabins and units at $50 a double. Also near the sanctuary and in a peaceful setting, *Sanctuary House Motel* (☎ 5962 5148) is set in 4 hectares of bushland and has singles/doubles starting at $45/65. *Strathvea* (☎ 5962 4109), 9km north of Healesville, is a restored Art Deco guesthouse and gourmet getaway with doubles ranging from $110 to $140.

Right in the centre of Yarra Glen, the *Grand Hotel* (☎ 9730 1230) is a National Trust-classified building dating to 1888, and one of the best country hotels in Victoria. Rooms start at $120.

The cosy *Motel Won-Wondah* (☎ 5966 2059), on Donna Buang Rd, has motel-style singles/doubles starting at $50/60. *Warburton Grange* (☎ 5966 9166), just south of Warburton, is a popular old-world guesthouse with guest lounges, reading rooms and open fires. B&B costs $150 a double.

Getting There & Away

The Met's suburban trains go as far from the city as Lilydale; two bus companies operate services from Lilydale train station into the Yarra Valley.

McKenzie's Bus Lines (☎ 5962 5088) has daily services from Lilydale to Healesville (zone 3 Met ticket) and Yarra Glen. It also operates direct services to Healesville from the Spencer St coach terminal in Melbourne (zone 1, 2 & 3 Met ticket).

Martyrs Bus Service (☎ 5966 2035) runs regular buses from Lilydale train station to Yarra Junction ($3.05) and Warburton ($3.85) – fares are cheaper if you show your train Met ticket.

KINGLAKE NATIONAL PARK

Known as the Forgotten Ranges, the Kinglake National Park is the largest national park near Melbourne, and one of the least visited. A huge eucalypt forest on the slopes of the Great Dividing Range, the park was established in 1928 to protect and preserve the native flora and fauna. There are dozens of walking tracks, good picnic areas and scenic lookout points in the three sections of the park. An admission fee is charged in some areas. For information about the park or to book a camp site, contact the park office (☎ 5786 5351) on National Park Rd, Pheasant Creek.

A scenic way to get here from the city is to drive out through Eltham (stopping to visit the **Montsalvat Gallery** – see Other Art Galleries in the Things to See & Do chapter), then up through Kangaroo Ground, Panton Hill and St Andrews.

In the centre of the park, **Kinglake** is a small township with a pub and a few shops and galleries (but no lake!). About 18km east is **Toolangi**, the home of the poet and writer CJ Dennis from 1915 to 1935. He wrote many of his famous works here, including *The Sentimental Bloke*. The Singing Garden Tearooms and gardens are named after his last published book.

Also in Toolangi is the NRE's impressive **Forest Discovery Centre** (☎ 5962 9314), which has educational displays and videos on various aspects of forest use. It's open from 10 am to 5 pm daily and entry costs $2/1 for adults/children. You can pick up leaflets here for the many bushwalks and scenic drives in the area, which include the **Wirrawilla Walk** – a 15-minute boardwalk circuit through a rainforest – and the **Toolangi Black Range Forest Drive** – a 44-km route from Toolangi north to Devlins Bridge, with a series of walks to picnic areas, waterfalls and historic sites along the way.

Camping areas in the national park include the *Gums*, on the Eucalyptus-Glenburn Rd, 10km north-east of Kinglake. It's a pretty area with a small stream nearby; there are eight tent sites and three caravan sites. There is also a *camping area*

north of Toolangi called the Murrindindi Scenic Reserve. It's on the Murrindindi River and has some great walks to places such as the **Cascades** and the **Wilhelmina Falls**, which are quite spectacular when the snow melts in spring.

DANDENONG RANGES

On a clear day, the Dandenong Ranges can be seen from the centre of Melbourne – Mt Dandenong is the highest point at 633m. The hills are about 35km (a one hour drive) east of the city, and their natural beauty has long made them a favoured destination for those wanting to escape the city.

Despite the effects of encroaching urban sprawl and constant droves of visitors, the Dandenongs have retained much of their unique charm and appeal. The attractions include magnificent public gardens and plant nurseries, tearooms and restaurants, potteries and galleries, antique shops and markets, birdlife and native animals, and bushwalks and picnic areas. Things can get a little hectic on the narrow winding roads, particularly on weekends during spring and autumn; midweek visits are usually much more sedate and peaceful.

The Dandenong Ranges & Knox Visitor Information Centre (☎ 9758 7522) is at 1211 Burwood Hwy, in Upper Ferntree Gully.

The Parks Victoria office (☎ 9758 1342) is in the Lower Picnic Ground in Ferntree Gully, at the start of the Mt Dandenong Tourist Rd. Rangers can supply maps of the parks and walking tracks; opening hours vary seasonally.

Dandenong Ranges National Park

The Dandenong Ranges National Park is made up of the three largest areas of forest remaining in the Melbourne region. All three sections have barbecue and picnic areas and good walking tracks. The **Ferntree Gully National Park**, named for its abundance of tree ferns, has four good walking trails, each of around two hours. **Sherbrooke Forest** has a towering cover of mountain ash trees and a lower level of silver wattles, sassafras, blackwoods and other exotic trees. This forest is home to a large number of birds, including rosellas, kookaburras, currawongs and honeyeaters. The **Doongalla Reserve**, on the western slopes of Mt Dandenong, is not as accessible as the other two areas, and so the forest areas here are less crowded.

William Ricketts Sanctuary

The William Ricketts Sanctuary (☎ 13 1963), on the Mt Dandenong Tourist Rd, is one of the area's highlights. The sanctuary and its sculptures are the work of William Ricketts, who worked here up until his death in 1993 at the age of 94. His work was inspired by the years he spent living with Aborigines in central Australia and by their affinity with the land. His personal philosophies permeate and shape the sanctuary, which is set in damp fern gardens with trickling waterfalls and sculptures rising out of moss-covered rocks like spirits from the ground. It's open from 10 am to 5 pm daily (last entry 4.30 pm) and admission is $5/2 for adults/children.

Concerts are also held here during the summer; phone the sanctuary or check the *Age* for details.

Gardens

The high rainfall and deep volcanic soils of the Dandenongs are perfect for agriculture, and the area has long provided Melbourne's markets with much of their produce. The gardens and nurseries overflow with visitors who come to see colourful displays of tulips, daffodils, azaleas, rhododendrons and other flora. The gardens are at their best in spring and autumn, but are worth a visit at any time.

The **National Rhododendron Gardens** are on the Georgian Rd, next to the Olinda State Forest. There are groves of cherry blossoms, oaks, maples and beeches, and over 15,000 rhododendrons and azaleas. The gardens are open from 10 am to 4.30 pm daily, until 5.30 pm during the autumn, spring festivals and daylight saving time. Admission is $6.50/$4.50 for adults/children during spring and autumn, and $5/4 at other times.

The **Alfred Nicholas Memorial Gardens**, on Sherbrooke Rd, Sherbrooke, originally formed the grounds of Burnham Beeches, the country mansion of Alfred Nicholas, co-founder of Aspro and the Nicholas Pharmaceutical Company. The gardens have in recent years been restored by Parks Victoria and are open from 10 am to 4.30 pm (admission is $4/2).

Nearby, to the east, **George Tindale Memorial Gardens** are smaller and more intimate. The gardens are open from 10 am to 4 pm daily (admission $4/2).

Puffing Billy

One of the major attractions of the Dandenongs is *Puffing Billy* (☎ 9754 6800 for bookings and recorded information), a restored steam train that puffs its way through the hills and fern gullies between Belgrave and the Emerald Lakeside Park. Billy is the last survivor of a series of experimental railway lines built at the end of the 19th century to link rural areas to the city. Along the way you can visit the historic **Steam Museum**, at Menzies Creek, and the pretty town of Emerald, with **Lakeside Park** and the **Emerald Lake Model Railway**.

Puffing Billy operates up to four times every day except Christmas Day. The round trip takes 2½ hours and costs $25/14/71 for adults/children/families (lunch specials are also available). The *Puffing Billy* train station is a short stroll from Belgrave train station, the last stop on the Belgrave suburban line.

Visit the Web site at www.pbr.org.au for more information.

Places to Stay

There are numerous motels, guesthouses, B&Bs and self-contained cottages in the Dandenong area. The comfy *Emerald Backpackers* (☎ 5968 4086), in Lakeview Court, charges $13 for dorm beds. The owners can often find work for travellers in local nurseries and gardens. In Belgrave, *Jaynes Retreat* (☎ 9752 6181, 27 Terrys Ave) is a budget B&B starting at $20 per person.

Opposite the Rhododendron Gardens in Olinda, *Arcadia Cottages B&B* (☎ 9751 1017) is an impressive two-storey cedar

View from Hanging Rock

Werribee Mansion and gardens

RICHARD I'ANSON

Sherbrooke Forest, Dandenong Ranges National Park

RODNEY HYETT

The Great Ocean Road kisses the shoreline

homestead in a delightful garden setting. B&B in the self-contained cottages is $155 to $185 a night during the week and $195 to $245 at weekends. Also in Olinda, *A Loft in the Mill (☎ 9751 1700, 1–3 Harold St)* is a romantic, restored mill complete with spas and log fires. Doubles start at $75, suites at $99 and spa suites range from $110 to $240.

Along the Mt Dandenong Tourist Rd, the old-English-style *Kenlock Manor (☎ 9751 1680)* has guestrooms ranging from $125 to $140 a double. Also on Mt Dandenong Tourist Rd, the charming *Como Cottages (☎ 9751 2264)* is in a garden setting and prices range from $130 to $160 a night during the week and $180 to $220 at weekends, breakfast included.

Getting There & Away

You really need your own transport to explore the Dandenongs properly – the Mt Dandenong Tourist Rd is the main route through the ranges.

The Met's suburban trains run on the Belgrave line to the foothills of the Dandenongs. From Upper Ferntree Gully train station it's a 10-minute walk to the start of the Ferntree Gully National Park. Belgrave train station is the last stop on the line and the starting point for *Puffing Billy*. It's a 15-minute walk from the train station to Sherbrooke Forest.

US Buslines (☎ 9754 8111) also runs from both stations along the Mt Dandenong Tourist Rd.

Mornington Peninsula

The boot-shaped Mornington Peninsula, which juts out between Port Phillip Bay and Western Port, is a little over an hour's drive from the city centre. Because of its great beaches and other attractions, it has been a favourite summer resort for Melburnians since the 1870s, when paddle-steamers used to carry droves of holiday-makers down to Portsea and Sorrento from the city.

The narrow spit of land at the end of the peninsula has calm beaches on Port Phillip Bay – known as the 'front beaches' – and rugged, beautiful ocean beaches – known as the 'back beaches'. At the far end of the spit, Portsea has a reputation as a playground for the wealthy, while nearby Sorrento has the peninsula's best range of accommodation and restaurants.

Swimming and surfing top the list of peninsula activities, but you can also try snorkelling, scuba diving, fishing and sailing. There are excellent bushwalking trails through the Point Nepean National Park, as well as horse-riding ranches, boat cruises, dolphin swims and several great golf courses.

The coastal strip fronting Bass Strait is protected as part of the Mornington Peninsula National Park, and along here you'll find more stunning coastal walking tracks and some great surf beaches. There are also good swimming and surf beaches in Western Port. Inland, the peninsula is a picturesque blend of rolling hills and green pastures, terraced vineyards and dense forests. It's a great area for leisurely tours and explorations – you can visit dozens of wineries and vineyards (see the boxed text 'Vineyards Around Melbourne' earlier in this chapter), pick your own fruit in orchards and berry farms, shop at craft and produce markets, wander through the bush, or discover one of the many fine local restaurants.

Peninsula Tourism's main visitor information office (☎ 5987 3078) is on the Nepean Hwy in Dromana, and is open from 9 am to 5 pm daily.

MORNINGTON TO SORRENTO

If you're not in a hurry, turn off the Nepean Hwy at Mornington and take the slower but more scenic route around the coast, which rejoins the highway at Dromana. In Mornington you can visit **Studio City**, at 1140 Nepean Hwy, which has memorabilia relating to TV, cinema and radio (it's open from 10 am to 5 pm daily). In Mt Martha there's the **Briars Historic Homestead**, which is open from 11 am to 5 pm daily.

Coolart homestead, Lord Somers Rd in Somers, dates to 1895 and is surrounded by

EXCURSIONS

landscaped grounds. There are adjacent wetlands and a wildlife sanctuary. The grounds are perfect for a picnic, with barbecues, tables and hot water on tap, and there's also a visitor centre and shop. A daily slide show, 'Introducing Coolart', is screened in the Wetlands Observatory at 1.30 pm weekdays, 2 pm on weekends. Coolart is open from 10 am to 5 pm daily except Christmas Day, Boxing Day and Good Friday. Admission is $6/4.50/3/15 for an adult/concession/child/family.

Arthur's Seat State Park is just inland from Dromana and signposted off the Nepean Hwy. A scenic drive winds up to the summit lookout at 305m, and you can also reach it by the **Arthur's Seat Scenic Chairlift**. The park has good picnic and barbecue facilities, walking tracks, a fauna park and car museum, a kiosk and restaurant, and great views of the bay and peninsula from several lookouts.

In McCrae, the National Trust's **McCrae Homestead** is a timber-slab cottage built in 1846. It houses the paintings and writings of pioneer Georgina McCrae. It's open from noon to 4.30 pm daily; entry is $5/4 for adults/children.

SORRENTO

The oldest town on the peninsula, Sorrento has a delightful seaside atmosphere. During the summer silly season it's a frenetic and fashionable resort; during the winter months it's more akin to a sleepy little village. It has some fine 19th-century buildings constructed from locally quarried limestone, and it boasts fine beaches, good accommodation and excellent cafes and restaurants. Dolphin-watching cruises in the bay are incredibly popular, and while you're here be sure to take a ferry trip across to Queenscliff (see Getting There & Away later in this section).

Local operators, including Polperro Dolphin Swims (☎ 5988 8437), Dolphin Discovery Tours (☎ 018 392 507) and Moonraker (☎ 018 591 033), offer a combination of sightseeing cruises of the bay, fishing trips and dolphin-watching cruises. Dolphin cruises run for four hours and cost

$35 for sightseeing, $60 if you want to swim with the dolphins.

Places to Stay

There are plenty of caravan parks along the bay. The **Rye Foreshore Reserve** (☎ 5985 2405) and **Sorrento Foreshore Reserve** (☎ 5984 2797) both have sites starting at $10.

In Sorrento **Bell's Environmental YHA Hostel** (☎ 5984 4323, 3 Miranda St) is a great place to stay. The facilities are excellent and the owners extremely helpful. Bunks start at $12. **The Oceanic Motel** (☎ 5984 4166, 234 Ocean Beach Rd) has rooms ranging from $90 to $150, breakfast included.

Carmel B&B (☎ 5984 3512, 142 Ocean Beach Rd) is a historic and stylish limestone cottage with B&B ranging from $120 to $150 a double, and self-contained units from $90 to $120. **Sorrento on the Park** (☎ 5984 4777, 15 Hotham Rd) is an impressive complex with modern timber apartments ranging from $120 to $140 a night during the week; a two-night weekend package is $340 to $440, cooked breakfast included.

PORTSEA

Portsea has some great beaches. On the back beach there's the impressive natural rock formation **London Bridge**, plus a cliff where hang-gliders leap into the void. This ocean beach has good surf but can be dangerous for swimming, so swim between the flags. The front beaches are safer for swimming. If things get too hot wander up to the Portsea pub and enjoy a drink in the pretty (and usually pretty crowded) beer garden which overlooks the pier.

Diver Instruction Services (☎ 5984 3155) charges $125 for two dive trips, all gear supplied. Dive Victoria (☎ 5984 3155) offers one-day beginner dives starting at $120, including gear and two dives, and snorkelling trips for $30, plus $15 gear hire.

Places to Stay

The cheapest option is the **Portsea Hotel** (☎ 5984 2213, 3746 Point Nepean Rd), which has comfy rooms with shared facilities starting at $85; rooms with en suites start at $140. The **Portsea Village Resort**

(☎ *5984 8484, 3765 Nepean Hwy)* has executive-style apartments ranging from $195 to $450 per night.

The ultimate in luxury accommodation is the ***Peppers Delgany Portsea*** *(☎ 5984 4000)*, on Point Nepean Rd. It's set in a magnificent old limestone castle on five hectares of private gardens. A weekend escape in a traditional-style room costs $748 two nights for two people; the price includes two breakfasts and one three-course dinner. The midweek escape for one night for two people ranges from $297 to $344.

MORNINGTON PENINSULA NATIONAL PARK

After being off-limits to the general public for over 100 years because it was a quarantine station and army base, Point Nepean National Park on the tip of the peninsula was opened to the public in 1988. It has been expanded (and renamed) to incorporate the ocean beaches up to Cape Schanck and Green Bush. There's an excellent visitor centre (☎ 5984 4276) near the Cape Schanck entrance. Admission costs $8.50 for adults, $4.50 for children and $19 for families if you take the two- to four-hour bus tour, less if you want to walk.

The main track through the park starts from the visitor centre and runs down to the point – a return distance of 14km. There are also walks branching off the main track, so it's not unlikely to find yourself alone on a wild surf beach.

PORTSEA TO FLINDERS

The peninsula's south-western coastline faces Bass Strait. Along here are the beautiful, rugged ocean beaches of Blairgowrie, Rye, St Andrews, Gunnamatta and Cape Schanck. There is a series of points and bays and a backdrop of cliffs, sand dunes, spectacular scenery and tidal rock pools – this is the fragile natural habitat of coastal birdlife.

Surf life-saving clubs operate at both Gunnamatta and Portsea during summer. If you're planning to swim, head for the patrolled beaches.

At Cape Schanck there's the **Cape Schanck Lighthouse & Museum** (☎ 5988 6154), an operational lighthouse built in 1859, which has a kiosk, museum and information centre. It's open from 10 am to around 4 pm daily and admission is $2. Cape Schanck is now part of the Mornington Peninsula National Park but admission to this section is free during the week and $3.50 per car on weekends. Cape Schanck is a great place for picnics and there are some good bushwalks.

Off the road from Cape Schanck to Flinders is a gravel turn-off to the **Blowhole**, and the rock platforms along here are accessible at low tide.

FLINDERS TO HASTINGS

Western Port starts at the town of Flinders, a pretty village with a busy fishing fleet, good rocky point breaks for surfers, an excellent ocean-side golf course and views across to Phillip Island from the point at West Head. If the wind is south-easterly you'll often see hang-gliders launching off the cliff tops here.

Towns on this coast are not as developed and crowded as those on Port Phillip Bay, and the natural environment on this part of the peninsula is more fertile and 'Europeanised', with pine trees and rolling green hills – in stark contrast with the sand dunes and coastal scrub of the western side of the peninsula. There are good beaches all the way along here at Shoreham, Point Leo (which also has good surf beaches), Merricks, Balnarring, Somers and Hastings.

Head inland from Shoreham for some great scenic drives, and to explore the country around Red Hill and Main Ridge. The hills and bushlands make an appealing change from the coastal scenery, and there are some great craft galleries, produce stores and wineries to stumble across.

Places to Stay

The ***Flinders Cove Motor Inn*** *(☎ 5989 0666, 32 Cook St)* has reasonable rooms starting at $89 during the week and at $99 on weekends. ***Flinders Country Inn B&B*** *(☎ 5989 0933, 165 Wood St, Flinders)* is a perfect weekend escape, with doubles costing $150.

The ***Black Rabbit*** (*☎ 5989 8500)* on Hill-crest Rd in Shoreham is a modern limestone villa on a bushland property. The double rooms in the main house range from $115 to $170, and self-contained units are $130.

GETTING THERE & AWAY
Train & Bus
The Met's suburban trains from the city to Frankston take about an hour; you'll need a zone 1, 2 & 3 Met ticket, which will cost $5.30 for two hours, $9.50 for a full day. From Frankston train station, Portsea Passenger Buses (*☎ 5986 5666)* runs a service along the Nepean Hwy to Portsea between 7 am and 7 pm, which costs $6.90 one way.

Ferry
Queenscliff Sorrento Ferry Service (*☎ 5258 3244)* operates the MV *Queenscliff* car and passenger ferry, linking Sorrento with Queenscliff on the Bellarine Peninsula. It runs every day year round and takes about half an hour to make the crossing, departing from Queenscliff at 7, 9 and 11 am and 1, 3 and 5 pm, and returning from Sorrento at 8 and 10 am, noon and 2, 4 and 6 pm. During the peak seasons – Friday and Sunday from mid-September to mid-December and then daily until Easter Tuesday – there is an additional departure from Queenscliff at 7 pm and from Sorrento at 8 pm. Cars cost $32 to $36, plus $3 per adult; a motorcycle and rider costs $13; without a vehicle it is $7/5 for adults/kids.

A passenger ferry (*☎ 5984 1602)* also operates regular daily crossings from Sorrento and Portsea to Queenscliff between Christmas and Easter and during school holidays; from November until Christmas it operates on weekends only.

Phillip Island

At the entrance to Western Port, 137km south-east of Melbourne, Phillip Island is a very popular holiday resort. The island itself is quite rugged and windswept and there are plenty of beaches – both sheltered and with surf – a fascinating collection of wildlife and several fairly sleepy and old-fashioned townships.

Phillip Island's famous Penguin Parade is one of Australia's most popular tourist attractions. Tourists come by the bus load, and while some people are disappointed by the high degree of commercialisation, the other side of the coin is that the parade and displays are educational and the money contributes towards protecting the penguins' natural habitat.

There is an excellent information centre (*☎ 5956 7447)* in Newhaven just after you cross the bridge to the island.

PENGUIN PARADE
Each evening at **Summerland Beach** in the south-west of the island, the little penguins nesting there perform their 'parade', emerging from the sea and waddling resolutely up the beach to their nests – seemingly oblivious to the sightseers. The penguins are there year round, but they arrive in larger numbers in the summer when they are rearing their young. The parade takes place like clockwork a few minutes after sunset each day. Not surprisingly there are crowds of up to 4000 people, especially on weekends and holidays, so bookings should be made in advance. Contact the information centre at Newhaven or the Phillip Island Nature Park (*☎ 5956 8300* for recorded information). Admission for the Penguin Parade is $10.50/5.50/26.50 for an adult/child/family.

THE NOBBIES & SEAL ROCKS
Off Point Grant, the extreme south-west tip of the island, a group of rocks called the Nobbies rises from the sea. Beyond these are Seal Rocks, which are inhabited by Australia's largest colony of fur seals. The rocks are most crowded during the breeding season from October to December, when up to 6000 seals arrive.

At the glass-walled **Sea Life Centre** (*☎ 9793 6767)* you can see seals in their natural environment via remote-viewing displays. Displays include live videos of the seals and a 180° Seal Watch Panorama. There's also a seaside kiosk, a brasserie and restaurant, and a souvenir shop. The centre is open from 10 am to dusk daily; admission is $15/7.50/38 for adults/children/families.

OTHER ATTRACTIONS

Phillip Island has always been promoted as a good place to see koalas 'in the wild', which in the last 20 years hasn't really been the case. The resident koalas lived in defoliated trees in badly managed roadside reserves, and through a combination of introduced diseases and road accidents, the population has been in continual decline.

The best place to see koalas is at the **Koala Conservation Centre**, at Fiveways on the Phillip Island Tourist Rd. The centre has a visitor area and elevated boardwalks running through a bush setting. It is open from 10 am until 6 pm daily; admission is $5/2 for adults/kids.

Phillip Island also has **mutton-bird colonies**, particularly in the sand dunes around Cape Woolamai. These birds, which are actually called shearwaters, are amazingly predictable: they arrive back on the island on exactly the same day each year – 24 September – from their migration flight from Japan and Alaska. The birds stay on the island until April. Your best chance of seeing them is at the Penguin Parade during the spring and summer months, as they fly in low over the sea each evening at dusk. Also try the Forest Caves Reserve at Woolamai Beach.

The **Phillip Island Wildlife Park** is 1km south of the township of Cowes. Visitors can walk through enclosures and wetlands and see native animals and birds – wallabies, kangaroos, wombats, emus and reptiles. The park is open daily and admission is $9/4.50/25 for adults/children/families.

Swimming and **surfing** are popular island activities. The ocean beaches are on the south side of the island and there's a life-saving club at Woolamai – this beach is notorious for its strong rips and currents, so swim only between the flags. If you're not a good swimmer, head for the bay beaches around Cowes, or the quieter ocean beaches such as Smith and Barry Beaches. There are quite a few surf shops on the island which rent equipment.

The old **Motor Racing Circuit** was revamped to stage the Australian Motorcycle Grand Prix for the first time in 1989. After moving to Sydney it has returned to Phillip Island and seems set to stay.

The area has some good walking tracks and cycling tracks. The walking track at rugged **Cape Woolamai** is particularly impressive. Access to the signposted walking trail is from the Woolami surf beach near the life-saving club.

ORGANISED FLIGHTS, TOURS & CRUISES

Island Scenic Tours (☎ 5952 1042) runs trips most evenings from Cowes out to the Penguin Parade ($18, including entry), as well as various scenic tours. Amaroo Park YHA also operates an evening service out to Penguin Parade. Phillip Island airport (☎ 5956 7316) operates scenic flights, which cost from $36 to $90 per person, with a minimum of two people. Bay Connections Cruises (☎ 5678 5642) runs cruises to Seal Rocks ($38/27 adult/child), French Island ($42/30) and evening 'shearwater cruises' ($27/18).

PLACES TO STAY

Phillip Island has hostels, guesthouses, B&Bs, motels, holiday flats and camping sites in Cowes, Newhaven, Rhyll, Ventnor and San Remo. Generally, you need to book ahead during Christmas, Easter and school holidays. The places mentioned below are all in Cowes.

The best backpacker accommodation is at the very friendly *Amaroo Park YHA* *(☎ 5952 2548)* on the corner of Church and Osborne Sts. Six-bed dorms cost $14 ($17 for nonmembers); doubles are $17 per person ($20) and tents $7 per person ($10). The facilities are good and a number of excursions can be arranged here. The owners run free courtesy buses from Melbourne (see the following Getting There & Around section). If you're after a caravan park in the area try *Anchor Belle Holiday Park* *(☎ 5952 2258, 272 Church St)*.

The *Isle of Wight Hotel (☎ 5952 2301)*, on The Esplanade, has motel rooms starting at $40/50 for a single/double (prices rise in summer). Farther along The Esplanade, the *Continental Resort (☎ 5952 2316)* is a modern executive-style complex with rooms ranging from $119 to $245 for a double. Also on The Esplanade is the *Anchor at Cowes (☎ 5952 1351)*, with a good restaurant and hotel units and suite from $62 to $72, and self-contained townhouses starting at $92.

Rhylston Park (☎ 5952 2730, 190 Thompson Ave) is a restored 1886 homestead with period fittings and furnishings, set in two hectares of gardens. Doubles range from $90 to $100. *Narabeen Cottage (☎ 5952 2062, 16 Steele St)* is a 'gourmet getaway' with five guestrooms and a small restaurant. B&B starts at $95 a double during the week, $210 at weekends with dinner included.

Cliff Top Country House (☎ 5952 1033, 1 Marlin St), overlooking Smith Beach, is a relaxed, kid-free retreat with doubles ranging from $150 to $300.

GETTING THERE & AROUND

V/Line's daily bus service between Melbourne and Cowes costs $13.80 and takes 3¼ hours.

Amaroo Park YHA (☎ 5952 2548) runs a courtesy bus to the island, leaving from the YHA's Queensberry Hill Hostel, in North Melbourne, at 1 pm every Tuesday and Friday. Transport is free if you're staying at Amaroo Park YHA.

There is no public transport on the island. You can hire bikes from Phillip Island Bike Hire (☎ 5952 1720), at 11 Findlay St in Cowes, or from Amaroo Park YHA.

LONELY PLANET

Guides by Region

Lonely Planet is known worldwide for publishing practical, reliable and no-nonsense travel information in our guides and on our Web site. The Lonely Planet list covers just about every accessible part of the world. Currently there are 15 series: travel guides, Shoestring guides, Condensed guides, Phrasebooks, Read This First, Healthy Travel, Walking guides, Cycling guides, Pisces Diving & Snorkeling guides, City Maps, Travel Atlases, Out to Eat, World Food, Journeys travel literature and Pictorials.

AFRICA Africa on a shoestring • Africa – the South • Arabic (Egyptian) phrasebook • Arabic (Moroccan) phrasebook • Cairo • Cape Town • Cape Town city map • Central Africa • East Africa • Egypt • Egypt travel atlas • Ethiopian (Amharic) phrasebook • The Gambia & Senegal • Healthy Travel Africa • Kenya • Kenya travel atlas • Malawi, Mozambique & Zambia • Morocco • North Africa • Read This First Africa • South Africa, Lesotho & Swaziland • South Africa, Lesotho & Swaziland travel atlas • Swahili phrasebook • Tanzania, Zanzibar & Pemba • Trekking in East Africa • Tunisia • West Africa • Zimbabwe, Botswana & Namibia • Zimbabwe, Botswana & Nambia Travel Atlas • World Food Morocco
Travel Literature: The Rainbird: A Central African Journey • Songs to an African Sunset: A Zimbabwean Story • Mali Blues: Traveling to an African Beat

AUSTRALIA & THE PACIFIC Auckland • Australia • Australian phrasebook • Bushwalking in Australia • Bushwalking in Papua New Guinea • Fiji • Fijian phrasebook • Healthy Travel Australia, NZ and the Pacific • Islands of Australia's Great Barrier Reef • Melbourne • Melbourne city map • Micronesia • New Caledonia • New South Wales & the ACT • New Zealand • Northern Territory • Outback Australia • Out to Eat – Melbourne • Out to Eat – Sydney • Papua New Guinea • Pidgin phrasebook • Queensland • Rarotonga & the Cook Islands • Samoa • Solomon Islands • South Australia • South Pacific • South Pacific Languages phrasebook • Sydney • Sydney city map • Sydney Condensed • Tahiti & French Polynesia • Tasmania • Tonga • Tramping in New Zealand • Vanuatu • Victoria • Western Australia
Travel Literature: Islands in the Clouds • Kiwi Tracks: A New Zealand Journey • Sean & David's Long Drive

CENTRAL AMERICA & THE CARIBBEAN Bahamas, Turks & Caicos • Bermuda • Central America on a shoestring • Costa Rica • Cuba • Dominican Republic & Haiti • Eastern Caribbean • Guatemala, Belize & Yucatán: La Ruta Maya • Jamaica • Mexico • Mexico City • Panama • Puerto Rico • Read This First Central & South America • World Food Mexico
Travel Literature: Green Dreams: Travels in Central America

EUROPE Amsterdam • Amsterdam city map • Andalucía • Austria • Baltic States phrasebook • Barcelona • Berlin • Berlin city map • Britain • British phrasebook • Brussels, Bruges & Antwerp • Budapest city map • Canary Islands • Central Europe • Central Europe phrasebook • Corfu & Ionians • Corsica • Crete • Crete Condensed • Croatia • Cyprus • Czech & Slovak Republics • Denmark • Dublin • Eastern Europe • Eastern Europe phrasebook • Edinburgh • Estonia, Latvia & Lithuania • Europe on a shoestring • Finland • Florence • France • French phrasebook • Germany • German phrasebook • Greece • Greek Islands • Greek phrasebook • Hungary • Iceland, Greenland & the Faroe Islands • Ireland • Italian phrasebook • Italy • Krakow • Lisbon • The Loire • London • London city map • London Condensed • Mediterranean Europe • Mediterranean Europe phrasebook • Munich • Norway • Paris • Paris city map • Paris Condensed • Poland • Portugal • Portugese phrasebook • Portugal travel atlas • Prague • Prague city map • Provence & the Côte d'Azur • Read This First Europe • Romania & Moldova • Rome • Russia, Ukraine & Belarus • Russian phrasebook • Scandinavian & Baltic Europe • Scandinavian Europe phrasebook • Scotland • Slovenia • Spain • Spanish phrasebook • St Petersburg • Sweden • Switzerland • Trekking in Spain • Tuscany • Ukrainian phrasebook • Venice • Vienna • Walking in Britain • Walking in Ireland • Walking in Italy • Walking in Spain • Walking in Switzerland • Western Europe • Western Europe phrasebook • World Food Ireland • World Food Italy • World Food Spain
Travel Literature: The Olive Grove: Travels in Greece

INDIAN SUBCONTINENT Bangladesh • Bengali phrasebook • Bhutan • Delhi • Goa • Hindi & Urdu phrasebook • India • India & Bangladesh travel atlas • Indian Himalaya • Karakoram Highway • Kerala • Mumbai (Bombay) • Nepal • Nepali phrasebook • Pakistan • Rajasthan • Read This First: Asia & India • South India • Sri Lanka • Sri Lanka phrasebook • Tibet • Tibetan phrasebook • Trekking in the Indian Himalaya • Trekking in the Karakoram & Hindukush • Trekking in the Nepal Himalaya
Travel Literature: In Rajasthan • Shopping for Buddhas • The Age Of Kali

LONELY PLANET

Mail Order

Lonely Planet products are distributed worldwide.They are also available by mail order from Lonely Planet, so if you have difficulty finding a title please write to us. North and South American residents should write to 150 Linden St, Oakland CA 94607, USA; European and African residents should write to 10a Spring Place, London, NW5 3BH, UK; and residents of other countries to PO Box 617, Hawthorn, Victoria 3122, Australia.

ISLANDS OF THE INDIAN OCEAN Madagascar & Comoros • Maldives • Mauritius, Réunion & Seychelles

MIDDLE EAST & CENTRAL ASIA Bahrain, Kuwait & Qatar • Central Asia • Central Asia phrasebook • Dubai • Hebrew phrasebook • Iran • Israel & the Palestinian Territories • Israel & the Palestinian Territories travel atlas • Istanbul • Istanbul City Map • Istanbul to Cairo on a shoestring • Jerusalem • Jerusalem City Map • Jordan • Jordan, Syria & Lebanon travel atlas • Lebanon • Middle East • Oman & the United Arab Emirates • Syria • Turkey • Turkey travel atlas • Turkish phrasebook • World Food Turkey • Yemen
Travel Literature: The Gates of Damascus • Kingdom of the Film Stars: Journey into Jordan • Black on Black: Iran Revisited

NORTH AMERICA Alaska • Backpacking in Alaska • Baja California • California & Nevada • California Condensed • Canada • Chicago • Chicago city map • Deep South • Florida • Hawaii • Honolulu • Las Vegas • Los Angeles • Miami • New England • New Orleans • New York City • New York city map • New York Condensed • New York, New Jersey & Pennsylvania • Oahu • Pacific Northwest USA • Puerto Rico • Rocky Mountain • San Francisco • San Francisco city map • Seattle • Southwest USA • Texas • USA • USA phrasebook • Vancouver • Washington, DC & the Capital Region • Washington DC city map
Travel Literature: Drive Thru America

NORTH-EAST ASIA Beijing • Cantonese phrasebook • China • Hong Kong • Hong Kong city map • Hong Kong, Macau & Guangzhou • Japan • Japanese phrasebook • Japanese audio pack • Korea • Korean phrasebook • Kyoto • Mandarin phrasebook • Mongolia • Mongolian phrasebook • Seoul • South-West China • Taiwan • Tokyo
Travel Literature: Lost Japan • In Xanadu

SOUTH AMERICA Argentina, Uruguay & Paraguay • Bolivia • Brazil • Brazilian phrasebook • Buenos Aires • Chile & Easter Island • Chile & Easter Island travel atlas • Colombia • Ecuador & the Galapagos Islands • Healthy Travel Central & South America • Latin American Spanish phrasebook • Peru • Quechua phrasebook • Rio de Janeiro • Rio de Janeiro city map • South America on a shoestring • Trekking in the Patagonian Andes • Venezuela
Travel Literature: Full Circle: A South American Journey

SOUTH-EAST ASIA Bali & Lombok • Bangkok • Bangkok city map • Burmese phrasebook • Cambodia • Hanoi • Healthy Travel Asia & India • Hill Tribes phrasebook • Ho Chi Minh City • Indonesia • Indonesia's Eastern Islands • Indonesian phrasebook • Indonesian audio pack • Jakarta • Java • Laos • Lao phrasebook • Laos travel atlas • Malay phrasebook • Malaysia, Singapore & Brunei • Myanmar (Burma) • Philippines • Pilipino (Tagalog) phrasebook • Read This First Asia & India • Singapore • South-East Asia on a shoestring • South-East Asia phrasebook • Thailand • Thailand's Islands & Beaches • Thailand travel atlas • Thai phrasebook • Thai audio pack • Vietnam • Vietnamese phrasebook • Vietnam travel atlas • World Food Thailand • World Food Vietnam

ALSO AVAILABLE: Antarctica • The Arctic • Brief Encounters: Stories of Love, Sex & Travel • Chasing Rickshaws • Lonely Planet Unpacked • Not the Only Planet: Travel Stories from Science Fiction • Sacred India • Travel with Children • Traveller's Tales

Index

Text

Boxed Text

Melbourne Maps

MAP 2 – CENTRAL MELBOURNE

To Flemington
(2.5km)

▼ 1

▼ 2

▼ 3

North
Melbourne

Victoria St

▼ 4

▼ 5

To
Melbourne Zoo
(3km)

■ 6

Miller St

Erol St

Roden St

Eades St

Chetwynd St

King St

Stanley St

Howard St

Capel St

Victoria St

Victoria St

Spencer St

To Footscray
(4km)

Ireland St

Hawke St

Adderley St

Stanley St

Roden St

Rosslyn St

Walsh St

William St

Peel St

Queen Victoria
Market

Therry St

Queen St

■ 20

21 ■

Elizabeth St

22

West
Melbourne

0   100   200m

100   200yd

Dudley St

Franklin St

Franklin St

A'Beckett St

Franklin St

24 ■

23 ■

Anthony St

Rosslyn St

Festival Hall

Dudley St

25 ✦

Batman St

Jeffcott St

Flagstaff
Gardens
✿

Flagstaff

M

Old Royal
Mint

Police
HQ ✦

Hardware
St

52 ◆

53 ■

To
Victoria Dock
(1km)

✦ 26

King St

Adderley St

Latrobe St

Niagara
La

77 ◆

77 ◆

Docklands

■ 83

Little Lonsdale St

The
Age

Lonsdale St

Law
Courts

82 ◆

81 ◆

80 ◆

Colonial Stadium

Wurundjeri Way

Spencer St

Little Bourke St

84 ▼

85 ▼

Bourke
Place

King St

Church St

William St

88 ■

87 ◆

Penfold Pl

Footscray Rd (Docklands Hwy)

Bourke St

Godfrey La

86 ■

Bank Pl

154 ▼

Little Collins St

Francis St

Collins St

King St

Church St

151 ■

152 ▼

153 ✦

Custom House La

William St

163 ☒

Market St

Spencer
Street

155 ■

156 ■

157 ■

158 ■

Flinders La

Flinders St

Queens Wharf Rd

Yarra
Turning
Basin

Queens
Bridge

To
Victoria Harbour
Precinct
(500m)

Pigott St

Charles Grimes Bridge Rd

Footscray Rd

Yarra Quay

North Wharf Rd

159 ☒

World
Trade
Centre

Batman
Park

Kings
Bridge

Queens Wharf Rd

162 ■

Kings Way

Queens Promenade

Crown
Entertainment
Complex

Ferry to
Williamstown

Wharves

20

30

Charles
Grimes
Bridge

Siddeley St

161

Yarra River Cruises

160 ☒

Spencer
Street
Bridge

Dukes
Dock

Orrs
Dock

Clarendon St

Yarra Promenade

Crown
Casino

Yarra Promenade

Whiteman St

Power St

Southbank

City Rd

Lorimer St

South Wharf Rd

Lorimer St

Melbourne
Exhibition
Centre

To
South Melbourne (3km)

Queensbridge St

Walsh St

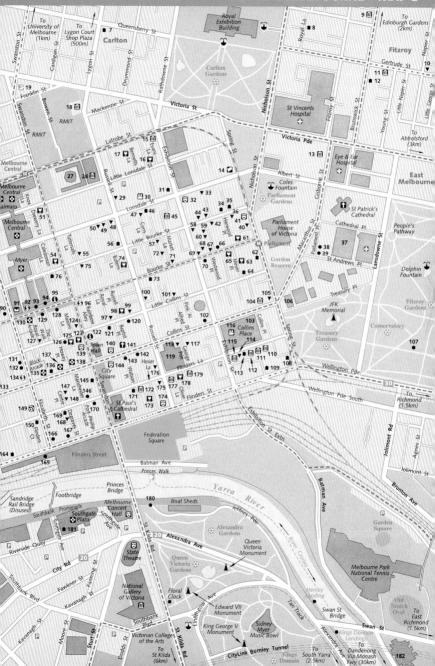

To University of Melbourne (1km)
To Lygon Court Shop Plaza (500m)
Queensberry St
Royal Exhibition Building
9
To Edinburgh Gardens (2km)

Carlton
7
8
Royal La
Fitzroy
Napier St

Swanston St
Cardigan St
Lygon St
Drummond St
Rathdowne St

Carlton Gardens
Nicholson St
Gertrude St
10
11
12
Little Napier St
Young St
Little George St

19
Franklin St
18
Mackenzie St
Victoria St
St Vincents Hospital
Fitzroy St
Brunswick St
To Abbotsford (3km)

Bowen St
RMIT
RMIT
Latrobe St
Victoria Pde
East Melbourne

Melbourne Central
15
17
16
Evans St
Bennetts La
Exhibition St
14
13
Eye & Ear Hospital
Gisborne St

Melbourne Central
Aimaru
51
27
28
Russell St
Little Lonsdale St
31
Albert St
Coles Fountain
Parliament Gardens
St Patrick's Cathedral
Cathedral Pl
People's Pathway

Melbourne Central
29
30
Lonsdale St
46
47
45
32
33
43
44
34
35
42
41
40
Harwood
36
37
Parliament House of Victoria
38
39
St Andrews Pl

Myer
50
49
48
58
59
60
61
62
39
Parliament
Gordon Reserve
Dolphin Fountain

54
55
56
57
72
71
70
68
67
66
65
69
63
64
Gisborne St
Macarthur St
Lansdowne St
Conservatory
Fitzroy Gardens

76
75
74
73
Bourke St
Treasury Pl
107

91
92
93
94
95
96
99
100
101
Little Collins St
104
105
106
JFK Memorial

90
128
129
124
98
97
120
102
103
116
Collins Place
114
Treasury Gardens

130
127
126
125
123
122
121
Collins St
115
113
112
110
111
109
108
Wellington Pde

131
132
133
134
135
136
137
138
139
140
141
142
143
144
Town Hall
City Square
119
118
117
176
Flinders La
30
To Richmond (1.5km)

147
148
145
146
171
172
173
174
177
178
Flinders St
Wellington Pde South
Wellington Pde-South

149
150
164
165
166
167
168
169
170
St Paul's Cathedral
Federation Square
Flinders Street

Batman Ave
Princes Walk
Yarra River
Batman Ave
Brunton Ave

180
Boat Sheds
Jeffries Pde
River Cruises
Jolimont Rd
Jolimont St

Sandridge Rail Bridge (Disused)
Footbridge
Princes Bridge
Melbourne Concert Hall
Southgate Plaza
181
St Kilda Rd
20
Alexandra Ave
Alexandra Gardens
Queen Victoria Monument
Garden Square
Old South Richmond (1.5km)

Riverside Quay
City Rd
20
State Theatre
Queen Victoria Gardens
Melbourne Park National Tennis Centre

Southbank Blvd
Fawkner St
Fanning St
National Gallery of Victoria
Floral Clock
Edward VII Monument
King George V Monument
Sidney Myer Music Bowl
Henley Landing
Swan St Bridge
Tan Track
Swan St
To East Richmond (1.5km)

Southbank Blvd
Kavanagh St
Moore St
Sturt St
Dodds St
Southbank Blvd
Victorian College of the Arts
To St Kilda (6km)
St Kilda Rd
Linlithgow Ave
CityLink Burnley Tunnel
Kings Domain
To South Yarra (2.5km)
To Dandenong Via Monash Fwy (30km)
182

CENTRAL MELBOURNE

Crown Towers Hotel presides over the glassy waters of the Yarra River.

MANFRED GOTTSCHALK

Maritime themes at Melbourne Aquarium

The public baths at Crown Entertainment Complex?

MAP 3 – CARLTON, FITZROY, NORTH & EAST MELBOURNE

Kensington

To
Melbourne Airport
via CityLink
(20km)

Victorian
Archive
Centre

Parkville

Map 4

University
High School

Story St

To
Melbourne
Zoo (2

Bruce St

Arden St

Lloyd St

To
Footscray
(3km)

To
Footscray
(3km)

North
Melbourne
Cricket Ground

Haines St

O'Shanassy St

Molesworth St

Harker St

3

Errol St

Curzon St

Arden St

Flemington Rd

Royal
Melbourne
Hospital

Grattan St

10

Dynon Rd

West
Melbourne

Moonee Ponds
(5km)

Harcourt St

Courtney St

Villiers St

6

North
Melbourne

Wreckyn St

Blackwood St

9

8

Pelham St

Elizabeth St

Royal Pde

Elizabeth St

Berkeley St

11

Queensberry St

Victoria St

Abbotsford St

Leveson St

Chetwynd St

Peel St

Howard St

Capel St

7

Errol St

5

4

North
Melbourne

See Map 2 – Central Melbourne

Spencer St

Ireland St

Hawke St

Roden St

Stanley St

Rosslyn St

Adderley Street

Railway Pl

Dudley St

King St

Queen
Victoria
Market

Therry St

Franklin St

A'Beckett St

Flagstaff
Gardens

Peel St

Queen St

Batman St

Jeffcott St

Latrobe St

Flagstaff

Little Lonsdale St

Lonsdale St

Little Bourke St

Bourke St

Little Collins St

Collins St

Rialto
Towers

Flinders La

Flinders St

William St

Spencer St

King St

Footscray Rd (Docklands Hwy)

Colonial
Stadium

Bourke St West

Spencer
Street

Victoria Harbour

Central Pier

North Wharf Promenade

North Wharf Rd

Docklands

Pigott St

Charles Grimes Bridge Rd

Footscray Rd

Yarra River

To
Fishermans Bend
(2km) &
Westgate Park
(3km)

Lorimer St

Yarra River
Cruises

Charles
Grimes
Bridge

Dukes Dock

Spencer St
Bridge

Kings
Bridge

Queen
Bridge

Crown
Casino

Queensbridge St

City Rd

Port
Melbourne

West Gate Freeway

Melbourne
Exhibition
Centre

To
Scienceworks (9km)
& Geelong
(70km)

Inglis St

Brady St

Fennell St

Boundary St

South
Melbourne

Montague St

Normanby Rd

Clarendon St

Map 7

King St

Brunswick St Enlargement

Rose St

34

35

36

37

Kerr St

33

38

39

40

41

Argyle St

Brunswick St

45

46

44

32

47

43

Johnston St

42

48

Young St

CARLTON, FITZROY, NORTH & EAST MELBOURNE

CHRIS MELLOR

Historic Ormond College, at the top of College Crescent, Parkville

Gates crafted in metal, Fitzroy

William Street stretching north to Flagstaff Gardens

Kebab meets barbie!

Lygon Street, Carlton, by night

Brunswick Street Parade

MAP 4 – PARKVILLE, NORTH FITZROY & BRUNSWICK

Clifton Park

Albert St

Victoria St

Brunswick

To Melbourne Holiday Park (5km), Fawkner Crematorium & Memorial Park (7km)

Gilpin Park

Albert St

Dawson St

Brunswick

Moule St

South Day St

Wylie Reserve

Munro St

Collier Cres

Brunswick Secondary College

Melbourne Institute of Textiles

RMIT

Blair St

Glenlyon Rd

Charles St

Cohuna St

Mincha St

Guthrie St

Centennial Ave

Grantham St

Fenton St

Edward

Fleming St

Heller St

Gray St

Temple Park

Gold St

Wilson St

Weston

Brunswick Rd

To Maribyrnong (4km)

Barkly St

Jewell

Black St

Sydney Rd

Brunswick City Shopping Centre

Barkly St

Park St

Royal Park Psychiatric Hospital

Melbourne Juvenile Justice Centre

Melbourne Extended Care & Rehabilitation Service

Poplar Rd

Western Oval

Ransford Oval

McAlister Oval

1

Park St

2

Holtom St

Pigdon St

Oak St

To Melbourne Airport (20km)

Royal Park Golf Course

Ryder Oval

Levers St

Bowen Cres

Arnold St

CityLink (Tullamarine Fwy)

Parkville Centre Psychiatric Hospital

McPherson Baseball Field

Royal Park

Poplar Oval

The Avenue

Milk La

Royal Pde

Optus Oval

Garton St

Richardson

Manningham St

Poplar Rd

Levers St

Walker St

Carlton Cricket Ground

MacPherson

Royal Melbourne Zoo

State Netball & Hockey Centre

Elliott Ave

Parkville

Brens Oval

HG Smith Oval

Leonard St

Princes Park

Princes Park Dve

Melbourne General Cemetery

Brens Dve

Women's Recreation Centre

MacArthur Rd

Flemington Bridge

Elliott Ave

Boundary Rd

Racecourse Rd

To Flemington Racecourse (2.5km)

6

Royal Park

Oxford Oval

Cemetery Rd

Cemetery

College Cres

Curran St

Brougham St

Flemington Rd

Native Plants Garden

Burnie St

Melrose St

Esrkine St

Drayton St

Abbotsford St

Aubil La

Royal Childrens Hospital

Gatehouse St

Levers Reserve

Fitzgibbon St

Royal Pde

College Cres

University of Melbourne

Swanston St

North Melbourne

National Archive Centre

Canning St

Macaulay Rd

Shiel St

Chapman St

7

Harker St

Map 3

Story St

University High School

8

Tin Alley

Melbourne Central Business District (2km)

9

Elgin St

Brunswick

Blyth St

To Northcote Municipal Golf Links (1.5km)

Thornbury

To Reservoir (6km)

Victoria St

Albert St

Fleming Park

Arthurton Rd

To Northcote (500m)

Greek Orthodox Monastery

Lygon St

Minnie St

Ewing St

Allan St

Home St

Huchinson St

John St

Nicholson St

Peers St

Sumner St

Rupert St

Dudley St

Merri Park

St Georges Rd

Park St

Charles Clarke St

Bridge St

Merri

Luscombe St

Balfe Park

Taylor St

White St

Rae St

Miller St

Clauscen St

Barkly St

Merri Pde

Union St

Merri Creek

1	The Princes Park Motor Inn
2	Ramada Inn
3	Empress Hotel
4	Moroccan Soup Bar
5	Carlton Library
6	Burke & Wills Memorial Cairn
7	Chapman Gardens YHA Hostel
8	Grainger Museum
9	Ian Potter Museum of Art
10	Dan O'Connell Hotel
11	Matteo's Ristorante
12	Rubira's
13	Fitzroy Swimming Pool
14	Retro Cafe

Brunswick Rd

Park St

Holden St

Park St

Holden St

McKillop La

Rushall Cres

Rushall

Mellwraith St

Keeley La

Drummond St

Rathdowne St

Mary St

Pigdon St

Moss St

Brunswick St

Birkenhead St

Best St

St Georges Rd

Scotchmer St

Bennett St

Kneen St

Sumner Ave

Paterson St

Amess St

Canning St

Station St

Richardson St

Scotchmer St

2 3

Reid St

Batman St

Rae St

Egremont St

Tranmere St

4 ▼

Ferrie St

Falconer St

Michael St

To Northcote (2.5km)

North Carlton

MacPherson St

Fenwick St

Taplin Pl

Boston Pl

Church St

Edinburgh Gardens

Alfred Cres

Delbridge St

Rowe St

Park Pde

Park Pde

North Fitzroy

Curtain St

5 ●

Newry St

Henty St

O'Grady St

Lee St

Davis St

Lygon St

Nicholson St

St Georges Rd

Freeman St

Percy St

WT Peterson Community Oval

Newry St

Napier St

Grant St

McKean St

Queens Pde

North Tce

Princes St

Drummond St

Rathdowne St

Victoria Pl

10 ☐

Neill St

Canning St

Station St

York St

Rae St

Brunswick St

11 ▼

Grace La

Hodgkinson St

Page St

Darling Gardens

South Tce

Hoddle St

Alexandra Pde

12 ▼

Cecil St

Westgarth St

14 ▼

Leicester St

Rose St

Kay St

Pitt St

Palmerston St

Carlton

Kerr St

To Melbourne Museum (500m)

Alexandra Pde

Young St

Napier St

George St

Gore St

13 ☐

Reeves St

Hilton St

Budd St

Smith St

To Yarra Bend Park (1.5km)

Council St

Emma St

Blanche St

Wellington St

Charlotte St

Noone St

Alexandra Pde

Eastern Fwy

Alexandra Pde

To St Patrick's Cathedral (3km)

Map 3

Map 5

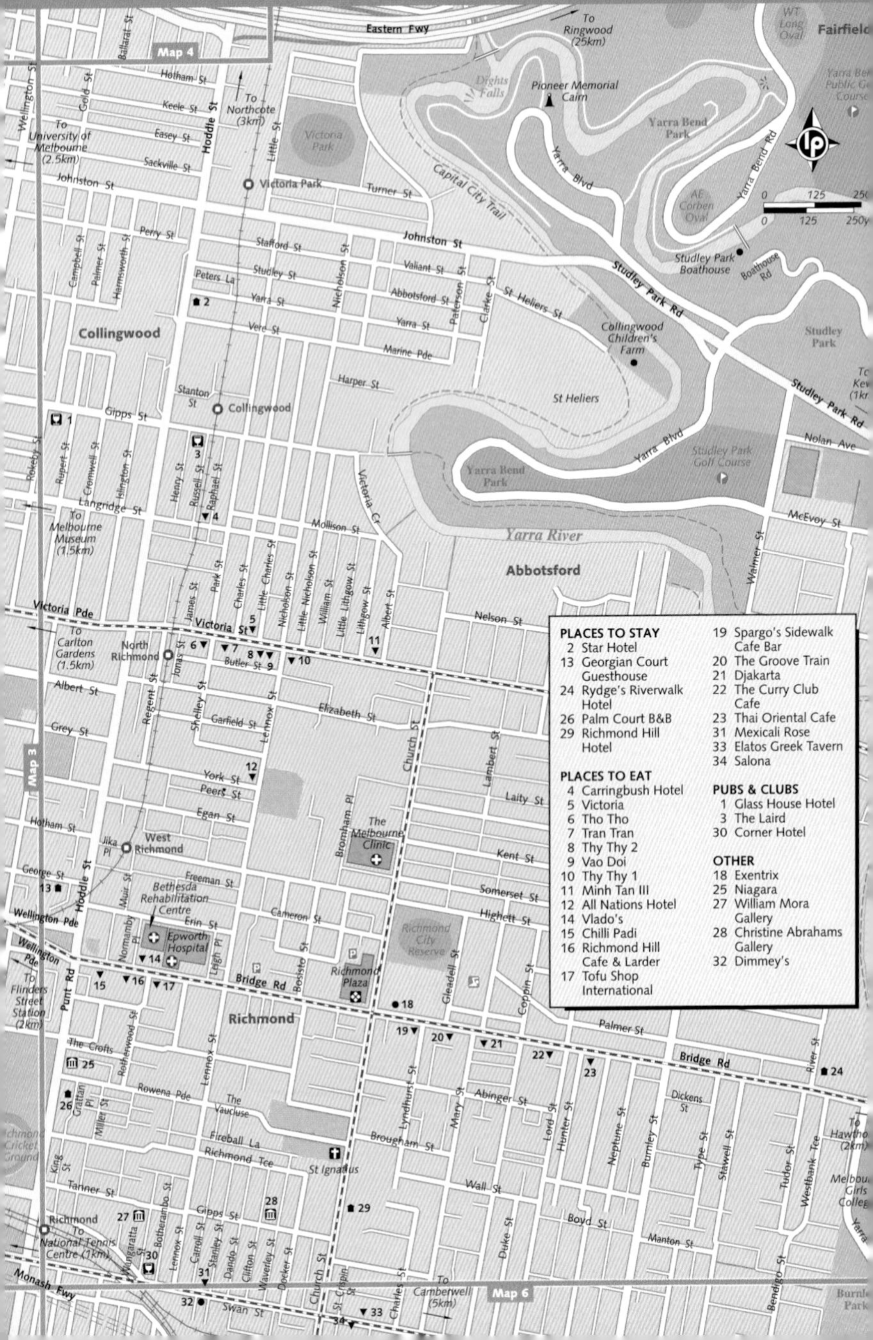

Map 4

To Ringwood (25km)

Eastern Fwy

WT Long Oval

Fairfield

Yarra Bend Public Golf Course

Drights Falls

Pioneer Memorial Cairn

Yarra Bend Park

AE Corben Oval

To Northcote (3km)

Hotham St
Keele St
Easey St
Sackville St

Johnston St

To University of Melbourne (2.5km)

Victoria Park

Turner St

Capital City Trail

Yarra Blvd

Yarra Bend Rd

125 250
125 250pf

Studley Park Rd

Studley Park Boathouse

Boathouse Rd

Perry St
Stafford St
Studley St
Nicholson St
Abbotsford St
Yarra St
Marine Pde

Johnston St

Valiant St
Paterson St
St Heliers St

Collingwood Children's Farm

Studley Park

To Kew (1k)

Collingwood

Harper St

St Heliers

Studley Park Rd

Stanton St

Collingwood

Nolan Ave

Gipps St

Yarra Blvd

Studley Park Golf Course

McEvoy St

To Melbourne Museum (1.5km)

Langridge St
Mollison St

Victoria Cr

Yarra Bend Park

Yarra River

Abbotsford

Nelson St

Victoria Pde

To Carlton Gardens (1.5km)

Victoria St

North Richmond

Albert St
Grey St
Hotham St

Elizabeth St
Garfield St
York St
Peel St
Egan St

Church St

Laity St
Lambert St

Kent St
Somerset St
Highett St

Wittner St

Map 3

West Richmond

Jika Pl
George St

Bethesda Rehabilitation Centre

The Melbourne Clinic

Bromham Pl

Wellington Pde

Epworth Hospital

Freeman St
Erin St
Cameron St

Richmond City Reserve

Richmond Plaza

Bridge Rd

To Flinders Street Station (2km)

Richmond

Bridge Rd

To Hawthe (2km)

The Crofts

Rowena Pde

The Vaucluse

Dickens St

To Hawtho (2km)

Richmond Cricket Ground

Fireball La
Richmond Tce

St Ignatius

Wall St
Boyd St
Manton St

Melbour Girls Colle

Richmond

To National Tennis Centre (1km)

Gipps St

St James St

Swan St

To Camberwell (5km)

Map 6

Burnle

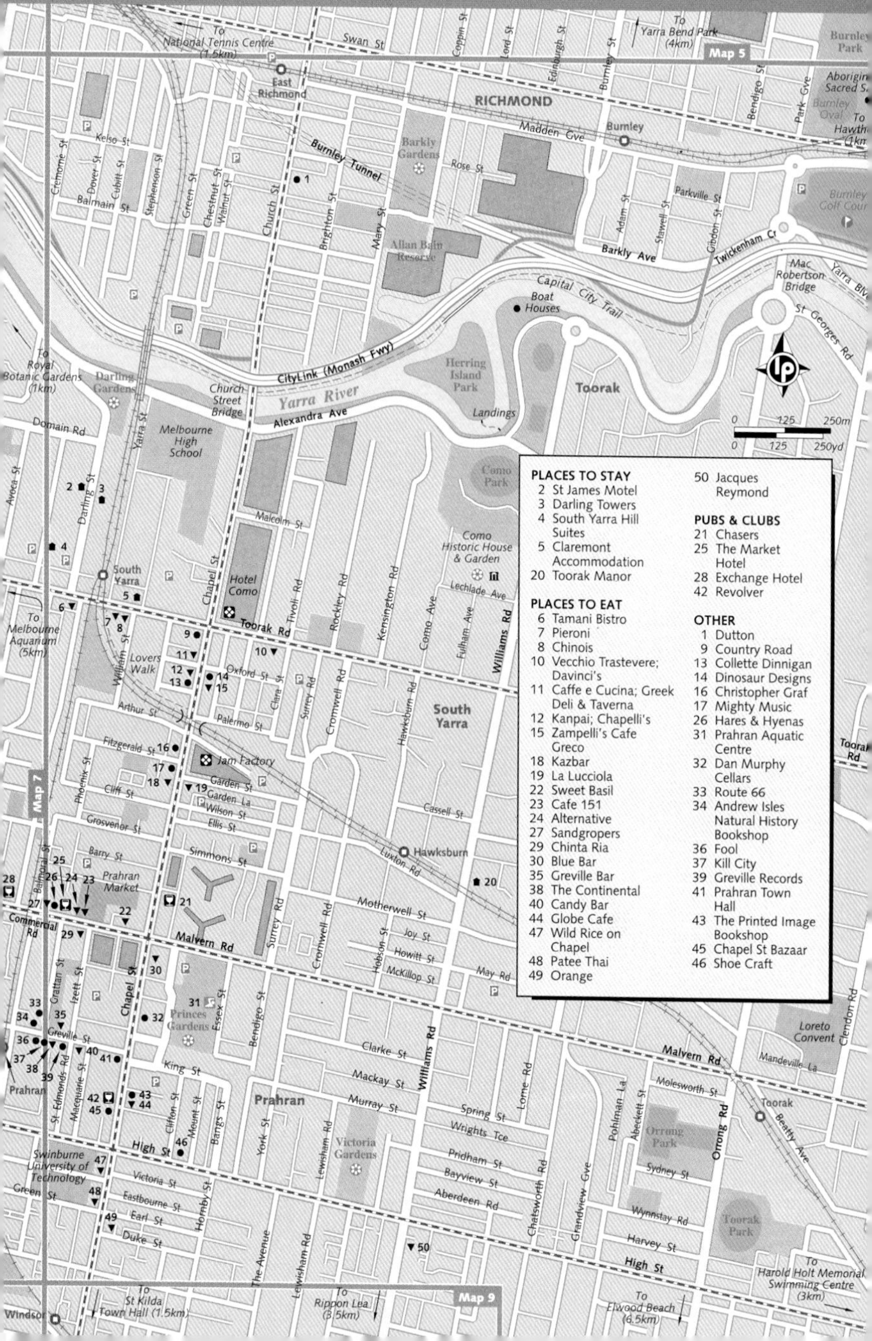

Map 5

RICHMOND

Yarra River

Toorak

South Yarra

South Yarra

Prahran

Prahran

Windsor

Map 7

Map 9

PLACES TO STAY
2 St James Motel
3 Darling Towers
4 South Yarra Hill Suites
5 Claremont Accommodation
20 Toorak Manor

PLACES TO EAT
6 Tamani Bistro
7 Pieroni
8 Chinois
10 Vecchio Trastevere; Davinci's
11 Caffe e Cucina; Greek Deli & Taverna
12 Kanpai; Chapelli's
15 Zampelli's Cafe Greco
18 Kazbar
19 La Lucciola
22 Sweet Basil
23 Cafe 151
24 Alternative
27 Sandgropers
29 Chinta Ria
30 Blue Bar
35 Greville Bar
38 The Continental
40 Candy Bar
44 Globe Cafe
47 Wild Rice on Chapel
48 Patee Thai
49 Orange

50 Jacques Reymond

PUBS & CLUBS
21 Chasers
25 The Market Hotel
28 Exchange Hotel
42 Revolver

OTHER
1 Dutton
9 Country Road
13 Collette Dinnigan
14 Dinosaur Designs
16 Christopher Graf
17 Mighty Music
26 Hares & Hyenas
31 Prahran Aquatic Centre
32 Dan Murphy Cellars
33 Route 66
34 Andrew Isles Natural History Bookshop
36 Fool
37 Kill City
39 Greville Records
41 Prahran Town Hall
43 The Printed Image Bookshop
45 Chapel St Bazaar
46 Shoe Craft

MAP 7 – SOUTH MELBOURNE & ALBERT PARK

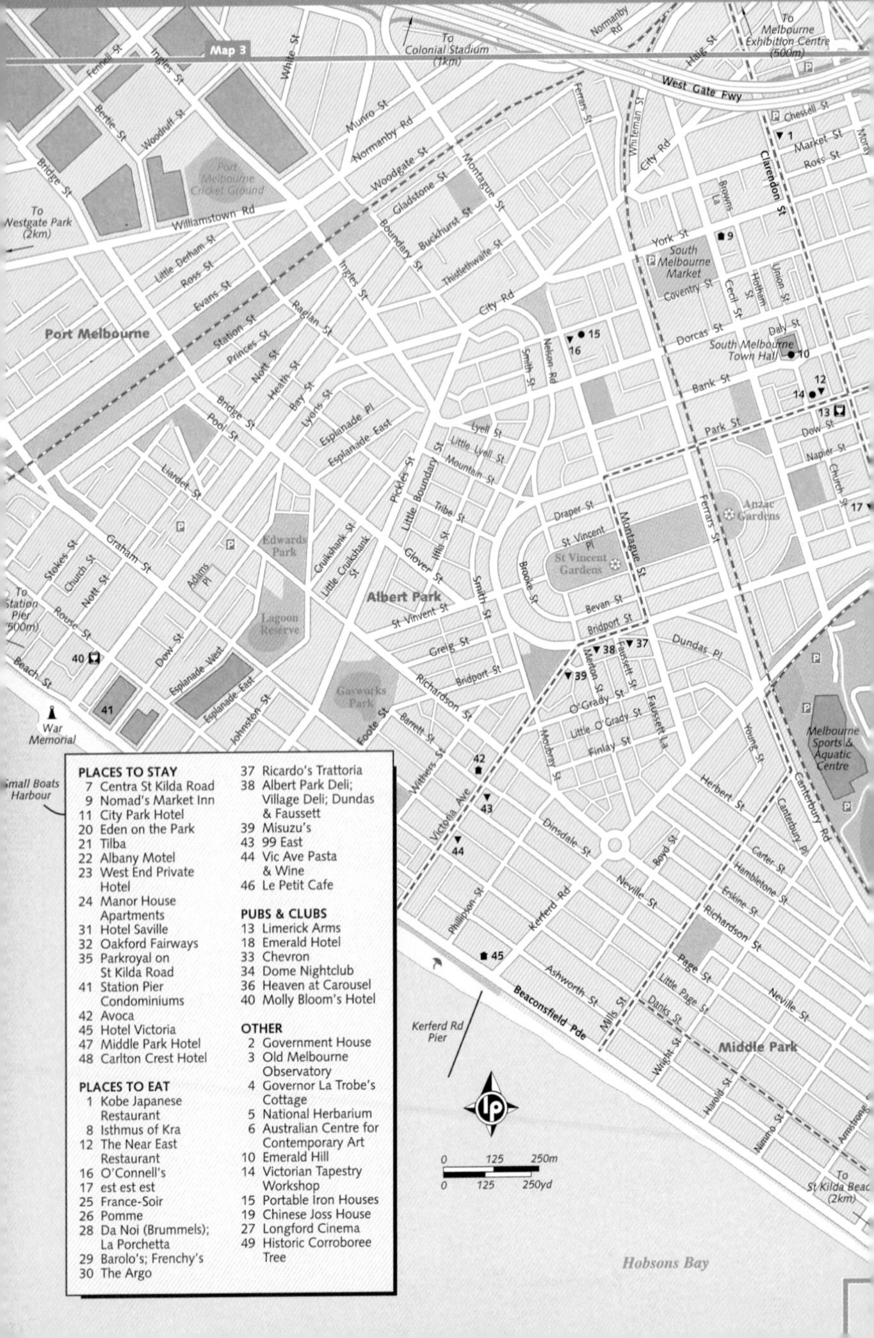

Map 3

To Colonial Stadium (1km)

To Melbourne Exhibition Centre (600m)

West Gate Fwy

Port Melbourne Cricket Ground

Williamstown Rd

To Westgate Park (2km)

Port Melbourne

South Melbourne Market

▼ 9

South Melbourne Town Hall ● 10

▼ 15
16

12
14 ▼ ●

13 □

Edwards Park

Albert Park

Anzac Gardens

17

St Vincent Gardens

Lagoon Reserve

▼ 38 ▼ 37

39

Gasworks Park

40 □

War Memorial

41

Small Boats Harbour

Melbourne Sports & Aquatic Centre

42
▪

43

44

Middle Park

▪ 45

Kerferd Rd Pier

Beaconsfield Pde

To St Kilda Beach (2km)

To Station Pier (900m)

Hobsons Bay

0   125   250m
0   125   250yd

LP

PLACES TO STAY
- 7 Centra St Kilda Road
- 9 Nomad's Market Inn
- 11 City Park Hotel
- 20 Eden on the Park
- 21 Tilba
- 22 Albany Motel
- 23 West End Private Hotel
- 24 Manor House Apartments
- 31 Hotel Saville
- 32 Oakford Fairways
- 35 Parkroyal on St Kilda Road
- 41 Station Pier Condominiums
- 42 Avoca
- 46 Hotel Victoria
- 47 Middle Park Hotel
- 48 Carlton Crest Hotel

PLACES TO EAT
- 1 Kobe Japanese Restaurant
- 8 Isthmus of Kra
- 12 The Near East Restaurant
- 16 O'Connell's
- 17 est est est
- 25 France-Soir
- 26 Pomme
- 28 Da Noi (Brummels); La Porchetta
- 29 Barolo's; Frenchy's
- 30 The Argo

- 37 Ricardo's Trattoria
- 38 Albert Park Deli; Village Deli; Dundas & Faussett
- 39 Misuzu's
- 43 99 East
- 44 Vic Ave Pasta & Wine
- 46 Le Petit Cafe

PUBS & CLUBS
- 13 Limerick Arms
- 18 Emerald Hotel
- 33 Chevron
- 34 Dome Nightclub
- 36 Heaven at Carousel
- 40 Molly Bloom's Hotel

OTHER
- 2 Government House
- 3 Old Melbourne Observatory
- 4 Governor La Trobe's Cottage
- 5 National Herbarium
- 6 Australian Centre for Contemporary Art
- 10 Emerald Hill
- 14 Victorian Tapestry Workshop
- 15 Portable Iron Houses
- 19 Chinese Joss House
- 27 Longford Cinema
- 49 Historic Corroboree Tree

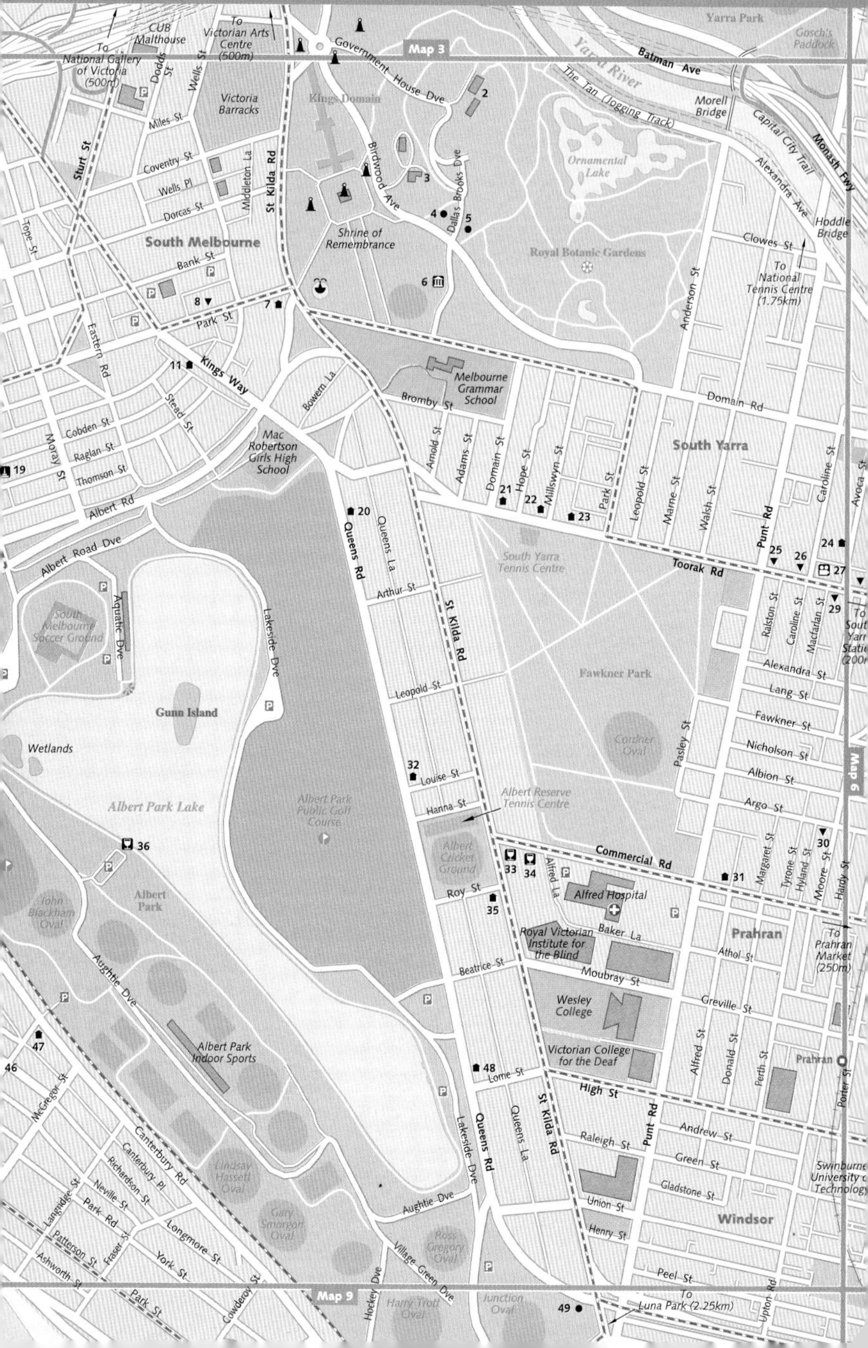

Yarra Park

Gosch's Paddock

CUB Malthouse

To Victorian Arts Centre (500m)

To National Gallery of Victoria (500m)

Government House Dve

Map 3

Batman Ave

Yarra River

The Tan (Jogging Track)

Morell Bridge

Capital City Trail

Victoria Barracks

Kings Domain

Dodds St

Wells St

Miles St

Coventry St

Wells Pl

Dorcas St

St Kilda Rd

Middleton La

Ornamental Lake

Alexandra Ave

Monash Fwy

Hoddle Bridge

South Melbourne

Bank St

Birdwood Ave

3

4

5

Shrine of Remembrance

6

Royal Botanic Gardens

Clowes St

To National Tennis Centre (1.75km)

Anderson St

Tepor St

Sturt St

8 ▼

7 ▪

Park St

Eastern Rd

11 ▪

Kings Way

Bowen La

Melbourne Grammar School

Bromby St

Domain Rd

South Yarra

Cobden St

Raglan St

Thomson St

Mac Robertson Girls High School

Arnold St

Adams St

Domain St

Hope St

Millswin St

Park St

Leopold St

Maine St

Walsh St

Caroline St

Avoca St

19

Moray St

Steed St

Albert Rd

21 ▪

22 ▪

23 ▪

25 ▪

26

24 ▪

27 ▣

Albert Road Dve

20 ▪

Queens Rd

Queens La

Arthur St

St Kilda Rd

South Yarra Tennis Centre

Toorak Rd

Punt Rd

29

To South Yarra Station (200m)

South Melbourne Soccer Ground

Aquatic Dve

Lakeside Dve

Leopold St

Fawkner Park

Alexandra St

Lang St

Fawkner St

Nicholson St

Albion St

Argo St

Pasley St

Gardiner Oval

Ma 6

Gunn Island

Wetlands

Albert Park Lake

Albert Park Public Golf Course

32 ▪

Louise St

Hanna St

Albert Reserve Tennis Centre

36 ▣

John Blackham Oval

Albert Park

Albert Cricket Ground

33 ▪ 34

Commercial Rd

30 ▼

31 ▪

Margaret St

Tyrone St

Hyland St

Moore St

Hardy St

Roy St

35

Alfred La

Alfred Hospital

Baker La

Prahran

Athol St

To Prahran Market (250m)

Royal Victorian Institute for the Blind

Moubray St

Greville St

Wesley College

Alfred St

Donald St

Perth St

Prahran

47

46

McGregor St

Lavender St

Neville St

Park Rd

Fraser St

Ashworth St

Patterson St

Canterbury Rd

Richardson Pl

Aughtie Dve

Albert Park Indoor Sports

Junction Oval

Lakeside Dve

Village Green Dve

Ross Gregory Oval

Gary Simmson Oval

48 ▪

Lorne St

Victorian College for the Deaf

High St

Queens Rd

Queens La

St Kilda Rd

Raleigh St

Andrew St

Green St

Gladstone St

Punt Rd

Union St

Henry St

Windsor

Swinburne University of Technology

Beatrice St

Peel St

Map 9

Hockey Dve

Harry Trott Oval

49 ▪

To Luna Park (2.25km)

Upton Rd

MAP 8 – WILLIAMSTOWN

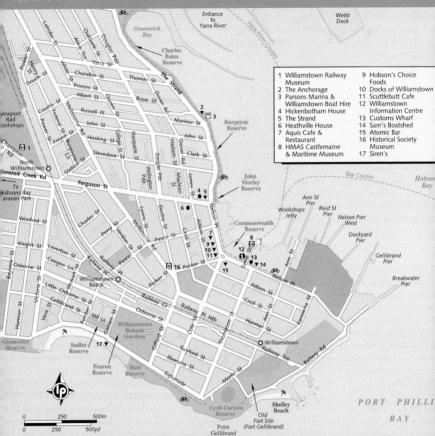

1 Williamstown Railway Museum
2 The Anchorage
3 Parsons Marina & Williamstown Boat Hire
4 Hickenbotham House
5 The Strand
6 Heathville House
7 Aquis Cafe & Restaurant
8 HMAS *Castlemaine* & Maritime Museum
9 Hobson's Choice Foods
10 Docks of Williamstown
11 Scuttlebutt Cafe
12 Williamstown Information Centre
13 Customs Wharf
14 Sam's Boatshed
15 Atomic Bar
16 Historical Society Museum
17 Siren's

Not quite a Sydney Harbour ferry – public transport Williamstown style

The bell of the *Alma Doepel*, Williamstown

The old pumphouse at Scienceworks, Spotswood

West Gate Bridge links Williamstown to the city

The city centre across Hobsons Bay from Williamstown

MAP 9 – ST KILDA, ELWOOD & BALACLAVA

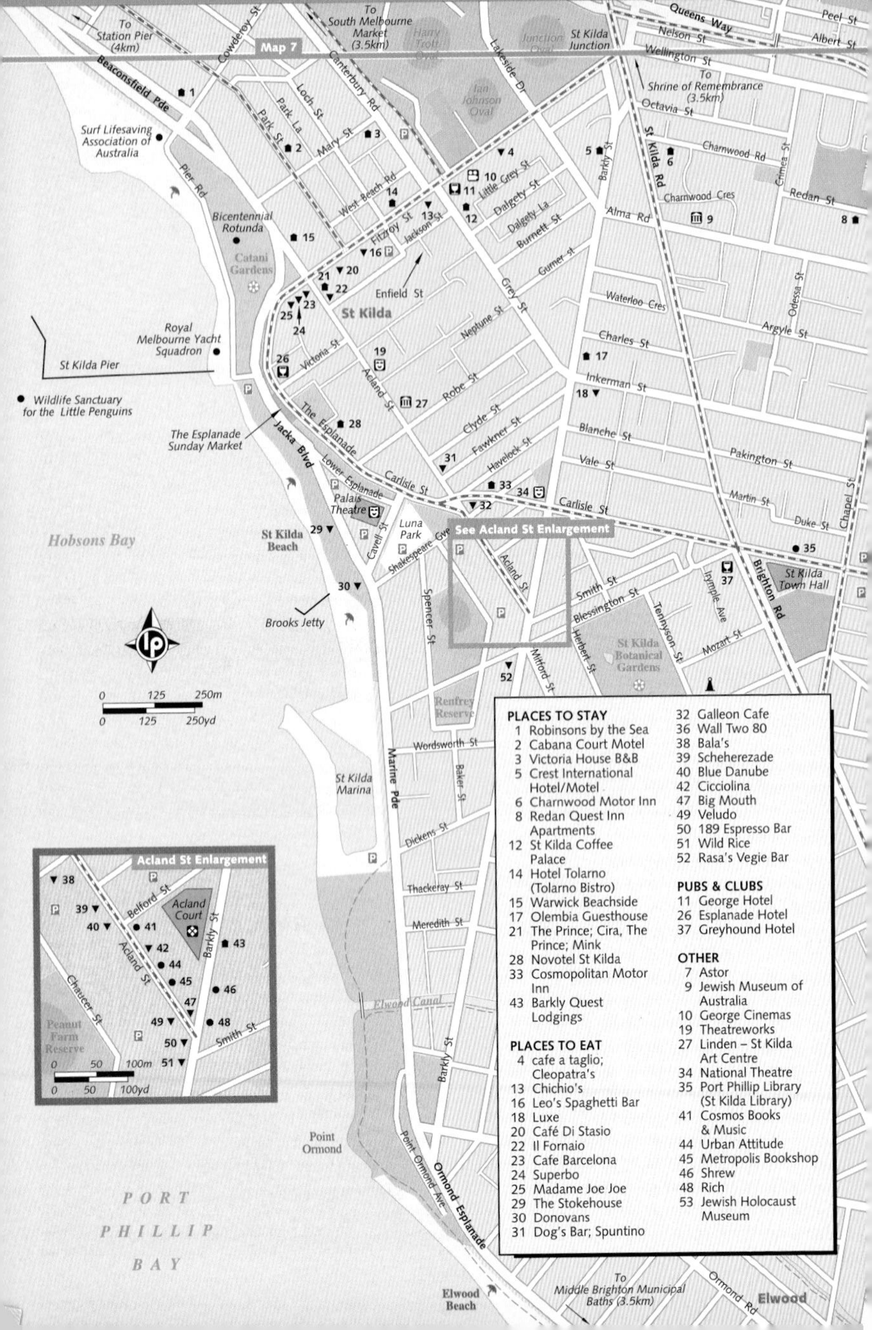

To Station Pier (4km)

To South Melbourne Market (3.5km)

Map 7

Queens Way

Peel St

Albert St

St Kilda Junction

To Shrine of Remembrance (3.5km)

Wellington St

Nelson St

Surf Lifesaving Association of Australia

Beaconsfield Pde

Pier Rd

Park La

Loch St

Park St

Mary St

West Beach Rd

Canterbury Rd

Lakeside Dr

Harry Trott

Junction Oval

St Kilda Troth

Bat Johnson Oval

Octavia St

Charnwood Rd

Charnwood Cres

Redan St

St Kilda Rd

Barkly St

Alma Rd

Charles St

Redan St

Bicentennial Rotunda

Catani Gardens

Royal Melbourne Yacht Squadron

St Kilda Pier

Wildlife Sanctuary for the Little Penguins

The Esplanade Sunday Market

Hobsons Bay

St Kilda Beach

Luna Park

Palais Theatre

Brooks Jetty

Little Grey St

Fitzroy St

Jackson St

Dalgety La

Enfield St

St Kilda

Victoria St

Acland St

Robe St

Clyde St

Fawkner St

Havelock St

Carlisle St

Grey St

Neptune St

Corner St

Waterloo Cres

Charles St

Inkerman St

Blanche St

Vale St

Martin St

Duke St

Pakington St

Chapel St

Argyle St

Odessa St

See Acland St Enlargement

St Kilda Beach

St Kilda Marina

Marine Pde

Shakespeare Gve

Spencer St

Wordsworth St

Dickens St

Thackeray St

Meredith St

St Kilda Botanical Gardens

Smith St

Blessington St

Herbert St

Mitford St

Tennyson St

Mozart St

George St

Dickens Av

Inner...

Brighton Rd

St Kilda Town Hall

Renfrey Reserve

Baker St

Elwood Canal

Barkly St

Point Ormond Rd

Point Ormond

PORT PHILLIP BAY

0   125   250m
0   125   250yd

Acland St Enlargement

Belford St

Acland St

Barkly St

Chaucer St

Acland Court

Peanut Farm Reserve

Smith St

0   50   100m
0   50   100yd

▼38   39▼   40▼   41   42   44   45   46   47   48   49▼   50▼   51▼   43

PLACES TO STAY
1 Robinsons by the Sea
2 Cabana Court Motel
3 Victoria House B&B
5 Crest International Hotel/Motel
6 Charnwood Motor Inn
8 Redan Quest Inn Apartments
12 St Kilda Coffee Palace
14 Hotel Tolarno (Tolarno Bistro)
15 Warwick Beachside
17 Olembia Guesthouse
21 The Prince; Cira; The Prince; Mink
28 Novotel St Kilda
33 Cosmopolitan Motor Inn
43 Barkly Quest Lodgings

PLACES TO EAT
4 cafe a taglio; Cleopatra's
13 Chichio's
16 Leo's Spaghetti Bar
18 Luxe
20 Café Di Stasio
22 Il Fornaio
23 Cafe Barcelona
24 Superbo
25 Madame Joe Joe
29 The Stokehouse
30 Donovans
31 Dog's Bar; Spuntino

32 Galleon Cafe
36 Wall Two 80
38 Bala's
39 Scheherezade
40 Blue Danube
42 Cicciolina
47 Big Mouth
49 Veludo
50 189 Espresso Bar
51 Wild Rice
52 Rasa's Vegie Bar

PUBS & CLUBS
11 George Hotel
26 Esplanade Hotel
37 Greyhound Hotel

OTHER
7 Astor
9 Jewish Museum of Australia
10 George Cinemas
19 Theatreworks
21 Linden – St Kilda Art Centre
34 National Theatre
35 Port Phillip Library (St Kilda Library)
41 Cosmos Books & Music
44 Urban Attitude
45 Metropolis Bookshop
46 Shrew
48 Rich
53 Jewish Holocaust Museum

To Elwood Beach

To Middle Brighton Municipal Baths (3.5km)

Ormond Rd

Ormond Esplanade

Elwood

Map (Prahran / Balaclava / Elsternwick area)

Map 6

Prahran

To Jam Factory (1.5km)
Windsor

Gertrude St
Bowen St
To Como Historic House & Garden (2km)
Gooch St
Wrexham Rd
The Avenue
Hornby St
Lewisham Rd
Ellesmere Rd
Williams Rd
Kelsimine Ave

Dandenong Rd

Alma Park
Westbury St
Fulton St
Hotham St
St Kilda Cemetery
To Chadstone Shopping Centre (7.5km)
Alexandra St

Alma Rd

Hammerdale Ave
Reaton St
Young St
Jervis St
Sebastopol St
Malakoff St
Leslie St
Prentice St
Cardigan St
To Malvern Station (2.5km)

Nelson St
Blenheim St
Orange Gve
Briton St
Wilgah St
Inkerman St
Empress Rd
Alexandra St

Carlisle St

Balaclava
Carlisle Ave
Hawksburn Ave
Balaclava Rd
To Labassa (500m)

Denman Ave

The Avenue
Melby Ave
Gourlay St
Talbot Ave
Grosvenor St
Glen Eira Ave
Sycamore Gve
Mayfield St
Elm Gve
Mchenry St
Oak Gve
Loch Ave
Ripponlea
Attley Gve
Bailey Ave
Myrtle St
McWhae Ave
Caulfield Grammar Senior School
Victoria Ave
Glen Eira Rd
Lyndoch St
Hotham St
Gordon St
Elizabeth St
Regent St
St Georges Rd
To Caulfield Racecourse & Lord Lodge B&B (2km)
Brighton Rd
Ernsdale Ave
Rippon Lea Historic Mansion
Allison Rd
Burns St
Rippon Gve
Sandham St
Heaton Ave
Sinclair St
53
Glen Huntly Rd
Elsternwick
Elsternwick Oval
To Southland Shoppingtown (10km)
To Glen Huntly Station (4.5km)
Elsternwick Parks Public Golf Course
Elsternwick

The historic kiosk on St Kilda Pier

Summer silliness on St Kilda beach…

…and St Kilda streets.

Dawn colours the jetties of Geelong's harbour.

The long, winding Great Ocean Road

Standing sentry off Cape Schanck

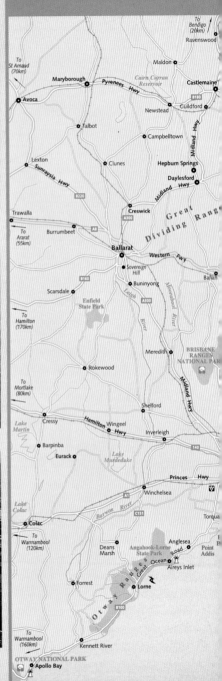

To Bendigo (20km)
Ravenswood
Maldon
Maryborough   Pyrenees Hwy   Castlemaine
To St Arnaud (70km)
Avoca
Guildford
Newstead
Talbot
Campbelltown
Lexton
Hepburn Springs
Clunes
Sunraysia Hwy
Daylesford
Midland Hwy
Creswick
Trawalla
Great Dividing Range
To Ararat (55km)
Burrumbeet
Ballarat
Western Hwy
Sovereign Hill
Ballan
Scarsdale
Buninyong
Moorabool River
Enfield State Park
Leigh River
To Hamilton (170km)
Meredith
BRISBANE RANGES NATIONAL PARK
Rokewood
To Mortlake (80km)
Shelford
Midland Hwy
Lake Martin
Cressy
Hamilton Hwy   Wingeel
Inverleigh
Barpinba
Lake Murdeduke
Eurack
Princes Hwy
Lake Colac
Winchelsea
Barwon River
Torqua
Colac
To Warrnambool (120km)
Deans Marsh
Angahook-Lorne State Park
Anglesea
Point Addis
Great Ocean Road
Aireys Inlet
Forrest
Lorne
Otway Ranges
To Warrnambool (160km)
Kennett River
OTWAY NATIONAL PARK
Apollo Bay

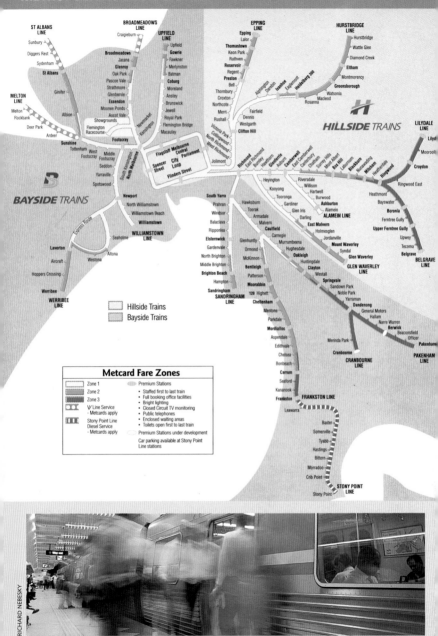

METROPOLITAN TRAIN SYSTEM

ST ALBANS LINE
Sunbury
Diggers Rest
Sydenham
St Albans
Ginifer

BROADMEADOWS LINE
Craigieburn
Broadmeadows
Jacana
Glenroy
Oak Park
Pascoe Vale
Strathmore
Glenbervie
Essendon
Moonee Ponds
Ascot Vale
Showgrounds
Flemington Racecourse

UPFIELD LINE
Upfield
Gowrie
Fawkner
Merlynston
Batman
Coburg
Moreland
Anstey
Brunswick
Royal Park
Flemington Bridge
Macaulay

EPPING LINE
Epping
Lalor
Thomastown
Keon Park
Ruthven
Reservoir
Regent
Preston
Bell
Thornbury
Croxton
Northcote
Merri
Rushall

HURSTBRIDGE LINE
Hurstbridge
Wattle Glen
Diamond Creek
Eltham
Montmorency
Greensborough
Watsonia
Macleod
Rosanna
Heidelberg
Eaglemont
Ivanhoe
Darebin
Alphington
Fairfield
Dennis
Westgarth
Clifton Hill

MELTON LINE
Melton
Rockbank
Deer Park
Ardeer
Albion
Sunshine
Tottenham
West Footscray
Middle Footscray
Seddon
Yarraville
Spotswood

Newmarket
Kensington
South Kensington
North Melbourne
Footscray
Newport

Flagstaff
Melbourne Central
Parliament
Spencer Street
City Loop
Flinders Street

Victoria Park
Collingwood
North Richmond
West Richmond
Jolimont
Richmond
East Richmond
Burnley
Hawthorn
Glenferrie
Auburn
Camberwell
East Camberwell
Canterbury
Chatham

HILLSIDE TRAINS

LILYDALE LINE
Lilydale
Mooroolbark
Croydon
Ringwood East
Ringwood
Heatherdale
Mitcham
Nunawading
Blackburn
Laburnum
Box Hill
Mont Albert
Surrey Hills

ALAMEIN LINE
Ashburton
Alamein
Burwood
Hartwell
Willison
Riversdale

Heyington
Kooyong
Tooronga
Gardiner
Glen Iris
Darling
East Malvern
Holmesglen
Jordanville
Mount Waverley
Syndal
Glen Waverley

GLEN WAVERLEY LINE

Heathmont
Bayswater
Boronia
Ferntree Gully
Upper Ferntree Gully
Upwey
Tecoma
Belgrave

BELGRAVE LINE

BAYSIDE TRAINS

WILLIAMSTOWN LINE
North Williamstown
Williamstown Beach
Williamstown
Seaholme
Laverton
Aircraft
Westona
Altona
Hoppers Crossing
Werribee

WERRIBEE LINE
Express Route

South Yarra
Prahran
Windsor
Balaclava
Ripponlea
Elsternwick
Gardenvale
North Brighton
Middle Brighton
Brighton Beach
Hampton

SANDRINGHAM LINE
Sandringham

Toorak
Armadale
Malvern
Caulfield
Carnegie
Murrumbeena
Hughesdale
Oakleigh
Huntingdale
Clayton
Westall
Springvale
Sandown Park
Noble Park
Yarraman
Dandenong
General Motors
Hallam
Narre Warren
Berwick
Beaconsfield
Officer

PAKENHAM LINE
Pakenham

Glenhuntly
Ormond
McKinnon
Bentleigh
Patterson
Moorabbin
Highett
Cheltenham
Mentone
Parkdale
Mordialloc
Aspendale
Edithvale
Chelsea
Bonbeach
Carrum
Seaford
Kananook
Frankston

FRANKSTON LINE
Leawarra

Merinda Park
Cranbourne

CRANBOURNE LINE

Baxter
Somerville
Tyabb
Hastings
Bittern
Morradoo
Crib Point
Stony Point

STONY POINT LINE

Metcard Fare Zones

- Zone 1
- Zone 2
- Zone 3
- V/Line Service – Metcards apply
- Stony Point Line Diesel Service – Metcards apply

Premium Stations
- Staffed first to last train
- Full booking office facilities
- Bright lighting
- Closed Circuit TV monitoring
- Public telephones
- Enclosed waiting areas
- Toilets open first to last train

Premium Stations under development

Car parking available at Stony Point Line stations

Hillside Trains
Bayside Trains

Melbourne Met – buy your ticket and ride!